Cambridge Imperial and Post-Colonial Studies Series

Series Editors
Richard Drayton
Department of History
King's College London
London, UK

Saul Dubow
Magdalene College
University of Cambridge
Cambridge, UK

The Cambridge Imperial and Post-Colonial Studies series is a collection of studies on empires in world history and on the societies and cultures which emerged from colonialism. It includes both transnational, comparative and connective studies, and studies which address where particular regions or nations participate in global phenomena. While in the past the series focused on the British Empire and Commonwealth, in its current incarnation there is no imperial system, period of human history or part of the world which lies outside of its compass. While we particularly welcome the first monographs of young researchers, we also seek major studies by more senior scholars, and welcome collections of essays with a strong thematic focus. The series includes work on politics, economics, culture, literature, science, art, medicine, and war. Our aim is to collect the most exciting new scholarship on world history with an imperial theme.

More information about this series at
http://www.palgrave.com/gp/series/13937

Maximilian Drephal

Afghanistan and the Coloniality of Diplomacy

The British Legation in Kabul, 1922–1948

Maximilian Drephal
Department of History
University of Sheffield
Sheffield, South Yorkshire, UK

Cambridge Imperial and Post-Colonial Studies Series
ISBN 978-3-030-23959-6   ISBN 978-3-030-23960-2 (eBook)
https://doi.org/10.1007/978-3-030-23960-2

© The Editor(s) (if applicable) and The Author(s), under exclusive license to Springer Nature Switzerland AG 2019
This work is subject to copyright. All rights are solely and exclusively licensed by the Publisher, whether the whole or part of the material is concerned, specifically the rights of translation, reprinting, reuse of illustrations, recitation, broadcasting, reproduction on microfilms or in any other physical way, and transmission or information storage and retrieval, electronic adaptation, computer software, or by similar or dissimilar methodology now known or hereafter developed.
The use of general descriptive names, registered names, trademarks, service marks, etc. in this publication does not imply, even in the absence of a specific statement, that such names are exempt from the relevant protective laws and regulations and therefore free for general use.
The publisher, the authors and the editors are safe to assume that the advice and information in this book are believed to be true and accurate at the date of publication. Neither the publisher nor the authors or the editors give a warranty, expressed or implied, with respect to the material contained herein or for any errors or omissions that may have been made. The publisher remains neutral with regard to jurisdictional claims in published maps and institutional affiliations.

Cover credit: Hulton Archive/Stringer

This Palgrave Macmillan imprint is published by the registered company Springer Nature Switzerland AG
The registered company address is: Gewerbestrasse 11, 6330 Cham, Switzerland

ACKNOWLEDGEMENTS

The making of this book has been a personal journey. Growing up in the German Democratic Republic, my decision to study history emerged from the realisation that moments, even when they came in the shape of such fundamental changes that re-unified Germany in 1989/1990, brought exciting freedoms as much as they encapsulated remnants of what had been overcome.

At the Freie Universität Berlin, Alexander Demandt introduced me to the Late Roman Empire and its long, unfinished endings. His patience, generosity and knowledge as a teacher inspired me. As I studied the history of imperial decline in antiquity, I also learned about Alexander the Great and Afghanistan. I was very fortunate to win an Erasmus scholarship, which allowed me to study modern empire with Anindita Ghosh and Till Geiger at the University of Manchester. One year became two. Back in Berlin, I wrote my MA dissertation on the end of colonial rule in India and the idea Pakistan.

Dominik Geppert, Uwe Puschner and Claudia Ulbrich volunteered suggestions during the early stages of my project on the British Legation in Kabul. Their research seminars in Berlin and Bonn provided me with a platform to articulate my ideas, and I am grateful to those who listened and commented on my work. At the Dahlem Research School, Reinhard Bernbeck drew a map of Kabul and also told me about a copy of William Kerr Fraser-Tytler's *Afghanistan* as I departed for the UK to pursue my Ph.D.

Loughborough University gave me a scholarship. Siobhan Lambert-Hurley and Thoralf Klein were dedicated supervisors, whose interest in my work allowed it to grow in the stimulating and supportive intellectual environment they created. They helped me organise the project and read its many drafts. They encouraged my research in so many different ways, and it is difficult to imagine the thesis eventually taking shape without them! Siobhan, especially, was a beacon of unfailing positivity and a fountain of advice.

As the project grew, I received comments and questions on my work at the conferences of the British Association for South Asian Studies, the British International History Group, the British Scholar Society, the Colonial/Postcolonial Researchers' Workshop at the Institute of Historical Research in London, the fifth Culture and International History conference at the John F. Kennedy Institute for North American Studies at the Freie Universität Berlin, the New Diplomatic History Network as well as the Sussex Afghanistan Forum.

The book has been shaped by a number of people. Benjamin D. Hopkins was a tirelessly encouraging mentor and examiner. Martin J. Bayly suggested additions and adjustments to the book manuscript. Raimund Bauer read the book when it was still a doctoral thesis. I am indebted to the reviewers at *Modern Asian Studies* and to J. Simon Rofe for their critical feedback on earlier versions of Chapter 6.

The German Historical Institute in London and the Royal Historical Society supported my work and travels. The archivists and librarians at the British Library in London, the British Red Cross, the Middle East Centre Archive in Oxford, The National Archives in Kew, the National Army Museum as well as the National Archives of India moved uncountable files to make the book possible. Special thanks are due to the digitisation departments at the British Library, The National Archives as well as MECA for making available the illustrations reproduced here.

I have received plenty of help in other ways. It has been a privilege and a pleasure to work with my colleagues at Loughborough University and the University of Sheffield. On many occasions, it has also been a revelation and an inspiration. The book has profited from the exceptional scholarship produced by others elsewhere, too. They are too many to mention here, but I am grateful they shared a stretch of way with me.

The intellectual curiosity and ability of my students at the University of Sheffield and Loughborough University made teaching a rewarding experience over the years. It was a particular pleasure to build an option module on "Afghanistan from the Great Game to the War on Terror" at Sheffield whose participants challenged my engagement with the subject and, in return, taught me plenty. It makes me immensely happy to acknowledge their contribution.

The book's historical subject is a surprisingly lively institution in the memory of some who are connected to it through their own professional lives or families. Many of them, including Nicholas Barrington, Charles Drace-Francis, Hazel Hastings, Katherine Himsworth, Owen Humphrys, Christopher and Hilary Knox-Johnston, Susan Loughhead, Martin Maconachie and Simon Parkes, shared with me parts of their private collections, stories, insights, personal papers or photographs. Mark Bertram sent the plan of the Legation compound, which is reproduced in the book. This dispersed archive awaits cataloguing. Ultimately, most of the book was written from publicly accessible materials. In the centenary year of Afghan independence, the moment for this book is now. But, like all history, it remains a fragment.

Molly Beck and Maeve Sinnott were exceptionally supportive, patient and enthusiastic editors at Palgrave Macmillan from day one. Sebastian Ballard created the maps.

My parents enabled my studies, encouraged and nurtured my independence. My family and friends supported me, freely and liberally. They all enrich my life and give meaning to it. None of this would have been possible without the love, care and wisdom of my wife, Pratibha. This book is dedicated to her.

London
April 2019

About This Book

The book offers an institutional history of the British Legation in Kabul, which was established in response to the independence of Afghanistan in 1919. It contextualises this diplomatic mission in the wider remit of Anglo-Afghan relations and diplomacy from the nineteenth to the twenty-first century, examining the networks of family and profession that established the institution's colonial foundations and its connections across South Asia and the Indian Ocean. The study presents the British Legation as a late imperial institution, which materialised colonialism's governmental practices in the age of independence. Ultimately, it demonstrates the continuation of asymmetries forged in the Anglo-Afghan encounter and shows how these were transformed into instances of diplomatic inequality in the realm of international relations. Approaching diplomacy through the themes of performance, the body and architecture, and in the context of knowledge transfers, this work offers new perspectives on international relations through a cultural history of diplomacy.

Contents

1 Introduction: Empire, Colony and Diplomacy   1

2 The Remaking of Anglo-Afghan Relations   47

3 Subaltern Biographies   81

4 Biography and Imperial Governance   117

5 Accreditation and Performance   173

6 Diplomatic Bodies   233

7 Architecture   277

8 From Colonial Legation to Postimperial Embassy   317

9 Conclusions: The Coloniality of Diplomacy   343

Glossary   351

Index   355

About the Author

Maximilian Drephal lectures in the School of Politics and International Studies at Loughborough University, UK, and is Research Associate in the Department of History at the University of Sheffield, UK, where he has taught as Lecturer in International History. He has previously published in *Modern Asian Studies* (Cambridge University Press) and the edited collection *Sport and Diplomacy: Games Within Games* (Manchester University Press).

A Note on Spelling

I have closely followed the sources in their spellings of names and terms. As a result, one and the same name and rank may appear in different forms throughout the thesis—for instance Mohammed and Muhammad, Sayyid and Saiyid, Sheikh and Shaikh. Non-English terms have been italicised throughout unless where they intend to express assimilation. Translations have been provided based on John T. Platts *A Dictionary of Urdu, Classical Hindi, and English* (London: W. H. Allen & Co., 1884) in a glossary at the end.

Abbreviations

BL British Library, London
BMJ British Medical Journal
EA External Affairs Department, Government of India
F&P Foreign and Political Department, Government of India
FCO Foreign and Commonwealth Office
FO Foreign Office
H.M. His/Her Majesty
IA Indian Army
ICS Indian Civil Service
IO India Office
IOBO India Office and Burma Office
IOR India Office Records
M.B.E. Member of the Order of the British Empire
MECA Middle East Centre Archive, St Antony's College, Oxford
NAI The National Archives of India
NAM National Army Museum
NWFP North-West Frontier Province
ODNB Oxford Dictionary of National Biography
TNA The National Archives, Kew

List of Figures

Fig. 3.1	A group photo, 1935/1936	84
Fig. 5.1	An accreditation scene, 1930	197
Fig. 7.1	The British Legation compound, 1933	287
Fig. 7.2	British Legation Kabul, site plan, 1948	294
Fig. 8.1	The site plan as palimpsest: Embassy as Legation as Afghanistan	332

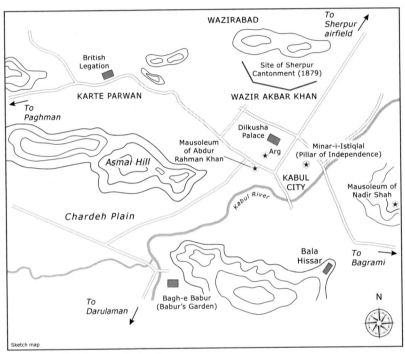

Kabul (*Credit* Sebastian Ballard)

Afghanistan, India and the Indo-Afghan borderland (*Credit* Sebastian Ballard)

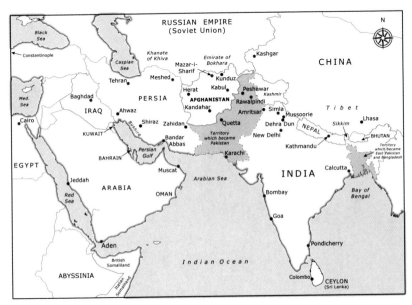

The Indian Empire (*Credit* Sebastian Ballard)

CHAPTER 1

Introduction: Empire, Colony and Diplomacy

THE RISE OF AN EMBASSY

Established in response to Afghan independence in 1919, the establishment of the British Legation in Kabul appeared to express the recognition of Afghanistan as a sovereign state in the realm of international relations by its former imperial suzerain. On paper, it conformed to Amanullah Khan's (r. 1919–1929) demands for direct relations between Afghanistan and the imperial metropole in London. In the nineteenth century, the colonial state had powerfully shaped the politics of Afghanistan, also directing its foreign affairs in return for cash payments to Abdur Rahman Khan (r. 1880–1901) and Habibullah Khan (r. 1901–1919), Amanullah Khan's grandfather and father respectively, from 1880 to 1919. Between 1919 and 1922, the colonial state in India adjusted to the new reality of Afghan independence without breaking from the past. The payment of colonial funds for the direction of Afghanistan's international relations to Afghan rulers ended with the peace treaty of Rawalpindi in 1919. However, funds now flowed into Afghanistan for other purposes, namely into the setup of a British-Indian diplomatic-colonial enclave, the Legation's structures and personnel. In late 1921, George Nathaniel Curzon, the former Viceroy of India (1899–1905) and then Foreign Secretary, decreed that the Legation building "should be one of the finest Residences in Asia".[1] From 1922 onwards, the Raj modelled the Legation according to its own ambitions, objectives and experiences. Colonial officers became diplomats, staffed the Legation

© The Author(s) 2019
M. Drephal, *Afghanistan and the Coloniality of Diplomacy*,
Cambridge Imperial and Post-Colonial Studies Series,
https://doi.org/10.1007/978-3-030-23960-2_1

1

and transferred colonialism's manifold asymmetries to Kabul, in essence recreating the colonial project *en miniature* in Kabul. As a twentieth-century diplomatic presence in Kabul, the British Legation accumulated a pool of actionable instructions, sourcing knowledge from other colonial contexts in South Asia. It ensured the continuity between a corpus of nineteenth-century knowledge of Afghanistan and twentieth-century British diplomacy.

In early 1989, Soviet troops prepared to withdraw from Afghanistan, ending the fourth major war that had violently entangled the country and imperial powers since the First Anglo-Afghan War in 1839. In January 1989, the British government, together with the USA, France, Italy and Japan, decided to remove its diplomatic mission from the Afghan capital, citing deteriorating security conditions.[2] The British Chargé d'Affaires in Afghanistan, Ian Mackley, was paraphrased as saying "[t]he US, Britain, West Germany and France have all written [Mohammad Najibullah] off, and have concluded that the sooner Kabul falls to the Mojahedin the better".[3] By departing, diplomatic missions effectively withdrew international recognition from the government of Mohammad Najibullah, which their presence in Kabul had until then rendered, and contributed to the erosion of Afghan politics in the following years. In the words of one commentator, the decision to leave was "wholly political, and contrary to the realistic and non-political traditions of British diplomacy".[4] Others, including India and Pakistan, maintained their diplomatic representations until well into the 1990s. Between 1989 and 1992, the regime of Najibullah, a remnant of the Soviet occupation of Afghanistan, was increasingly embattled as Kabul became a fighting ground. In 1992, the government collapsed following the end of Russian aid. The *mujahideen* took control of Kabul.

The departure of the British Embassy in January 1989 brought back to memory Britain's past encounters in Afghanistan since the early nineteenth century. In 1989, "a few elderly survivors of the British Raj" remembered events, which had played out almost exactly sixty years before. In February 1929, the advance of an army of 'rebels' had been halted by Amanullah Khan's troops in the vicinity of the British Legation, trapping the Empire's diplomatic mission in the crossfire of bullets and shrapnel. Sixty years on, Richard Gould, the son of the Legation's Counsellor, spoke of a "hair-raising three-mile walk through enemy lines" from the British Legation to the airfield, where aeroplanes would eventually take the Legation's women and children to safety in India.[5] The Legation returned to Kabul in 1930 after relations with the government of Nadir Shah (r. 1929–1933) had been re-established. For the second time in the twentieth century, a British mission left Afghanistan during a moment of profound political and international crisis.

For Peter Hopkirk, too, writing for *The Times*, the past held the key to explaining events in Afghanistan in 1989. Looking for clues in a two-page piece dating from May 1990, he went "back to square one" to the immediate aftermath of the First Anglo-Afghan War.[6] Hopkirk drew a large frame around the killing of two "British officers" in Bokhara in 1842, Charles Stoddart and Arthur Conolly:

> Stoddart and Conolly were paying the price of engaging in a highly dangerous game – the Great Game, as it became known to those who risked their life in pursuit. The Great Game was played against Russia, then engaged in carving out a vast empire in the Caucasus and Central Asia. Today, as violent unrest threatens the survival of that empire, the events of those times have taken on a new significance; the seeds of the present turmoil were sown during the Great Game years. The current bitterness and resentment of the Central Asian peoples towards their Soviet rulers dates back to their forcible, and often brutal, subjugation by Tsarist generals. For their part, the British tried to pre-empt Russian moves.[7]

In this reading, the Cold War *was* the Great Game. British characters in the nineteenth and twentieth centuries had died attempting to contain several expansionist Russian empires. Soviet soldiers became Tsarist generals. Later that year, Hopkirk published *The Great Game: On Secret Service in High Asia*, which became a widely referenced text. The past was precedent. The "secret heroes" of Britain's imperial history came back to life.[8] The end of the Cold War made glorified imperial history popular.

In 1989, British diplomats left behind "a 25-acre haven of Edwardian comfort and security", "an oasis of tranquillity".[9] In 1994, the British government handed over the abandoned Embassy buildings to its owner, and one of its postcolonial successor states in South Asia, the government of Pakistan. Work on the buildings had been completed in 1927. They had housed the British Legation since 1926, and from 1948 the British Embassy. Pakistan took possession of an imperial monument in Kabul's Karte Parwan district. For both Pakistan and the UK, empire and its history in South Asia were living concepts in their relations with Afghanistan. Pakistan and the UK were joined by their common imperial history, and in particular the governance of the historical Indo-Afghan borderland through which ran the Durand Line, now referred to as AfPak. The occupation of the premises of the former British Legation visualised that common inheritance. As during the uprising against Amanullah Khan in the winter of 1928/1929, the Embassy structures became targets for anti-imperial sentiment. In 1995, the buildings were attacked by 5000 Afghans protesting the government of Pakistan's "creeping invasion" of Afghanistan and, especially, its employment of the Taliban as a "military instrument".[10] Now it was the Pakistani Embassy's turn to be withdrawn from Kabul.

The British Embassy returned to Kabul seven years later in 2001, in the wake of the 'Fourth Anglo-Afghan War', the fifth for Afghanistan involving imperial powers of the day. As with previous occupations in 1839 and 1878 as well as in 1922, a British diplomatic mission, once again, found itself in search of 'permanent' accommodation. The British and Pakistani governments entered discussions about a sale of the Legation buildings, which eventually failed. For a moment, the "return to magnificence for British diplomats" had seemed possible.[11] "Remarkably, the ambassadorial china, silver teapots and crystal glasses survived years of Taliban rule, hidden away and kept safe by two Afghan caretakers".[12] In 2010, the former Minister's residence was refurbished. In 2012, it reopened as the Embassy of Pakistan. At the moment of writing, a picture of the former Legation buildings adorns the diplomatic representation in digital space.[13] At the same time, the British Embassy is located in Kabul's Wazir Akbar Khan district, named after the son of Dost Mohammed Khan, who besieged the Indian occupation army in 1841 and eventually forced its withdrawal during the imperial catastrophe of the First Anglo-Afghan War. The very diplomatic institution that emerged in response to Afghan independence in 1919 has become geographically entangled with the icon of Afghanistan's anti-imperial resistance to the first British military occupation. The idea of Afghan independence has been inscribed twice onto this diplomatic mission; by means of its own history as well as its location in Afghanistan's capital.

The history of the British Legation in Kabul, the British Empire's diplomatic mission from 1922 to 1948, is a funnel for these events. In 1919, Afghanistan was the first South Asian polity under imperial rule to be internationally recognised as an independent, sovereign state. In the following years, Afghanistan sent its representatives into capitals around the world and, at the same time, received the diplomatic agents from other states according to the principle of diplomatic reciprocity and equality. As diplomats, staff and families arrived in Kabul, the cityscape was populated with diplomatic buildings and enclaves. The history of one of these, the British

1 INTRODUCTION: EMPIRE, COLONY AND DIPLOMACY 5

Legation in Kabul, throws light on the processes that preceded the development of a new diplomatic post in Asia in the first half of the twentieth century. The institution visualises the transformation of the Indian colonial state into a conduit of international relations. Its history enhances our understanding of the practical application of colonial ideas beyond colonialism's remit and the manifold transformations of empire occurring into the present.[14] This particular diplomatic mission came to life as a site of imperial power. It shaped the practice of diplomacy as a form of imperial governance in the twentieth century. Until 1947, Afghanistan existed in the neighbourhood of the colonial state in India, which in this period repurposed its technologies of rule for application in the realm of international relations. This process provides insights into the continuities of colonial knowledge and of the practices employed in the Anglo-Afghan encounter during the nineteenth century. It further complicates our understanding of the age of decolonisation as well as of the ideas underlying the organisation of inter-state relations in the twentieth century and at the beginning of the twenty-first. We begin to recognise the duplication and employment of colonial governing practices into the postcolonial era across thresholds of statal independence and beyond state institutions.

The Legation in Kabul transitioned Anglo-Afghan relations from colonial rule to the age of independence. The book captures the presences of this diplomatic mission's colonial past. The subtitle hints at its contentious label as a 'British' Legation. In its discussion of Anglo-Afghan relations, the book uses the descriptor 'Anglo-Afghan' with caution because of its implied ethnocentricity. The term suggests a holistic opposition between two distinct parties. Several governments administered the political relations between Afghanistan, India and the United Kingdom. Ruling elites in South Asia were multinational in character and included European families with deep historical ties to British colonialism in South Asia and imperialism on a global scale as well as South Asian stakeholders. In addition, the term 'Afghan' subsumes several ethnic and state identities. And yet, contemporaries thought of Britain's and India's international relations with Afghanistan in terms of 'Anglo-Afghan' relations. By the twentieth century, the term 'Anglo-Afghan' relations represented Afghanistan's interaction with empire, in particular with the Indian colonial state, in asymmetrical terms. In the period between 1919 and 1947, the Anglo-Afghan relations between empire and vassal state of the nineteenth century were remade. A 'British' Legation became their conduit. It was itself heavily informed by the colonial state's ideologies that had shaped these Anglo-Afghan relations in the nineteenth century. The institution's imperial label represented the internationalisation of the colonial state, but it also captured an uncertain and ambiguous remaking of historical diplomatic ties.

The tradition and transformation of empire are at the heart of the Legation's institutional history and its afterlife. This book discusses the proliferation of the colonial state and its subsequent introduction into a global system of inter-state relations based on mutual recognition and diplomatic institutions. The history of the British Legation in Kabul shows that the period between 1919 and 1947 was instrumental in reshaping colonial sites and properties of the Government of India in the Indian Empire into the diplomatic representations of the British state. It challenges assumed fundamental ruptures that coincide with the recognition of the sovereignty of Afghan statehood in 1919 on the one hand and the independence of Pakistan and India in 1947 on the other. Rather, we see significant continuities in the colonial state's effort to harness technologies of rule and utilise them in the time after colonialism. This book is about the creation of a colonial enclave, its institutional life to the present day, colonial India's relations with Afghanistan since the nineteenth century as well as the coloniality of power in the modern world. It is also about the numerous and interconnected temporary illusions of permanence surrounding Britain's relations with Afghanistan as well as their repeated rupture and reinvention from the early nineteenth to the twenty-first century.

The Historiography of Afghan Space: The Great Game, Frontiers and Borderlands

This section and the next establish the book's location in current historiographical thinking about Afghanistan through space and time. Constructed as a triple frontier between South, Central and West Asia, Afghanistan has often been considered to exist outside of global history's normative spatial and temporal orders. Since 2001, Afghanistan studies have become a populated, productive and creative subject. At the same time that fresh ideas and frameworks are being established, the resilience of colonial inheritances has also resurfaced. Perhaps the most well-known example is the notion of the 'Great Game', which has constituted a recurring feature in writings on Central Asia since the mid-nineteenth century.[15] The term dates back to the colonial exploration of Afghanistan in the nineteenth century and was as an established academic paradigm by 1926.[16] Since then, there have been several renaissances. The first occurred in the late 1940s coinciding with the end of the colonial Indian Empire and the emerging Cold War in Asia.[17] In the late 1970s and early 1980s, Western imperial anxieties were recycled in response to the Soviet invasion of Afghanistan.[18] Peter Hopkirk's book was an outcome of this historiographical rediscovery. The third, and most recent reinvention, has been on-going since 2001.[19] As a concept, the Great Game's endurance is unbroken, and many contributions have pronounced various "endgames" in a competition that is seemingly never-ending.[20]

The Great Game's deep history is contemporaneous with the articulation of the earliest ambitions of modern empires in relation to Afghanistan. This approach to studying the history of Afghanistan combines a telescopic focus from the perspective of imperial governments, predominantly nineteenth-century Britain and Russia, with the accounts of colonial explorers and administrators, resulting in the contextualisation of Afghanistan as a 'buffer state' in the defence of India and British imperial strategy. In 1980, Malcolm Yapp's well-researched *Strategies of British India*, for instance, considered Afghanistan from the perspective of a colonial state that expanded across northern India in the first half of the nineteenth century.[21] The resultant framework of Yapp's work and similar studies narrows the study of Afghanistan on the planning and articulation of imperial grand strategy and is ultimately defined by the military and political objectives of that strategy's many authors. It subordinates the history of Afghanistan to a master narrative of imperial rivalry. This imperial lens and its methodological limitations restrict the visibility of colonial realities to the reproduction of colonial intentions.[22]

Although still a widely popular framework to explain events on the 'periphery' of empire, the Great Game has been rightly scrutinised in recent studies, mostly for its conceptual rigidity, exclusivity and repetitiveness, which sidelines local agency, circumstances and conditions in the context of imperial expansion in the nineteenth century.[23] There is no doubt that imperial competition and cooperation played a role in the history of Afghanistan as a multifaceted polity, but that role has received undue attention relative to other fields of enquiry. But, the international history of Afghanistan has been distorted as an imperial problem through the very process of its reconstruction from imperial sources in national archives, which minutely reconstruct policy and military deliberations of individuals complicit in imperial expansion and colonial administration. The same sources usually focus on men in the corridors of political and military power in metropolitan ministries, colonial headquarters or frontier 'outposts'. Despite painstaking and attentive archival work, scholarship has not always been critical enough of the vantage point of a colonial 'centre' of authority and power, from which the history of the Afghan frontier was written. At times, studies of Afghanistan and the frontier operate in close proximity to their material, leading to the reconstruction of a particular historical reality based on colonial accounts and perspectives.[24] In addition, colonial, imperial and foreign political narratives on occasion display an identity of language, enabled through the appropriation of historical perspectives for the purposes of writing history. The results are, depending on the subject matter, a methodological mix of nationalism, colonialism and imperialism. Most problematically, imperial formations of the present have on occasion shaped and prompted scholarly investigation of past models of "cultural understanding" and "pacification" in the Indo-Afghan borderland in an effort to inform military operations ongoing in Afghanistan since 2001.[25]

Scholarship has responded to this challenge of the Great Game in two ways in particular. On the one hand, it has sought to refocus the history of Afghanistan "through Afghan eyes".[26] Robert Crews and Magnus Marsden have moved beyond Afghanistan as a geopolity, highlighting the movement of people, ideas and goods in global perspective.[27] On the other, critical approaches have engaged with previous histories, revisiting their sources and subjecting them to innovative methodological techniques, which directly enquire into the construction of knowledge on Afghanistan. This book arises from the scholarship of Christopher A. Bayly, Bernard S. Cohn, Nicholas B. Dirks and Thomas R. Metcalf, who have studied the pathways and power of colonial knowledge in Indian history in response to Edward Said's thesis on the mutual shaping of the 'West' and the 'East'.[28] Scholarship on the history of Afghanistan specifically provides several leading examples on the formation of colonial knowledge and its impact on present frameworks of thought. Since Mountstuart Elphinstone's *Account of the Kingdom of Caubul* in 1815, the history of Afghanistan has repeatedly taken the shape of ethnography, combining insights of colonial anthropology and studies of the environment with social, economic and political vectors. These "stylistic modalities of colonial knowledge" sought to make Afghanistan legible for colonial policymakers.[29] From the earliest colonial encounter at the beginning of the nineteenth century, British colonial officers 'made' the Afghan state in several ways.[30] Benjamin D. Hopkins has established that the creation of the Afghan state was closely connected with the colonial project in India. As a "para-colonial" state, Afghanistan was neither fully incorporated into nor fully excluded from its neighbouring colonial state in India. Elphinstone's mission to Peshawar in the early nineteenth century and the subsequent publication of his *Account of the Kingdom of Caubul* has had a lasting impact on generations of colonial and imperial administrators.[31] This "Elphinstonian episteme" provided an archive of the knowable on Afghanistan.[32] In addition to shaping 'Afghanistan' itself, it was populated it with 'war-like' Pashtun tribes, who first appeared as the South Asian likenesses of Scottish clans and later as imperial problems. As Nivi Manchanda has shown, the notion of 'tribe' has played, and continues to play, a crucial role in imperial constructions of Afghanistan.[33] In the course of the nineteenth century, Pathans were grouped in the colonial imagination of India's 'martial races'.[34] Martin J. Bayly has charted the extent and limits of colonial knowledge on Afghanistan from Elphinstone, to the First and Second Anglo-Afghan Wars, underlining the dialogic nature of colonial knowledge production, which included "moments of collaboration, collusion, alliance, and dialogue" between European "knowledge entrepreneurs" and South Asian informants.[35] At the same time, the colonial state contributed to the shaping of the Afghan state in cartographic exercises and boundary delineations since the early nineteenth century.[36] Together, these scholarly contributions reveal the inherent ambition of the colonial state in India to understand Afghanistan and solidify that knowledge for purposes of imperial administration along various pathways.

The very form, in which this kind of knowledge on Afghanistan was enshrined and transported, has itself had a long afterlife.[37] Several handbooks on Afghanistan written on either side of 1947 begin their narratives of the Afghan state with descriptions of geology and nature, on "the land and the people".[38] As Ranajit Guha has shown for colonial India, the very act of writing histories of India was modelled on the demands of colonial rule itself inasmuch as it served separate colonial from precolonial eras.[39] Several works on Afghanistan mimic a corpus on South Asian history sanctioned by the colonial government, such as the section on "Indian history" published in the annual *India Office List* prior to 1937. Examples of handbooks on Afghanistan from the early twentieth century suggest that the place generated particular characteristics in its inhabitants as a response to the various demands of nature. Afghans, this suggests, were determined by their ecology. According to these accounts, Afghanistan's primordial origins locked it in premodernity and implied the impermeability of an essential Afghan character that prevented progress into civilisation as defined by colonial rulers and authors.

The state-history nexus is most clear in the question of authorship. State servants have shaped the historiography of Afghanistan in ethnographic handbooks since the early nineteenth century, beginning with Elphinstone.[40] The nineteenth-century entanglement of state and history has outlived even the twentieth century. In addition to sharing a colonial tradition of writing about Afghanistan, the historiography of Afghanistan and early independent India also share similar contents and conclusions. William Kerr Fraser-Tytler's *Afghanistan*, first published in 1950, is a particularly important example. As a former colonial officer whose diplomatic experience in Kabul spanned almost two decades between 1922 and 1941, culminating in his Ministership (1935–1941), Fraser-Tytler believed in "the great physical and moral power" of the Raj. He provided an apologetic and heroic account of British rule in India, like many of his contemporaries also suffering from 'Raj nostalgia' did for India.[41] He perpetuated the myth of British India's efficient administration and thought in colonial categories, labelling the Indo-Afghan border as a boundary "between civilization and barbarism", which was also coupled with "the problem of the tribes".[42] In addition, he displayed patronising tendencies in his infantilising descriptions of independent Afghanistan, arguing that "the Afghans, like other young people, are liable to be volatile and fickle in their allegiance".[43] Fraser-Tytler implied a feudal notion of loyalty and societal organisation, which applied to Afghanistan as well as to the colonial state, both of which dispensed monetary payments and honours in return for the acceptance of overrule. Fraser-Tytler, thus, blended a history of Afghanistan with a positive assessment of British rule in South Asia.[44] He preserved his personal perceptions of Afghanistan in writing, perpetuating colonial history through publication. His account was originally designed as a handbook on Afghan affairs for the Foreign Office, indicating an immediate transfer of knowledge across the colonial-postcolonial divide.[45] Percy Sykes' *A History of Afghanistan*, published in 1940, also began as an official account.[46] In Nicholas Dirks' words, "[l]ike the aftermath of colonialism itself, colonial history lives on".[47]

Fraser-Tytler is one example among many others. Terence Creagh Coen wrote a history of his employer, *The Indian Political Service*, and included a section on Afghanistan.[48] Basil John Gould and George Leslie Mallam provide colonial service autobiographies with chapters on Kabul.[49] Olaf Caroe, former Governor of the North-West Frontier Province and India's Minister for External Affairs, wrote an influential international history of *The Pathans* that capitalised on ethnography's overlaps with colonial administration.[50] People, who had professional connections to Afghanistan after 1947, continued the tradition set by former colonial officers of describing Afghanistan through "imperial eyes".[51] This practice also generated the only, intensely nostalgic, retrospective on the later British Embassy.[52] Throughout the twentieth century, members of Britain's diplomatic services have provided commentaries on Afghanistan that were shaped by their own experiences, including Nicholas Barrington, Sherard Cowper-Coles and Martin Ewans.[53] This diplomatic genealogy was by no means only limited to British institutions. Several other former diplomats from Pakistan and the United States, Akbar S. Ahmed, Leon B. Poullada and James W. Spain have authored accounts on the frontier and Afghanistan, thus adopting a tradition of colonial administrators who turned into scholars, historians and ethnographers as well as inheriting the challenges of their methodological toolkits.[54] As a narrativised technology of rule, history-writing ensured colonialism's lively afterlife. The power of these colonial genealogies of thinking about Afghanistan explains why writing on Afghanistan still struggles to overcome a frontier mentality that captures the polity as a place 'beyond' or 'between'.[55] In these examples, we recognise the challenge that Ashis Nandy refers to as the "second colonization" as well as "colonialism that survives the demise of empires".[56]

Recent studies on the Indo-Afghan borderland have tugged at previously resolute definitions of imperial space and moved beyond the geographical and ideational borders imposed by the colonial state to perceive India's north-west frontier in terms of "connecting histories".[57] Shah Mahmoud Hanifi firmly "situates nineteenth-century Afghanistan in the context of British Indian colonialism".[58] David B. Edwards and Sana Haroon have pointed to the manifold personal, political, intellectual, religious, economic and societal links existing across the Indo-Afghan borderland's territorial delineations.[59] In the course of the nineteenth century, Afghanistan was created as an inter-imperial space.[60] The colonial state participated in the territorial delineation of the Afghan state, redefining the relationship between territory, people and the sovereignty of the state according to European notions.[61] Crucially, the colonial state was closely involved in Afghan boundary-making.[62] However, while the territories of Afghanistan and India were cartographically determined, the colonial state treated the region in between the two as ethnically defined space by means of the Frontier Crimes Regulation, effectively excluding the frontier from the fabric of the colonial state applied elsewhere in India. The people living on the frontier were treated as "imperial objects" as opposed to "colonial subjects".[63] As a consequence, the frontier itself was defined as inter-imperial, yet extra-colonial. Afghanistan lay beyond the reach of the India's colonial bureaucracy, yet within its 'sphere of influence'. Consequently, Elisabeth Leake shows how the Indo-Afghan, and later Afghan-Pakistani, borderland remained largely independent of colonial and postcolonial state control in the middle of the twentieth century.[64]

The history of the British Legation in Kabul also speaks to a recent body of scholarship that 'decenters empire' and positions colonial India in its wider oceanic and transcontinental connections.[65] Thomas R. Metcalf's *Imperial Connections* frames India as "both colonizer and colonized".[66] India "made possible British imperial conquest, control, and governance" elsewhere and was "a nodal point from which peoples, ideas, goods and institutions—everything that enables empire to exist—radiated outward".[67] Reaching from Southeast Asia to Eastern Africa, this "empire of the Raj" was an imperial centre with a high degree of agency in its own right and constituting much more than just a peripheral appendage to the imperial metropolis London.[68] Since John Gallagher and Ronald Robinson's seminal article of 1953, the periphery of empire had been at the forefront of scholarly attention.[69] According to Robinson and Gallagher, empires did not need to claim sovereignty to exert their claims; they could rule 'informally', enacting "the imperialism of free trade". Unlike imperial formations at the point of becoming, postcolonial nations explicitly claimed sovereignty during the dissolution of empires in the twentieth century in the name of 'independence'. As Ann Laura Stoler indicates, "'indirect rule' and 'informal empire' are unhelpful euphemisms, not working concepts".[70] They assume empire to be a bounded space or territory. If considered as an "imperial formation", empire emerges as producing "scaled genres of sovereignty and gradations of rights", which generated "new zones of exclusion and new sites of […] privileged exemption".[71] Imperial formations are "processes of becoming, not fixed things".[72] In addition to breaking up the spatial rigidity of 'empire', Stoler's also work prompts us to read archives "along the grain" and identify imperial archives as a technology of rule in themselves rather than as mere repositories that supply sources for the study of past events.[73]

The engagement with Afghanistan and empire in terms of space allows us to see the manifold shapes in which empire manoeuvred, negotiated and made Afghanistan's geographies before 1919. Afghanistan, the frontier and empire moved in and were constructed as liminal spaces. The field opens up for a discussion of empire as multicentred space and as a processual cluster in constant flux, of which diplomatic practice formed one dimension. Considering the history of the British Legation in Kabul in the geographical context of the 'oceanic turn' leaves behind the assumption that diplomacy emanated outward from one definitive imperial centre.[74] The book captures the British Legation in Kabul as an imperial node that embodied the transformation of the Indian Empire and its principles of governance at the same time that Afghanistan emerged as an independent state. The book links the history of the British Legation in Kabul to the moment of Afghanistan's statal independence in 1919 and problematises the early history of Afghanistan as an independent, sovereign entity in the context of imperial transformation. The dual process that entangled imperial transformation after independence with the making of independent postcolonial states occurred in other colonial settings around the world in the course of twentieth century.

Whilst colonial knowledge of Afghanistan is traceable over long stretches of time, it is also subject to transformation and relocation. The history of the Legation connects Afghanistan in the nineteenth, twentieth and twenty-first centuries. From Kabul, colonial practices of diplomacy were reproduced and exported to other localities and institutions. In this way, colonial practice went from colonial administration in India to a system of international relations that expanded in the course of the twentieth century in the shape of both state and non-state actors. The Legation itself was a "laboratory" where these processes of imperial communication, administration, bureaucracy and governance were set up, tested and refined in the age of imperial reconfiguration and experimentation.[75] From the Legation, diplomats distributed these techniques of governance across the Indian Empire. The Legation provided a model for a wider global phenomenon, potentially linking Kabul to other emerging diplomatic missions in the remit of the Indian Empire and beyond. Indeed, Kabul was conceived as a model institution, from which other colonial outputs and representations-in-the-making drew their inspiration. In other words, Afghanistan presents is a case of 'unique universality': it was unique in that the British Legation drew on specific knowledge and discourses that emerged from the Anglo-Afghan encounter; it was universal in that it represented broader imperial developments across the Indian Ocean in spatial terms as well as in the contexts of emerging independent nation-states in postcolonial time.

Afghanistan and the Timescales of Modernity, Development and Independence

In addition to space, colonial understandings of time have similarly marginalised Afghanistan. Contributions to global history have shown how the history of empire led to the integration of concepts of time, creating a shared sense of linear progress.[76] For Fraser-Tytler, the tutelage of colonialism necessarily preceded the later 'freedoms' of colonised peoples. In the age of post-independence, similar notions have persisted in the idea of 'development', which tended to organise postcolonial time along a linear, one-dimensional, unidirectional scale. This gave a sense of temporal localisation to colonial rulers as well as their 'dependents' and came to dominate approaches to histories of the "Third World" in the course of the twentieth century.[77] As much as the beginnings of colonial rule were, in retrospect, cast as fundamental ruptures from the precolonial, moments of independence in South Asia, whether 1919 or 1947, have likewise been treated as rigid divisions into a 'before' and an 'after'.[78] But, moments of statal independence in themselves acknowledged continuing imbalances of power. They perpetuated the categories of imperial masters and former colonial subjects in a system of international relations based on nominally independent nations.

The 1960s saw a range of studies engaging with the subject of 'modern Afghanistan' after 1919. They carried the stamp of that era's intellectual occupation with development and modernisation.[79] This 'modern Afghanistan' was a historical period in which the making of the state and its relations with tribes and people from the nineteenth century onwards were given preeminent scholarly attention.[80] Modernisation equated to the adoption of the state as a societal organising principle and the resistances created in the process. The idea of modernising Afghanistan was closely aligned to the centralisation and expansion of state structures. This political modernisation in Afghanistan gave prominent attention to elite bureaucratic administrators, including Amanullah Khan. How society is organised and how power is distributed is particularly pertinent when it comes to the history of law-making, in particular constitution-writing. Amanullah Khan sealed his revolutionary ambition with a range of legal codes (*nezam-nama*) and a constitution in 1923 as well as a second set of reforms regulating more specific areas of Afghan life and behaviour after his return from Europe in 1928. In the Afghanistan of Amanullah Khan ideas of modernity were implemented from the top at the expense of subaltern imaginings.

Amanullah Khan's secular reforms, especially those relating to women, challenged the religious authority of the *ulema*, its reach on education and, consequently, its position to administer social control independently of a central government. Francis Robinson has argued that "much of the discourse on modernity took place over how women should clothe themselves and move in public".[81] Modernisation came with challenges to the way the organisation of society, and the relations between the state and tribe as well as between secular and religious law therein were perceived. After overcoming the Khost rebellion of 1924, another armed insurgency in the winter of 1928/1929 ultimately forced Amanullah Khan's abdication in 1929 and led to the reign of Habibullah Kalakani. Leon B. Poullada concludes that "[t]he modernization program was more the victim than the cause of the revolution [against Amanullah Khan in 1928/1929]".[82] To Poullada, this was a conflict between "tribal power and centralized authority" that had "all the classical elements of historical tribal conflict".[83] To Senzil Nawid, Amanullah Khan's reign ended because of his failure to legitimise his reforms.[84] Whilst Amanullah Khan styled himself as a leader of the Muslim world after the disintegration of the Ottoman Empire, he lost religious authority as a consequence of undermining existing elites at home.[85] As Nawid points out, the "government that Aman-Allah forged after independence was a modernizing despotic monarchy".[86] Amanullah Khan saw his reign as "one of the pen and not the sword", a phrase with practical consequences.[87] The underfunding of the army, "potentially his best weapon" according to Vartan Gregorian, at the expense of other areas of reform, did not help matters when urban support for socioeconomic reforms crumbled.[88]

Historical commentators have tended to posit insurgency and tradition as rejections of modernity. As James Caron points out in his discussion of the historiography of Afghan modernisation in the 1920s, the backlash against Amanullah Khan's reforms has been captured in terms of 'insurgency' and as an embodiment of archaic 'tradition'.[89] The events of 1928/1929 have been variously framed as a "rebellion", "revolution", "uprising" or "revolt" against the government of Amanullah Khan.[90] Whilst each term suggests a different scope for agency and resistance, together the references firmly establish the insurgents' illegitimacy. Habibullah Kalakani's reign in 1929 often appears as the 'interregnum' of a "bandit amir" between the reigns by Amanullah Khan and Nadir Shah, giving its demise after a few months a sense of inevitability.[91] However, 'tradition' and 'modernity' are more than just a binary opposing pair of alternate timescales. As Alessandro Monsutti argues, it is restrictive to "emphasize the resilience of tradition in the face of modernity, the persistence of tribalism and ethnic loyalties, the rise of Islamic fundamentalism, international terrorism, drug trafficking, and corruption", as large sections of scholarship on Afghanistan have been wont to do.[92] Rather, scholars are urged to capture the idea of "entangled modernities", which removes from modernity its "teleological narrative" and captures the "fuzzy sovereignties" shared by international and national, elite and non-elite actors alike.[93]

Studies of twentieth-century Afghanistan have also focused on modernisation's international dimensions in the shapes of aid and development. Rooted in colonial notions, archaic conceptualisations of modernisation saw it as emanating from the 'West' to emerging nations. This kind of 'international' modernisation was inherently Eurocentric, flowing from imperial centres into colonial peripheries. As Astri Suhrke has pointed out, the history of development in Afghanistan created new powerful international hierarchies:

> A voluminous social science literature developed on this subject, which equated 'modern' with 'Western', and assigned Western capital, political influence and knowledge an important role in promoting the modernisation process. For a generation of these theorists, moreover, modernisation was seen as a package. Economic growth, political democracy, modern attitudes and Weberian rationality in state bureaucracies were all viewed as interdependent and mutually sustaining elements.[94]

After 2001, the power asymmetries inherent in international aid have resulted in a 'sovereignty gap' in Afghanistan that owes its existence to the proportionately higher weightage attributed to foreign donors over Afghans in decision-making processes.[95]

Whilst Afghan modernity is pursued in these avenues of enquiry, this book adds to them a modern history of diplomacy. Diplomacy, and a state's capacity to represent itself and project its sovereignty abroad, forms a crucial part of the histories of modernity and modernisation. Histories of the state are not synonymous with histories of the nation, but the formalisation of diplomatic representations through accredited missions is a key aspect of the modern world and its understandings of sovereignty. After 1919, the independent Afghan state sent its emissaries abroad to formalise its bilateral contacts in order to expand the reach of the state beyond a domestic realm on an international scale. At the same time, and in reverse direction, people, diplomats, staff, engineers and travellers arrived in Kabul. The resulting international encounter in Kabul also posed challenges to Afghanistan's sovereignty in legal terms. During the 1920s, two incidents, in particular, threw light on Afghanistan's systems of law enforcement and justice. Transgressions of the law, in particular by non-Afghan perpetrators at the expense of Afghans, carried the threat of undermining the sovereignty of the Afghan state both domestically and internationally. In 1924, an Italian engineer Piparno shot an Afghan policemen. He paid an indemnity to the victim's family that equated to a settlement. In addition, the Afghan state, and its supreme representative Amanullah Khan, sought to enforce its law, sending Piparno to prison, from where he escaped before he was apprehended, tried, sentenced and eventually hanged. In 1925, the German geography professor, Gustav Stratil-Sauer travelled to Kabul on a motorcycle. On his way, he shot an Afghan, claiming he had done so in self-defence. Like Piparno, Stratil-Sauer attempted to escape, assisted by the German Minister Fritz Grobba in whose car he was found seated near Jalalabad. Stratil-Sauer was apprehended, tried in Kabul and sentenced, but eventually pardoned by Amanullah Khan. In addition to international newspaper coverage both instances also caused fallout on Afghanistan's diplomatic relations with Italy and Germany, respectively. The Italian Legation threatened withdrawal from Kabul, which was averted by the return of the indemnity originally paid by Piparno to the victim's family as well as an official statement of regret by the Afghan state. In Stratil-Sauer's case, the German Minister had assisted the subversion of due process and was eventually withdrawn from Kabul in 1926.[96]

As a set of laws guiding the conduct of states with one another, the history of formalised diplomacy between states is a narrative of modernisation that affected both the 'West' and colonial nations alike. Whilst scholarship has furthered our understanding of 'Western' development affecting Afghanistan and Afghans, very little work has been undertaken to study the changes affecting the imperial system of governance to which Afghanistan was so intricately connected before and after 1919. The British Legation in Kabul was a product of Afghan independence, but also a unique institution that was not simply shaped according to a readily available, universally applicable, Eurocentric blueprint of diplomatic practice. Afghan independence prompted a rethinking of imperial governance. The book's perspective captures the emergence of a diplomatic institution as an instance of modern international history. As such, it trains the idea of modernisation as effected by spaces construed as imperial peripheries back onto the 'West'. Recent scholarship on Afghanistan has rightly pointed to a "'re-turn' to empire", in that international history and its disciplinary associate diplomatic history have been inextricably entangled with imperial history since the beginnings of both disciplines.[97] The British Legation's institutional history and its eclectic set of diplomatic practices illustrate the convergence of at least two temporalities. On the one hand, the Legation owed its very existence to notions of inter-state relations as laid down in the Treaty of Vienna of 1815. On the other hand, this European modernity joined its colonial variant in Kabul, where the international took on different proportions altogether.

The construction of these different temporal orders is closely entangled with conceptions of space. The British Legation in Kabul illustrates the shaping of empire by a buffer state on its frontier. It connected Afghanistan to a formalised world of diplomacy. As territorially limited, international extensions of sovereign states, that world was mostly, though not exclusively, reserved for the 'great powers' or, in other words, European imperial monarchies in the early twentieth century. Speaking in terms of linear understandings of time that both the imperial and colonial teleologies themselves implied, the Legation represented the synchronicity of the asynchronous. In Kabul, diplomatic relations were placed on a reciprocal footing between former imperial masters and colonial subjects without relinquishing the former imperial and colonial asymmetries that became visible in the uses of imperial channels and colonial materiality. As a meeting site of Afghan, colonial and imperial timescales, knowledge and modernities, the history of the British Legation in Kabul was a uniquely hybrid institution through which the colonial past of international relations intruded upon the Anglo-Afghan diplomatic interaction in the present.[98] It complicates our approach to thinking about state institutions that have predominantly been understood as products of Western statecraft alone.

POSTCOLONIALISM, DECOLONISATION AND COLONIALITY

Colonial and, supposedly, *post*colonial dimensions collapsed into one another between 1919 and 1947, making visible also parallel conceptions of modernity. Gyan Prakash has pointed to the linear understanding of history, as "history with a clear trajectory originating in the early modern European expansions and ending with the postwar anticolonial nationalism and decolonization".[99] Modernity cannot exist outside of the framework provided by European colonialism:

> This view is complicit with Western domination, but offers itself nonetheless as a clear lens through which we can understand colonialism. It sequesters colonialism tightly in the airless container of History, and casts postcoloniality as a new beginning, one in which certain old modes of domination may persist and acquire new forms of sustenance but one that marks the end of an era. To pry open the reading of colonialism from this prison-house of historicism requires more than the concept of neocolonialism. For at stake is not simply the issue as to whether or not former colonies have become free from domination, but also the question as to how the history of colonialism and colonialism's disciplining of history can be shaken loose from the domination of categories and ideas it produced – colonizer and colonized; white, black, and brown; civilized and uncivilized; modern and archaic; cultural identity; tribe and nation.[100]

The resilience of colonial frameworks of thought resonates here. More importantly, Prakash points to the fluidity of paradigms and timeframes during the 'end of empire'. But, this thought-process has not fully broken down more conventional ways of periodising the process of decolonisation, which separates colonialism from postcolonialism. There is considerable debate as to how long and how complete decolonisation really was (or is).[101] Derek Gregory dismisses the completeness of the decolonising process, suggesting instead that we live in a "colonial present".[102] In fact, there was uncertainty whether decolonisation described a process or a singular moment in time, such as the achievement of independent statehood in the case of former colonial nations.[103] Colonial administrators framed decolonisation in South Asia as a moment in time, as the benevolent retreat of colonial rule and bureaucracies during a 'transfer of power and responsibility' to India and Pakistan. Over time, decolonisation assumed new meanings that moved its interpretation beyond moments in time towards sequences of events. The 'end of empire' became a drawn-out, incomplete process.[104] Stoler's idea of "ruin" is a handy device to reconsidering colonialism's messy endings: "At issue is the political life of imperial debris, the longevity of structures of dominance, and the uneven pace with which people can extricate themselves from the colonial order of things".[105] This has important repercussions on the temporal structuring of history, as the *post*colonial follows the colonial. The term of *post*colonialism, or *post*coloniality, defined as the era following *after colonialism*, is not synonymous with colonialism's disappearance.[106] In the linear compartmentalisation of history, the temporal-postcolonial is not the same as the decolonial, when colonialism's "old modes of domination" (Prakash's words) would be entirely absent.[107] Historians of South Asia have grappled with the idea that historiography itself perpetuates colonial notions.[108] Decolonisation is the process, which creates, or re-establishes, the decolonial through "delinking". It denotes more than just the disappearance of colonial bureaucracies. In Walter Mignolo's words, "delinking" is a "de-colonial epistemic shift leading to other-universality, that is, to pluriversality as a universal project".[109] The means to achieve this is "epistemic disobedience".[110] For Nandy, decolonisation is a "moral and cognitive venture against oppression" that takes aim at "a colonialism which survives the demise of empire".[111] "[F]or us, the once-colonized", wrote Partha Chatterjee, decolonisation denoted "our freedom of imagination".[112]

While terms like postcolonialism, postcoloniality and decolonisation provide crucially important meanings for the study of the colonial past as well as its present and futures, this book adopts the notion of coloniality to capture colonialism's presences and the consciously prevented disappearance of the colonial.[113] Studies located in the history of ideas and the history of knowledge have pointed to colonialism's lingering constituents and elements.[114] Coloniality describes the continued impact of colonialism in the absence of colonialism itself.[115] It liberates the historiography of colonialism from previously rigid binary concepts proposed by early postcolonial thinkers, such as Frantz Fanon and Edward Said, who despite their insightful and influential critiques of colonial concepts, arguably, still thought in terms of them.[116] In 1989, Anibal Quijano reflected on "Colonialidad y modernidad/racionalidad" in an edited collection on the quincentennial of 1492.[117] In the context of this fitting occasion for a reconsideration of the global impact of European colonialism, Quijano established coloniality as "the invisible and constitutive side of 'modernity'".[118] Coloniality lends itself particularly well to analyses of colonialism's lasting power structures.[119] This "coloniality of power" expresses itself in many registers, including knowledge. Whilst the coloniality of power is particularly pertinent in areas that came under direct colonial control in the past, Afghanistan was the subject of a colonial epistemic structuring. Elphinstone's mission in 1808/1809 laid the epistemological foundations for a Western understanding Afghanistan.[120] Whilst no lasting colonial bureaucracy was installed, the influx of Indian money linked Afghanistan to colonial markets and created economic dependencies.[121] Moreover, Afghanistan's borders were drawn by Russian, Indian and Persian empires. The Goldsmid and Durand Missions physically shaped Afghanistan by delineating its territorial boundaries and defining its eastern and western borders in 1870–1872 and 1893, respectively.[122] The making of the Durand Line in 1893 is one among many similar instances of border-making. Yet, this colonial border continues to present challenges of a global scale until today. Afghanistan's independence in 1919 was not synchronic with a process of decolonisation, because the colonial state continued to exist until 1947. Arguably, the colonial state lives on in Afghanistan's geographical shape. Equally, the objectives and practices of British diplomacy in Kabul between 1922 and 1947 cannot be considered postcolonial, let alone decolonial. The Raj impacted on the diplomatic practices of the British Legation in Kabul, its structure, its staff and its representations. Its knowledge shaped Anglo-Afghan diplomatic relations. British diplomacy in Afghanistan as practised by the Legation was characteristically colonial. The very existence of the Legation represented a materialisation of colonial power.

The concept of coloniality captures the hybridity of the modern world and the colonial presences therein, both from a contemporary and from a historical perspective. From a historical perspective, the Legation in Kabul was colonial as long as the Raj existed and the storehouse of colonial knowledge provided a repertoire of intellectual as well as material inspirations for the conduct of Anglo-Afghan diplomacy. As such, this coloniality was synchronic with colonialism. From a contemporary perspective, its coloniality was later incorporated into a Foreign Office network of British diplomacy after 1947 by way of an inner-imperial transfer of ideas from the former colony to the metropolis. As such, the Legation's coloniality was diachronic, existing on both sides of colonialism's formal end in South Asia when it became an Embassy in 1948. The book's chapters are dedicated to explorations of the Legation's colonialities in synchronic and diachronic dimensions.

THE REINVENTION OF DIPLOMATIC HISTORY

This book is not a conventional diplomatic history. As one of the oldest forms of historiography, the beginnings of history as an academic discipline are intimately interwoven with accounts of states and the diplomatic representatives of nations. Since the nineteenth century, the discipline of history has moved far beyond the remit of the state. Although histories of the nation-state may now only constitute one among other genres its relevance is unbroken even at the beginning of the twenty-first century.[123] Once considered an outdated form of historiography, diplomatic history has shown signs of renewal and scholarly vigour for several decades, applying a series of innovative turns, whilst diplomatic histories of a more conventional variety also continue to be produced.[124] Resting on advances made in the study of colonial India, Afghanistan as well as the methodologies of what has been called 'new' diplomatic history since the 1990s following several methodological turns, the book's chapters confront the colonial past of the British state's diplomatic history. Statal independence, and the subsequent emergence of diplomatic missions in capitals around the world, has for a long time been defined as a paradigmatic shift. But, the discipline has shown a remarkable reluctance to meaningfully engage with its colonial origins both in terms of the academic discipline, its epistemologies and its frameworks of thought as well as their implications for the study of diplomatic institutions of inter-state relations. The discipline's present-day relevance is beyond doubt, but its methodology is well primed for rejuvenation and expansion. It is time to address the decolonisation of diplomatic history's epistemological foundations, which continue to distort the study of the modern world. A growing body of scholarship on diplomatic history written from Indian perspectives is a testament to this need.[125]

In a widely used guidebook published in 1917, Ernest Satow defined diplomacy as "the application of intelligence and tact to the conduct of official relations between the governments of independent states, extending sometimes also to their relations to their vassal states".[126] Studies of diplomatic history, by convention, identify a set of state interests and reconstruct the process of international negotiation. In this variety of the term, diplomatic history represents a particular form of historiography whose focus on political decision-making amongst a selected few state representatives and officials make it an almost exclusive domain of high politics. Confined by the constraints set by the state, diplomatic history has also often focused on the narration of individual ambassadors' lives or collective studies of diplomatic heads of mission in a certain place.[127] As shown above, the former employees of several states have contributed to the history of Afghanistan as editors and authors. The overlap of diplomatic and historiographical practices underlines for the specific case of Afghanistan what holds true to the discipline of diplomatic history as a whole. Due to their privileged access both to historical decision-making processes and to the people involved in them, diplomatic history has often been *about* diplomats as much as it has also been framed *by* them. The resultant accounts are often privileged and elitist both in terms of social distinction and the richness of the archival record on diplomatic decisions, lives and institutions.

Conventional diplomatic history shares many similarities with its colonialist avatar. The writing of diplomatic history has been, and in some cases still is, marked by the absence of reflection on the subject's theoretical assumptions as well as by the omnipresence of narratives of power. Together with the often teleological nature of state histories, they have impeded the probing of the tools and limits of diplomatic history in favour of positivist histories of events. Studies of this kind seemingly reinforce diplomatic history's explanatory utility for the present. However, this output-oriented approach to diplomatic history suppresses a reflection on why certain individuals and organisations have been chosen for description while others have not or why certain methods and assumptions have been made and not others. Diplomatic history, at times, resembles a stage play, in which a number of characters enter and exit. It is often marked by a methodological focus on the nation and chronological narratives, rather than analytical-thematic approaches. Conventional diplomatic history reconstructs a specific process of policy formulation and consequently suffers from the process of its description in the pursuit of an essentially teleological perspective.

Michael J. Hogan and Thomas G. Paterson's *Explaining the History of American Foreign Relations* broke important ground in the reframing of diplomatic history.[128] The beginning of the third millennium saw several other edited collections aimed at redrawing disciplinary boundaries. Several international and global approaches were articulated in order to remove diplomatic history from the restraints of the nation-state and illuminate its theoretical blind spots. An important step in the process was the reshaping of diplomatic history as international history through foci of culture.[129] Jessica C. E. Gienow-Hecht and Frank Schumacher pursued a "merger between international history and cultural studies".[130] The results of this multifaceted moulding of disciplines have decentred diplomatic history and brought forth advances in the meaning of culture itself, which emerged in terms of "social affinities, comparative analyses, cultural connections, psychological influences, local traditions, and unspoken assumptions".[131] Rather than generating a new synthesis, Volker Depkat's and Eckart Conze's debate on the usability of culture for the study of international relations history illuminated the divisions within the field. The spectrum of historiographical activities ranged from attempts to change the field cautiously to radical transformations. Depkat, for instance, urged caution in the application of concepts of culture to the study of international history, arguing that these should only be employed to serve conventional diplomatic or international history and leave its main objectives in place.[132] By comparison, Conze argued that concepts of culture, if properly defined, could in themselves represent worthwhile contributions to the field of diplomatic history, for "patterns of causality" cannot simply forget the "contingent nature of history" itself.[133] In other words, diplomatic history cannot produce meaningful interpretations by being shielded from the larger patterns of history. Today, diplomatic and international histories range from the conventional to the transdisciplinary. The former explain foreign policy, the latter strip it of policy altogether by locating diplomatic history in the contexts of places, people and ideas far removed from the centres of power in the decision-making process.

Several additional contributions have since been made to the theoretical apparatus underlying international and diplomatic historiography in an attempt to move it beyond the bounds of "decisive moments and pivotal people".[134] Diplomatic history moved to include the study of diplomats, diplomacy-related personnel and organisations.[135] But, there have also been countercurrents. Timothy J. Lynch, for instance, was critical of the "trendier, and leftier approaches" as well as of the "modern bias against elitism and 'great men'".[136] In light of this engaging debate on the methods of international and diplomatic historiography, there has been an important shift away from "high politics" to diplomats as important historical actors.[137] Kenneth Weisbrode, for instance, has urged a more detailed analysis of personal and professional networks, "critical networks of persuasion", as well as life histories of individual diplomats in order to place diplomats in "their proper place of innovation at the center of international history".[138] The growing corpus of research on diplomatic women, the League of Nations, other international organisations and non-governmental organisations are cases in point.[139] This focus on individuals rather than policy formulation, however, has raised further questions as to who should qualify as a diplomat. As the boundaries of diplomatic, international and transnational histories continue to shift, people involved in diplomacy, but not officially attached to a political setup, still only exist in diplomatic history's "fringes".[140]

It is important to note that the above summary is to a large extent a reflection of a transatlantic debate.[141] But, it helps to bridge two disconnected fields of study located in Europe and Northern America on the one hand and South Asia on the other. One notable exception is Andrew

Rotter's *Comrades at Odds*, a study of Indian-American international relations from 1947 to the mid-1960s, which broke with the chronological determinism of policy-making and instead organised its discussion into chapters along cultural themes.[142] Another helpful bridge from the transatlantic debate on diplomatic history's methodology to South Asia is Michael H. Fisher's work, which has pointed to the overlap of diplomacy and colonialism in the age of independence: "In the broadest sense, indirect control – or at least determining influence over other states – remains the goal of many governments and trans-national corporations today. Often this control or influence is exercised through the medium of its embassy or local corporate headquarters".[143]

In contrast to more tangible shapes of state power, violence for instance, diplomacy is yet to be subjected to analysis around the colonial-postcolonial divide. In a revealing article on diplomacy and empire, John Darwin argued that "[t]he main task of imperial diplomacy [in the nineteenth century] was managing the endemic disputes, which arose where the demarcation of colonial domains had still to be finalized".[144] Between 1954 and 1956, diplomacy's main task was "maintaining empire by influence".[145] In this reading, diplomacy shaped colonial spaces. Later, in the age of decolonisation, it followed empire in a temporal sense. In between the two thresholds, before and after colonialism, lay the period of colonial rule. Crucially, however, diplomacy appears separate from either colonialism, empire or decolonisation. It was an imperial statecraft that managed the process of decolonisation for receding colonial powers. As a discipline it appeared unaffected by a need to decolonise, although it inherited empire's legacies, was inspired by power-laden narratives and, to some degree, was justified by a previous existence of empire. In this sense, coloniality can be understood as a deliberate mechanism employed to counter the decolonisation of power. To paraphrase Anibal Quijano, when coloniality is modernity's other, then diplomacy is empire's invisible and constitutive side. Rather than treating diplomacy and empire as different entities, this book argues that diplomacy bridged the end of empire, existing before and after as one and the same. Diplomacy's colonial past continues to inspire its present.[146] It is in itself a form of empire that acquired global proportions in the twentieth century. If, for a moment, we consider diplomacy as empire, then it, too, can be subjected to the paths of enquiry that imperial history has opened up, including violence. This is a particularly promising thought with regard to usual assumptions about the 'peaceful statecraft' of diplomacy. If, in addition to conceiving of diplomacy as empire, we then think of the imperial origins of international history, then the global adoption of embassies as representations of nation-states virtually everywhere appears both as a democratisation of empire among nation-states as well as the adoption of empire as a universally applied concept in the postcolonial world. In other words, if diplomacy is empire, then empire spread everywhere and to everyone in the twentieth century. This suggestion opens up new avenues for the study of postcolonial nation-states and their engagement with twentieth-century imperial formations. In the same way that postcolonial studies overcame colonial binary divisions into colonial masters and anticolonial nationalists, the study of diplomacy is relevant if it can take up the study of diplomatic representations as emerging forms of empire. As a field, diplomatic history awaits further engagement with postcolonial critique and enquiry.

Writing 'New' Diplomatic History in Paracolonial Space and Time

The book is the result of several research agendas. First, the book provides a dedicated historical account of the British Legation in Kabul and of the larger framework of the Afghan state's international relations from the 1920s to the late 1940s. The Legation surfaces only occasionally and in histories of Afghanistan's foreign relations. From the late 1960s to the early 1980s, Ludwig W. Adamec and Milan Hauner achieved a meticulous and pioneering assembly of archival records in important compendia sourced from several national repositories in India, the UK, Germany and the USA, on Afghanistan's foreign relations in the first half of the twentieth century.[147] Owing to their focus on accessing and collating, these works were, however, heavily focused on the realm of the high politics of Afghanistan's international relations from the vantage point of Western metropoles. Unlike the 1920s, the history of Afghanistan's relations with India and the UK in the 1930s and 1940s has been largely neglected.[148] In addition to these academic ventures, Rhea Talley Stewart's *Fire in Afghanistan* of 1973 provides a fast-paced history of Anglo-Afghan relations between 1914 and 1929.[149] Anne Baker and Ronald Ivelaw-Chapman's *Wings Over Kabul* of 1975 celebrates the aerial evacuation of the Legation to India during the rebellion against Amanullah Khan.[150] In Susan Loughhead's *The Endgame*, the Legation is the historical backdrop to the "final chapter in Britain's Great Game in Afghanistan" that played out between 1948 and 1950.[151]

Second, in order to write a diplomatic history of a new variety, the book assembles a distinct methodological apparatus consisting of four approaches—biographical, performative, bodily, material-architectural. Instead of reiterating the logic imposed by the abstract deliberations of diplomats as well as of archives, which house them in abundance, these approaches organise the book's discussion. It adopts a purposely fragmented approach focusing firmly on the technologies of colonial power that connect the era of colonialism with the realm of international relations. These approaches offer fresh reflections on the material used to write diplomatic histories in general. For instance, the book engages with notions of gender in order to upset the taken-for-granted availability of scores of archival materials written and provided by men.[152] Several chapters engage with ideas of masculinity, whilst a dedicated section (see Chapter 3) foregrounds the history of the so-called "Legation Ladies". It is important to note that Joan W. Scott's assessment still holds true: "High politics itself is a gendered concept, for it establishes its crucial importance and public power, the reasons for and the fact of its highest authority, precisely in its exclusion of women from its work".[153] In this way, the book follows in the path of much current scholarship that aims at rereading, reinterpreting and reassessing material relevant to the writing of diplomatic history in addition to exploring previously untapped materials, among them biographical dictionaries, private letters, personal career files and the colonial state's accounting documents. The organisation of the book is an application of its research objective to remove diplomatic history from purely teleological trajectories. Rhea Talley Stewart's *Fire in Afghanistan* is an extreme example of a chronologically organised narrative. Adamec's work is explicitly structured in "chronological order", though "examination of the complexities of Afghan foreign relations with various powers and their implications in domestic Afghan politics necessitated interruptions of the chronological sequence with accounts of concurrent events".[154] This book fundamentally implements the necessity of rupturing the chronology of diplomatic histories hinted at by Adamec.

Third, as a result of the preceding two points, the book presents a range of connections between colonial India and independent Afghanistan in terms of a history of ideas. Heeding Adamec's observation that "India, rather than Britain, was still in command of Anglo-Afghan relations", it supplies a whole register of both synchronic and diachronic colonial links between British diplomacy as practiced in Kabul and colonial rule in India. The discussion in the book's chapters investigates the colonial realities that have been confined to the backgrounds of previous studies. Through the life history of the institution the book is able to focus on a hitherto understudied area of history and offer a reassessment of colonialism's continuities in the age of statal independence. The book's chapters explore the origins of British diplomacy in precolonial and colonial contexts, revealing the inherent tensions in the setup of British diplomacy.[155] They expand diplomatic history's narrow borders through an exploration of the overlapping colonial and imperial practices of British diplomacy in a place that has for a long time been considered peripheral, marginal and ahistorical.[156] The history of the British Legation in Kabul illustrates developments of global significance from colonial rule to independence for both colonisers and colonised. British diplomats in Kabul were exposed to, borrowed from and contributed to a colonial archive on Afghanistan.[157] An investigation of this archive and British diplomats' complicity in its circulation, expansion and maintenance in professional and public arenas widens the scope of diplomatic history from narrow output-oriented, foreign policy decision-making to a deeper appreciation of diplomats and diplomacy-related staff as historical actors in their own right. In essence, the book explores diplomatic history's postcolonial turn.

Diplomatic History as Imperial History, Diplomacy as Empire

Prior to and after 1919, Afghanistan existed outside of, but not disconnected from, the system of colonial bureaucracy in India. From 1922, the British Legation in Kabul regulated Afghanistan's diplomatic relations with its a former suzerain or imperial overlord, the colonial power in South Asia until 1947. Like the imperial spaces of 'Afghanistan', the 'frontier' and 'empire', in which it was shaped and with which it engaged, the British Legation in Kabul took on characteristics of spatial and temporal liminality. Its history fits into a larger transitory period both in the histories of Afghanistan and empire from independence to decolonisation that the book's chapters address in detail. From 1922, 'British' diplomacy in Afghanistan was characteristically colonial. A generation of colonial officers from the same colonial service that had shaped Afghanistan during the nineteenth century now became diplomats in Kabul. While these colonial officers observed Afghanistan's transition to an independent sovereign state very acutely, they were less perceptive of their own transition from colonial officers with authoritarian ideas of statehood to practitioners of international diplomacy based on the recognition of equality between states. Contemporary definitions of the person of the diplomat did not distinguish between colonial officers and diplomats.[158] Diplomats in Afghanistan entertained and applied qualified understandings of independent Afghanistan's sovereignty, which were grounded in the colonial state's perception of its imperial periphery. The Legation was an inter-space, located outside of, but not removed from, the shifting parameters of colonial rule in India. It was the diplomatic representation of an imperial government and a colonial outpost in an independent state that throws light on the paradoxical emergence of colonial presences during the 'end of empire' in South Asia. When the Legation became the British Embassy in 1948, many of its colonial foundations, most materially in the shape of its compound structures and buildings, survived into the postcolonial era, where they were purposely utilised to harness bygone imperial glory for the purposes of a British metropolitan government's foreign policy in Afghanistan after 1947. The Legation was a uniquely multifaceted institution whose grounding in colonial culture, imperial rule and diplomatic inequality is contradictory, polyvalent and spatially dislodged between independent Afghanistan, colonial India and metropolitan Britain.

Chapter 2 begins in 1919 and draws up the wider context of Anglo-Afghan relations before and after the moment of Afghan independence. It offers an overview of the negotiations that shaped the nature of Afghan independence and the creation of the Legation before its arrival in Kabul in 1922. It also offers a brief history of the Legation until 1948, thus presenting a narrative framework for the discussion that follows in the later chapters. Chapters 3 and 4 make visible the transmitters of knowledge at the Legation in Kabul. Chapter 3 inverts colonial hierarchies and excavates the Legation's subordinated operative staff from a variety of archival sources. Rebalancing common asymmetries in favour of a European colonial elite, the chapter gives primary importance to the previously neglected layers of British diplomacy's setup in recognition of advances effected by Subaltern Studies, postcolonial critique and engagements with the historiography of diplomacy and international relations. The collective biography struggles against the anonymising tendencies of elitist colonialist and diplomatic historiography and reveals intricate and long-lasting connections on the Legation's clerical and support staff levels. The chapter exposes the intensity of the Legation's connections with colonial India in its human foundations and the organisation of its labour.

Chapter 4 reveals the career geographies of the Legation's political leadership in colonial India before and after their postings in Kabul. It conceptualises the Legation's political staff against the background of their career geographies, networks of family and profession. It treats the Legation's structure as a manifestation of colonial hierarchies at work in neighbouring India and addresses questions of recruitment in a changing world of international relations. It argues that the Legation was modelled on similar institutions in colonial India, to which it was effectively assimilated by means of a circular system of colonial staff movements. The chapter also lays the groundwork for the discussion in the following chapters by introducing the main characters of British diplomacy in Afghanistan between 1922 and 1947 as agents in the transfer of colonial culture to independent Afghanistan.

Chapters 5 through 7 focus on the Legation's colonial practices. Chapter 5 highlights the process that turned colonial servants into international diplomats. It explores the accreditations of British Ministers in Kabul through the theme of performance and embeds its discussion in a wider history of Anglo-Afghan relations. It flags the repercussions of the performative aspects in diplomatic reporting and ultimately casts doubt on their credibility as true recordings of a past reality. British Ministers in Kabul emerge as performers in a double sense. On the one hand, their role during the actual historical encounter with Afghan kings was delimited by Afghan state protocol. On the other hand, by writing it down, with almost supreme authority over the text production process, they performed the encounter again, borrowing heavily from the storehouse of the colonial archive that was established during the nineteenth century. The ultimate text constituted a dramatised version of the encounter during the accreditation as it presented itself to the recorder or as the recorder wished to present it. Following this avenue of inquiry, the chapter interrogates British diplomatic records against their claim of factually representing Anglo-Afghan encounters and relations. By reading those records as textual end products, which can reveal their authors' objectives, motivations and political frameworks, and instead of treating them as ur-texts for the reconstruction of narrative histories of events, the chapter generates insights for reading and writing Anglo-Afghan diplomatic interaction and diplomatic history in general. The chapter conceptualises diplomacy as a string of performances. It reveals the tensions between colonial and diplomatic identities and between international bureaucrats as persons and state officials. It displays the colonial archive at the very moment of its production and in repeated action through its rich supply of literary portraits of Afghan rulers.

Chapter 6 uses the body as a thematic bundle and discusses its ubiquity in British diplomacy in Afghanistan through the themes of space, language and medicine. It explores the Legation's many diplomatic bodies. Having established colonial diplomats' intimate links with the colonial state, the chapter explores the pervasiveness of colonial physicality in diplomatic society in Kabul. It looks at how British diplomacy was practiced in corporeal dimensions. The chapter argues that the body fulfilled several crucial roles. Through the body, Afghanistan was perceived in intensely physical dimensions. The colonial body defined the very circumstances of British diplomacy in Afghanistan in terms of comfort, hygiene and pastimes. It also provided a powerful trope in the language of diplomatic reporting. Most intimately, the Afghan body in need of medical attention provided British diplomacy with the opportunity to unleash the technological means at colonial India's disposal on to a wider Afghan public. In sum, British diplomats in Kabul introduced into Afghanistan several aspects of the physicality of the Raj, consisting of its concomitant athletic traditions, competition and education as well as its discourses on nature, climate and hygiene. Colonial diplomats applied these discourses to Kabul, which was consequently perceived in colonial terms. Independent Afghanistan was, thus, subjected to colonial concepts of the body, which had been developed by generations of colonial administrators in India.

Chapter 7 extends the discussion of Afghan space into an analysis of the Legation's material foundations and examines the Legation's architecture and material representations in the context of the ambitions of British diplomacy in Afghanistan until 1947/1948. It focuses on the Legation's architectural evidence in the context of a transfer of culture from India to Afghanistan. The Legation premises highlight the asymmetry in British-Afghan relations as the Raj provided the intellectual background to many of the Legation's designs. The Legation's localisation and structuring followed colonial rationales as it was established at a distance from Kabul's allegedly dirty and dangerous crowds. India provided the means and ideas for the construction of the Legation in Kabul, which was physically imposed onto Kabul's suburban landscape. In itself, the Legation compound further implemented ideas of racial segregation by placing domestic labourers and the Indian Oriental Secretary either marginally or entirely outside. The Legation also effectively ordered Afghan nature through its horticultural reorganisation and by supplanting an Afghan landscape under British architectural structures. The colonial state's material representation in Kabul illustrates one of the longest-lasting legacies of the Raj.

Chapters 5–7 reveal the discursive colonialism of British diplomacy in Afghanistan, with each chapter building on the insights of the previous one. The book moves from a historical introduction to populating the Legation (biography), to performative interactions with Afghans (accreditations), to physical practices (the body) and to spaces of diplomacy and recreation (architecture). Chapter 8 takes the historical frame beyond 1947, picking up the chronological threads spun throughout the book, also touching on the history of British-Afghan relations in the second half of the twentieth century and the early twenty-first century. Chapter 9 offers concluding reflections and elaborates on the idea of coloniality, colonial presences outside of colonialism's territorial reach and beyond its ends. As a whole, the book reveals the Legation's coloniality, from 1922 to 1948, and its afterlives. It encourages a rethinking of previous binary divides into colonial and postcolonial chronologies and also provides a long-overdue study into the colonial inspirations of the British state's interactions with the world after 1945.

The book produces several methodological insights. As a result of the biographical approach in Chapters 3 and 4, British diplomacy in Afghanistan appears as a multilayered undertaking, removed from the reserve of particular elites, which understands all its participants as enabling the conduct of international relations. In return, these chapters articulate approaches to the study of biography in order to uncover the seemingly 'unimportant' individuals of elite-centrist colonial and national archives, for instance through reading the colonial state's accounting documents. Chapter 4 extends biography's scope to include genealogies through networks of family and profession. It reads service biographies as accumulated career geographies. Chapter 5 establishes the staged, performative and particular character of diplomatic reality, casting doubt on previously unchallenged diplomatic reporting. This has important repercussions for approaches to colonial and diplomatic archives, whose sources must, as a consequence, undergo intense scrutiny as performances. Chapter 6 establishes the body's omnipresence in diplomatic encounters and reporting. As a result, diplomatic history ventures beyond a political domain and further into studies of the everyday. In the other direction, the relevance of the body in international relations thinking is further expanded. Chapter 7 lifts diplomatic architecture beyond the awe-inspiring and intimidating, revealing its flaws and purposely hidden elements. Owing to this multitransdisciplinary approach, the book highlights multiple aspects of diplomatic life in Kabul, from the very personal to the communal, from the private to the official, from the political to the casual, from the physical to the metaphysical, from the leisurely to the competitive, from the natural to the cultural, thus giving an account of diplomatic reality that goes beyond studies focused on the essential political. Together, the chapters explore the discursive colonialism of British diplomacy in Afghanistan.

Notes

1. Transcript of interview of Hugh Michael Carless, 23 February 2002, 5, https://www.chu.cam.ac.uk/media/uploads/files/Carless.pdf [accessed: 26 May 2018].
2. Michael Evans, "Britain Follows US Lead to Close Down Embassy in Kabul", *The Times*, 28 January 1989, 6; Liz Thurgood and Hella Pick, "Britain Joins Exodus from Afghanistan", *The Guardian*, 28 January 1989, 24.
3. Hella Pick, "Regime Written Off", *The Guardian*, 7 February 1989, 10
4. Evan Luard, "British Decision to Quit Kabul", *The Times*, 15 February 1989, 15.
5. David Fairhall, "60 Years After, Raj Survivors Recall Our Own Kabul Airlift", *The Guardian*, 15 February 1989, 7.
6. Peter Hopkirk, "Secret Heroes of the Great Game", *The Times*, 5 May 1990, 29–30.
7. Ibid.
8. Ibid.
9. Michael Binyon, "Our Man in Splendour", *The Times*, 6 May 1992, 12.
10. "Afghans Attack Pakistan Mission", *The Times*, 7 September 1995, 10; "Pakistan Evacuates Kabul Mission Staff", *The Times of India*, 8 September 1995, 14. See also William Maley, *The Afghanistan Wars* (Basingstoke: Palgrave Macmillan, 2009), 180, 184.
11. Jon Boone, "A Return to Magnificence for British Diplomats", 17 May 2009, https://www.guardian.co.uk/politics/2009/may/17/british-embassy-afghanistan [accessed: 6 February 2013].
12. Eleanor Mayne, "Raj-Era Embassy in Afghanistan to Be Rebuilt", 11 November 2007, https://www.telegraph.co.uk/news/uknews/1569018/Raj-era-embassy-in-Afghanistan-to-be-rebuilt.html [accessed: 12 June 2014].
13. https://www.flickr.com/photos/140537288@N04/albums [accessed: 18 April 2019].
14. See also Spencer Mawby, *The Transformation and Decline of the British Empire: Decolonisation After the First World War* (London: Palgrave Macmillan, 2015).
15. See, for instance, the sizable corpus produced by Garry John Alder, John Lowe Duthie and Edward Ingram, among others: Garry John Alder, "The

Key to India? Britain and the Herat Problem 1830–1863 (I)", *Middle Eastern Studies* 10, no. 2 (1974): 186–209; Garry John Alder, "The Key to India? Britain and the Herat Problem, 1830–1863 (II)", *Middle Eastern Studies* 10, no. 3 (1974): 287–311; John Lowe Duthie, "Some Further Insights into the Working of Mid-Victorian Imperialism: Lord Salisbury, the 'Forward' Group and Anglo-Afghan Relations: 1874–1878", *The Journal of Imperial and Commonwealth History* 8 (1980): 181–208; John Lowe Duthie, "Pressure from Within: The 'Forward' Group in the India Office During Gladstone's First Ministry", *Journal of Asian History* 15 (1981): 36–72; John Lowe Duthie, "Sir Henry Creswicke Rawlinson and the Art of Great Gamesmanship", *The Journal of Imperial and Commonwealth History* 11, no. 3 (1983): 253–274; John Lowe Duthie, "Pragmatic Diplomacy or Imperial Encroachment? British Policy Towards Afghanistan, 1874–1879", *The International History Review* 5, no. 4 (1983): 475–495; John Lowe Duthie, "Lord Lytton and the Second Afghan War: A Psychohistorical Study", *Victorian Studies* 27, no. 4 (1984): 461–475; Edward Ingram, *The Beginning of the Great Game in Asia, 1828–1834* (Oxford: Clarendon Press, 1979); Edward Ingram, *Commitment to Empire: Prophecies of the Great Game in Asia 1797–1800* (Oxford: Clarendon Press, 1981); Edward Ingram, *In Defence of British India: Great Britain and the Middle East, 1775–1842* (London: Frank Cass, 1984); Edward Ingram, *Britain's Persian Connection, 1798–1828: Prelude to the Great Game in Asia* (Oxford: Clarendon Press, 1992). For a history of the term 'Great Game' see Seymour Becker, "The 'Great Game': The History of an Evocative Phrase", *Asian Affairs* 43, no. 1 (2012): 61–80 and Malcolm E. Yapp, "The Legend of the Great Game", *Proceedings of the British Academy* 111 (2001): 179–198.

16. Henry William Carless Davis, "The Great Game in Asia (1800–1844)", in *Henry William Carless Davis, 1874–1928: A Memoir*, ed. J. R. H. Weaver and Austin Lane Poole (London: Constable and Company, Ltd., 1933), 164–202.

17. Peter John Brobst, "Rediscovering the Great Game. Sir Olaf Caroe, the Cold War and the Pacific Century", in *Rediscovering the British Empire*, ed. Barry J. Ward (Malabar, Florida: Krieger Publishing Company, 2002), 95–109; Peter John Brobst, *The Future of the Great Game: Sir Olaf Caroe, India's Independence, and the Defense of Asia* (Akron: University of Akron Press, 2005); Elisabeth Leake, "The Great Game Anew: US Cold-War Policy and Pakistan's North-West Frontier, 1947–65", *The International History Review* 35, no. 4 (2013): 783–806; Andrew J. Rotter, *Comrades at Odds: The United States and India, 1947–1964* (Ithaca: Cornell University Press, 2000), 37–76.

18. For instance Stanley A. Wolpert, *Roots of Confrontation in South Asia: Afghanistan, Pakistan, India and the Superpowers* (Oxford: Oxford University Press, 1982).
19. For instance Evgeny Sergeev, *The Great Game, 1856–1907: Russo-British Relations in Central and East Asia* (Washington: Woodrow Wilson Center Press, 2013).
20. Mark Jacobsen, "The Great Game Resumed: Afghanistan and the Defense of India, 1919–1939", in *Rediscovering the British Empire*, ed. Barry J. Ward (Malabar: Krieger Publishing Company, 2002), 77–94; Susan Loughhead, *The End Game: The Final Chapter in Britain's Great Game in Afghanistan* (Stroud: Amberley, 2016); Barnett R. Rubin and Ahmed Rashid, "From Great Game to Grand Bargain: Ending Chaos in Afghanistan and Pakistan", *Foreign Affairs* 87, no. 6 (2008): 30–44; Jennifer Siegel, *Endgame: Britain, Russia, and the Final Struggle for Central Asia* (London: I.B. Tauris, 2002).
21. Malcolm E. Yapp, *Strategies of British India: Britain, Iran and Afghanistan, 1798–1850* (Oxford: Clarendon Press, 1980).
22. For studies employing the concept of the Great Game as great power rivalry for the period covered in this book see Ludwig W. Adamec, *Afghanistan's Foreign Affairs to the Mid-Twentieth Century: Relations with the U.S.S.R., Germany, and Britain* (Tucson: University of Arizona Press, 1974), 66–72; Pradeep Barua, "Strategies and Doctrines of Imperial Defence: Britain and India, 1919–45", *The Journal of Imperial and Commonwealth History* 25, no. 2 (1997): 240–266; Suhash Chakravarty, *Afghanistan and the Great Game* (Delhi: New Century, 2002); Rose Greaves, "Themes in British Policy Towards Afghanistan in Its Relation to Indian Frontier Defence, 1798–1947", *Asian Affairs* 24, no. 1 (1993): 30–46; Milan Hauner, "Afghanistan Between the Great Powers, 1938–1945", *International Journal of Middle East Studies* 14, no. 4 (1982): 481–499; Milan Hauner, "The Last Great Game", *Middle East Journal* 38, no. 1 (1984): 72; Lesley Margaret Jackman, *Afghanistan in British Imperial Strategy and Diplomacy, 1919–1941* (Unpublished PhD thesis, University of Cambridge, 1979); Christopher Wyatt, *Afghanistan and the Defence of Empire: Diplomacy and Strategy During the Great Game* (London: I.B. Tauris, 2011); Malcolm E. Yapp, "British Perceptions of the Russian Threat to India", *Modern Asian Studies* 21, no. 4 (1987): 647–665.
23. For instance Benjamin D. Hopkins, *The Making of Modern Afghanistan* (Basingstoke: Palgrave Macmillan, 2008), 34–60; Benjamin D. Hopkins and Magnus Marsden, "Introduction: Rethinking Swat: Militancy and Modernity Along the Afghanistan-Pakistan Frontier", in *Beyond Swat: History, Society and Economy Along the Afghanistan-Pakistan Frontier*, ed. Benjamin D. Hopkins and Magnus Marsden (London: Hurst, 2013),

1–16; Magnus Marsden and Benjamin D. Hopkins, *Fragments of the Afghan Frontier* (London: Hurst & Company, 2011), 1–22; Alexander Morrison, "Introduction: Killing the Cotton Canard and Getting Rid of the Great Game: Rewriting the Russian Conquest of Central Asia, 1814–1895", *Central Asian Survey* 33, no. 2 (2014): 131–142.

24. Brandon Marsh, *Ramparts of Empire: British Imperialism and India's Afghan Frontier, 1918–1948* (Basingstoke: Palgrave Macmillan, 2015); Christian Tripodi, *Edge of Empire: The British Political Officer and Tribal Administration on the North-West Frontier, 1877–1947* (Aldershot: Ashgate, 2011); Christian Tripodi, "'Good for One but Not the Other': The 'Sandeman System' of Pacification as Applied to Baluchistan and the North-West Frontier, 1877–1947", *The Journal of Military History* 73, no. 3 (2009): 767–802; Christian Tripodi, "Grand Strategy and the Graveyard of Assumptions: Britain and Afghanistan, 1839–1919", *Journal of Strategic Studies* 33, no. 5 (2010): 701–725; Christian Tripodi, "Negotiating with the Enemy: 'Politicals' and Tribes 1901–47", *The Journal of Imperial and Commonwealth History* 39, no. 4 (2011): 589–606.

25. Christian Tripodi, "Enlightened Pacification: Imperial Precedents for Current Stabilisation Operations", *Defence Studies* 10, no. 1–2 (2010): 40–74; Christian Tripodi, "Peacemaking Through Bribes or Cultural Empathy? The Political Officer and Britain's Strategy Towards the North-West Frontier, 1901–1945", *Journal of Strategic Studies* 31, no. 1 (2008): 123–151.

26. Tamin Ansary, *Games Without Rules: The Often-Interrupted History of Afghanistan* (New York: Public Affairs, 2012); Nile Green, ed., *Afghan History Through Afghan Eyes* (London: Hurst & Company, 2015); Pirouz Mojtahed-Zadeh, *Small Players of the Great Game: The Settlement of Iran's Eastern Borderlands and the Creation of Afghanistan* (London: RoutledgeCurzon, 2004).

27. Robert D. Crews, *Afghan Modern: The History of a Global Nation* (Cambridge, MA: Harvard University Press, 2015); Magnus Marsden, *Trading Worlds: Afghan Merchants Across Modern Frontiers* (London: Hurst & Company, 2016).

28. Christopher A. Bayly, *Empire and Information: Intelligence Gathering and Social Communication in India, 1780–1870* (Cambridge: Cambridge University Press, 1999); Bernard S. Cohn, *Colonialism and Its Forms of Knowledge: The British in India* (Princeton: Princeton University Press, 1996); Nicholas B. Dirks, *Castes of Mind: Colonialism and the Making of Modern India* (Princeton: Princeton University Press, 2001); Thomas R. Metcalf, *Ideologies of the Raj* (Cambridge: Cambridge University Press, 1994); Edward W. Said, *Orientalism* (London: Penguin, 1995).

29. Martin J. Bayly, "The 'Re-turn' to Empire in IR: Colonial Knowledge Communities and the Construction of the Idea of the Afghan Polity, 1809–38", *Review of International Studies* 40, no. 3 (2014): 452.
30. Nigel J. R. Allan, "Defining Place and People in Afghanistan", *Post-Soviet Geography and Economics* 42, no. 8 (2001): 545–560.
31. Mountstuart Elphinstone, *An Account of the Kingdom of Caubul and Its Dependencies in Persia, Tartary, and India: Comprising a View of the Afghaun Nation and a History of the Dooraunee Monarchy* (London, 1815).
32. Hopkins, *The Making of Modern Afghanistan*, 11–33.
33. Nivi Manchanda, "The Imperial Sociology of the 'Tribe' in Afghanistan", *Millennium: Journal of International Studies* 46, no. 2 (2018): 165–89.
34. Tarak Barkawi, *Soldiers of Empire: Indian and British Armies in World War II* (Cambridge: Cambridge University Press, 2017), 17–48.
35. Martin J. Bayly, *Taming the Imperial Imagination: Colonial Knowledge, International Relations, and the Anglo-Afghan Encounter, 1808–1878* (Cambridge: Cambridge University Press, 2016), 45–47. See also Bayly, *Empire and Information*, 369–370.
36. Benjamin D. Hopkins, "The Bounds of Identity: The Goldsmid Mission and the Delineation of the Perso-Afghan Border in the Nineteenth Century", *Journal of Global History* 2, no. 2 (2007): 233–254.
37. Cohn, *Colonialism and Its Forms of Knowledge*; Nicholas B. Dirks, *Castes of Mind*, 43–60.
38. Thomas Jefferson Barfield, *Afghanistan: A Cultural and Political History* (Princeton: Princeton University Press, 2010); Louis Dupree, *Afghanistan* (Karachi: Oxford University Press, 1997); Martin Ewans, *Afghanistan: A New History* (Richmond: Curzon, 2000); William Kerr Fraser-Tytler, *Afghanistan: A Study of Political Developments in Central and Southern Asia*, 2nd ed. (London: Oxford University Press, 1953); Anthony Hyman, *Afghanistan Under Soviet Domination, 1964–83* (London: Macmillan Press, 1984); George Fletcher MacMunn, *Afghanistan from Darius to Amanullah* (London: G. Bell & Sons, 1929); Arnold Fletcher, *Afghanistan: Highway of Conquest* (Ithaca: Cornell University Press, 1965); Percy Molesworth Sykes, *A History of Afghanistan*, vol. 2, 2 vols. (London: Macmillan, 1940).
39. Ranajit Guha, "Dominance Without Hegemony and Its Historiography", in *Subaltern Studies VI: Writings on South Asian History and Society*, ed. Ranajit Guha (Delhi: Oxford University Press, 1992), 210–309.
40. For indirect example of oral history: Vartan Gregorian, *The Emergence of Modern Afghanistan: Politics of Reform and Modernization, 1880–1946* (Stanford: Stanford University Press, 1969).
41. Purnima Bose, *Organizing Empire: Individualism, Collective Agency, and India* (Durham: Duke University Press, 2003), 1–28, 169–222.

42. Fraser-Tytler, *Afghanistan*, 181–191, 193, 299.
43. Ibid., 195.
44. Ibid., 277.
45. IOR/L/PS/12/701B, "Ext 1192/42(1) Preparation of handbook on Afghanistan by Sir W Kerr Fraser Tytler; safe custody of despatch box key"; IOR/L/PS/12/701C, "Ext 1192/42(1) Preparation of handbook of Afghanistan by Sir W Kerr Fraser Tytler; safe custody of despatch box key; books, etc., lent to Sir W Kerr Fraser Tytler", BL; FO 371/75651, 1949, "Comments on handbook on Afghanistan prepared by Sir Kerr Fraser-Tytler. Code 97, file 1673", TNA.
46. Sykes, *A History of Afghanistan*; 555-F, F&P, 1925, "Proposal of Sir P. Sykes to write a history of Afghanistan. Decision that the work should be carried out by an officer of the Political Department of the Government of India", NAI.
47. Dirks, *Castes of Mind*, 306.
48. Terence Creagh Coen, *The Indian Political Service: A Study in Indirect Rule* (London: Chatto & Windus, 1971), 237–239.
49. Basil John Gould, *The Jewel in the Lotus: Recollections of an Indian Political* (London: Chatto & Windus, 1957), 91–107; Diana Day and George L. Mallam, *Frogs in the Well* (Moray: Librario, 2010), 131–146.
50. Olaf Kirkpatrick Caroe, *The Pathans, 550 BC–AD 1957* (London: Macmillan, 1958).
51. Mary Louise Pratt, *Imperial Eyes: Studies in Travel Writing and Transculturation* (London: Routledge, 1992).
52. Katherine Himsworth, *A History of the British Embassy in Kabul, Afghanistan* (Kabul: British Embassy, 1976). See also Chapter 7.
53. Nicholas Barrington, Joseph T. Kendrick, and Reinhard Schlagintweit, *A Passage to Nuristan: Exploring the Mysterious Afghan Hinterland* (London: I.B. Tauris, 2006); Nicholas Barrington, *Envoy: A Diplomatic Journey* (London: I.B. Tauris, 2014); Sherard Cowper-Coles, *Cables from Kabul: The Inside Story of the West's Afghanistan Campaign* (London: HarperPress, 2012); Ewans, *Afghanistan*.
54. Akbar S. Ahmed, "An Aspect of the Colonial Encounter in the North-West Frontier Province", *Asian Affairs* 9, no. 3 (1978): 319–327; Akbar S. Ahmed, *Pukhtun Economy and Society: Traditional Structure and Economic Development in a Tribal Society* (London: Routledge, 2011); James W. Spain, *The Way of the Pathans* (London: Robert Hale, 1962); James W. Spain, *The Pathan Borderland* (The Hague: Mouton, 1963); James W. Spain, *Pathans of the Latter Day* (Karachi: Oxford University Press, 1995); William Patey, "Future of Afghanistan", *Asian Affairs* 45, no. 3 (2014): 401–412; Leon B. Poullada, *Reform and Rebellion in Afghanistan, 1919–1929: King Amanullah's Failure to Modernize a Tribal Society* (Ithaca: Cornell University Press, 1973).

55. For example Rory Stewart, *The Places in Between* (London: Picador, 2005). See also Nivi Manchanda, "Rendering Afghanistan Legible: Borders, Frontiers and the 'State' of Afghanistan", *Politics* 37, no. 4 (2017): 386–401.
56. Ashis Nandy, *The Intimate Enemy: Loss and Recovery of Self Under Colonialism* (Oxford: Oxford University Press, 1983), xi; Frédérique Appfel Marglin, "Towards the Decolonization of the Mind", in *Dominating Knowledge*, ed. Frédérique Appfel Marglin and Stephen A. Marglin (Oxford University Press, 1990), 1–28.
57. Shah Mahmoud Hanifi, *Connecting Histories in Afghanistan: Market Relations and State Formation on a Colonial Frontier* (Stanford: Stanford University Press, 2011); Shah Mahmoud Hanifi, "Impoverishing a Colonial Frontier: Cash, Credit, and Debt in Nineteenth-Century Afghanistan", *Iranian Studies* 37, no. 2 (2004): 199–218.
58. Ibid.
59. David B. Edwards, *Heroes of the Age: Moral Fault Lines on the Afghan Frontier* (Berkeley: University of California Press, 1996); David B. Edwards, *Before Taliban: Genealogies of the Afghan Jihad* (Berkeley: University of California Press, 2002); Sana Haroon, *Frontier of Faith: Islam in the Indo-Afghan Borderland* (London: Hurst, 2007).
60. Hopkins, *The Making of Modern Afghanistan*, 170.
61. Benjamin D. Hopkins and Magnus Marsden, eds., *Beyond Swat: History, Society and Economy Along the Afghanistan-Pakistan Frontier* (London: Hurst, 2013); Marsden and Hopkins, *Fragments of the Afghan Frontier*.
62. Francesca Fuoli, "Incorporating North-Western Afghanistan into the British Empire: Experiments in Indirect Rule Through the Making of an Imperial Frontier, 1884–87", *Afghanistan* 1, no. 1 (2018): 4–25.
63. Benjamin D. Hopkins, "The Frontier Crimes Regulation and Frontier Governmentality", *The Journal of Asian Studies* 74, no. 2 (2015): 369–389.
64. Elisabeth Leake, *The Defiant Border: The Afghan-Pakistan Borderlands in the Era of Decolonization, 1936–1965* (Cambridge: Cambridge University Press, 2016).
65. Durba Ghosh and Dane Keith Kennedy, eds., *Decentring Empire: Britain, India and the Transcolonial World* (Hyderabad: Orient Longman, 2006).
66. Thomas R. Metcalf, *Imperial Connections: India in the Indian Ocean Arena, 1860–1920* (Berkeley: University of California Press, 2007), 204.
67. Ibid., 1.
68. Robert J. Blyth, *The Empire of the Raj: Eastern Africa and the Middle East, 1850–1947* (Basingstoke: Palgrave, 2003); Robert J. Blyth, "Britain Versus India in the Persian Gulf: The Struggle for Political Control, c. 1928–48", *The Journal of Imperial and Commonwealth History* 28, no. 1 (2000): 90–111; James Onley, *The Arabian Frontier of the British Raj:*

Merchants, Rulers, and the British in the Nineteenth-Century Gulf (New York: Oxford University Press, 2007); James Onley, "The Raj Reconsidered: British India's Informal Empire and Spheres of Influence in Asia and Africa", *Asian Affairs* 40, no. 1 (2009): 44–62.
69. John Gallagher and Ronald Robinson, "The Imperialism of Free Trade", *The Economic History Review* 6, no. 1 (1953): 1–15.
70. Ann Laura Stoler, "On Degrees of Imperial Sovereignty", *Public Culture* 18, no. 1 (2006): 136.
71. Ibid., 128.
72. Ann Laura Stoler, "Imperial Debris: Reflections on Ruins and Ruination", *Cultural Anthropology* 23, no. 2 (2008): 193.
73. Ann Laura Stoler, *Along the Archival Grain: Epistemic Anxieties and Colonial Common Sense* (Princeton: Princeton University Press, 2008); Ann Laura Stoler, "Colonial Archives and the Arts of Governance", *Archival Science* 2, no. 1–2 (2002): 87–109.
74. Nile Green, "Rethinking the 'Middle East' After the Oceanic Turn", *Comparative Studies of South Asia, Africa and the Middle East* 34, no. 3 (2015): 556–564.
75. For the idea of Afghanistan as a humanitarian "laboratory" see Nunan, *Humanitarian Invasion*.
76. Christopher A. Bayly, *The Birth of the Modern World, 1780–1914: Global Connections and Comparisons* (Oxford: Blackwell, 2004); Sebastian Conrad, *What Is Global History?* (Princeton: Princeton University Press, 2016), 141–161; Nile Green, "Spacetime and the Muslim Journey West: Industrial Communications in the Making of the 'Muslim World'", *The American Historical Review* 118, no. 2 (2013): 401–429.
77. Nick Cullather, "Damming Afghanistan: Modernization in a Buffer State", *The Journal of American History* 89, no. 2 (2002): 513. See also Rotter, *Comrades at Odds*, 77–115.
78. By way of exception see Leake, *The Defiant Border*.
79. Gregorian, *The Emergence of Modern Afghanistan*; George Grassmuck, Ludwig W. Adamec, and Frances H. Irwin, eds. *Afghanistan: Some New Approaches* (Ann Arbor: Center for Near Eastern and North African Studies, The University of Michigan, 1969).
80. Christine Noelle, *State and Tribe in Nineteenth-Century Afghanistan: The Reign of Amir Dost Muhammad Khan, 1826–1863* (Richmond: Curzon Press, 1997); M. Hasan Kakar, *Government and Society in Afghanistan: The Reign of Amir 'Abd Al-Rahman Khan* (Austin: University of Texas Press, 1979); Amin Saikal, *Modern Afghanistan: A History of Struggle and Survival* (London: I.B. Tauris, 2012).
81. Francis Robinson, *Islam and Muslim History in South Asia* (New Delhi: Oxford University Press, 2003), 38–39.
82. Poullada, *Reform and Rebellion in Afghanistan*, 159.

83. Ibid., 217, 266.
84. Senzil K. Nawid, *Religious Response to Social Change in Afghanistan, 1919–29: King Aman-Allah and the Afghan Ulama* (Costa Mesa: Mazda Publishers, 1999). See also Asta Olesen, *Islam and Politics in Afghanistan* (Richmond, Surrey: Curzon, 1995), 111–171.
85. Olesen, *Islam and Politics in Afghanistan*, 111.
86. Nawid, *Religious Response to Social Change in Afghanistan*, 187.
87. As quoted ibid., 170.
88. Gregorian, *The Emergence of Modern Afghanistan*, 273.
89. James M. Caron, "Afghanistan Historiography and Pashtun Islam: Modernization Theory's Afterimage", *History Compass* 5, no. 2 (2007): 314–329.
90. See also Barfield, *Afghanistan*, 194. See also Robert McChesney, *Kabul Under Siege: Fayz Muhammad's Account of the 1929 Uprising* (Princeton: Markus Wiener Publishers, 1999).
91. Gregorian has one of the more substantial chapters: Gregorian, *The Emergence of Modern Afghanistan*, 275–292. See also Chapter 5.
92. Alessandro Monsutti, "Anthropologizing Afghanistan: Colonial and Postcolonial Encounters", *Annual Review of Anthropology* 42, no. 1 (2013): 270.
93. Ibid., 279.
94. Astri Suhrke, "Reconstruction as Modernisation: The 'Post-conflict' Project in Afghanistan", *Third World Quarterly* 28, no. 7 (2007): 1293.
95. Astri Suhrke, "Democratizing a Dependent State: The Case of Afghanistan", *Democratization* 15, no. 3 (2008): 630–648.
96. Sykes, *A History of Afghanistan*, 299–300.
97. Bayly, "The 'Re-turn' to Empire in IR"; Martin J. Bayly, "Imperial Ontological (In)Security: 'Buffer States', International Relations and the Case of Anglo-Afghan Relations, 1808–1878", *European Journal of International Relations* 21, no. 4 (2014): 816–840.
98. For the idea of 'hybridity' see Homi Bhabha, "Of Mimicry and Man: The Ambivalence of Colonial Discourse", in *Tensions of Empire Colonial Cultures in a Bourgeois World*, ed. Frederick Cooper and Ann Laura Stoler (Berkeley: University of California Press, 1997), 153–160; Homi K. Bhabha, *The Location of Culture* (Abingdon: Routledge, 1994).
99. Gyan Prakash, "Introduction: After Colonialism", in *After Colonialism: Imperial Histories and Postcolonial Displacements* (Princeton: Princeton University Press, 1995), 4.
100. Ibid., 5.
101. Dipesh Chakrabarty, "Postcolonial Studies and the Challenge of Climate Change", *New Literary History* 43, no. 1 (2012): 2; John Darwin, "British Decolonization Since 1945: A Pattern or a Puzzle?", *The Journal of Imperial and Commonwealth History* 12, no. 2 (1984): 187–209; D. K. Fieldhouse, "'Imperialism': An Historiographical Revision", *The Economic*

History Review 14, no. 2 (1961): 187–209; Paul Gilroy, *After Empire: Melancholia or Convivial Culture?* (London: Routledge, 2004); Stephen Howe, "When (If Ever) Did Empire End? International Decolonisation in British Culture Since the 1950s", in *The British Empire in the 1950s: Retreat or Revival?*, ed. Martin Lynn (Basingstoke: Palgrave Macmillan, 2006), 214–237; Ronald Hyam, *Britain's Declining Empire: The Road to Decolonisation, 1918–1968* (Cambridge: Cambridge University Press, 2006); Ronald Robinson, "Imperial Theory and the Question of Imperialism After Empire", *The Journal of Imperial and Commonwealth History* 12, no. 2 (1984): 42–54; Martin Thomas and Andrew Thompson, "Empire and Globalisation: From 'High Imperialism' to Decolonisation", *The International History Review* 36, no. 1 (2014): 142–170.

102. Derek Gregory, *The Colonial Present: Afghanistan, Palestine, and Iraq* (Oxford: Blackwell, 2004).
103. Sebastian Conrad, "Dekolonisierung in den Metropolen", *Geschichte und Gesellschaft* 37, no. 2 (2011): 135–156.
104. E.g. John Darwin, "Decolonization and the End of Empire", in *The Oxford History of the British Empire*, ed. William Roger Louis et al. (Oxford: Oxford University Press, 1999), 541–557.
105. Stoler, "Imperial Debris", 193.
106. Anne McClintock, "The Angel of Progress: Pitfalls of the Term 'Postcolonialism'", *Social Text*, no. 31/32 (1992): 84.
107. See note 99 above.
108. Dipesh Chakrabarty, "Postcoloniality and the Artifice of History: Who Speaks for 'Indian' Pasts?", *Representations* 37, Special issue: *Imperial Fantasies and Postcolonial Histories* (1992): 1–26; Dipesh Chakrabarty, *Provincializing Europe: Postcolonial Thought and Historical Difference* (Princeton: Princeton University Press, 2000).
109. Walter D. Mignolo, "Delinking", *Cultural Studies* 21, no. 2–3 (2007): 453.
110. Walter D. Mignolo, "Epistemic Disobedience, Independent Thought and DE-colonial Freedom", *Theory, Culture, and Society* 26, no. 7–8 (2009): 1–23.
111. Nandy, *The Intimate Enemy*, xiv, xi.
112. Partha Chatterjee, *The Nation and Its Fragments: Colonial and Postcolonial Histories* (Princeton: Princeton University Press, 1993), 13.
113. The term "postcolonialism" has come under particular scrutiny. Among many others see Dipesh Chakrabarty, "Introduction: From the Colonial to the Postcolonial: India and Pakistan in Transition", in *From the Colonial to the Postcolonial: India and Pakistan in Transition*, ed. Dipesh Chakrabarty, Rochona Majumdar, and Andrew Sartori (New Delhi: Oxford University Press, 2007), 1–12; McClintock, "The Angel of Progress".

114. Corinne Fowler, *Chasing Tales Travel Writing, Journalism and the History of British Ideas About Afghanistan* (Amsterdam: Rodopi, 2007); Gregory, *The Colonial Present*; Hopkins, *The Making of Modern Afghanistan*.
115. See also Angelika Epple and Ulrike Lindner, "Introduction", *Comparativ: Zeitschrift für Globalgeschichte und vergleichende Gesellschaftsforschung* 21, no. 1 (2011): 7.
116. Frantz Fanon, *A Dying Colonialism* (London: Writers and Readers Publishing Cooperative, 1980); Frantz Fanon, *The Wretched of the Earth* (Harmondsworth: Penguin Books, 1967); Said, *Orientalism*. For further critical reading see Emily S. Rosenberg, "Considering Borders", in *Explaining the History of American Foreign Relations*, ed. Michael J. Hogan and Thomas G. Paterson, 2nd ed. (Cambridge: Cambridge University Press, 2004), 177–179, n. 2.
117. Mignolo, "Delinking", 451.
118. Ibid.
119. E.g. Linda Martin Alcoff, "Mignolo's Epistemology of Coloniality", *CR: The New Centennial Review* 7, no. 3 (2007): 79–101; Michael Ennis and Aníbal Quijano, "Coloniality of Power, Eurocentrism, and Latin America", *Nepantla: Views from South* 1, no. 3 (2000): 533–580; Olaf Kaltmeier, Ulrike Lindner, and Binu Mallaparambil, "Reflecting on Concepts of Coloniality: Postcoloniality in Latin American, South Asian and African Historiography", *Comparativ: Zeitschrift für Globalgeschichte Und Vergleichende Gesellschaftsforschung* 21, no. 1 (2011): 14–31; Walter D. Mignolo, "Coloniality at Large: Knowledge at the Late Stage of the Modern/Colonial World System", *Journal of Iberian and Latin American Research* 5, no. 2 (1999): 1–10; Walter Mignolo, *Local Histories/Global Designs: Coloniality, Subaltern Knowledges, and Border Thinking* (Princeton: Princeton University Press, 2000); Aníbal Quijano, "Coloniality and Modernity/Rationality", *Cultural Studies* 21, no. 2 (2007): 168–178; Gayatri Chakravorty Spivak, *A Critique of Postcolonial Reason: Toward a History of the Vanishing Present* (Cambridge: Harvard University Press, 1999).
120. Hopkins, *The Making of Modern Afghanistan*.
121. Hanifi, "Impoverishing a Colonial Frontier".
122. Marsden and Hopkins, *Fragments of the Afghan Frontier*.
123. See, for instance, Dipesh Chakrabarty, "Postcolonial Studies and the Challenge of Climate Change", 5.
124. For a useful introduction in German see Doris Bachmann-Medick, *Cultural Turns: Neuorientierungen in den Kulturwissenschaften* (Reinbek: Rowohlt Taschenbuch Verlag, 2006); Doris Bachmann-Medick, "Introduction: The Translational Turn", *Translation Studies* 2, no. 1 (2009): 2–16.

125. Amongst many others see Deep K. Datta-Ray, *The Making of Indian Diplomacy: A Critique of Eurocentrism* (Oxford University Press, 2015).
126. Ernest Satow, *A Guide to Diplomatic Practice*, vol. 1 (London: Longmans, Green and Co., 1917), 1.
127. Hugh Arbuthnott, Terence Clark, and Clark Muir, eds., *British Missions around the Gulf, 1575–2005: Iran, Iraq, Kuwait, Oman* (Folkestone: Global Oriental, 2008); Geoff R. Berridge, *British Diplomacy in Turkey, 1583 to the Present: A Study in the Evolution of the Resident Embassy* (Leiden: Martinus Nijhoff, 2009); Geoff R. Berridge, *Embassies in Armed Conflict* (New York: Continuum, 2012); Hugh Cortazzi et al., *British Envoys in Japan, 1859–1972* (Folkestone: Global Oriental, 2004); Sabine Freitag, Peter Wende, and Markus Mößlang, eds., *British Envoys to Germany, 1816–1866*, 4 vols. (Cambridge: Cambridge University Press, 2000); Donald Gillies, *Radical Diplomat. The Life of Archibald Clark Kerr, Lord Inverchapel, 1882–1951* (London: I.B. Tauris, 1999); James. E. Hoare, *Embassies in the East. The Story of the British Embassies in Japan, China and Korea from 1859 to the Present* (Richmond: Curzon, 1999); Ernst Schütz, *Die Gesandtschaft Grossbritanniens am immerwährenden Reichstag zu Regensburg und am Kur(Pfalz-)Bayerischen Hof zu München, 1683–1806* (München: Beck, 2007).
128. Michael J. Hogan and Thomas G. Paterson, eds., *Explaining the History of American Foreign Relations*, 2nd ed. (Cambridge: Cambridge University Press, 2004).
129. Wilfried Loth and Jürgen Osterhammel, eds., *Internationale Geschichte: Themen, Ergebnisse, Aussichten* (München: Oldenbourg, 2000); Ursula Lehmkuhl, "Diplomatiegeschichte als internationale Kulturgeschichte: Theoretische Ansätze und empirische Forschung zwischen historischer Kulturwissenschaft und soziologischem Institutionalismus", *Geschichte und Gesellschaft* 37 (2001): 394–423; Ursula Lehmkuhl, "Entscheidungsprozesse in der internationalen Geschichte: Möglichkeiten und Grenzen einer kulturwissenschaftlichen Fundierung außenpolitischer Entscheidungsmodelle", in *Internationale Geschichte: Themen, Ergebnisse, Aussichten*, ed. Wilfried Loth and Jürgen Osterhammel (München: Oldenbourg, 2000), 187–207; Ursula Lehmkuhl, "Zur kulturwissenschaftlichen Fundierung der Analyse außenpolitischen Entscheidungsverhaltens", *Politische Meinung* 1 (2002): 51–59.
130. Jessica C. E. Gienow-Hecht and Frank Schumacher, eds., *Culture and International History* (New York: Berghahn Books, 2003).
131. Jessica C. E. Gienow-Hecht, "Introduction: On the Division of Knowledge and the Community of Thought: Culture and International History", in *Culture and International History*, ed. Jessica C. E. Gienow-Hecht and Frank Schumacher (New York: Berghahn Books, 2003), 4.

132. Volker Depkat, "Cultural Approaches to International Relations. A Challenge?", in *Culture and International History*, ed. Jessica C. E. Gienow-Hecht and Frank Schumacher (New York: Berghahn Books, 2003), 175–197.
133. Eckart Conze, "States, International Systems, and Intercultural Transfer: A Commentary", in *Culture and International History*, ed. Jessica C. E. Gienow-Hecht and Frank Schumacher (New York: Berghahn Books, 2003), 203.
134. See also Laura Mcenaney, "Personal, Political, and International: A Reflection on Diplomacy and Methodology", *Diplomatic History* 36, no. 4 (2012): 772; Patrick Finney, ed., *Palgrave Advances in International History*, Palgrave Advances (Basingstoke: Palgrave Macmillan, 2005).
135. Geoff R. Berridge, *Diplomacy: Theory and Practice*, 3rd ed. (Basingstoke: Palgrave Macmillan, 2005); Geoff R. Berridge, Alan James, and Lorna Lloyd, *The Palgrave Macmillan Dictionary of Diplomacy* (Basingstoke: Palgrave Macmillan, 2012); Keith Hamilton and Richard Langhorne, *The Practice of Diplomacy: Its Evolution, Theory, and Administration*, 2nd ed. (London: Routledge, 2011); Iver B. Neumann, *At Home with the Diplomats: Inside a European Foreign Ministry* (Ithaca: Cornell University Press, 2012); Iver B. Neumann, *Diplomatic Sites: A Critical Enquiry* (London: Hurst, 2013).
136. Timothy J. Lynch, "Is Diplomatic History Dying?", OUPblog, 3 May 2013, https://blog.oup.com/2013/05/is-diplomatic-history-dying [accessed: 14 October 2013]. See also Cara L. Burnidge, "Is Diplomatic History Dying?: And Other Considerations in Preparation for the SHAFR Annual Meeting", 12 June 2013, https://burnidge.wordpress.com/2013/06/12/is-diplomatic-history-dying-and-other-considerations-in-preparation-for-the-shafr-annual-meeting [accessed: 14 October 2013].
137. Kenneth Weisbrode, "The New Diplomatic History: An Open Letter to the Membership of SHAFR", 2008, https://www.shafr.org/passport/2008/december/Weisbrode.pdf [accessed: 11 April 2012].
138. Ibid.
139. For examples see https://newdiplomatichistory.org/literature [accessed: 18 April 2019].
140. John Fisher and Antony Best, *On the Fringes of Diplomacy: Influences on British Foreign Policy, 1800–1945* (Aldershot: Ashgate, 2011).
141. E.g. Christopher Baxter and Andrew Stewart, *Diplomats at War: British and Commonwealth Diplomacy in Wartime* (Leiden: Martinus Nijhoff, 2008); Markus Mößlang and Thomas Riotte, eds., *The Diplomats' World: A Cultural History of Diplomacy, 1815–1914* (Oxford: German Historical Institute London, 2008).
142. Rotter, *Comrades at Odds*; Andrew J. Rotter, "Culture", in *Palgrave Advances in International History*, ed. Patrick Finney, Palgrave Advances

in International History (Basingstoke: Palgrave Macmillan, 2005), 267–99; Andrew J. Rotter, "Gender Relations, Foreign Relations: The United States and South Asia, 1947–1964", *The Journal of American History* 81, no. 2 (1994): 518.
143. Michael H. Fisher, *Indirect Rule in India: Residents and the Residency System, 1764–1858* (Oxford: Oxford University Press, 1991), 3.
144. John Darwin, "Diplomacy and Decolonization", *The Journal of Imperial and Commonwealth History* 28, no. 3 (2000): 9, 18.
145. Ibid.
146. See also Catherine Hall and Sonya O. Rose, eds., *At Home with the Empire: Metropolitan Culture and the Imperial World* (Cambridge: Cambridge University Press, 2006).
147. Ludwig W. Adamec, *Afghanistan, 1900–1923: A Diplomatic History* (Berkeley: University of California Press, 1967); Adamec, *Afghanistan's Foreign Affairs to the Mid-Twentieth Century*, 1; Ludwig W. Adamec, "Germany, Third Power in Afghanistan's Foreign Relations", in *Afghanistan: Some New Approaches*, ed. George Grassmuck, Ludwig W. Adamec, and Frances H. Irwin (Ann Arbor: Center for Near Eastern and North African Studies, The University of Michigan, 1969), 204–259; Milan Hauner, *India in Axis Strategy: Germany, Japan, and Indian Nationalists in the Second World War* (Stuttgart: Klett-Cotta, 1981).
148. Christian Tripodi, "'Politicals', Tribes and Musahibans: The Indian Political Service and Anglo-Afghan Relations 1929–39", *The International History Review* 34, no. 4 (2012): 865–886.
149. Rhea Talley Stewart, *Fire in Afghanistan, 1914–1929: Faith, Hope and the British Empire* (Garden City: Doubleday, 1973).
150. Anne Baker and Ronald Ivelaw-Chapman, *Wings Over Kabul: The First Airlift* (London: Kimber, 1975).
151. Subtitle of Loughhead's *The Endgame*.
152. See also Maryam Khalid, "Gender, Orientalism and Representations of the 'Other' in the War on Terror", *Global Change, Peace & Security* 23, no. 1 (2011): 15–29.
153. Joan W. Scott, "Gender: A Useful Category of Historical Analysis", *The American Historical Review* 91, no. 5 (1986): 1073.
154. Adamec, *Afghanistan's Foreign Affairs to the Mid-Twentieth Century*, 5.
155. See also Rupali Mishra, "Diplomacy at the Edge: Split Interests in the Roe Embassy to the Mughal Court", *Journal of British Studies* 53, no. 1 (2014): 5–28.
156. See also Rosenberg, "Considering Borders".
157. C. Kamissek and J. Kreienbaum, "An Imperial Cloud? Conceptualising Interimperial Connections & Transimperial Knowledge", *Journal of Modern European History* 14, no. 2 (2016): 164–182.
158. Satow, *A Guide to Diplomatic Practice*, vol. 1, para. 1.

CHAPTER 2

The Remaking of Anglo-Afghan Relations

INDEPENDENCE CAPTURED

The independence of Afghanistan in 1919 cast a complex colonial question in the terminology of international relations. Afghan independence was international in character, not a legal act based on constitutional change. This "full diplomatic independence"[1] complemented Afghanistan's "independence in all aspects of its governance".[2] In this sense, the year 1919 provides a noteworthy, though not fundamental watershed in the history of Afghanistan internationally. 1919 was momentous as much as it was one moment among many others in a deep history of independence and empire that played out in an even broader intellectual, social, cultural, economic, political and material history of Indo-Afghan interaction. 1919 was certainly not the beginning of Afghanistan's 'international' history, especially if the 'international' signifies more than the diplomatic engagement between political representatives of state, such as, among many other examples, the long history of cross-border relations.[3] Even within the complex of 'inter-state' relations, questions of authority and legitimacy unsettled secure notions of who represented 'India' and 'Afghanistan'. In 1915, for instance, Mahendra Pratap established the Provisional Government of India in Kabul.[4] Yet, 1919 is important as the Afghan state's international relations were redefined. In response to independence, the previous system of suzerainty or shared power, of 'layered' or 'divided' sovereignty, was rearranged, with Afghanistan now exercising its sovereignty also internationally.

At the same time, the idea of suzerainty did not disappear.[5] Powerful imperial and colonial trends continued to influence Afghanistan's international relations. The framework that shaped the Legation's diplomatic action was the colonial past and present of Afghanistan's international relations with the colonial state. Between 1919 and 1947, Afghanistan's relations with the Indian and British empires existed in a colonial twilight. Questions surrounding the ideas of independence and sovereignty were not new phenomena, but in 1919 they jumped scale, from within the colonial system of the Raj to an imperial-global arrangement among sovereign states.

RAWALPINDI, 1919

In April 1919, the orders of Amanullah Khan set in motion the Third Anglo-Afghan War of 1919. The military encounter ended a forty-year period that began with the Treaty of Gandamak in 1879 during which the Government of India conducted Afghanistan's foreign affairs. Amanullah Khan succeeded his father, Habibullah Khan, in 1919 after the latter's assassination during a hunting trip in Jalalabad. He outbid his father's brother, Nasrullah, and his older brothers, Inayatullah and Hayatullah, in the succession of the late Afghan king. On 13 April 1919, the day of the violent crackdown on an unarmed gathering at Jallianwala Bagh in Amritsar, Amanullah Khan unilaterally declared Afghanistan independent in *durbar*.[6] Amanullah Khan's government demanded Afghanistan's "complete internal and external independence and entire freedom to have all free political relations and equal status with any or all the world Powers great or small".[7] In addition, it called for the removal of the Anarchical and Revolutionary Crimes Act in India, better known as the Rowlatt Act, out of "strong sympathy with the oppression" suffered by Indians as well as for the restitution of "usurped" lands in Peshawar, the winter capital of the Durrani Empire, as well as in Baluchistan and Derajat.[8]

In March, Amanullah Khan had sent letters to the Viceroy of India, Lord Chelmsford (1916–1921), requesting, as soon as possible, the conclusion of a new treaty following the death of his father. The government of India referred to Amanullah Khan's mourning and put off discussions until a later date. In the previous year, the Government of India had already denied Habibullah Khan's request to represent Afghanistan at the peace conference in Paris in return for Afghanistan's neutrality during the First World War. In May 1919, Amanullah Khan sent another letter to the Viceroy asking for negotiations for a treaty of friendship as soon as possible. At the same time, Amanullah Khan instructed Afghan troops to secure Afghanistan's border with India and protect it from "quickly approaching revolution" incited by the Rowlatt Act. Amanullah Khan simultaneously calculated that Afghanistan's demand for independence would help unite growing political disaffection in India. Troops were concentrated on Afghanistan's border with India. Throughout the month of May, Afghan and Indian forces were repeatedly engaged in battle. Both sides also deployed information as a weapon. Afghanistan mobilised soldiers by means of a *firman* issued by Amanullah Khan as well as from India, most notably from the office of the Afghan Postmaster General in Peshawar. The inability of the government of the North-West Frontier Province to shut down the Postmaster General's Office, one point of Indo-Afghan contact, indicated the limited reach of colonial control. Kabul and Jalalabad also became targets for the new military technology of aerial warfare. In a stroke of bitter irony, the bombing destroyed the tombs of Habibullah Khan in Jalalabad and of Abdur Rahman Khan in Kabul.[9] Amanullah Khan had invoked the memory of his father and grandfather when he had asked the Government of India for negotiations of a new personal treaty. At the same time, Amanullah Khan and Chelmsford continued an exchange of letters. On 24 May 1919, Amanullah Khan began negotiations for peace. On 3 June 1919, the Government of India agreed to the ceasefire. In retrospect, a border clash became the Third Anglo-Afghan War that had no winners. In Ludwig W. Adamec's words:

> Both the Afghans and the British held enemy territory, and no decisive battles were fought and no one was definitely defeated. But this war did result in an end to Britain's suzerainty over Afghanistan and for this reason is justly called a victorious war by the Afghans – even though the victory was finally won in the field of diplomacy rather than the field of military action.[10]

This was the Afghan War of Independence. It failed to convert the forces that later fuelled the Khilafat movement into a widespread uprising against the colonial state, but it served to enhance the cause of Amanullah Khan's rule as a unifying undertaking both at home and abroad. As *jihad*, the war was framed in intensely emotive language that set out to defend the "honour" and "prestige" of the "motherland".[11] In his memoirs, Shah Wali Khan, the brother of Nadir Khan and a commander during the war, wrote that "[t]he British, finding the situation extremely delicate and detrimental to their interests, decided to end the war and come to terms with the Afghans".[12] Indian colonial officers, on the other hand, judged the course of military events to have forced Amanullah Khan into an armistice. According to them, he and his advisers had "realised the gravity of their mistake", forcing the withdrawal of troops from the Khyber: "Jalalabad and Kandahar were threatened, our aeroplanes bombed Kabul, and we obviously meant business".[13]

An armistice was agreed in June 1919. It was followed by negotiations for a peace treaty in Rawalpindi in Punjab, which began in July. A peace treaty was signed in August 1919, whose terms did not explicitly recognise Afghan independence but ended the practice of subsidising Afghan rulers. As on previous occasions when Indian-Afghan relations were redefined, legal changes that carried the force of international treaties arose from the informality of letter-writing among aristocratic elites. The relationship of Afghanistan with India during the reign of Abdur Rahman Khan, for instance, was first articulated in an exchange of letters with Lepel Henry Griffin.[14] Four decades later, it was again a letter appended to the peace treaty that specified that "the said Treaty and this letter leave Afghanistan officially free and independent in its internal and external affairs".[15] On 10 September 1919, Amanullah Khan himself sent out no less than three letters to Hamilton Grant, Chelmsford and King George V (r. 1910–1936), all documenting in escalating terminology Afghanistan's "internal and external independence", the "internal and external *freedom and* independence", as well as the "internal and external independence, *freedom and liberty of the Government of Afghanistan*".[16] By referring to it as having been "officially agreed to, and acknowledged", Amanullah Khan reinscribed Afghanistan's dependence on foreign recognition after the fact.[17] The ontological reasoning of independence required empire from whose dependence it had sprung.

Prior to 1919, the legal terms of the Treaty of Gandamak had restricted the exercise of Afghan sovereignty by Afghans to Afghan territory. In 1880, Abdur Rahman Khan had agreed that "he should have no direct political relations with any foreign Power".[18] The payment of subsidies or allowances formed a crucial part of the colonial state's administration in India as well as in the context of Afghanistan's foreign affairs. Subsidies were directed at specific people, tribal *khans* for instance, not territories. The Government of India had paid an annual sum of Rs. 12 lakh to Abdur Rahman Khan and Habibullah Khan, in exchange for the control of Afghan international agency.[19] This subsidy was a deposit in an

Indian bank account, which could be withdrawn by a representative of the Afghan government to which it had been made out. Short of transferring large amounts of money to Afghanistan, the practice of depositing funds meant that the government of India continued to hold control over them until their withdrawal. Unless the funds were cashed, they remained on the accounting books of the government of India as little more than a credit note. After 1893, the year of the agreement of the Durand Line, the subsidy to Abdur Rahman Khan went up to Rs. 18 lakh *per annum*. Twenty years later, Habibullah Khan's subsidy was increased to Rs 20.5 lakh in 1915, and he was offered a "special gift" in the vicinity of Rs. 1 crore (Rs. 10,000,000) for maintaining Afghanistan's neutrality during the First World War.[20] The subsidy paid by the colonial state to Afghan rulers played only a minor role in Afghan finances. It was reserved for the person of the *amir* as well as military considerations, the payment of troops, import of arms and defensive installations.[21] Its utility was limited by the fact that its withdrawal from an Indian bank account required the collaboration of the colonial state. Still, given a broader history of Afghan elites in Indian exile, the subsidy cushioned against the potential fallout of sharing sovereignty by collaborating with the neighbouring imperial bureaucracy.

The division or layering of sovereignty did not affect Afghan rulers' understanding of independence, however. Abdur Rahman Khan had considered himself an independent ruler despite the fact that he received a subsidy from India and was bound by an agreement that obliged him to consult with India when it came to Afghanistan's international political relations.[22] Habibullah Khan shared his father's sentiment. He saw the subsidy as a salary paid for services rendered to empire and as rent for the cession of Afghan territories.[23] Both Abdur Rahman Khan and Habibullah Khan considered themselves sovereign. The princely states in India were ruled according to this principle internally. Their external relations were restricted by Residents who oversaw the states' relations with the central government. In reference to the princely state of Hyderabad, Eric Beverley refers to this setup as the creation of "minor sovereignty" for a "minor state".[24] The absence of a colonial bureaucracy in the states and in Afghanistan turned both into practical examples of 'independence'. On India's north-western border, too, the 'independence' of tribes was the corner stone of their organisation within a colonial system that bound them externally. The Indo-Afghan border drawn in 1893, the Durand Line, was more than a delimitation of the sovereignty of the Afghan and Indian political orders. It was an instrument of imperial control that divided communities and Pashtuns in particular. Pashtuns on the Indian side were integrated into India's defences against the Pashtun tribes on the Afghan side by means of Indian arms and money. India's Pashtuns were handed the means to suppress their contenders in Afghanistan, "benefiting from British power without being fully constrained by it".[25] This border did not just separate India and Afghanistan. It connected, moulding Afghanistan into India's imperial formation. Colonial military thought conceived of the frontier and its inhabitants as "ramparts of empire".[26] But, the same logic also offered protection for Afghanistan. As much as the colonial state had sought to direct policy in Kabul, Afghanistan's rulers fostered patronage among the inhabitants of the Indo-Afghan borderland through payments of allowances.[27] Even after 1919, the Durand Line continued to work in both directions, towards India and Afghanistan, sometimes even simultaneously. In 1936/1937, for instance, the two revolutionary episodes spearheaded by the Shami Pir and the Faqir of Ipi moved across the Indo-Afghan border in opposite directions with opposite political intentions. The Faqir of Ipi's target was the government of India in the North-West Frontier Province, whilst the Shami Pir, a relation of Queen Soraya, Amanullah Khan's wife, opposed the rule of the new dynasty of the Musahiban installed by Nadir Shah in Kabul in 1929.[28] Colonial officers considered Afghan connections to Pashtuns living in India as a "principal weapon", whose disarmament prompted violent 'pacification' campaigns on the frontier the decades following 1919.[29] In the early 1940s, colonial statistics counted half a million fighting men and a quarter of a million rifles in the North-West Frontier Province and Baluchistan.[30] This wide distribution of arms encouraged a militarisation of the colonial state's responses to the question of frontier administration.

In 1919, Afghanistan's right to conduct its own foreign relations was committed to paper. The international recognition of Afghanistan as an independent sovereign, territorial power was an important stage in the making of the modern Afghan state. In theory, independence was synonymous with undivided sovereignty.[31] Internationally recognised independence became a global hallmark of modern statehood during the twentieth century.[32] Although restrictions had been placed on Afghanistan's sovereignty in the 1880s, cross-border mobility had been undermining these limitations for a while before 1919. During a mission to Afghanistan to supervise the repair of pillars along the Afghan-Russian boundary in 1903, Henry Dobbs, a colonial officer building a career in north-western India and Afghanistan, had realised that the isolation of Afghanistan was practically impossible. Correspondence and commerce flowed with ease across Afghanistan's northern borders.[33] In 1915, Habibullah Khan had even signed a draft agreement with the Turkish-German military mission that arrived in Kabul, promising arms and money in return for Afghanistan's military involvement on India's frontier without knowledge of the Government of India. Given the permeability of Afghanistan's borders and the inability to control movements of any kind across them, Grant, the chief delegate of the Government of India at the Rawalpindi conference in 1919, acknowledged that "[t]he old arrangement had unquestionably served a very useful purpose vis-à-vis Russia: but it had practically failed when the first big strain was put upon it. […] [W]e had no power to enforce it. The change was bound to come".[34] In other words, Afghanistan had been practicing international sovereignty for a while before 1919. The Government of India agreed with its chief representative:

> True, we have relinquished the shadow – the war proved it to be nothing more – of our formal control over Afghanistan's foreign affairs. But Afghanistan's economic and geographical dependence on India justifies the hope that we may exert our control in the substance, provided that we do nothing to drive her elsewhere for that help of which she stands in need.[35]

Contrary to the imperial government in London, the other imperial government in New Delhi interpreted Afghanistan's independence in terms of "satisfaction".[36] The outcome at Rawalpindi left India in a "commanding position" to extend power in material terms: "for the first time in history of our dealings with Afghanistan, we have taught Afghanistan her true position—the position of a petty State in relation to her powerful neighbour".[37] The acknowledgement of Afghanistan's new international status prompted a reordering of its relations with the colonial state in India and the imperial government in London. To the colonial government, the new reality of Afghan independence shifted attention to the question of controlling the Afghan state in the setting of international relations. As the Government of India put it in 1919: "We have now attempted to teach [Afghanistan] that all we require of her is that peaceful neighbourliness which a great Power can demand of any weak State on her borders".[38] 1919 opened a new chapter, yet in familiar asymmetrical frameworks of power.

Behind the gendered-paternalist rhetoric adopted in communication, imperial authorities also recognised a "newly-awakened democratic spirit in Afghanistan".[39] Rather than travelling to Rawalpindi himself, Amanullah

Khan had nominated diplomatic representatives and equipped them with plenary powers, an "amazing departure from the old autocratic system" in Grant's view.[40] The events of 1919 were received as the "beginning of [...] a really constitutional and almost democratic régime" and a "revolutionary power" in Afghanistan. Previous *amirs* had conducted Afghanistan's foreign relations as a representation of their sovereignty. In the course of the events following 1919, Afghan sovereignty was gradually distributed away from the person of the *amir*. The English translation of the peace treaty of Rawalpindi invoked the "Afghan Government", not the *amir* personally. Amanullah Khan gave powers of negotiation to his cousin, Ali Ahmad Khan, in 1919 and to Mahmud Beg Tarzi, a leading reformer, advisor and his father-in-law, in 1920. The creation of governmental offices was seen as nascent democratisation that was itself attributed to the "general democratic upheaval in the world and especially to Bolshevist influence".[41] There was a global dimension, too, noted Grant:

> The ideal of independence, always a war-cry in Afghanistan, became a popular passion. Democratic impulses, stimulated in part by Bolshevik catchwords, partly by the pronouncements of President Wilson and other politicians, and partly by a general political awakening, manifested themselves throughout the country, and the days of autocracy were numbered.[42]

Altogether, the year 1919 brought about multiple fundamental challenges to the system of imperial governance in South Asia. In the words of the Government of India:

> We must face facts squarely. [...] We have to deal with an Afghan nation, impregnated with the world-spirit of self-determination and national freedom, inordinately self-confident in its new-found emancipation from autocracy and in its supposed escape from all menace from Russia, impatient of any restraint on its absolute independence.[43]

Mussoorie, 1920

After establishing Afghan independence in 1919, another round of negotiations took place in the Savoy hotel in Mussoorie in India in 1920.[44] It sought to assess the respective positions of the two negotiating parties regarding a treaty that would define Afghanistan's future relationship with India and empire at large. Since it had made itself independent of the Indian imperial formation, the onus of requesting a "treaty of friendship" that remodelled its future international relations lay with Afghanistan. Former colonial subjects sought recognition, whilst imperial powers granted it. In 1919, Woodrow Wilson's war-time declaration contributed to Afghanistan's drive for independence. Amanullah Khan's declaration of independence explicitly referenced evolving protest movements in India. Although the principle of self-determination invoked legitimacy as a new discourse in international relations, the "old imperial logic of international relations, which abridged or entirely obliterated the sovereignty of most non-European peoples, would remain largely in place" after 1919, as Erez Manela has shown.[45] And yet, even "the collapse of 'this Wilsonian moment' [...] launched the transformation of the self-determining nation-state as the only legitimate political form throughout the globe".[46] As Manu Goswami argues, the "cascading crises of the interwar period" also informed non-state political activists and intellectuals, who forged "colonial internationalisms" that were united in their future-oriented, anti-imperial, transnational and radical reimaginings of an egalitarian world order.[47] In part, Afghan independence emerged in response to the Wilsonian moment. That moment's betrayal also echoed in Mussoorie and Kabul in 1920 and 1921, when Afghan delegations championed the "cession to Afghanistan on the principle of self-determination of those tribes within the British frontier who might express a desire for such cession".[48] Tarzi challenged colonial India's implementation of the Durand Line of 1893. The Wilsonian moment, long after its demise, empowered Afghanistan to establish not only its own independence but also make an argument for the future of the tribes of the Indo-Afghan borderland.

Dobbs represented these arguments as "absurdly exaggerated demands".[49] To him, self-determination applied only to "the nations over whom we had been victorious and would release from their rule the oppressed subjects who differed from them in terms of language and race".[50] The universal application of the principle of self-determination would render nations under imperial rule 'oppressed': "They are not oppressed. It is purely a matter sentiment".[51] In order to avoid the "death-warrant of the British Empire" encapsulated in the principle of self-determination, Dobbs suggested that 'oppression' was a feeling, not a fact. He attempted to regulate the emotions of empire's subjects to empire. Yet, Abdul Hadi Khan reminded Dobbs that "as long as this question of the tribes is not settled on national lines, we cannot get this out of our hearts. For 100 years we have not forgotten that Peshawar really belongs to us".[52] As the former winter capital of the Durrani Empire, Peshawar evoked Afghanistan's own imperial past. In Mussoorie, the idea of empire was alive for both parties. The Afghan Empire of the past met in Dobbs a representative of the Indian Empire of the present. The Indo-Afghan conference in Mussoorie was a diplomatic meeting of competing imperial designs and their sovereign claims over South Asia's people.

The argument of self-determination did not just work in Afghanistan's favour. In a multi-ethnic polity, Pashtuns exercised a form of internal imperialism over Hazara, Tajik, Uzbek, Jewish, Hindu, Sikh and other minorities. From Abdur Rahman Khan to Nadir Shah, these groups fell victim to the often-violent implementation of Pashtun nationalism.[53] Dobbs reminded Tarzi of the legacy of Afghanistan's imperial past:

> The Afghan argument was that the new doctrine of self-determination warranted the suggestion that our Pashtu-speaking tribes should be transferred to their control. I disposed of this by showing that the same doctrine, if applied to Afghanistan, would release from her rule almost the whole of her territory which is inhabited by non-Afghan races held down by her military force.[54]

The imperial experience of independent Afghanistan sought to redraw the borders that the colonial encounter of the past century had created. As radical decolonial reimaginings of the Afghan polity such visions invited the label of 'irredentism'.[55] Ironically, the principle of national sovereignty that was won in 1919 simultaneously reinforced colonialism's boundary lines as the new delineations of that principle in international relations. From 1919 onwards, attempts to reverse the history of colonially shaped borders came to be seen as Afghanistan's failure to come to terms with the past. The preoccupation of Afghan rulers with Afghanistan's imperial past was exploited by the several German governments in the first half of the twentieth century. In the 1930s, for instance, the German Minister in Kabul offered assistance in the reconstitution of the Durrani Empire and the inclusion of the port city of Karachi into Afghan territory in return for "intrigue" along the Indo-Afghan frontier.[56] The idea also infused the movement for an independent state Pashtunistan from the 1940s onwards.[57]

In 1920, self-determination was an inconvenient concept for colonial India to contemplate because it carried force. The "safety of our Empire and our frontier" was at stake[58]:

I [Dobbs] insisted on the impossibility of our ever yielding up to a nation of whose permanent friendship we had no assurance the keys of our frontier gates. In the course of these discussions the Afghans officially admitted that they had intrigued among our tribes in order to maintain their influence over them and had not wished to let drop so potent a weapon until they were convinced of our friendship.[59]

Dobbs' writings make clear that the Indo-Afghan conference in 1920 was driven by imperial insecurities, anxiety and fear. 1919 and 1920 had been turbulent years:

When the Treaty of Peace was signed with Afghanistan [in 1919], the political predominance of Great Britain, from Constantinople to Meshed, seemed almost unchallenged. [...] From such a zenith there was a rapid decline. [...] [I]n view of the deterioration of the situation in the Middle East, [...] it seemed essential to regain close touch with the Amir and [...] important to tide over the critical period of the Spring and Summer of 1920, during which the British military position in India would, for various reasons, be comparatively weak and internal difficulties might be expected to arise from the excitement over the Turkish Peace Terms.[60]

Towards the end of 1920, "the difficulties in Ireland had increased, and in December outrage succeeded outrage, impressing the Afghans with an idea of weakness at the heart of the Empire".[61] In this context, the colonial state's tried practice of deploying money in return for a sense of control was a handy device. With the accession of Amanullah Khan in 1919, the payment of subsidies deposited in the name of Habibullah Khan had ended. But, the practice itself did not disappear even though Afghanistan's independence was recognised later in the year. The idea of applying the fiscal means of the Raj for its international relations survived the temporal threshold of statal independence. Since the contents of Habibullah Khan's Indian bank account, including the bonus for maintaining neutrality in wartime and leftovers of past subsidies, had not been withdrawn by the time of the late *amir*'s death, the Afghan delegation at the Indo-Afghan conference in Mussoorie in 1920 asked to have this account transferred over to the new government of Afghanistan of Amanullah Khan. At the same time, the offer of despoting a fresh subsidy of Rs. 18 lakh to the government of Amanullah Khan was on the table. In addition to this transfer of monetary funds, the Afghan delegation asked for a comprehensive programme of economic assistance in "the construction of railways, telegraphs and factories, in the development of their mines, and in the education of their youths in Europe".[62] Dobbs calculated that "we should in practice not incur very onerous obligations" owing to the "exceeding slowness against every kind of obstruction" frequently occurring in Afghanistan and such "unpractical visionaries" like Tarzi. Dobbs recommended that "it would be worth our while to incur considerable expenditure on the[se projects], since they would be a great solvent of ignorant hostility and fanaticism and would *permanently establish our influence in Afghanistan*".[63] In Dobbs' vision of empire, colonial funds put into practice "benevolent intentions" that turned Afghanistan into a materially dependent financial black hole.[64]

At the end of the Indo-Afghan Conference in Mussoorie in 1920, the two parties agreed on a note, which listed the conditions upon which a treaty of friendship could be concluded. In return for India's and Afghanistan's recognition of each other's territory and sovereignty, Afghanistan would receive a whole catalogue of humanitarian assistance in material, financial and economic shapes. The *aide-mémoire* also listed an annual subsidy of Rs. 18 lakh, the ability to send students to Europe, assistance in the construction of railways, telegraph lines and factories and the development of mines. Further, Afghanistan would receive technical knowledge relating to irrigation, paper and machines to print currency as well as advice on the establishment of a banking and credit system. Goods in transit through India originating in India or Afghanistan would not be subjected to customs duty. As a producer and manufacturer of opium and cannabis (*charas*), Afghanistan would be allowed to use Indian ports for export unless this was prohibited at places of destination.[65] By the end of 1920, Afghan independence appeared to have a concrete price tag.

And yet, in addition to contemporary historical circumstances, history weighed on the minds of colonial administrators. In late 1920, one historical precedent in particular made George Nathaniel Curzon wary. The precendent was the Dane Mission to Afghanistan of 1904/1905 during Curzon's tenure as Viceroy of India and its failure to mould Afghanistan more intimately into the Indian Empire. Taking advantage of the legal ambiguity of letter-treaties in 1903, Curzon had tried to talk Habibullah Khan into travelling to Delhi and negotiating anew the terms of Afghanistan's relationship with India. Having visited Afghanistan in 1894, Curzon knew father and son, Abdur Rahman Khan and Habibullah Khan, personally. On that basis, according to Ludwig W. Adamec, Curzon had hoped "to tie [Habibullah Khan] and his country closer to India".[66] But, Habibullah Khan could not be moved. Instead, India's Foreign Secretary, Louis Dane, was sent to Kabul. With Dane went Dobbs, Grant and an entire entourage of assistants and doctors.[67] The outcome was an agreement that continued the practices adopted at the beginning Abdur Rahman Khan's reign. From Curzon's viewpoint, the Dane Mission achieved the exact opposite of his own intentions and expectations, namely "a complete victory for the Amir".[68] The legal framework of the political relationship of Habibullah Khan's Afghanistan with India was moulded on the terms his father had agreed to in the early 1880s. The display of Afghan diplomatic ability in 1904 was on Curzon's mind again in late 1920. It was this experience of the diplomatic intricacies of Anglo-Afghan relations that led him to weigh in and advise against sending Dobbs to Kabul in 1921.[69] An anxious Curzon needed no reminding of empire's limited reach.

KABUL, 1921

Nonetheless, Dobbs went to Kabul the next year where he spent most of 1921 in Kabul negotiating the terms of 'treaty of friendship' with Afghan representatives and Amanullah Khan. By then, two years of negotiations had passed. The extended process of moving from a 'treaty of peace' in 1919, to a conference that defined the framework of a potential 'treaty of friendship' in 1920 that eventually became a 'treaty of neighbourly relations' in 1921 was deliberate. In addition to playing for time during one of "the most critical periods in the recent history of the East", the British delegations were also reluctant to release Afghanistan from its subordinate international legal status.[70]

Negotiations continued on the basis of the note crafted in Mussoorie the year before, which posited sovereignty against material assistance. In addition, the Afghan delegates were prepared to exclude Russian influence in Afghanistan altogether. In return for an 'exclusive treaty' of this kind, Dobbs had been authorised to accept a long list of material demands including:

> [A]n annual subsidy [...] 40 lakhs of rupees, an immediate gift of 20,000 rifles, 200 machine guns, 12 mountain guns and two 18-pdr. batteries, with adequate supplies of ammunition for all these weapons, a gift of six aeroplanes after six months, with telegraph material sufficient for a line from Kabul via Kandahar to Herat, and a promise of further assistance in money, munitions and aeroplanes to the extent deemed necessary by the two Governments after consultation, in the event of unprovoked Russian aggression.[71]

Amanullah Khan, Dobbs and the Government of India appeared close to reaching an agreement that would have, in essence, provided a continuation of Afghanistan within a South Asian imperial arrangement on significantly improved, yet familiar material terms. But, Afghanistan could not commit to a clause that bound it to consulting with India on any future agreements with third parties that could impact Indian-Afghan relations. Dobbs reported that Afghan delegates "could not accept the formula put forward by us for consultation about future agreements affecting our mutual interests, as this would amount to a virtual British control of their foreign policy".[72] Instead of a 'treaty of friendship', the parties agreed on a 'treaty of neighbourly relations'.

The Treaty of Kabul of 1921 acknowledged Afghanistan's "internal and external independence".[73] It "fully recognised Afghan independence and embodied the neighbourly relations existing between the great nations of the world".[74] But, to both parties the outcome appeared less than what they had hoped for. Dobbs "recognised that it was not ideal", whilst Amanullah Khan appeared intent on rejecting the treaty "since it gave no advantages to Afghanistan".[75] The discontinuation of a subsidy removed an imperial tool and "much hold over the Amir", but provided, "far more cheaply" than anticipated, for the "the permanent location at Kabul of a British Minister".[76] That Minister would now be able to make "more effective and energetic protest than was possible in the past".[77] The empire's diplomatic representative would become the colonial state's executor in Afghanistan. Amanullah Khan attempted to sell the deal as a victory nonetheless: "He would only be prepared to make close friendship with us if we showed generosity towards Turkey and our frontier tribes and treated the inhabitants of India with kindness".[78] To Dobbs, "[t]his speech was plainly an act of propaganda designed to forestall the reproaches which the Amir foresaw would be directed against him by the Khilafat party, the malcontent tribesmen of Waziristan and the Indian extremists for what they would describe as his desertion of their causes".[79] Whilst Amanullah Khan gauged the limits of independence, Dobbs tested its reach.

In 1919, empire had been threatened from within by the emotions of its 'conquered' subjects. It had since also been exposed to the emotions of those outside. In the report on his mission, Dobbs concluded:

> If I have correctly gauged [Amanullah Khan's] character and ambitions, his ruling passion is for expansion. He can satisfy this in only three directions, towards India, Central Asia, and Persia. India is in herself the most attractive,

because of her riches and because the Pathan tribes, restive under her control, appeal to ties of blood and language and are a ready-made and formidable fighting force which may with luck be turned against her.[80]

In order to blunt "so potent a weapon" in Afghan hands, Dobbs recommended "dominating" Waziristan, the Indo-Afghan border crossing of the Khyber Pass as well as the Afridi tribe.[81] Amanullah Khan appeared to him "ambitious and greedy for expansion", determined "to take advantage of weakness in any quarter":

> It was belief in our *strength* and persistence which induced him to sign the Treaty; and he will not keep it unless we continue to show ourselves *strong*. *Strength*, immediately beneath his eyes, in our dealings with the frontier tribes will make the greatest impression on him.[82]

Dobbs was determined to eliminate any sense of imperial decline from his report on the negotiations in 1921, which had been a dominating trope in his report on the discussions in Mussoorie little over a year before. Dobbs projected onto Amanullah Khan his own policy. Whilst he pointed to the potential of Amanullah Khan seeking territorial 'enlargement', he advocated the colonial control of the Indo-Afghan borderland. Applying both carrot and stick, Dobbs also made provisions for occasional gifts to both entice and satisfy Afghanistan's and Amanullah Khan's material demands.[83]

In 1922, the world of international relations was the domain of 'developed' nations. The India Office saw independence as an economic burden for Afghanistan. International law did not exist for everyone equally. It had to be acquired in material terms:

> Very little experience of the heavy expenditure entailed by the upkeep of the Legations [Amanullah Khan] is seeking to establish, and also of the trade expectations of the Powers whose Legations he seeks to attract to Kabul, will be needed to make the Ameer realise the necessity for the development of Afghanistan's internal resources, before she can afford to take up the rôle of a civilised nation seriously, or indulge in fantastic schemes of expansion.[84]

Practicing international relations was costly and required resources. Afghanistan's political independence was qualified by its economic means. The Government of India suggested that "no obstacles" should be placed in Afghanistan's way: "This, it is true, is a reversal of our traditional policy with Afghanistan, but in the changed conditions of to-day it seems the safest line to follow".[85] Afghanistan's appearance on the world stage was held in the gendered language of imperial patriarchy. Afghan independence was a momentary aberration that would eventually be corrected, not the conclusion of 'natural' process towards international self-determination. "[A]ctual experience of Afghanistan's backwardness and the poverty of her resources [will] convince most, if not all, the other Powers that the upkeep of Legations in Kabul is not worth the expense, [leading to] their gradual defection from Kabul".[86] Crucially, the connectivities provided by the Indian Ocean were turned into a ruling device: "Already she is relying on our postal and telegraphic system and our rail and sea communications for her intercourse with the outside world, and the more that intercourse grows, the more will she realise her dependence on India and the British Empire".[87] Whilst diverting Afghanistan's independence "into other channels", the colonial state capitalised on the mobility of its own technologies of rule which were directed into the world of international relations. Paraphrasing the Wilsonian intention to 'make the world safe for democracy' in 1917, 1919 prompted empires to make the "world safe for empire".[88] This meant making Afghan "independence safe for empire".[89]

The colonial state's response to the challenges articulated against its imperial rule materialised in the remaking of 'Anglo-Afghan' relations and, eventually, the establishment of a diplomatic mission to be located in Kabul. The Treaty of Kabul brought about the exchange of diplomatic missions, resulting in the establishment of the British Legation in Kabul and of the Afghan Legation in London.[90] British Consulates were established in Afghanistan (Kandahar and Jalalabad), but Afghan Consulates opened only in India (Calcutta, Bombay and Karachi), not in the UK. The post of an Afghan Consul-General was established at the seat of the colonial government in India. This emerging network of diplomatic and consular institutions reflected India's continued importance in the triangular relationship of the British, Indian and Afghan governments.[91] 1919 brought independence, but it did not make present empires or their history go away. Empire persisted in this era of independence, and its history remained a constant presence in Afghanistan's diplomatic relations after 1919 and also after 1947.

INDEPENDENCE IN THE AGE OF EMPIRE

The independence of Afghanistan, like that of other postcolonial and postimperial nation-states in the twentieth century, entangled questions of sovereignty, modernisation and development. There was an economy to Afghan independence. As the Governor of Kabul at the time of his father's death, Amanullah Khan's access to the state's treasury and army ensured his success in the struggle for succession. But, the achievement of Afghan independence came with significant limiting factors. As Amanullah Khan continued the Afghan state's centralisation, the expansion of the Afghan state's bureaucracy required revenue. Independence triggered modernisation in manifold shapes, including the redefinition of the state itself as well as in terms of education, healthcare, infrastructure and communication.[92] Prior to 1919, Afghanistan generated little revenue in absolute terms, but it was self-sufficient.[93] As Chapter 1 shows, Amanullah Khan's rule has a pride of place in narratives of modernisation.[94] In the late nineteenth century, Afghanistan had taken part in a transfer of ideas with imperial and industrialised forerunners, in particular the Ottoman Empire.[95] Abdur Rahman Khan had employed 13 English professionals at court.[96] After his tour of India in 1907, Habibullah Khan accelerated the process of material modernisation, attracting specialists, including architects and infrastructure engineers.[97] Money enabled the implementation of Amanullah Khan's own reform programme. It entailed science and technology programmes that sent Afghan students abroad and invited international teachers and engineers to Afghanistan. The programme grew in scope after Amanullah Khan's tour of 1927/1928 that took him to India, Egypt, Italy, France, Belgium, Switzerland, Germany and England, Russia, Turkey and Persia. Afghan money was often spent in outrageous amounts on outdated industrial and military equipment. As the Afghan state also internationalised its presence abroad by means of formalised diplomatic missions, significant stresses emerged on the affordability of independence or the statal apparatus of institutions that came with it.

As the state's revenues dwindled, references to Afghanistan's precarious financial state became more frequent and public knowledge. The price of independence was dependence on newly emerging regimes of social control on a global scale. Amanullah Khan attempted to balance Afghanistan's independence with a rising necessity to generate revenues. He increased the tax burden on merchants, urban and rural populations in order to pay for the state's burgeoning administration whilst simultaneously limiting the impact of foreign investment, such as mining rights, in order to protect sovereignty rooted in Afghanistan's soil.[98] In 1928, the Afghan state collected thirty percent of the administration's income from taxes on land.[99] Amanullah Khan's reforms, and cuts to the funding of the army, form a crucial role in his abdication and exile. Beyond his reign, they also speak to a larger story of the Afghan state in its relation to existing regimes of fiscal dependency. In this sense, the 1920s are illustrative in terms of setting the stage for later development initiatives.

The story of this book is embedded in a larger history of independent Afghanistan's international relations that go well beyond an 'Anglo-Afghan' remit. The Soviet Union, Turkey, Persia, Germany, Italy and France established diplomatic missions in Kabul, populating Kabul with an international diplomatic society and the ancillary movements of people connected to it as labourers, travellers, visitors or 'specialists' and others. The British Legation began producing regular biographical reports on the personnel of other diplomatic mission, keeping track of these competing international presences in India's colonial domain. In 1942, the US American Legation arrived. Successive German states sought to establish themselves as a "third force" in addition to the British and Soviet empires in Asia. Following the military expedition of 1915, the 1920s saw increased German engagement. As much as Afghanistan's international relations were redefined, so were the imperial formations with which it interacted. After 1919, German imperialism made its mark by means of finance and 'experts'. Amanullah Khan's experience laid the foundations for the later activities of humanitarian regimes who, attracted by Afghanistan's potential as a recipient of ideas produced by 'Western progress', began flocking there in increasing numbers from the 1930s and 1940s.[100] In its international dimensions, Afghan independence highlighted the continuation of dependence in other, often new, realms and on an even larger scale.

Between 1919 and 1921 Afghanistan went from limited agency in the international practice of its sovereignty through an experiment of independence and on to the realisation that economic dependence was the reality of postcolonial states in the age of empire and capitalism. The question of what Afghan independence meant, how far it reached and where it ended has been asked several times since 1919. As freedom from foreign intervention, the first articles of the Treaty of Kabul of 1921, which defined Afghan independence, and of the first Geneva Accord of 1988, which provided the legal framework for the withdrawal of Soviet troops from Afghanistan, become comparable. The text from 1921 certified "all rights of internal and external independence", whilst in 1988 relations between the signatories of the accords were held to "the principle of non-interference and non-intervention".[101] In other respects, the 'sovereignty gap' of foreign humanitarian and developmental involvement speaks to the infringement of the power of the people of Afghanistan and of Afghanistan's constitutional independence as a state in the context of unprecedeted payments by foreign donors and their subversive effects on societal power sharing structures at the beginning of the twenty-first century.[102] The Afghan state's interaction with other stakeholders continues to occupy the minds of both scholars and statesmen.[103]

Administering Anglo-Afghan Relations

Like Afghanistan, the colonial state, too, had to respond to the remaking of the Afghan state's international relations after 1919. It designed a diplomatic mission that followed a late-imperial logic on multiple aspects at the same time that the Afghan state 'internationalised'. Afghanistan insisted on establishing direct relations with the British government in London through the Foreign Office after 1919 as opposed to its fellow colonial ministry, the India Office. The "[m]ain purpose of Afghan[istan]", wrote Dobbs, "is to claim equality with other nations".[104] This claim rested on "manifestations of independence", the most important of which was "emancipation from the tutelage of [the] Government of India". The pathways of Afghanistan's international relations symbolised the practice of Afghan independence internationally.

This diplomatic mission encapsulated a long and varied history of 'Anglo-Afghan' diplomatic interaction. In the late nineteenth-century, the title of "Resident" was applied to diplomatic heads of mission in princely India, who, posing as 'advisors', oversaw the implementation of governmental policy. In the late nineteenth century, these techniques of rule were exported from India to Afghanistan as the latter came to be seen as another South Asian principality.[105] In 1895, Abdur Rahman Khan had attempted to connect Kabul with London. "[H]e was informed that an Afghan Embassy could not be established in London while it was still unsafe for a British Envoy to live in Kabul".[106] On several occasions, Abdur Rahman Khan pointed to Pierre Louis Napoleon Cavagnari's fate in order to prevent an unwanted colonial representation in Afghanistan. Cavagnari, the last Resident and chief political representative during Afghanistan's occupation in the Second Anglo-Afghan War, was killed in 1879. Ḥabibullah Khan followed the tactic in his encounter with Dane.[107] In 1919, Afghanistan reiterated the intention to host the diplomatic representation of the British Empire and not that of the Raj, which had restricted the Afghan state's international relations and, hence, the exercise of its sovereignty. The Afghan demands for diplomatic representation were also driven by broader anti-imperialist movements that originated in the late nineteenth century.[108] Cemil Aydin has shown how pan-Islamic and pan-Asianist thought were aligned with Wilsonian ideas, socialism and nationalism at the time when the international order found itself in a profound crisis of legitimacy following World War I.[109]

In 1921, Curzon told an Afghan mission led by Mohammed Wali that the Foreign Office "had nothing to do with the negotiations proceeding in Kabul, which were solely the concern of the India Office and the Government of India".[110] The refusal had repercussions for the negotiations ongoing in Kabul, causing "indignant telegrams" and "the most serious outburst of unfriendliness" there.[111] Eventually, Dobbs offered "the establishment of the long desired Afghan Legation in London".[112] The Afghan Legation in London seemed to conclude Afghanistan's demand for the international recognition of its sovereignty, but really only preserved the "outward appearance" of diplomatic equality.[113] The British Legation in Kabul was placed only under the "nominal" political guidance of the London Foreign Office, its staff appearing on the annual *Foreign Office List* to give the setup wider, particularly Afghan, publicity.[114] Afghanistan required "altogether exceptional treatment", and, to the India Office, this setup awarded "full recognition of India's predominant and almost exclusive interest in Afghan affairs".[115] India remained the primary point of reference for British-Afghan relations until the end of colonial rule in 1947. Afghanistan's diplomatic mission in the imperial capital did not ensure its unqualified treatment as independent, sovereign state. Instead, Afghanistan was compartmentalised into the Indian domain of that empire until 1947: "the conduct of our relations with Afghanistan depends so much on Indian interests and knowledge of India, that it is almost essential to have an Indian Service officer rather than Foreign Office diplomatist [as Minister]".[116] Giving the British Legation in Kabul a "British" label was, therefore, a racialised misnomer. Not only was knowledge of India the institution's epistemological fundament. Its setup, too, was predominantly Indian in terms of people, ideas and materials.

The ideational construction of the Legation did not follow normative processes. The regulation of Afghanistan's relations with India and Britain after 1919 wrote its own rulebook. The Legation was both a unique and a model state institution, whose emergence, life and transformation provide insights into the complex processes taking place with regard to the political history between Afghanistan, India and empire in the first half of the twentieth century. The order of political entities comprised a whole diplomatic register ranging from the European 'great powers' to the Indian princely states. The very status of Britain's diplomatic mission as a Legation ranked it below that of an Embassy. The Congress of Vienna in 1815 defined diplomatic agents in three groups. Only the first, Ambassadors, Legates and Nuncios "have the represented character".[117] Ministers, and also Envoys, were heads of mission "of the second class".[118] At the time of the establishment of the British Legation in Kabul, five out of nine British Ambassadors were based in Europe, one in Asia and none in the capital of a former subject state.[119] Of the thirty-one British Ministers, half resided in Europe. The British Legation and its head of mission, His Majesty's Envoy Extraordinary and Minister Plenipotentiary, reflected Afghanistan's subordinate international status. The international network of diplomatic institutions in the early 1920s captured the layered imperial asymmetries existing between international polities. The Legation formalised Anglo-Afghan diplomatic inequality.

The Legation reincarnated previous missions to Afghanistan as well as violent military occupations. Mountstuart Elphinstone's mission was accommodated in the Durrani Empire's winter capital in Peshawar. Arguably, the invasion of 1839 attempted to establish a long-term colonial presence in Kabul in continuation of a rapid expansion of the East India Company state across northern India. The Afghan response to the First Anglo-Afghan War (1839–1842) inspired the reluctance during the Second Anglo-Afghan War (1878–1880) on the part of the invading army to insist on the establishment of a colonial post headed by a European colonial officer. Instead, Yakub Khan (r. 1879) relinquished Afghanistan's international sovereignty in return for an annual payment under the terms of the Treaty of Gandamak, which were later accepted by Abdur Rahman Khan. Griffin, who articulated the terms of Abdur Rahman Khan's accession in 1880, wrote:

> The British Government desires to exercise no interference in your internal government of these territories, nor will you be required to admit an English Resident anywhere; although, for convenience of ordinary friendly intercourse between two contiguous States, it may be advisable to station, by agreement, a Muhammadan Agent of the British Government at Kabul.[120]

Abdur Rahman Khan and Habibullah Khan successfully resisted the establishment of colonial officers as diplomatic representatives in Kabul, but accepted Indians who embodied Afghanistan's subordination in international politics nonetheless. The position of an Indian Newswriter in Kabul between 1882 and 1919 emerged as a compromise in the administration of Anglo-Afghan relations.[121] At the same time the colonial state also extended its structures and governmental practices into Afghanistan after the Second Anglo-Afghan War, by means including the diplomatic missions of Mortimer Durand in 1893, Dobbs in 1903 and Dane in 1904/1905.[122]

Under Amanullah Khan, Afghanistan regained in 1919 the international status that it had held prior to 1879. Only in 1922 did Afghanistan's international status usher into the mutual recognition of diplomatic missions between this newly independent state and empire. And yet, between 1922 and 1948, the British Legation in Kabul was purposely situated at the intersection of global and local colonial concerns. The system of correspondence that the Foreign and India Offices devised in order to communicate with a multitude of imperial and colonial localities reflects the localisation of Afghanistan in the ideational interstices of empire until 1947. The British Minister in Kabul reported to the Secretary of State for Foreign Affairs at the Foreign Office in London. A copy of the Minister's despatch was simultaneously sent to the Government of India, which sent its viewpoints on the Minister's despatch to the India Office in London. This process sometimes also involved the opinions of colonial officers posted along India's north-western territories. In London, the India Office added its own concerns, comments and recommendations and forwarded them to the Foreign Office. From there, a despatch was returned to Kabul by the authority of the Secretary of State for Foreign Affairs. At the same time, the India Office returned its reply to the Government of India, which in turn informed its local officers. In Kabul, the British Minister represented the Foreign Office's conclusion to Afghan statesmen, who informed their Minister in London.[123] Thus, the Legation introduced colonial concerns into British diplomacy towards Afghanistan and raised colonial concerns to the level of imperial importance. British diplomacy as exercised in Kabul was a palimpsest of imperial and colonial instructions, viewpoints and attitudes. As a system of communication, it worked slowly to the point of systematic "procrastination".[124]

The system of correspondence between Kabul and London precluded direct communication between the Legation and India's north-western districts although India and Afghanistan constituted neighbouring geopolities. Afghanistan was neither fully excluded from Indian concerns, nor was it fully integrated in terms of information flows. In late 1938, the Minister in Kabul, William Kerr Fraser-Tytler, suggested opening a direct line of communication between the Legation and frontier districts in the shape of regular letters written by him to the British officers in those districts on subjects relating to both Afghanistan and the Government of India's frontier policy. The result was a series of nine "unofficial quarterly letters" between 1939 and 1941, which aimed at balancing the "disjointed and often garbled form" of information given to Indian officers on Afghanistan.[125] The initiative exposed the deliberate communicative marginalisation of Afghanistan in international affairs. The first British Minister after Afghan independence, Francis Henry Humphrys (1922–1929), rejected the idea of discussions with Afghan representatives on India's external affairs entirely.[126] Afghan concerns with regard to the Government of India were presented either to the British Minister in Kabul or to the British Foreign Secretary through the Afghan Minister in London. In London, such communication went to the India Office, to the Government of India, back to the India Office, to the Foreign Office and finally to the Legation in Kabul. Afghan protests against its neighbouring state were passed through Britain's global imperial bureaucracies several times before the British Minister in Kabul received his instructions from the Foreign Office in London, which only had token authority in Anglo-Afghan relations by its own admission.[127] In the words of Ann Laura Stoler, the administration of 'Anglo-Afghan' diplomatic relations worked along "elusive vectors of accountability".[128]

This significant imbalance between publicised and actual authority in British-Afghan relations was cemented into the setup of Britain's diplomatic structure in Afghanistan. While diplomatic missions were set up in the capitals of Afghanistan and the United Kingdom on the highest diplomatic level, London had only little political interest in conducting these relations. By contrast, Afghanistan hosted two Indian Consuls, who represented British interests, and India hosted a total of four Afghan Consuls and Consul-Generals. These Consulates connected Afghanistan with India on diplomacy's subsidiary consular level and offered a realistic representation of the intricate diplomatic connections existing between Afghanistan and India after 1919. Yet, while India did not have any authority over British diplomacy in Afghanistan on paper, the Legation was effectively incorporated into the Government of India's external relations apparatus through the provision of its personnel and its funds. The Legation's material circumstances were solely defined by the colonial state in India, which did not carry the political responsibility for the conduct of these diplomatic relations. The colonial state, thus, exploited the ambiguity arising from the tensions between metropolitan-colonial and colonial-colonial concerns for its own benefits. It created a veritable "state of exception".[129] The system of bureaucratic communication between Afghanistan, India and Britain was purposely dysfunctional, leaving Afghanistan exposed to the colonial state's diplomatic objectives whilst its recourse to tools of diplomatic protest risked getting lost in transition between Britain's Asian and global imperial formations.

The Government of India regulated its external relations and those with the princely states by means of political officers, who were organised in the Foreign and Political Department (from 1914) and in the Indian Political Service (from 1937).[130] The so-called Politicals were considered the "diplomatic corps" of the Government of India whose area of activity was identical with the expanse of the Indian Empire from the Himalayas to Southeast Asia, the Gulf and East Africa.[131] The terms "political", "diplomatic" and "colonial" were synonymous.[132] As Chapter 4 discusses in detail, the Legation diplomats were drawn from this colonial cadre. The majority of the political officers of the Government of India were themselves recruited from a variety of colonial services, but mostly from the Indian Civil Service and the Indian Army. Glossing over fine distinctions between the colonial and the diplomatic, Curzon called India's political service "the Asiatic Branch of the Foreign Office in England".[133] Afghanistan may have outwardly been awarded the treatment of a sovereign, independent state by hosting a 'British' Minister from 1922, but it continued to be framed in terms of British-Indian colonial governance. The system devised for British diplomacy after 1919 favoured the colonial state over the imperial capital until the former merged with the latter in 1947.

In 1919, Afghanistan's international relations did not conform to the normative of the "secular, sovereign, independent and equal" state, which was grounded in the Peace of Westphalia of 1648.[134] On the one hand, transborder tribal relationships between India and Afghanistan persisted. On the other, even as the international relations of the Afghan state were formalised, the arrival of the British Legation in Kabul in 1922 continuously challenged the notion of Afghanistan's egalitarian engagement in international diplomacy. "[G]radated variations and degrees of sovereignty and disenfranchisement", continued after 1919.[135] Afghanistan's "forced integration into the Eurocentric state system as a buffer" during the 1800s continued to shape its international relations.[136] A clause in the Treaty of Kabul prevented the opening of Russian consulates in eastern Afghanistan.[137] The colonial state that had shaped Afghanistan during the previous century, now expected Afghan representatives to act according to the "comity of nations", a synonym for the cultures of international diplomacy set by the European imperial powers, including Afghanistan's colonial neighbour, that also reinforced old hierarchies between nations after 1919.[138]

In Kabul, colonial Indian practices of diplomacy *took place*. British diplomacy in Kabul was inspired and materially shaped by the colonial state in India. When the Legation became the British Embassy in 1948 it conserved its colonial practices and material representations by linking British diplomacy of the twentieth century, and arguably of the twenty-first, with the historical interactions of the East India Company in colonial South Asia in the nineteenth. A state-centred narrative on Afghanistan's international history in the nineteenth and twentieth century of this kind cannot, and does not, claim exclusivity when it comes to explaining Afghanistan's interaction with the wider world. If anything, the history of inter-state relations presents only one of many others, though of extremely rich documentation. However, the book visualises the colonisation of international relations by the colonial state in India in the shape of the British Legation in Kabul. The global rise of the embassy as the key to statal recognition is an integral and understudied part of the history of independence movements around the world, including Afghanistan's. Empires responded in different ways to this democratisation, in principle, among all nation-states. Far from ending or withdrawing, the colonial state in India spawned a diplomatic institution in Afghanistan that transitioned imperial rule into a theoretically democratic world of nation-states. Empire did not cease to exist in 1919 or 1947: its knowledge, practices and power were reshaped and relocated. The British Legation in Kabul was the colonial state's response to the challenge of its system of imperial governance generated by the Wilsonian moment. Its history refines our understanding of the colonial state's significant epistemological and material continuities as well as of its decidedly and finely tuned interstitial registers. Histories of the state continue to be relevant, and history's disciplinary development does not stop short of the study of diplomats.

It is in this sense that the British Legation in Kabul warrants treatment as an insightful chapter in the history of Afghanistan's international relations: one that connects the history of Afghanistan's long nineteenth century with the globalising standard of reciprocal diplomatic representation in the context of widespread independence movements and the creation of new sovereign entities emerging from colonial nations in the twentieth century. From the perspective of the twentieth century, which saw the globalisation of embassies as a universal system of regulating inter-state relations that was virtually adopted everywhere and everyone, especially so after 1945, the history of the British Legation in Kabul provides insights into the history of empire, illustrating as it does the colonial state's transformation into a conduit of postcolonial international relations. More than just a transmitter, this was also a node in its own right.

Notes

1. Alessandro Monsutti, "Anthropologizing Afghanistan: Colonial and Postcolonial Encounters", *Annual Review of Anthropology* 42, no. 1 (2013): 271.
2. Elisabeth Leake, *The Defiant Border: The Afghan-Pakistan Borderlands in the Era of Decolonization, 1936–1965* (Cambridge: Cambridge University Press, 2016), 29.
3. For example, the history of the "Hindustani Fanatics" in Afghanistan: Benjamin D. Hopkins, "A History of the 'Hindustani Fanatics' on the Frontier", in *Beyond Swat: History, Society and Economy Along the Afghanistan-Pakistan Frontier*, ed. Benjamin D. Hopkins and Magnus Marsden (London: Hurst, 2013), 39–50. See also the discussion of Afghanistan as more than a geopolity in Chapter 1.
4. Carolien Stolte, "'Enough of the Great Napoleons!' Raja Mahendra Pratap's Pan-Asian Projects (1929–1939)", *Modern Asian Studies* 46, no. 2 (2012): 403–423.
5. Benjamin D. Hopkins, "The Frontier Crimes Regulation and Frontier Governmentality", *The Journal of Asian Studies* 74, no. 2 (2015): 370, 372. See also "paramountcy of the Raj", Benjamin D. Hopkins and Magnus Marsden, "Introduction: Rethinking Swat: Militancy and Modernity Along the Afghanistan-Pakistan Frontier", in *Beyond Swat: History, Society and Economy Along the Afghanistan-Pakistan Frontier*, ed. Benjamin D. Hopkins and Magnus Marsden (London: Hurst, 2013), 4.
6. Ludwig W. Adamec, *Afghanistan, 1900–1923: A Diplomatic History* (Berkeley: University of California Press, 1967), 110.
7. "The message of Amir Amanullah Khan to the Government of India", "Diary of the British Agent at Kabul for the period 9th May to 22nd September 1919", 7, file 1061/1919, pt 6, IOR/L/PS/10/809, "File 1061/1919 Pt 3-4, 6-7, 10 Afghan War", BL.
8. Ibid.
9. Adamec, *Afghanistan, 1900–1923*, 117.
10. Ibid., 122–123. See also 108–123.

11. Shah Wali, *My Memoirs* (Kabul, 1970). See also Benjamin D. Hopkins, "Jihad on the Frontier: A History of Religious Revolt on the North-West Frontier, 1800–1947", *History Compass* 7, no. 6 (2009): 1459–1469.
12. Wali, *My Memoirs*, 27.
13. Hamilton Grant, No. 108-P.C., Nathia Gali, 6 September 1919, para. 3, 2, IOR/L/PS/10/808, "File 1061/1919, Pt 1-2 Afghanistan", BL.
14. M. Hasan Kakar, *A Political and Diplomatic History of Afghanistan, 1863–1901* (Leiden: Brill, 2006), 168–169.
15. "A survey of Anglo-Afghan relations", 11, F 1161/108/97, FO 371/69451, 1948, "Corrections to the Foreign Office Research Department memorandum on Anglo-Afghan relations from 1747 to the present day", TNA.
16. Emphasis added. Translation of a letter from Amir Amanullah Khan to Lord Chelmsford, 10 September 1919; Translation of a letter from Amir Amanullah Khan to King George, 10 September 1919; Translation of a letter from Amir Amanullah Khan, 10 September 1919, 1061/1919, pt 11, IOR/L/PS/10/811, "File 1061/1919 Pt 11 Relations with Afghanistan: detailed reports of the Mussoori [Mussoorie] meetings leading up to the despatch of the Kabul mission Jan 1920", BL.
17. Ibid.
18. "A survey of Anglo-Afghan relations", 6, F 1161/108/97, FO 371/69451, 1948, op. cit., TNA.
19. No. VI, C. U. Aitchison, ed., *The Treaties, &c., Relating to Persia and Afghanistan*, vol. 13, A Collection of Treaties, Engagements and Sanads Relating to India and Neighbouring Countries (Calcutta: Government of India Central Publication Branch, 1933), 240–242.
20. Adamec, *Afghanistan, 1900–1923*, 106.
21. Ibid., 44.
22. Ibid., 21.
23. Ibid., 129.
24. Eric Lewis Beverley, *Hyderabad, British India, and the World: Muslim Networks and Minor Sovereignty, c. 1850–1950* (Cambridge: Cambridge University Press, 2015).
25. Nick Cullather, "Damming Afghanistan: Modernization in a Buffer State", *The Journal of American History* 89, no. 2 (2002): 516–517. See also Adamec, *Afghanistan, 1900–1923*, 6.
26. Brandon Marsh, *Ramparts of Empire: British Imperialism and India's Afghan Frontier, 1918–1948* (Basingstoke: Palgrave Macmillan, 2015).
27. Sana Haroon, *Frontier of Faith: Islam in the Indo-Afghan Borderland* (London: Hurst, 2007), 91–124.
28. Milan Hauner, "One Man Against the Empire: The Faqir of Ipi and the British in Central Asia on the Eve of and During the Second World War", *Journal of Contemporary History* 16, no. 1 (1981): 192, 195–196.

29. Dobbs, No. 178-M.C., 6 August 1920, para. 29, 12, N 127/127/97, FO 371/5381, 1920, "Proceedings of the British-Afghan Conference at Mussoorie, 1920", TNA. Leake, *The Defiant Border*, 20–65.
30. Hauner, "One Man Against the Empire", 187.
31. See "independence" and "sovereignty" in Geoff R. Berridge and Alan James, *A Dictionary of Diplomacy* (Basingstoke: Palgrave, 2001), 122, 222–223.
32. E.g. Charles S. Maier, "Consigning the Twentieth Century to History", *The American Historical Review* 105, no. 3 (2000): 807–831.
33. Adamec, *Afghanistan, 1900–1923*, 36–37.
34. Hamilton Grant, No. 108-P.C., Nathia Gali, 6 September 1919, para. 6, 5, IOR/L/PS/10/808, op. cit., BL.
35. Government of India, Foreign and Political Department, no. 73, 2 October 1919, para. 6, IOR/L/PS/10/808, op. cit., BL.
36. Ibid., para. 7.
37. Ibid.
38. Government of India, Foreign and Political Department, no. 73, 2 October 1919, para. 7, IOR/L/PS/10/808, op. cit., BL.
39. Ibid., para. 4.
40. Hamilton Grant, No. 108-P.C., Nathia Gali, 6 September 1919, para. 4, 3, IOR/L/PS/10/808, op. cit., BL.
41. "Report on the Kabul Mission, by Sir H. R. C. Dobbs, K.C.S.I., K.C.I.E.", para. 10–11, 5, N 1450/59/97, FO 371/8076, 1922, "Negotiations conducted by British Mission in Kabul during 1921", TNA.
42. Hamilton Grant, No. 108-P.C., Nathia Gali, 6 September 1919, para. 2, 1, IOR/L/PS/10/808, op. cit., BL.
43. Government of India, Foreign and Political Department, no. 73, 2 October 1919, para. 5, IOR/L/PS/10/808, op. cit., BL.
44. "Proceedings of the Indo-Afghan Conference", N 127/127/97, FO 371/5381, 1920, op. cit., TNA.
45. Erez Manela, *The Wilsonian Moment: Self-Determination and the International Origins of Anticolonial Nationalism* (Oxford: Oxford University Press, 2007), 5.
46. Ibid.
47. Manu Goswami, "Imaginary Futures and Colonial Internationalisms", *American Historical Review* 117, no. 5 (2012): 1463–1464.
48. "Report on the Kabul Mission, by Sir H. R. C. Dobbs, K.C.S.I., K.C.I.E.", para. 24, 11, N 1450/59/97, FO 371/8076, 1922, op. cit., TNA.
49. Ibid.
50. "Proceedings of the eighth meeting of the Indo-Afghan Conference, held at the Savoy Hotel, Mussoorie, on the 23rd June 1920", N 127/127/97, FO 371/5381, 1920, op. cit., TNA.
51. Ibid.

52. Ibid.
53. Anthony Hyman, "Nationalism in Afghanistan", *International Journal of Middle East Studies* 34, no. 2 (2002): 299–315.
54. Dobbs, No. 178-M.C., 6 August 1920, para. 22, 9, N 127/127/97, FO 371/5381, 1920, op. cit., TNA.
55. For instance, "Political review for 1942", para. 4, E 2233/86/97, FO 371/34920, 1943, "Political review of Afghanistan", TNA.
56. "A survey of Anglo-Afghan relations", 20, F 1161/108/97, FO 371/69451, 1948, op. cit., TNA.
57. Leake, *The Defiant Border*, 104–145.
58. "Proceedings of the eighth meeting of the Indo-Afghan Conference, held at the Savoy Hotel, Mussoorie, on the 23rd June 1920", N 127/127/97, FO 371/5381, 1920, op. cit., TNA.
59. Dobbs, No. 178-M.C., 6 August 1920, para. 22, 9, N 127/127/97, FO 371/5381, 1920, op. cit., TNA.
60. Dobbs, No. 178-M.C., 6 August 1920, para. 3/4/9, 1-4, N 127/127/97, FO 371/5381, 1920, op. cit., TNA.
61. "Report on the Kabul Mission, by Sir H. R. C. Dobbs, K.C.S.I., K.C.I.E.", para. 8, 4, N 1450/59/97, FO 371/8076, 1922, op. cit., TNA.
62. Dobbs, No. 178-M.C., 6 August 1920, para. 24, 9, N 127/127/97, FO 371/5381, 1920, op. cit., TNA.
63. Ibid., para. 24, 10, emphasis added.
64. Ibid., para. 25, 10.
65. "Note on proposals of the British and Afghan Governments discussed by the delegates of the two States at the Conference held at Mussoorie between the months of April and July 1920, as a preliminary to definite negotiations for a Treaty of Friendship", 125–127, ser. 32, "Proceedings of the seventeenth meeting of the Indo-Afghan Conference, held at the Savoy Hotel, Mussoorie, on the 24th July 1920", N 127/127/97, FO 371/5381, 1920, op. cit., TNA.
66. Adamec, *Afghanistan, 1900–1923*, 62.
67. Ibid., 49, n. 31.
68. Ibid., 63.
69. Handwritten note by Curzon, 29 November 1920, ser. 62, 1061/1919 pt 9, IOR/L/PS/10/810, "File 1061/1919 Pt 8-9 Relations with Afghanistan", BL.
70. Dobbs, No. 178-M.C., 6 August 1920, para. 28, p. 11, N 127/127/97, FO 371/5381, 1920, op. cit., TNA; Amin Saikal, *Modern Afghanistan: A History of Struggle and Survival* (London: I.B. Tauris, 2012), 64.
71. "Report on the Kabul Mission, by Sir H. R. C. Dobbs, K.C.S.I., K.C.I.E.", para. 25, 11–12, N 1450/59/97, FO 371/8076, 1922, op. cit., TNA.
72. Ibid.

73. No. XXIV, Aitchison, *The Treaties*, vol. 13, 288–292. See Adamec for a detailed account of the negotiations that took place after 1919: Adamec, *Afghanistan, 1900–1923*; Ludwig W. Adamec, *Afghanistan's Foreign Affairs to the Mid-Twentieth Century: Relations with the U.S.S.R., Germany, and Britain* (Tucson: University of Arizona Press, 1974).
74. "Report on the Kabul Mission, by Sir H. R. C. Dobbs, K.C.S.I., K.C.I.E.", para. 27, 14–16, N 1450/59/97, FO 371/8076, 1922, op. cit., TNA.
75. Ibid.
76. Ibid., para. 29, 17.
77. Ibid., para. 31, 18.
78. Ibid., para. 28, 16.
79. Ibid.
80. Ibid., para. 32, 18.
81. Ibid. See also note 60 above.
82. Ibid., para. 30, 17, emphasis added.
83. Ibid., para. 31, 18.
84. Government of India to India Office, 23 March 1922, para. 6, N 3998/59/97, FO 371/8077, 1922, "Sir H. Dobb's [Dobbs] report on his mission to Kabul", TNA.
85. Ibid.
86. Ibid.
87. Ibid.
88. Title of chapter 10 in Manela, *The Wilsonian Moment*, 197–214.
89. Title of chapter 9 in Susan Pedersen, *The Guardians: The League of Nations and the Crisis of Empire* (Oxford, UK: Oxford University Press, 2015), 261–285.
90. Article III, Aitchison, *The Treaties*, vol. 13, 289.
91. Article IV, ibid.
92. Vartan Gregorian, *The Emergence of Modern Afghanistan: Politics of Reform and Modernization, 1880–1946* (Stanford: Stanford University Press, 1969), 227–274.
93. Adamec, *Afghanistan, 1900–1923*, 90.
94. Leon B. Poullada, "Political Modernization in Afghanistan: The Amanullah Reforms", in *Afghanistan: Some New Approaches*, ed. George Grassmuck, Ludwig W. Adamec, and Frances H. Irwin (Ann Arbor: Center for Near Eastern and North African Studies, The University of Michigan, 1969), 99–148.
95. Faiz Ahmed, *Afghanistan Rising: Islamic Law and Statecraft Between the Ottoman and British Empires* (Cambridge: Harvard University Press, 2017); Michael O'Sullivan, "'The Little Brother of the Ottoman State': Ottoman Technocrats in Kabul and Afghanistan's Development in the Ottoman Imagination, 1908–23", *Modern Asian Studies* 50, no. 6 (2016): 1846–1887.

96. Adamec, *Afghanistan, 1900–1923*, 21, n. 33.
97. Ibid., 66, 81.
98. Gregorian, *The Emergence of Modern Afghanistan*, 227–274.
99. Ibid., 270.
100. See Cullather, "Damming Afghanistan"; Timothy Nunan, *Humanitarian Invasion: Global Development in Cold War Afghanistan* (Cambridge: Cambridge University Press, 2016), 46–118.
101. For the Treaty of Kabul see Adamec, *Afghanistan, 1900–1923*, 184. For the text of the Geneva Accords see Maley, *The Afghanistan Wars*, 116.
102. William Maley, *The Afghanistan Wars* (Basingstoke: Palgrave Macmillan, 2009), 230–274; Astri Suhrke, "Democratizing a Dependent State: The Case of Afghanistan", *Democratization* 15, no. 3 (2008): 630–648; Astri Suhrke, "Reconstruction as Modernisation: The 'Post-conflict' Project in Afghanistan", *Third World Quarterly* 28, no. 7 (2007): 1291–1308. See also Chapter 1.
103. Ashraf Ghani and Clare Lockhart, *Fixing Failed States: A Framework for Rebuilding a Fractured World* (Oxford: Oxford University Press, 2008).
104. Viceroy, Foreign and Political Department, to Secretary of State for India, copy of telegram, 4 July 1921, no. 113, P. 2984 "Afghanistan: the question of the British Minister at Kabul", IOR/L/PS/10/957/2, "File 15/1921 Pt 4 Afghanistan: Kabul Mission 1921; question of consular establishments; British minister at Kabul; Afghan objection to Mr S E Pears; appointment of Major Humphrys", BL.
105. Francesca Fuoli, "Incorporating North-Western Afghanistan into the British Empire: Experiments in Indirect Rule Through the Making of an Imperial Frontier, 1884–1887", *Afghanistan* 1, no. 1 (2018): 4–25.
106. "A survey of Anglo-Afghan relations", 8, F 1161/108/97, FO 371/69451, 1948, op. cit., TNA.
107. Adamec, *Afghanistan, 1900–1923*, 60.
108. Pankaj Mishra, *From the Ruins of Empire: The Revolt Against the West and the Remaking of Asia* (London: Penguin Books, 2013), 46–123; Umar Ryad, "Anti-imperialism and the Pan-Islamic Movement", in *Islam and the European Empires*, ed. David Motadel (Oxford: Oxford University Press, 2014), 131–149; Benjamin D. Hopkins, "Islam and Resistance in the British Empire", in *Islam and the European Empires*, ed. David Motadel (Oxford: Oxford University Press, 2014), 150–169.
109. Cemil Aydin, *The Politics of Anti-Westernism in Asia: Visions of World Order in Pan Islamic and Pan-Asian Thought* (New York: Columbia University Press, 2007).
110. "A survey of Anglo-Afghan relations", 11, F 1161/108/97, FO 371/69451, 1948, op. cit., TNA.
111. "Report on the Kabul Mission, by Sir H. R. C. Dobbs, K.C.S.I., K.C.I.E.", para. 26, 12–23, N 1450/59/97, FO 371/8076, 1922, op. cit., TNA.

112. Ibid., para. 24, 11.
113. Telegram no. 259, 18 January 1922, N 1838/59/97, FO 371/8076, 1922, "Communication between Foreign Office and British Legation at Kabul", TNA.
114. "Rough note on the proposal for a British Minister at Kabul", S. E. Pears, 24 November 1921, 1, 68(20)-Est, F&P, 1923, "Note by Mr S. E. Pears, C.S.I., C.I.E., on the proposed establishment of a British Legation at Kabul", NAI.
115. Draft letter by Wakely, 13 December 1921, no. 207, P. 5408, "Afghanistan: proposed arrangements with the F.O. as to conduct & control of correspondence, relations with Afghan Minister, etc.", IOR/L/PS/10/959, "File 15/1921 Pt 8 Afghanistan: arrangements for correspondence between Kabul Legation and FO, Govt of India and India Office; Afghan Minister, London and FO; co-operation between Northern Dept FO and Govt of India; British and Afghan frontier officials", BL.
116. Draft paragraph "in reply to the Viceroy's para. 9", no date, IOR/L/PS/12/1913, "Coll 4/54 British Legation: appointment of Lt Col Sir W Kerr Frazer-Tytler [sic], Sir Francis Wylie and Mr G F Squire", BL.
117. "Precedence of diplomatic agents. Regulations annexed to the Vienna Congress Treaty, of June 9, 1815" in *Foreign Office List for 1922*, 109; "The Right of Legation", Ernest Satow, *A Guide to Diplomatic Practice*, vol. 1 (London: Longmans, Green and Co., 1917), 175–180.
118. See "Legation", Berridge and James, *A Dictionary of Diplomacy*, 147.
119. Berlin, Brussels, Constantinople, Madrid, Paris, Rio de Janeiro, Rome, Tokyo and Washington.
120. "Letter from Lepel Griffin to Sirdar Abdur Rahman Khan, June 14, 1880", Adamec, *Afghanistan, 1900–1923*, 171–172.
121. James Onley, *The Arabian Frontier of the British Raj: Merchants, Rulers, and the British in the Nineteenth-Century Gulf* (New York: Oxford University Press, 2007), 17.
122. Adamec, *Afghanistan, 1900–1923*, 39–64, 157–166; Christopher Wyatt, *Afghanistan and the Defence of Empire: Diplomacy and Strategy During the Great Game* (London: I.B. Tauris, 2011), 46–50, 114–139.
123. See "Memorandum: System of dealing with correspondence, etc., relating to Afghanistan", P. 2758, "Correspondence regarding Afghanistan", no. 136–145, IOR/L/PS/10/959, op. cit., BL and no. 23–32, N 6344/6344/97, FO 371/8084, 1922, "Correspondence regarding Afghanistan", TNA.
124. Milan Hauner, "The Soviet Threat to Afghanistan and India 1938–1940", *Modern Asian Studies* 15, no. 2 (1981): 289.

125. Fraser-Tytler to Metcalfe, 14 December 1938, IOR/L/PS/12/1765, "Coll 3/166 Indo-Afghan frontier: measures to give British frontier officials a better understanding of Afghanistan; A) issues of quarterly unofficial letter by British Legation Kabul; B) proposed mutual exchange of visits by British and Afghan frontier officials", BL.
126. Adamec, *Afghanistan's Foreign Affairs to the Mid-Twentieth Century*, 98.
127. 542-F, EA, 1938, "Objections raised by the Afghan government against the 'Forward Policy' of the Government of India", NAI.
128. Ann Laura Stoler, "Imperial Debris: Reflections on Ruins and Ruination", *Cultural Anthropology* 23, no. 2 (2008): 194.
129. Ann Laura Stoler, "On Degrees of Imperial Sovereignty", *Public Culture* 18, no. 1 (2006): 125–146.
130. Terence Creagh Coen, *The Indian Political Service: A Study in Indirect Rule* (London: Chatto & Windus, 1971); Onley, *The Arabian Frontier of the British Raj*, 38–43; Barbara N. Ramusack, *The Indian Princes and Their States* (Cambridge: Cambridge University Press, 2004), 98–105; Christian Tripodi, *Edge of Empire: The British Political Officer and Tribal Administration on the North-West Frontier, 1877–1947* (Aldershot: Ashgate, 2011), 22.
131. Edward Blunt, *The I.C.S.: The Indian Civil Service* (London: Faber & Faber, 1937), 165.
132. Coen, *The Indian Political Service*, 5; Ian Copland, "The Other Guardians: Ideology and Performance in the Indian Political Service", in *People, Princes and Paramount Power: Society and Politics in the Indian Princely States*, ed. Robert Jeffrey (Oxford: Oxford University Press, 1978), 286; W. Murray Hogben, "British Civil-Military Relations on the North-West Frontier of India", in *Swords and Covenants*, ed. Adrian W. Preston and Peter Dennis (London: Croom Helm, 1976), 124; W. Murray Hogben, "An Imperial Dilemma: The Reluctant Indianization of the Indian Political Service", *Modern Asian Studies* 15, no. 4 (1981): 756; James Onley, "The Raj Reconsidered: British India's Informal Empire and Spheres of Influence in Asia and Africa", *Asian Affairs* 40, no. 1 (2009): 39.
133. Cited in Onley, *The Arabian Frontier of the British Raj*, 38. See also Copland, "The Other Guardians", 293; The "Foreign Office of the Government of India".
134. See "Westphalia, Congress of (1644–8)", Berridge and James, *A Dictionary of Diplomacy*, 249–250; Luke Glanville, "The Myth of 'Traditional' Sovereignty", *International Studies Quarterly* 57, no. 1 (2013): 79–90.
135. Stoler, "On Degrees of Imperial Sovereignty". See also Lauren A. Benton, *A Search for Sovereignty: Law and Geography in European Empires, 1400–1900* (Cambridge: Cambridge University Press, 2010); Lauren Benton, "Colonial Law and Cultural Difference: Jurisdictional Politics

and the Formation of the Colonial State", *Comparative Studies in Society and History* 41, no. 3 (1999): 563–588.
136. Barnett R. Rubin, *The Fragmentation of Afghanistan: State Formation and Collapse in the International System*, 2nd ed. (New Haven: Yale University Press, 2002).
137. "Report on the Kabul Mission, by Sir H. R. C. Dobbs, K.C.S.I., K.C.I.E.", para. 27, 15, N 1450/59/97, FO 371/8076, 1922, op. cit., TNA.
138. Humphrys, telegram no. 80, 4 April 1924, no. 58, FO 402/3, 1924, "Further correspondence regarding Afghanistan: Part III" and N 3100/4/97, FO 371/10393, 1924, "Demands from His Majesty's Government from Afghan Government", TNA.

CHAPTER 3

Subaltern Biographies

MAKING AND UNMAKING DIPLOMATIC SUBALTERNS

The British Legation arrived in Kabul in 1922. By 1923, its population had risen to "nearly one hundred souls".[1] As the first British Minister, Francis Henry Humphrys, acknowledged, this diplomatic mission-in-the-making was more than the sum of its 'diplomats'. "[I]n a place like Kabul", wrote Humphrys' successor Richard Roy Maconachie (1930–1935), "[a] small and isolated cadre like the Kabul Legation is bound to appear overstaffed to the superficial observer, and if no one ever needed leave or was ever off duty because of sickness, no doubt some reduction of staff could be possible, but one must always maintain a sick and leave reserve".[2] Contrary to these documentary gestures, diplomatic labourers rarely emerge from the depths of archival anonymity into histories of international relations. Almost never are they afforded 'diplomatic status' as enablers of diplomatic practice. As Chapter 1 notes, biography and diplomatic history converge into individual career autobiographies on the one hand and into institutional histories of diplomatic posts on the other. This chapter offers a history of the Legation in the shape of a biography from below that breaks with conventional diplomatic historiography. On the one hand, it resists the temptation to mould the history of the Legation as a linear, chronological reconstruction of diplomatic engagement. On the other hand, it counters the widespread practice of favouring state-centred elites in narratives of international relations. The chapter is premised on the idea that the making of elites demands

© The Author(s) 2019
M. Drephal, *Afghanistan and the Coloniality of Diplomacy*,
Cambridge Imperial and Post-Colonial Studies Series,
https://doi.org/10.1007/978-3-030-23960-2_3

subordination. In recognition of this process, the discussion of the Legation's collective biography has been split into two separate chapters. This chapter conceives of the Legation's hierarchies as the outcome of processes of subordination along lines of race, class and gender. It refers to 'subordinated' instead of 'subordinate' persons in hierarchies, underlining the deliberate nature of the making of both elites and subalterns. As a whole, the chapter insubordinates the Legation's hierarchies.

This chapter is the first part of the Legation's collective biography. Together with Chapter 4 it reconstructs the institution's "life history".[3] According to Judith Brown, life histories highlight "the shared lives of people within or moulded by important social and political institutions, as well as the lives of such institutions themselves".[4] In this vein, the two chapters provide a 'thick biography', in variation of Clifford Geertz' method of "thick description".[5] They are also an effort in prosopography. The application of biographical methods is a productive undertaking that overcomes two of diplomatic historiography's inclinations: to focus on the reconstruction of abstract policy-formulation processes and on 'elites' therein. Histories of inter-state relations have often favoured 'eminent' diplomatic agents and men particularly so. The fact that some persons are more visible than others in diplomatic archives has echoed into diplomatic histories.[6] Diplomatic practice and processes of archiving determined diplomatic history's foci. Diplomats became visible as the authors of reports or the brokers of treaties, which were circulated among a diplomatic audience, archived and found important enough to survive instances of 'weeding', consequently spoiling historians for choice in the pursuit of material for their reconstructions of the past. Diplomacy's writers, or those credited with authorship, emerge from anonymity, become identifiable individuals and so ensure their place in history. While there are several thousands of despatches, telegrams and reports from successive Ministers in Kabul, we know very little about the processes or people involved in their production. For instance, Harold Carter, Personal Assistant to the Minister in the 1920s, "seemed to be able at any hour of the day or night to produce flawless typescript in minimum time".[7] Yet, he is virtually unknown to the archive that he helped build. The reproduction of diplomatic texts together with the original logic of their creation has restricted diplomatic historiography's remit. Naming and evidence ensured prominence in the archive. At the same time, policy and chronology have often been deemed as essences of what diplomacy is all about: the management of inter-state relations at a personal level. As a result, diplomatic history has often reproduced diplomacy's frameworks and their contents. This chapter is interested in the people behind and outside of diplomatic texts as well as those who made diplomatic life and action possible. It goes up against the two entangled and confining parameters of elitism and 'policy'. A sociology of the kind that Tarak Barkawi has presented for army-society relations in *Soldiers of Empire* can situate diplomatic history in a wider interpretive frame that acknowledges the co-constitution of diplomats and society.[8] The chapter widens diplomacy beyond a select set of people who are often too easily and readily recognised as the 'real' diplomats.

The diplomatic and colonial services published annual lists of its staff. This process of gazetting colonial officers and diplomats defined who was who or what. It also resulted in a division of the visible and the invisible, producing and cementing colonial and diplomatic hierarchies. Between 1922 and 1940, the Legation's gazetted political officers, its diplomats, included a Minister, a Counsellor, a Secretary, an Oriental Secretary, a Surgeon and a Military Attaché. According to the logic of the *Foreign Office List* and the *India Office List*, they *were* the Legation. The chapter inverts the colonial hierarchies that these *Lists* expressed. To achieve this, the chapter's focus lies on individuals who were not captured in these hierarchies and especially the Legation's subaltern operative and support staff. The chapter applies the term of the subaltern as the opposite of a dominant elite, in relation to which the subaltern's subordinated, inferior rank is expressed "in terms of class, caste, age, gender and office or in any other way".[9] In regard to Afghanistan, the notion of tribe needs to be added to this list of differentiating markers. There were several degrees of subalternity, which this chapter explores in the process of writing the Legation's biography from below. In its subordinated positions, the Legation revealed the significant depth of the colonial foundations of its labourers. The chapter complements and mirrors Chapter 4 showing the making of diplomatic subalterns in Kabul, whilst Chapter 4 shows the making of a diplomatic elite (Fig. 3.1).

The Legation's structure takes the shape of a pyramid at whose top power, historical visibility and identifiability converge. Its base consists of several larger anonymous groups. The spectrum, which segregates the top from the base, includes virtually permanent visibility, partial anonymity as well as comprehensive invisibility in archival as well as historical records. The Legation's operative staff was divided into skilled office clerks, a "ministerial establishment", and into unskilled labour, a "menial establishment". Members of the latter were almost never recorded as individuals. In general terms, the colonial state recorded and archived information on its

Fig. 3.1 A group photo, 1935/1936 (*Credit* Photo 2/3, GB165-0326, Fraser-Tytler Collection, MECA)

operative employees in terms of financial accounting and not, in contrast to its gazetted officers, in terms of professional achievement. The same sources that comprehensively list the Legation's political personnel equally subordinated other staff to the margins of anonymity. Colonial and diplomatic archives' biases in favour of elites in terms of both volume and detail of materials seriously challenge the search for subordinated individuals.[10] And yet, the look behind the most obvious archival visibilities is rewarding. The very process of visualising subordinated individuals and groups reveals the very pathways in which power was distributed inside the Legation. In its search for the Legation's neglected and glossed-over, the chapter shows the diplomatic mission's layered authorities and sheds light on the inherent social and professional gradations in its colonial and diplomatic society.[11] If viewed as a holistic social microcosm, even the Legation's most subordinated individual can no longer be overlooked as a diplomatic agent.

Three sets of sources provide the chapter's primary source base. First, there is a multitude of scattered single files, which minutely document job applications, employment, salaries and allowances.[12] Those who are occasionally named straddle biography's boundaries because they are neither fully elusive nor fully visible. This partial anonymity distinguishes certain individuals from others who are resigned to obscurity by reason of their archival namelessness. Anonymity, in particular, prevents identification in finding aids.[13] As a result, large parts of the Legation's subordinated personnel are visible only through the larger groups to which they were assigned or belonged to and whose professions they shared. The second set of sources, therefore, consists of the annual budgets and accounts of the Legation, which visualise the Legation's "ministerial" and "menial establishments" and occasionally name otherwise anonymous individuals. It is indicative of the meticulous financial working of the colonial bureaucracy that these budgets and accounts are the single most important complement to the published governmental lists. The third is the Legation's *Office Manual*, written by George Leslie Mallam, the Counsellor in 1933. It provides an important document for the definition of some of the Legation's professional communities and groups, specific jobs as well as their regulation by means of standing orders. Although it does not elevate subordinate individuals beyond the bounds of anonymity, the *Office Manual* offers the job descriptions of the Legation's ministerial establishment in a detailed survey. The following sections build the Legation's biography from the ground up.

The "Menial Establishment"

The Legation's operative levels were designated its "menial establishment" or "inferior staff".[14] While it is almost impossible to identify individuals, the existence of particular labour groups indicates the foundations of the Legation, which were modelled on the needs of colonial households in India.[15] The Legation's employees comprised launderers (*dhobi, dhoban*, sg.), cleaners and sweepers, horse-keepers at the stables (*syce*, sg.), water-carriers (*bhisti*, sg.), cooks or "servants" in general, "house bearers" (*ferrash*, sg.) and watchmen (*chowkidar*, sg.).[16] At one point, the Legation employed no less than twenty-four gardeners (*mali*, sg.).[17] The initial plans for the Legation alleged that "there seems little hope that reliable menials will be obtainable in Kabul, at any rate to start with. Also for obvious reasons it will not be advisable to have despatchers and other subordinates of this type, whose work gives them access to the office, unless they are more or less reliable".[18] Mistrust of Afghan labour both in terms of productivity and secrecy prompted the recruitment of similar workers from the North-West Frontier Province whose pay rate in the cantonments had to be doubled for service in Kabul. Domestic staff, water carriers and sweepers were, in the long term, also recruited in Afghanistan. Indian workers generally reported to the Counsellor. Afghan labourers reported to the Nazir. As a collective, potential Afghan employees had to undergo background checks after one had been accused of theft.[19] Thus, both Indian clerks and Afghan labourers were collectively subjected to colonial suspicions.

The Legation's operative establishment remained largely anonymous. A rare reference identifies Masjidi as the head gardener. It documents that Masjidi negotiated with the Legation's neighbouring farmers the Legation's use of water from a shared canal, which had contributed to draught and crop failure on their fields.[20] This instance is revealing of the Legation's multiple points of contact with its Afghan neighbourhood at a local level. Moreover, British diplomats' representations of individual gardeners commonly labelled them as "usually lazy" and lacking intelligence.[21] William Kerr Fraser-Tytler referred to the gardeners as having a particularly strong olfactory "effect on the atmosphere of the room" during the viewing of a political cinematic performance at the Legation in 1940: "The gardeners are all right in the open air, though not exactly sweet smelling, but indoors – my word!!. The small cat house at the Zoo is a bed of roses in comparison".[22] Writing on the British Embassy in Kabul of 1959, Nicholas Barrington describes their quarters as a "doghouse" and suggests that they extracted opium from the Legation's poppy flowers.[23]

The very denomination of the Legation's "ministerial" and "menial establishments" implied an impersonal machine, which prevented the documentation of individuals as individuals due to the subordination of their labour along the notions of race. The colonial state's perceptions of and mentalities towards labour and race were, thus, acutely felt in the organisation of the Legation's personnel. Another group so marginalised, was the Legation's bodyguard. Initial plans for the recruitment of fitting soldiers specified that it would have to consist of "Pathans from the North-West Frontier Province", as Indian Pashtuns were to look after colonial bodies in Kabul.[24] As the personified 'ramparts of empire', they also represented the colonial regimentation of India's north-west frontier. Primary importance was given to the "smartness of individuals selected and their turn out".[25] The guard only carried sabre and lance, as it did not primarily serve protective purposes. It consisted of "old soldiers" and "time-expired" men from a "smart cavalry regiment".[26] In order to minimise the risk of "corruption" and to increase their "incentive to smartness" the men selected according to these criteria served only six months in Kabul.[27] The escort mainly fulfilled representational tasks, "as in Kabul appearances are likely to count for a good deal it appears very desirable that Minister should be accompanied by escort too small in number to be provocative but adequate for performance of orderly duties".[28]

George Nathaniel Curzon himself had "laid great stress" on this in an interview with Humphrys before the latter's departure to Kabul.[29] The escort comprised Indian cavalry sergeants (*daffadar*, sg.), cavalry troopers (*sowar*, sg.) and a farrier, comprising a total of about a dozen individuals.[30] As a collective, the Legation's operative staff were crucial for the everyday operation of the Legation as a whole. Yet, in the colonial archive these Indians and Afghans hardly ever emerge from anonymity. In September 1933, after the attack on the Legation, the Minister singled out the "extremely gallant behaviour" of Naurez Khan:

> He is not a young man, and neither his mind nor his body moves very quickly. He had about 50 yards to traverse, without any cover whatever, between the gate of the dispensary and the well, before he could close with Muhammad Azim [the attacker], who had by then fired seven shots, killing three men without a single miss, and was obviously desperate. Naurez Khan had no weapon on any kind, and his only comment on his action was that as he had 'eaten the Government's salt' there was nothing else to be done. He was, however, anxious to explain why he was unable to reach Muhammad Azim in time to save Mr. Stranger and Yakub. Recognition of his action is under consideration.[31]

While the Legation relied heavily on Indian and Afghan labour, the security and comfort it provided as well as on the effect of representation, which this labour generated, it never overcame its race-based organisation. Subalternity was established through the skills required for a job and through the ethnicity of its incumbents. It expressed itself in anonymity.

THE "ORIENTAL OFFICE"

The ministerial establishment provided support staff for the Legation's office-related tasks. In 1933, it included a Superintendent, a Second Clerk, a Third Clerk, a Fourth Clerk, an Accountant, a Mir Munshi (chief adviser), a Passport Clerk and a Nazir (overseer).[32] The Legation's ministerial establishment was divided by notions of race into "Europeans" in the "English office" on the one hand and Indians in the "Oriental Office" on the other. This was an adaptation, although in reverse, of the setup at Residencies across the Indian Empire, where the so-called Persian Office under the leadership of a *mir munshi* ranked higher than the English Office.[33] European descent was a race-based misnomer as most of the clerks were British. The Legation kept occasional lists of its "European personnel", but not of its South Asian employees.[34] India, thus, provided both the personnel and the ideology underlying the organisation of the Legation's clerical staff.

The Legation's Indian clerks were organised in a separate Oriental Office, which comprised the positions of the Accountant, the Mir Munshi, the Passport Clerk and the Nazir in 1933.[35] In terms of the Accountant and the Passport Clerk, Indians held offices which also existed in other diplomatic posts. In terms of the Mir Munshi and the Nazir, South Asians fulfilled recognisably South Asian offices that originated in the Persianate bureaucracy of Mughal India. The capitalisation and Anglicisation of indigenous job titles underlined the incorporation of South Asian bureaucracy into British diplomacy's office vocabulary and practices. The employment of indigenous persons in diplomatic posts was by no means a practice restricted to Kabul or peculiar to the colonial state in India. But, here and in case of the upper positions of the clerical establishment, Kabul's office practices were specifically inspired by similar colonial institutions in India.

Indians were segregated from their 'British' colleagues who had access to confidential office communications. While the latter could be elevated to the heroic by mastering the physical demands of their work, Indian employees of the Legation came under persistent scrutiny. For instance, arguing for the employment of another European clerk in October 1926, Humphrys highlighted the "enormous" pressure of work on the two European clerks, who worked "unconscionably long hours [...] forgoing all holidays, except a Sunday occasionally".[36] By contrast, the Legation's Indian employees were subject to control by the Superintendent and the Legation's political staff. In general, they had to relinquish their passports until the day before their planned return to India, receiving them only "on proper application".[37] Indian clerks faced tough restrictions that limited their mobility.

The Accountant recorded the Legation's financial transactions, prepared monthly and annual accounts and safeguarded cash deposits in Indian and Afghan currency under the close supervision of the Counsellor. He had to provide a security of Indian Rs. 1000 and was "required to make good any loss which may be proved to be due to his negligence".[38] The inbuilt threat of financial punishment for professional mistakes seems to have been the result of a case in which one Accountant embezzled Rs. 20,000, subsequently receiving a prison sentence of seven years.[39] Yet, the individual case seemed to confirm more general colonial impressions of Indian unreliability. It also subjected successive Legation Accountants to a similar suspicion. By comparison, the Legation's political staff were not subjected to such punitive clauses while they also benefitted from far superior pay. For instance, in 1932, the Minister's annual income of Rs. 48,000 dwarfed the Accountant's pay of Rs. 5100.[40]

Although the Accountant was "[o]ne of the most important members of the office establishment", very little is known about individuals. An initial proposal to employ them from "one of the Peshawar firms of Sethi[']s", a private banking firm, echoed a widespread practice in India's Residency system.[41] An early Legation Accountant, Rai Sahib Pundit Shiva Dayal Jha, was on deputation from the Rajputana Agency, an administrative unit in northern central India comprising several princely states.[42] The Accountants were not restricted to a single religious community, as the examples of Khan Sahib Sheikh Muhammad Qasim (in 1931 and 1932) and Sahib Amir Ali Shah (in 1942) indicate.[43] But, they were drawn from Indian services until August 1947, when the Legation in Kabul was informed about the upcoming introduction of Foreign Office accounting procedures.[44] Judging from the honorific titles among the Accountants, Rai Sahib, Khan Sahib and Sahib, which the colonial state bestowed only on Indians, the Accountants were established members of the colonial state's bureaucracy. These honours were borrowed from Mughal *durbar* practices and sought to incorporate Indians into the society of colonial governors.[45] As such, the Accountants qualify as subalterns only in a relative sense by comparison with India's colonial elite and other clerks. In relation to their societal origins, however, they were invested in the colonial administration to which they aligned their careers and lives.

The Legation's Mir Munshi was its Persian language specialist, handling correspondence with the Persian Embassy and the Afghan Foreign Office.[46] Originally, a *mir munshi* was a "native adviser to the head of mission on local politics, customs, protocol, etc.".[47] At the Legation, aspects of the connecting role between British Residents and local rulers in India were still tangible. The importance of the *mir munshi* as interpreter of an alien court ritual, language and diplomacy at the top of the Residency's bureaucracy was reduced over time, as British Political Agents increasingly attempted to master these skills in order to make themselves independent of native middlemen, who were not always considered trustworthy or reliable. At the Legation, the Mir Munshi translated receipts into English and issues into Persian, all of which were checked by the Oriental Secretary, Counsellor or Minister, diminishing the importance which once had been placed on the sole interpreter of Mughal court ritual and as translator of diplomatic correspondence.[48] However, in Kabul the Mir Munshi provided an important link to the further subordinated levels of the Legation's subordinate staff, for instance by distributing all "vernacular" mail items to its "inferior servants".[49] The imbalance of the colonial record reveals itself in the anonymity of the Mir Munshi, whose translations enabled British diplomacy in Kabul in the first place. We know little about them, but they, too, were recruited from existing cadres in India, most notably from the North-West Frontier Province.[50] In 1935, the permanent office of Assistant Mir Munshi was established due to an increase in the Mir Munshi's workload.[51] In the absence of concrete biographical evidence, it seems that knowledge of Persian, familiarity with Afghan court protocol and customs as well as personal faith qualified individuals for the position. We know of one translator in particular, Syed Irshad Husain, who lost his life in the attack on the Legation in September 1933. In a rare deviation from regular correspondence practices, Syed Irshad Husain was mentioned in Maconachie's letter to the British Foreign Secretary: "Syed Irshad Husain had served in the Foreign and Political Department for sixteen years and, since May 1930 in His Majesty's Legation. He was regarded by the Moslem employees as their leader in religious matters and was much respected. He has left a widow and a large family".[52]

The Passport Clerk's job description was wider than its denomination suggests. The post owed its existence to the large amount of consular work.[53] He primarily dealt with Afghan visa applications and *rahdari* (transit duty). He also issued the relevant travel permissions on passports and green passes for the Legation's subordinate Indian personnel after receiving instructions from the Oriental Secretary and from the Superintendent. Like several other clerks, the job was split between the main office and that of the Military Attaché. For the latter, he kept a "clothing register", which documented sheets of cloth for every government employee to be issued to a *durzi* for tailoring.[54] Despite work in several of the Legation's areas, both consular and mundane, there is very little information in terms of individual histories. There is an indication, however, that Passport Clerks were also appointed from the Secretariat of the North-West Frontier Province.[55]

As the last member of the Legation's Oriental Office, the Nazir ensured the Legation's material supplies, buying and distributing firewood and maintaining a *godown* (store). According to the Legation's *Office Manual*, the Nazir "performs a large number of miscellaneous duties of an official nature, many of which entail journeys from the Legation to the Kabul bazar and back, for which he receives a conveyance allowance for the maintenance of a tonga and pony".[56] Like the Legation's other Indian clerks, the Nazir's agency was significantly circumscribed. He reported to the Counsellor who gave permission to the Oriental Secretary to invite tenders from local contractors when stocks were running low. But, like his Indian colleagues, the Nazir provided an important link to the Legation's Indian as well as Afghan employees, as he performed *gumrukh* (toll clearing) duties and allotted quarters to the Legation's domestic staff of Indian or Afghan origins for whom he also obtained residence cards. For the Military Attaché, the Nazir oversaw the custody of tents and camp furniture and purchased fodder and bedding for the Legation's horses. By involving both the Nazir and the *daffadar* at the stables, the Legation made its subordinate Indian staff collectively responsible for the correct weight, quantity and quality of the broken straw (*bhoosa*), barley and bran supplied by local contractors.[57] These positions also involved their holders in the care of the Legation's diplomatic animals.

Created in 1925, three Muslim incumbents emerge from anonymity, Rahmat Khan in 1925, Fazal Rahman in 1932 and Muhammad Munif in 1942.[58] It is not improbable that Rahmat Khan was identical to the "caretaker" of the Legation buildings between 1929 and 1930, when the Legation was temporarily withdrawn during the rebellion against Amanullah Khan.[59] Rahmat Khan was then charged with safeguarding the government property left behind in Kabul.[60] With him stayed several "Pathan British subjects", the lorry drivers, and no less than fifteen Afghan "nightwatchmen" (*chowkidar*, sg.) eight Afghan gardeners and six Afghan grooms for the Legation's horses.[61] Reports on Rahmat's work suggested that he used the absence of diplomats to establish "for himself a position of greater importance than his functions warrant"[62]:

> The rumours of Rehmat's [sic] riotous living are without foundation. It is true [that Baron von Plessen] once saw Rahmat in an elevated condition which Rehmat [sic] admitted was the result of a bout with a friend over a bottle of

country liquor, excusing himself with the hopeless dulness [sic] of his life. But the Legation buildings are in first class condition, and the furniture, horses etc., are looked after really well. And from various anecdotes I have got the clear impression that Rahmat is abiding strictly by Sir Francis Humphrys' injunctions. The garden seems to have been allowed to go to seed.[63]

The very existence of largely unfounded rumours reflected the fear of colonial officers that their absence from Kabul would cause the natural havoc of South Asian subordinates to break free. The acknowledgment that Rahmat proved to fulfil his duties by following the orders of the absent British Minister is effectively sidelined by the reference to the overgrowing garden attached to the temporarily abandoned Legation. The stereotypes already encountered in connection with the Legation's Indian Accountants recur here in anecdotal form.

When the Legation returned in 1930, the Counsellor, Arthur Edward Broadbent Parsons, and Secretary, Arthur Ernest Henry Macann, interrogated Rahmat Khan as well as the gardeners Masjidi and Sher Muhammed. In a rare example, the Legation's subordinated staff speak in their own words in these statements. Maconachie also reached out to Humphrys in Baghdad. Humphrys was "furious" that the Legation, "my house", had been "invaded by Rahmat's visitors" and that Rahmat Khan had opened the wine cellar:

> I impressed on him in the clearest possible language that he was left behind merely as a caretaker and not as a British Representative in Kabul. He should therefore refuse to allow any person to enter my house for any purpose whatever and should receive visitors in any of the Indian quarters outside. It is a monstrous thing that he allowed visitors into the big house to drink wine, use the lavatories (which of course had no water laid on) and to play billiards, and I hope that you will let Rahmat have it in the neck for his gross disobedience of my orders. I know he is very fond of the bottle himself and this may account for his violation of the cellar.[64]

Humphrys listed Rahmat Khan's several shortcomings, whilst also expressing an inclination for violent disciplinary action for the alleged transgressions. Rahmat Khan was dehumanised. His alleged alcoholism drove his alleged insubordination. Humphrys included in his letter to Maconachie a list of bottles that had been left behind in 1929. By contrast, Rahmat Khan's testimony shows that he protected the Legation's watchmen and guard by taking them from the Oriental Secretary's house in the hospital compound into the main Legation compound during the retreat of Habibullah Kalakani's soldiers, the Saqavis, in October 1929. That night, Rahmat Khan said, the Oriental Secretary's house outside and the Surgeon's house inside the compound were broken in whilst three guards were killed and one *chowkidar*, Murad Khan, was "badly bruised".[65] The next day, another party attempted to steal the Legation's horses, but Rahmat Khan managed to prevent this by turning some of the Legation's sheep into a feast. For a month, he also catered to around thirty soldiers sent by the Shah Wali Khan to protect the Legation grounds. In Rahmat Khan's own words:

> I used stores and wines for entertainment when members of other Legations and Afghans came. I also had to feed about twentyfour Indian motor lorry drivers, who took refuge in the Legation for about six weeks during the time of Bacha Saqao. There were eight lorries. I was given no proper charge of anything, but Sir Francis Humphrys merely informed me the evening before the evacuation that I should remain.[66]

Regardless, Rahmat Khan's time in Kabul was over. Parsons and Maconachie agreed that, in material terms, Rahmat Khan's "stewardship" was "worthy of commendation": "He has delivered valuable property practically intact after a disturbed period of more than a year. He volunteered to remain behind, & single handed fulfilled his trust, no small achievement for a man of his status & antecedents".[67] And yet, that was exactly the problem. By making use of the Legation's resources to protect it and those left behind, Rahmat Khan had irreversibly overstepped important boundaries of race and imperial sovereignty: "His departure was inevitable as it was clear that after the liberty—not to say licence—he has enjoyed for the last year or so he would never again fit into his proper place".[68] Humphrys was "furious" because Rahmat Khan had not submitted himself or his colleagues to the logic of imperial sovereignty that the Legation embodied. To save himself and others, Rahmat Khan had emerged from the "*Indian* quarters *outside*" to "invade" the main building inside the compound.[69] Seeking shelter within the imperial sovereignty that the Minister's residence represented was interpreted as an act of insubordination on Rahmat Khan's part. Subordinated Indian employees were not entitled to the material representation of empire. Maconachie tried to assuage Humphrys, arguing that this insubordination was based on Rahmat Khan's "natural defects of character".[70] In other words, Indians were prone to challenging the 'natural' order of empire in the absence of colonial masters. As a permanent non-gazetted officer, Rahmat Khan could not be dismissed from colonial service as there were no grounds for this, such as "inefficiency".[71] Maconachie tried to persuade Steuart Edmund Pears, the Chief Commissioner in the North-West Frontier Province, to employ Rahmat Khan in exchange for Fazal Ilahi, but Pears declined owing to what "he's heard about the latter's character and history".[72] Despite preventing the 'looting' of the Legation compound, protecting the left-behind as well as feeding its guards, Rahmat Khan himself came to embody a challenge to the colonial order in Kabul as well as the North-West Frontier Province.

The "English Office"

The Legation's clerical establishment shows diminishing degrees of biographical information and individuality. The Superintendent and the "European" clerks had access to most of the Legation's written correspondence and transactions. At the head of the Legation's ministerial establishment, the Superintendent's duties included the "supervision of office staff [...] registering and filing papers, putting up cases, typing, stenography, assisting gazetted officers in cypher work".[73] The Superintendent's office was the Legation's communications hub, which tracked all incoming and outgoing written correspondence, circulated files to the Legation's political officers for action and information, and enables today's historians to track and connect the Legation's correspondence in archives in India and the United Kingdom. The Superintendent also safeguarded the *toshakhana* (a store of gifts), blank passports and the passports of the Legation personnel. He implemented the Legation's standing orders, which regulated the Legation's routines, stored character rolls and annual confidential reports on the Legation staff.[74] He was directly subordinated to the Counsellor, the Legation's second-in-command. From 1939 onwards, the Superintendent was relabelled as the Archivist, a designation which also survived the Legation's merger into the later Embassy.[75] Humphrys needed the ideal Superintendent to be "a man who can type, keep his mouth shut, run a small office really well, remain impervious to fat bribes, and be happy in comparative solitude [...]. He should be an Englishman as he will have a British clerk under him & his work is super confidential".[76] Race defined the Legation's hierarchies and the processes of subordination. Indian clerks were not trusted with confidential paper work. Moreover, the limited space at the temporary Legation houses meant that the early members of the mission came to Kabul without partners. If married candidates were selected, they had to initially separate from their families for the time of their posting in Kabul. Being free from debt was a prerequisite in all colonial services. It reduced the risk of bribery and corruptibility. While race implied general trustworthiness, the job still required a "good moral character".[77]

The same characteristics applied to the other clerks. The Second Clerk, or Stenographer, typed letters, despatches, memoranda and notes to the Afghan Foreign Office, creating the very files which historians use today.[78] He handled the Legation's private mail, which shuttled weekly between Kabul and Peshawar, checked the incoming and prepared the outgoing *chalan* (register) for the *yakdan* (mail bag).[79] As organiser of the Legation's reminder register, the Second Clerk was crucial for the timing of the Legation's office routines. As the Legation's office workload increased, more clerks were added over time. The Third Clerk prepared the Legation's official mail. During the week, he contributed to the overall office workload, that is "[a]ll the routine work that in India would be carried out by *duftries* [*daftari*, an office clerk]".[80] He had a language specialism in French and registered the mail circulating between the Afghan Foreign Office and the British Legation. A Fourth Clerk or "Military Attaché's Clerk" worked in the Military Attaché's office, typing correspondence, keeping a running summary of events, circulated weekly by the Military Attaché under his own name, and maintaining maps. In the "Main Office", the Fourth Clerk typed radio news and was occasionally seconded to the Legation Surgeon and the Superintendent, maintaining, for instance, the Legation's library catalogue and its stationery.[81] Originally a separate post entirely, the Military Attaché's Clerk was incorporated into the dynamic hierarchy of the Legation's ministerial establishment.[82] As the duties involved the handling of military intelligence, incumbents were, unsurprisingly, European. But, the post is also one of the very few which were not held exclusively by men alone.[83] In 1935, it was held by the wife of one of the Legation's other clerks, combining an economy of space in terms of accommodation and finances.[84] The Persianate terms in the job descriptions of the Legation's Oriental Office reveal the inspiration informing the Legation's clerical setup. The numbering of the clerks in the English Office underlines the evolution of their positions over time. It also introduced a hierarchy into the clerical establishment, which was upwardly mobile. Lower-ranking clerks accumulated knowledge of the Legation's office routines, which enabled them to move into higher positions when those offices fell vacant.

The selection process for the Legation's ministerial establishment reveals intricate bureaucratic connections with the colonial state in India, which provided the Legation with clerks from its existing cadres. Vacancies at the Legation in Kabul were advertised as departmental circulars in several branches of the Indian Army establishment.[85] Candidates directed their applications to the British Minister in Kabul who selected the incumbents. As a result, the selected clerks were closely connected with and well versed in the day-to-day military administration of the colonial state.[86] The most important pool for the recruitment of the Legation's clerical establishment was the General Staff Branch at the Army Headquarters in India. The General Staff branch supervised Indian Army personnel, its training and education and developed operational schemes for the army's deployment.[87] These tasks were the reserve of the Indian Army's commissioned officers. But, the General Staff Branch's pool of clerks, which included retired army officers, circulated into and out of Kabul. These clerks were styled "military subordinates" and were grouped in separate divisions.[88] Examples for clerks from the General Staff Branch at the Legation in Kabul include the Superintendents J. Carter in 1924 and J. H. Milnes in 1939, whose names are on record only as initials.[89] There were also commissioned officers, such as Captain Bowtell-Harris, who officiated as Superintendent in 1924 and whose name is reduced to rank and surname.[90] B. S. Burgess, Second Clerk in 1922, was deputed from the Military Secretary's Branch at Army Headquarters.[91] L. H. Spinks, both Second Clerk between 1925 and 1927 and later Superintendent, offers an exceptionally visible example. Having served as a clerk in the Foreign and Political Department since 1919, he was present at the Indo-Afghan peace conference in Rawalpindi in 1919 and during Henry Dobbs' mission to Kabul in 1921. When he applied for the job of Superintendent in 1930, all British members of the Legation's political leadership, except the Secretary, provided references.[92] Finally, the Legation's clerks were also seconded from other clerical cadres in India, the North-West Frontier Province Secretariat, for instance, as evidenced by the Second Clerk in 1938, M. R. Gallyôt, who reverted to his substantial appointment after his tour in Afghanistan.[93]

The Legation's ministerial establishment expanded further in the late 1930s, moving beyond the snapshot provided by the *Office Manual* in 1933. Not only did the clerks employ their own "house bearer" or "servant", a Fifth and a Sixth Clerk were added in 1937 and 1938, respectively.[94] The Sixth Clerk was originally designated as "Leave Reserve Clerk". Shortly after, the post became the "propaganda clerk" and was charged with the typing and circulation of BBC broadcasts in October 1939 as part of the Legation's "propaganda offensive" in the wake of the Second World War.[95] In late 1941, there was an opening for a Confidential Clerk tasked with collecting and collating information from local sources.[96] The Legation's English Office changed the denominations of its multiple jobs to Assistants in 1942.[97] While the clerical positions were mostly occupied by men, there were two "lady stenographers", C. Carvello and S. Broughton, in 1947. The very description underlined that the employment of women as colonial clerks took place in an exclusively male preserve. In the same year, the only remaining Assistant, Truter, the Military Attaché's clerk, Baker, and the two stenographers chose to continue their employment with the newly independent state of India.[98] By contrast, W. S. Sinclair, who from 1935 climbed up the Legation's clerical ladder from Third to Second Clerk and Superintendent, was still the Embassy's Archivist in 1950, by then with an M.B.E. to his name.[99] The Archivist's employment as master of the Legation's colonial records and office routines marked a colonial continuity which linked the colonial and postcolonial dimensions of British diplomacy in Kabul.

The Garage Superintendent

The Legation's Garage Superintendent provides an important mirror image to the South Asian labourers at the Legation.[100] He supervised all arrangements of a mechanical and electrical nature related to the Legation. Most importantly, he looked after its fleet of cars, which in 1922 included Wolseley and Austin touring cars, a Rolls Royce limousine, as well as two Crossley tenders and Albion lorries for the Legation's mail service between Kabul and Peshawar.[101] Initial requests for the Legation's representative car went in the direction of a Napier or a Landaulette. In 1940, the Legation possessed a Humber limousine.[102] Like the escort, cars were important status symbols and repeatedly considered as valuable gifts, especially since Amanullah Khan was renowned for driving himself.[103] The Legation's lorries were also used for transport to outdoor pursuits, such as *shikar* (hunting) or fishing.[104] The Garage Superintendent was later put in charge of fire safety arrangements. Geoffrey Herbert Stranger, also a later recipient of imperial honours, was the Legation's Garage Superintendent since its inception in February 1922. He was killed in the attempt on the Minister's life in 1933 that has already brought into view other subordinated members of the Legation's personnel.[105] Through the event, we also get glimpse of the person and of Stranger's position in the Legation's structures:

> Mr. Stranger was in his 38th year. He enlisted in the army in 1915 and served in France during the two following years. In 1918, he received a commission in the Machine-Gun Corps, and after demobilisation was employed in Wolseley Motors, Bombay. In 1922 he joined the staff of His Majesty's Legation, where with the exception of a year after the evacuation of 1929, he served continuously until his death. For his services during the disturbances of 1928-29, he received the Membership of the Order of the British Empire. His official title of garage superintendent gives a very inadequate idea of his value to this Legation. He was a born mechanic, and his ability was equally evident whether he was adjusting the shutter of a camera, repairing a clock, or replacing the back axle of a lorry in a snow storm. The efficiency of the Legation mail service, over what my predecessor [Humphrys] described as 'some of the worst roads in the world,' is locally proverbial and entirely due to Mr. Stranger. While no day was too long for himself and no conditions to severe, his consideration for his Indian subordinates was unfailing, and explains their remarkable outburst of grief when they heard the news of his death. He has left a widow and a daughter.[106]

The Garage Superintendent reported to the Counsellor but was himself in charge of a number of garage staff, including a mechanic (*mistri*), cleaners and drivers.[107] The Garage Superintendent was removed from the Legation's office routines and in charge of his own, mostly Indian and Afghan workforce. As an Anglo-Indian, his position was comparable to that of Legation's European clerks, but he was not part of the clerical hierarchy. Moreover, the mechanical nature of the job defined him as a maintenance person, who was not only of European extraction, and, therefore, trustworthy, but also equipped with the requisite knowledge of the Legation's material operations. By contrast, the very people who drove the Legation's mail lorries from and to Peshawar, do not appear anywhere apart from occasional references to their Pashtun, or "Pathan", tribal identities.[108] Their jobs, too, were regulated in the *Office Manual*.[109] The Indian Forwarding Clerk in Peshawar, the point of destination for the Legation's mail lorry, also remained largely anonymous.[110] Skilled labour alone did not by itself provide a means to break out of the subaltern position which British diplomacy in Afghanistan imposed on most of its employees. In combination with race, labourers with certain skills could at least emerge from absolute subalternity.[111]

The "Legation Ladies", Women and Diplomacy

In a historiographical field dominated by men, women have been persistently marginalised in diplomatic histories. As Cynthia Enloe has argued in *Bananas, Beaches and Bases*, "[m]en are seen as having the skills and resources that the government needs if its international status is to be enhanced", whilst women often appear as "objects of worry for the makers of foreign policy chiefly as 'wives'".[112] The Legation was a patriarchal community, whose dozens of members included women in numerous roles, including domestic labourers in its several individual households, as children's nurses (*ayah*, sg.), organisers as well as visitors. Women also appear as more distant, yet involved confidantes. Christian Alice Scott-Kerr, Fraser-Tytler's mother, received her son's regular weekly letters over a period of close to two decades until the end of his career in colonial service.

Amongst these women, the so-called "Legation Ladies" formed a group at the top of the Legation's female hierchary.[113] The Legation Ladies were the wives of the Legation's political offers. The group also included the wives of office administrators, such as the Office Superintendent. They mirrored, along lines of race, the social and professional hierarchies implemented in the world of the Legation men. The very term "Legation Ladies" both included and excluded them from the institution, whilst also establishing a class-based hierarchy between 'ladies' and other women. Despite its biologically divisive implications, the term was adopted by these "diplomatic wives" themselves in their own life writing in an act of self-subjection.[114] While the Legation Ladies were not given 'official' state roles, they were not private individuals either. The Legation Ladies supervised domestic aids, including the cooks, sweepers and private bearers mentioned above. They also took up nursing tasks at the Legation hospital and clerical duties in the Legation's administration. In a taped interview, Mary Irene Squire, the wife of the last British Minister in Kabul, Giles Frederick Squire (1943–1948), remembered the material dimensions of daily life at the Legation, including an "extraordinarily good" personal bearer and a "table boy", but also the management of "difficult servants".[115] There are also references to food, such as her cook's shopping in local markets, the weekly lorry to a Parsi shop in Peshawar that supplied the Legation's groceries as well as "cooking under godowns".[116] The Legation Ladies acted as nodes between the Legation's "menial" setup and its domestic households. In this sense, the Legation Ladies were women at the Legation, resembling the role of the *memsahib* in elite colonial society in India.[117] In

Kabul, their task was to "creat[e] an atmosphere where men from different states can get to know one another 'man to man'".[118] Diplomatic wives did not always meet men's expectations, however. Fraser-Tytler ridiculed Gertrude Humphrys' contributions to the interior design of the Legation as "atrocities" in letters to his mother.[119]

In another sense, the Legation Ladies were also women *of* the Legation when they acted as representatives the diplomatic institution outside of the Legation compound. Mary Irene Squire, for instance, refers to the public diplomacy of her visits of mosques in Kabul. Women were enlisted in support of men's diplomacy and in diplomatic initiatives. In late 1923, the women and children of the Legation were sent to India in order to force the Afghan government to arrest persons suspected of killing British officers in the Indo-Afghan borderland. The move intended to suggest the impending departure of the entire British Legation. Francis Henry Humphrys reported that some foreign Legations and the Afghan government had shown themselves "powerfully impressed".[120] The Legation Ladies returned in March 1924.

During the rebellion against Amanullah Khan in 1928/1929, the advancing army of Habibullah Kalakani and Amanullah Khan's troops defending Kabul met in the vicinity of the British Legation. The British Legation and several other members of Kabul's diplomatic society, though mostly Europeans, were eventually evacuated from Kabul by air in early 1929. The removal of the Legation's women and children from Kabul to "safety" in India was a popular theme in the British press that echoed the liberation of women and children by the "Army of Retribution" during the First Anglo-Afghan War in 1842.[121] According to Richard Gould, his governess Violet Pulford remembered Habibullah Kalakani playing to these fears in 1929: "'I know you have white women in there', she recalled the rebel leader telling Sir Francis, 'I shall not hurt them'".[122] In Anglo-Afghan relations, women had the potential to be powerfully 'embarassing'.

In the history of the Legation, the voices of women occur only sporadically. When they do, they are often described in terms of the men's reactions to their bodies, subjected in private to the scrutinising literary gaze of diplomatic men. Women were objects in men's sexual fantasies. Fraser-Tytler referred to Audrey Harris, a travel writer and novelist as "a most attractive young woman to look at, tall & fair".[123] He introduced Rosita Forbes as a "vamp" in a letter to his mother.[124] Lucy Eileen Moody, the Surgeon's wife, was "S.A. or Sex Attraction" and "insatiable".[125] This practice also included women beyond the Legation. George Kirkbride,

Secretary in the 1920s, referred to the Italian Minister's wife as "most alluring and Madonna-like".[126] Together, these manifold subjections of women by men, by other women and by themselves to the patriarchal structures of diplomacy are indicative of the marginalisation of women in diplomatic history more broadly.

On occasion, women's own voices can be recovered. The *Legation Diary* was written by several anonymous authors, most probably the Legation's senior officers. As a record of life at the Legation, the diary covers the years 1922–1924. It also contains five sections, which were written by women. Four out of five passages were written by Gertrude Humphrys, who also maintained a separate diary of her own. Women's voices are fragments in this instance. They are marginal in relation to the overall *Legation Diary*, constituting less than ten percent of text. But, as the 'inofficial' head of the Legation Ladies establishment, Gertrude Humphrys' diary constitutes a comparatively privileged account. Because of this, it is contentious to classify the Legation Ladies as subalterns. And, yet, there are only a few examples of women's voices, which do deserve closer attention.

The *Legation Diary* indicates that Gertrude Humphrys adopted multiple roles in different spatial contexts. Owing to the separation of Afghan women from men, the Legation Ladies provided the requisite female bodies to access spaces, which were otherwise locked to outsiders. The Legation Ladies extended the means of male diplomacy by virtue of their bodies. This led to the establishment of social networks by women, and in particular with the wives of Afghan statesmen. In one particularly intimate instance, Gertrude Humphrys was even considered to act as a midwife to Queen Soraya, Amanullah Khan's wife. At the same time, some passages from the *Legation Diary* indicate that the Legation Ladies emulated the official business of their husbands in terms of documenting their transactions with the wives of Afghan officials. For instance, Gertrude Humphrys was chauffeured in the Legation's Rolls Royce, and she wrote down reports assessing the success of her meetings with the Queen and the latter's mother.[127] Chapter 5 discusses in more detail her husband's documentation of his meetings with Amanullah Khan. The Legation Ladies feminised diplomacy as much as they adopted the masculine dimensions of their husbands' profession.

The overarching reason for inclusion of these excerpts in the *Legation Diary* was their portrayal of "life beyond the veil" in Kabul. The passages provide a close-up of Afghan interiors, fashion, make-up, bodies, sports, dance, singing, eating, talking and children.[128] Through women's eyes, the closed spaces of Afghan homes were opened up to a male readership in great detail. Diplomatic recording, to a degree, broke the bounds of *purdah*. Gertrude Humphrys' descriptions of Queen Soraya are steeped in references to the queen's body, clothes and demeanour:

> The Queen is young and very handsome in a buxom way, with curly dark hair and big brown eyes and a clear complexion, much rouged and powdered; her eyebrown and lashes are heavily pencilled in. She is plump and awkward in her movements, partly, I think, because of tight garments and high heels. She was wearing a cotton frock embroidered with mauve wistaria [sic], very tight as to the bodice and waist and very short as to the skirt, with pink stockings and very high heeled white canvas shoes, which would have been much improved by the use of 'blanco'. Enormous yellowish diamonds were in her ears and on her fingers.[129]

Coming exceptionally close to the queen's body, Gertrude Humphrys mimicked the male gaze and curiosity with regard to female bodies. Gertrude Humphrys applied similar terms in her description of Queen Soraya during a game of tennis: "Her Majesty is not a stayer and was very warm and exhausted after so much play".[130] Queen Soraya appears particularly feminine. The set of masculine behavioural practices, that is sportsmanship, gentlemanliness and fair play, which Akbar S. Ahmed has called the "Frontier Code", were not only geographically transferred to Kabul but also into the domain of diplomatic relations between women.[131] Gertrude Humphrys was the daughter of Harold Deane, the first Chief Commissioner of the North-West Frontier Province, which was created in 1901 by Curzon. She was aware of the code of conduct which existed along India's north-western border region. Her husband had served in the North-West Frontier Province since 1903. The application of aspects of this essentially code of masculine conduct is visible in the Queen's demeanour during a game of badminton. Gertrude Humphrys pointed out that "though I think she really tried to play fair, [she] took a much larger number of services than the rules of the game would allow amongst commoners".[132] Gertrude Humphrys also rode, making her "the object of much curiosity on the part of Afghan ladies, who take off their veils to get a clearer view".[133] Women, who were exposed to the "Frontier Code", could also act in accordance with it and make gender boundaries less discernible.[134] As Mary Procida has argued, "the ideal imperial wife combined the best of both genders".[135] Extending this argument to Gertrude Humphrys' diplomatic other, Queen

Soraya, feminine women were considered in more doubtful terms that constructed a 'soft' and 'sensual East'.

Two Legation Ladies also documented exceptional events. Gertrude Humphrys and Lorraine Gould left personal accounts of the rebellion against Amanullah Khan in 1928/1929 and its effects on the Legation, the damage to buildings as well as injuries to people and animals. Lorraine Gould's letter to her mother captures a heightened sense of confusion and conflicting loyalties, myth making and rumour, as she documented her admiration for Habibullah Kalakani, who was known as Bacha-i-Saqao, the son or "Brat" of the water carrier.[136] "Personally I prefer the B.S.'s people who are gentlemen so far! *but of course we want the King's* [Amanullah Khan's] *troops to get in control*".[137] The documents at the time refer to Habibullah Kalakani as a "gentleman", "Robin Hood", "a notorious highwayman, merciless to Afghan officials and wealthy travellers, but generous to the poor".[138] In addition to this romanticisation of the contender, a sense of crisis pervades Lorraine Gould's account that is only settled by the figure of the British Minister, Francis Henry Humphrys. As Habibullah Kalakani advanced on Kabul, Humphrys went to meet him: "Sir Francis is the bravest man I have ever known. He walked out quite calmly smoking a pipe and talked to the B.S. through the gate".[139] In Gertrude Humphrys' account of the rebellion, her husband's pipe also takes centre stage in the defense of the Legation's diplomatic inviolability. Whereas Habibullah Kalakani ordered his troops to respect the extraterritoriality of the Legation, soldiers of Amanullah Khan at one point forced their way into the compound. For a moment, one soldier even aimed a rifle at the Minister. The clearing of the Legation compound of "combatants" took some time, requiring "relays of tobacco": "Nothing calms our servants so much as the Minister's pipe nor so disarms the invaders".[140] Whilst the Minister and his pipe stood on patrol, the Legation's bodyguard was "sitting under the back wall with their rifles buried".[141] Lorraine Gould's son, Richard, recalled sixty years later that Humphrys "used his pipe deliberately as a theatrical prop, to convey that while the legation might be surrounded, the Brits inside were not in the least rattled".[142]

Lorraine Gould also volunteered a personal assessment of Amanullah's relations with the Legation:

> We are more than furious and astonished that there is *still* no message from the Afghan Government, considering the King's troops have been at our gates for days, and today have passed beyond us. We now know what a perfectly

rotten lot they all are. I can't understand the King's attitude at all – it's amazing. [...] I am afraid it's the end of the King. I am not so sorry as I might be, as he and his Government have treated us so badly. [...] Damned dirty dogs – they have done absolutely nothing for us.[143]

By revealing these emotions, Lorraine Gould's account challenges the muted nature of men's renderings of these events. It reveals a community of anxious sufferers at the hands of Amanullah Khan. At the same time, the internalisation of gender roles at the Legation is written into the fabric of both Gertrude Humphrys' and Lorraine Gould's records. While notions of male bravery, honour and gentility are reinforced, the limited agency of the Legation Ladies finds expression only in private outrage. In the same way that the Legation Ladies entered otherwise hidden Afghan space, the accounts left by them open a dimension in the realm of patriarchal domesticity at the Legation. Outside of the routinised forms of communication between men, these accounts broaden our understanding of the emotional life at the Legation at a moment of significant crisis when the institution became the focal point of an international media audience.

Biography and Insubordination

Despite the limits imposed on the study of life histories by the archival visibility of individuals, this chapter excavates the Legation's largely unregarded layers and restores them to their proper place of investigation. The Legation's subordinated staff fulfilled a wide spectrum of clerical and operative tasks, which are commonly hidden under the tip of the "small and isolated cadre" that Maconachie referred to in the opening paragraph of this chapter. In fact, by struggling 'against the archival grain', the chapter unearths fragments of individual lives that lay bare the considerable scale and manifold connections of the Legation's labourers, administrators, operators and women with the colonial state, across a region as well as their interactions with people locally.

Moving 'along the archival grain', the chapter reveals the Legation's many principles of subordination along the lines of race, class and gender. Subalternity came in degrees, and the Legation's hierarchies are plain in the *Office Manual*, budgets and accounts. Europeans from colonial India's clerical professions occupied leading positions in the Legation's administration. As members of Anglo-Indian society, the Legation's clerks worked in close proximity to the Legation's political leadership and shared its correspondence-related tasks. The office staff were established clerks of the colonial state, and the Indians among them were recognised "servants" of the Raj. Other Indians fulfilled crucial tasks, such as the Nazir, who ensured the running of the administrative machine by providing a point of contact between the Legation's material needs and Kabul's markets. For the political undertaking to work, it needed a person with knowledge of local supply chains. In a similar way, the Mir Munshi provided a crucial linguistic intermediary for the Legation and other diplomatic institutions. These two positions alone were vital connecting points between the Legation and its local environments, without which it is difficult to imagine the diplomatic machine's daily running. The same argument applies to the Legation's women and to the entirety of its household staff, bodyguard, orderlies, its gardeners, drivers, cleaners and many others. European office staff are not necessarily more visible than their Indian colleagues, but unskilled labour was the least well-recorded and is, by consequence, the most elusive category from the historian's perspective. Entire groups of Indian or Afghan origins are no longer recognisable as individuals. The sources discussed in this chapter illustrate the fashioning of the Legation's subalterns by means of regulations, such as the *Office Manual* and its standing orders. 'Menial' personnel was kept out of office spaces, subordinated into entire anonymous labour communities and, quite literally, written out of history. At the same time and at the other end of the Legation's hierarchy, the next chapter shows the self-fashioning of an elite, who capitalised on the labour of those whose gradated subalternities it created, sometimes simply by means of putting a signature under the work of a clerk.

A microcosmic representation of colonial Indian society, authority and hierarchies emerges. 'British' diplomacy in Afghanistan did not only draw its personnel from the colonial state's various administrative networks. It also recreated that structure for the purposes of international representation in Kabul. Inside the Legation, international hierarchies were moulded as Europeans were divided from Indians and Afghans in order to supervise them. Indians, in turn, supervised and managed Indians and Afghans, but ultimately followed the orders of a European Superintendent or elite political officers. Unlike Europeans, Indians and Afghans were also held collectively responsible for intentional or accidental transgressions on their jobs. Whilst European clerks were upwardly mobile professionally, the occupational reach of Indian and Afghan labourers in the Legation's structure was restricted by ideas of race. Alongside this marker of difference, women also internalised and reproduced the Legation's patriarchal and class-based setup.

The analysis of the Legation's structures outside of its political leadership establishes the mission's coloniality in several dimensions. It borrowed from the past the very organisation of labour that implemented existing colonial ideas about how to establish a diplomatic mission. The Legation was informed by practical knowledge accumulated by generations of colonial administrators. The political staff defined the tasks and responsibilities of office clerks and those in charge of the everyday maintenance of the Legation. It also disciplined women's bodies, a point that will be discussed further in Chapter 6. The jobs, which they designed and prescribed for themselves, other Europeans, Indians and Afghans, are reminiscent of well-established attitudes in colonial contexts. Mistrust of indigenous persons, doubts about the productivity of colonial labour as well as the need for a detailed regulation of tasks, all coupled with a low position in the Legation's social structure and equally low pay. The operative structure of 'British' diplomacy in Afghanistan borrowed heavily from the treasure trove of colonial knowledge, not least by also acculturating Persianate jobs for several of its positions, gradually assimilating them into the Legation's day-to-day life. In the present, the Legation was a product of the colonial Anglo-Indian-Afghan encounter, modelled on the needs generated by the place. The significant movement of people between India and Afghanistan, including the Pashtun drivers of the Legation lorries, connects the Legation to lively cross-border exchanges with India's colonial realm. Personnel was drawn from existing colonial cadres, and labour was recruited from among tribesmen of the North-West Frontier Province or in Kabul itself. Looking beyond 1947, and into the future of the Legation, the position of the Archivist that was established in the Legation's paracolonial times survived the end of colonial rule and merged into the setup of the later British Embassy in Kabul. In other words, the British Legation borrowed from the Anglo-Afghan encounter of the past and the storehouse of knowledge that spanned colonial India's diplomatic engagement across the Indian Ocean, whilst, as a product of these manifold interactions, it was itself incorporated into a 'postcolonial' diplomatic network after 1947.

NOTES

1. Letter from Humphrys, no. 241, 7 July 1923, no. 59, 212-F, F&P, 1922, "Construction of British Legation Buildings at Kabul", NAI.
2. 413-A, F&P, 1931, "Budget estimates Kabul Legation for 1932–33", NAI.
3. For a differentiation between the terms "biography", "life narratives" and "life writing" see Sidonie Smith, *Reading Autobiography: A Guide for Interpreting Life Narratives* (Minneapolis, MN: University of Minnesota Press, 2001), 4.
4. Judith Margaret Brown, "'Life Histories' and the History of South Asia", *The American Historical Review* 114, no. 3 (2009): 591.
5. Clifford Geertz, *Interpretation of Cultures* (London: Hutchinson, 1975).
6. For instance: Ludwig W. Adamec, *Afghanistan, 1900–1923: A Diplomatic History* (Berkeley: University of California Press, 1967); Ludwig W. Adamec, *Afghanistan's Foreign Affairs to the Mid-Twentieth Century: Relations with the U.S.S.R., Germany, and Britain* (Tucson: University of Arizona Press, 1974); Abdul Ali Arghandawi, *British Imperialism and Afghanistan's Struggle for Independence, 1914–21* (New Delhi: Munshiram Manoharlal Publishers, 1989); Jackman, *Afghanistan in British Imperial Strategy and Diplomacy*; Christopher Wyatt, *Afghanistan and the Defence of Empire: Diplomacy and Strategy During the Great Game* (London: I.B. Tauris, 2011).
7. Basil John Gould, *The Jewel in the Lotus: Recollections of an Indian Political* (London: Chatto & Windus, 1957), 95.
8. Tarak Barkawi, *Soldiers of Empire: Indian and British Armies in World War II* (Cambridge: Cambridge University Press, 2017).
9. Ranajit Guha, "Preface", in *Subaltern Studies I: Writings on South Asian History and Society*, ed. Ranajit Guha (Delhi: Oxford University Press, 1982); Edward W. Said, "Foreword", in *Selected Subaltern Studies*, ed. Ranajit Guha and Gayatri Chakravorty Spivak (Oxford: Oxford University Press, 1988), v–x.
10. See in particular James Onley, *The Arabian Frontier of the British Raj: Merchants, Rulers, and the British in the Nineteenth-Century Gulf* (New York: Oxford University Press, 2007), 43 and n. 62–63 on researching subaltern individuals and communities.
11. For a similar undertaking on undocumented subordinated staff see Michael H. Fisher, *Indirect Rule in India: Residents and the Residency System, 1764–1858* (Oxford: Oxford University Press, 1991), 316–374.
12. Ibid., 316. See also Onley, *The Arabian Frontier of the British Raj*, 43.
13. David E. Pelteret, "Should One Include Unnamed People in a Prosopography?", in *Prosopography Approaches and Applications: A Handbook*, ed. K. S. B. Keats-Rohan (Oxford: Unit for Prosopographical Research, Linacre College, University of Oxford, 2007), 183–196.

14. The Counsellor, British Legation, Kabul to the Under Secretary to the Government of India in the Foreign and Political Department, New Delhi, memorandum no. 609, 2 January 1932, 413-A, F&P, 1931, op. cit., NAI.
15. E.g. Elizabeth M. Collingham, *Imperial Bodies: The Physical Experience of the Raj, c. 1800–1947* (Cambridge: Polity Press, 2001), 103–113.
16. 68(9)-E, F&P, 1922, "Menial Establishment for the British Legation in Afghanistan and their emoluments"; "Rough note on the proposal for a British Minister at Kabul", S. E. Pears, 24 November 1921, 3–4, 68(20)-Est, F&P, 1923, "Note by Mr S. E. Pears, C.S.I., C.I.E., on the proposed establishment of a British Legation at Kabul"; 68(16)-E, F&P, 1923, "Status of the ministerial establishment employed with British Legation, Kabul. Agreement in regard to Mr. Miller's appointment as Superintendent, Legation Office. Resignation by Mr. Miller of his appointment as Supdt., Kabul Legation Office"; 256-A, F&P, 1924, "Budget estimates of the British Legation Kabul for the year 1925–26", NAI.
17. Fraser-Tytler to his mother, 20 November 1930, no. 13–14, file 1/1/3, GB165-0326, MECA. See also Gould, *The Jewel in the Lotus*, 96–97.
18. "Rough note on the proposal for a British Minister at Kabul", S. E. Pears, 24 November 1921, 3, 68(20)-Est, F&P, 1923, op. cit., NAI.
19. "Standing Order No. 10: Registration of Servants" and "Standing Order No. 16: Employment of Afghan Servants", 55–56, 62, IOR/R/12/200, "British Legation, Kabul: Office Manual", BL.
20. Fraser-Tytler to his mother, 27 July 1939, no. 91–94, file 1/1/10, GB165-0326, MECA; Handwritten note by Fraser-Tytler, IOR NEG 1869, "File 695A Irrigation of Legation Property and Water Rights (1933–47 Omnibus File)", BL.
21. Fraser-Tytler to his mother, 27 July 1939, no. 91–94, file 1/1/10, GB165-0326; Fraser-Tytler to his mother, 19 June 1931, no. 26, file 1/1/4, GB165-0326, MECA.
22. Fraser-Tytler to his mother, 5 October 1940, no. 129–131, file 1/1/11, GB165-0326, MECA; Chapter 6.4 further explores the likening of Afghan to animal bodies.
23. Nicholas Barrington, *Envoy: A Diplomatic Journey* (London: I.B. Tauris, 2014), 29.
24. "Rough note on the proposal for a British Minister at Kabul", S. E. Pears, 24 November 1921, 4, 68(20)-Est, F&P, 1923, op. cit., NAI.
25. Ibid.
26. Ibid.
27. Copy of telegram no. 126, 11 January 1922, FO 371/8076, N 411/59/97, 1922, "Staff of Kabul Legation", TNA. See also copy of telegram no. 18S, 7 January 1922, N 296/59/97, FO 371/8076, 1922, "Relations between Great Britain and Afghanistan", TNA.

28. Foreign and Political Department to Secretary of State for India, telegram no. 57, 5 January 1922, 68(5)-E, F&P, 1922, "Appointment of Military Attache to the Legation in Kabul", NAI.
29. Copy of telegram no. 126, 11 January 1922, FO 371/8076, N 411/59/97, 1922, op. cit., TNA.
30. See "daffadar" and "sowar" in Onley, *The Arabian Frontier of the British Raj*, xxv, xxix. 256-A, F&P, 1924, op. cit.; 165(2)-A, F&P, 1927, "Budget estimates of the British Legation Kabul for the year 1928–29", NAI. See also Gould, *The Jewel in the Lotus*, 94.
31. Maconachie to Simon, no. 120, 28 September 1933, no. 25, FO 402/16, 1933, "Further correspondence respecting Afghanistan: Part XVI", TNA.
32. "Table of contents", ii, IOR/R/12/200, op. cit., BL.
33. Fisher, *Indirect Rule in India*, 349–352.
34. "List of European personnel attached to British Legation, Kabul, on 9th August, 1924", N 7034/7034/97, FO 371/10410, 1924, "British Legation at Kabul"; "List of European personnel attached to the British Legation, Kabul", N 9394/7034/97, FO 371/10410, 1924, "British Legation at Kabul", TNA; 60(5)-E, F&P, 1924, "Orders regarding the assumption and delivery of charge by members of the Kabul Legation on transfer or when proceeding on leave from Kabul. Extension of the provision of Supplementary rules 303 and 304 to Government Servants employed in the British Legation, Kabul and in the British Consulates at Jalalabad and Kandahar", NAI.
35. Hailey to Weightman, 24 October 1941, 12(14)-E, EA, 1940, "Appointment of a British Commercial Attache at Kabul and his staff. 2. Appointment of a Confidential Clerk to the Counsellor, British Legation, Kabul, for commercial work", NAI.
36. "Kabul Legation Budget, 1927–1928: Annexure 2", 15 October 1926, 165-A, F&P, 1926, "Budget estimates of the British Legation Kabul for the year 1927–1928", NAI.
37. "Passport Clerk", 19–24, IOR/R/12/200, op. cit., BL.
38. "Accountant", 8–16, ibid.
39. Diana Day and George L. Mallam, *Frogs in the Well* (Moray: Librario, 2010), 142–143; "Afghanistan: Annual Report, 1932", para. 269, N 1626/1626/97, FO 371/17198, 1933, "Annual Report on Afghanistan", TNA.
40. 313-A, F&P, 1932, "Budget estimates of the British Legation at Kabul for the year 1933–34", NAI
41. "Rough note on the proposal for a British Minister at Kabul", S. E. Pears, 24 November 1921, 3, 68(20)-Est, F&P, 1923, op. cit., NAI. Fisher, *Indirect Rule in India*, 357–360. See also Shah Mahmoud Hanifi, *Connecting Histories in Afghanistan: Market Relations and State Formation on a Colonial Frontier* (Stanford: Stanford University Press, 2011), 153–164.

42. 68(16)-E, F&P, 1923, op. cit.; 60(5)-E, F&P, 1924, op. cit., NAI.
43. 413-A, F&P, 1931, op. cit.; 313-A, F&P, 1932, op. cit.; 314-A, EA, 1942, "Budget estimates of the Kabul Legation for 1943–44", NAI.
44. Secretary of State for India to Government of India, External Affairs and Commonwealth Relations Department, Delhi, 8 August 1947, 11(12)-IA, EA, 1947, "Future of the British Legation at Kabul", NAI.
45. See in particular Bernard S. Cohn, "Representing Authority in Victorian India", in *The Invention of Tradition*, ed. Eric J. Hobsbawm and T. O. Ranger (Cambridge: Cambridge University Press, 2013), 165–209; Thomas R. Metcalf, *Ideologies of the Raj* (Cambridge: Cambridge University Press, 1994), 194–196.
46. Fisher, *Indirect Rule in India*, 360–362; 60(19)-E, F&P, 1925, "Appointment of Mr. S.M. Kamaruddin, as Mir Munshi, Kabul Legation. Resignation by Mr. S. M. Kamaruddin of his appointment of Mir Munshi, Kabul Legation", NAI.
47. See "dragoman" in Onley, *The Arabian Frontier of the British Raj*, xxvi. See also section "The Role of the Munshi as Ritual Specialist" in Michael H. Fisher, "The Resident in Court Ritual, 1764–1858", *Modern Asian Studies* 24, no. 3 (1990): 435–447. For further reading on dragomans, see Geoff R. Berridge, *British Diplomacy in Turkey, 1583 to the Present: A Study in the Evolution of the Resident Embassy* (Leiden: Martinus Nijhoff, 2009), 49–74; G. R. Berridge, "English Dragomans and Oriental Secretaries: The Early Nineteenth Century Origins of the Anglicization of the British Embassy Dragomanate in Constantinople", *Diplomacy & Statecraft* 14, no. 4 (2003): 137–152.
48. See also Fisher, *Indirect Rule in India*, 319–331, 363–364, 438–440.
49. "Mir Munshi", 16–19, IOR/R/12/200, op. cit., BL.
50. See "subordinate officer" in Onley, *The Arabian Frontier of the British Raj*, xxix; 68(16)-E, F&P, 1923, op. cit.; 24(3)-E, F&P, 1926, "Emoluments of Mr. Fazal Hussain, Forwarding Clerk to the British Legation, Kabul. Appointment of Syed Ahmad Shah, Mir Munshi in the office of the Political Agent, Khyber, as Passport Clerk to the British Legation, Kabul, and his emoluments", NAI.
51. A. Macann to C. A. G. Savidge, demi-official no. 1023-A(E), 28 October 1938, 314-A, EA, 1938, "Budget estimates of the Kabul Legation for 1939–40", NAI.
52. Maconachie to Simon, no. 120, 28 September 1933, no. 25, FO 402/16, 1933, op. cit., TNA.
53. Cunningham, April 1926, 24(3)-E, F&P, 1923, op. cit., NAI.
54. "Passport Clerk", 19–24, IOR/R/12/200, op. cit., BL.
55. 179-E, F&P, 1931, "Question of defining certain posts in Afghanistan as tenure posts and to fix a period of tenure in each case. Question whether the incumbents of the posts of Superintendent, 2nd and 3rd Clerks, British

Legation, Kabul, who are Military subordinates can get benefit of Kabul rates of pay while on leave", NAI.
56. "Nazir", 25–33, IOR/R/12/200, op. cit., BL; 24(30)-E, F&P, 1927, "Grant of a maintenance allowance of Rs. 60 p. m. to the Nazir, British Legation, Kabul for the upkeep of a horse, tonga and harness purchased by him"; 226-A, F&P, 1931, "Grant of an advance to Fazal Rahman, Nazir, British Legation, Kabul, for the purchase of a horse and a tonga", NAI.
57. "Nazir", 25–33, IOR/R/12/200, op. cit., BL; 60(22)-E, F&P, 1925, "Creation of two new appointments of a Nazir and a Hospital Dresser in the British Legation", NAI.
58. Ibid.; 313-A, F&P, 1932, op. cit.; 314-A, EA, 1942, op. cit., NAI.
59. Maconachie, telegram no. 6, 7 April 1930, N 2306/6/97, FO 371/14786, 1930, "Employment of Rahmat at Kabul", TNA.
60. Adamec, *Afghanistan's Foreign Affairs to the Mid-Twentieth Century*, 184–185.
61. Humphrys, telegram no. 217, 16 February 1929, N 1112/1/97, FO 371/13993, 1929, "Withdrawal of British Legation from Kabul", TNA.
62. Note by P. J. Patrick, 29 August 1929, N 3915/1/97, FO 371/13998, 1929, "Conversation between Foreign Secretary to the Government of India and Baron von Plessen", TNA.
63. "Note by the Foreign Secretary on his conversation with Baron Plessen on the general Afghan situation", para. 13, N 3915/1/97, FO 371/13998, 1929, op. cit., TNA.
64. Humphrys to Maconachie, 12 June 1930, no. 1–3, IOR/R/12/189, "Statements re attacks on the Legation during the revolution", BL.
65. "Nazir Rahmat Khan states", 4 July 1930, no. 5–8, ibid.
66. Ibid.
67. Minutes by AP, 7 July 1930, para. 6, no. 12–15, ibid.
68. Maconachie to Howell, 10 July 1930, no. 16, ibid.
69. See note 64 above.
70. Maconachie to Humphrys, 10 July 1930, no. 17, IOR/R/12/189, op. cit., BL.
71. Typescript note, October 1929, no. 25, ibid.
72. Howell to Maconachie, 3 September 1930, no. 23, ibid.
73. 60(10)-E, F&P, 1924, "Appointment of Mr. J. Carter, as Superintendent in the office of the British Legation, Kabul & his emoluments", NAI.
74. "Superintendent", 1–2, IOR/R/12/200, op. cit., BL.
75. C. A. G. Savidge to Counsellor, Kabul, 26 October 1939, 55-F.O., EA, 1939, "Staff for the British Legation Kabul", NAI.
76. 68(6)-E, F&P, 1922, "Resignation of Mr Rees Harris and Appointment of a Successor", NAI.

77. Ibid.; 60(10)-E, F&P, 1924, op. cit.; 10(11)-E, F&P, 1930, "Selection of candidates to the post of Superintendent and Second Clerk in the Kabul Legation Office and their allowances etc.", NAI.
78. "Second Clerk", 3, IOR/R/12/200, op. cit., BL.
79. "Standing Order No. 5: Procedure for check and distribution of the dâk", 49–50, ibid.
80. "Third Clerk", 3–5, ibid.; "Kabul Legation Budget, 1927–1928: Annexure 2", 15 October 1926, 165-A, F&P, 1926, op. cit., NAI.
81. "Fourth Clerk", 6–8, IOR/R/12/200, op. cit., BL.
82. Counsellor, Kabul, to The Under-Secretary of the Government of India in the External Affairs Department, Simla, 20 September 1939, 55-F.O., EA, 1939, op. cit., NAI.
83. Army Headquarters, General Staff Branch, Simla, J. J. Kingston to Military Attaché, Kabul, 27 October 1922, 68(5)-E, F&P, 1922, op. cit.; Gould to Acheson, 10 September 1927, 114-F, F&P, 1924, "Proposed measure for the protection of the British Legation, Kabul, in times of crisis. Question of the installation of a wireless set in the said Legation"; Alban to Hay, 21 October 1939, 55-F.O., EA, 1939, op. cit., NAI; "Note in continuation of Legation telegram, Katodon, No. 76, dated 8th August, 1947", Ext. 7798, IOR/L/PS/12/1914, "Coll 4/54(1) Future Diplomatic Representation in Kabul (British and Indian)", BL.
84. 313-A, F&P, 1935, "Budget estimates of the Kabul Legation for the year 1936–37", NAI.
85. These departments included: the Chief of General Staff, the Adjutant General in India, the Quartermaster General in India, the Engineer-in-Chief, Army Headquarters, the Master General of Supply, the Military Secretary, Army Headquarters, the Assistant Military Secretary (Personal) to His Excellency The Commander-in-Chief, the Medical Directorate, the Air Officer Commanding, RAF, and the Judge Advocate General.
86. 60(10)-E, F&P, 1924, op. cit., NAI.
87. For further reading on the General Staff Branch see James Louis Hevia, *The Imperial Security State: British Colonial Knowledge and Empire-Building in Asia* (Cambridge: Cambridge University Press, 2012), 17–33; Dallas D. Irvine, "The Origin of Capital Staffs", *The Journal of Modern History* 10, no. 2 (1938): 161–179; Timothy Moreman, "Lord Kitchener, the General Staff and the Army in India, 1902–1904", in *The British General Staff: Reform and Innovation, 1890–1939*, ed. David French and Brian Holden Reid (London: Frank Cass, 2002), 57–74.
88. 60(8)-E, F&P, 1924, "Treatment as regards leave of military subordinates transferred temporarily to the Kabul Legation", NAI.
89. 60(10)-E, F&P, 1924, op. cit.; W. R. Hay to R. W. Parkes, 16 January 1939, 55-F.O., EA, 1939, op. cit., NAI.
90. 60(5)-E, F&P, 1924, op. cit., NAI.

91. Humphrys, 27 March 1923, no. 77–79, 68(16)-E, F&P, 1923, op. cit., NAI.
92. 10(11)-E, F&P, 1930, op. cit., NAI: F. H. Humphrys (Minister), B. J. Gould (Counsellor), G. Cunningham (Counsellor), P. C. R. Dodd (Counsellor) and H. H. Thorburn (Surgeon). "Report on the Kabul Mission, by Sir H. R. C. Dobbs, K.C.S.I., K.C.I.E", N 1450/59/97, FO 371/8076, 1922, "Negotiations conducted by British Mission in Kabul during 1921", TNA: Although Dobbs has left a detailed appreciation of the political staff who accompanied him to Kabul he did not mention Spinks' clerical services.
93. R. W. Parkes to W. R. Hay, 17 December 1938, 55-F.O., EA, 1939, op. cit., NAI. See also 179-E, F&P, 1931, op. cit., NAI.
94. 314-A, EA, 1938, op. cit., NAI.
95. External Affairs Department, office memorandum, 24 March 1939, 55-F.O., EA, 1939, op. cit., NAI; Alban to Hay, 21 October 1939, ibid.
96. Draft circular, External Affairs Department, 11 September 1941, 12(14)-E, EA, 1940, op. cit., NAI.
97. 314-A, EA, 1942, op. cit., NAI.
98. Note by P. N. Krishnaswamy, 30 July 1947, 11(12)-IA, EA, 1947, op. cit., NAI; "Note in continuation of Legation telegram, Katodon, No. 76, dated 8th August, 1947", Ext. 7798, IOR/L/PS/12/1914, op. cit., BL.
99. *Foreign Office List for 1950*, 78.
100. "Garage Standing Orders: Di[s]cipline", 40–42, IOR/R/12/200, op. cit., BL.
101. Humphrys, memorandum no. 45, 9 February 1924, "Pay of Mr. G. H. Stranger, Garage Superintendent, British Legation, Kabul", 60-E, 1924, F&P, NAI.
102. Fraser-Tytler to his mother, 19 July 1940, no. 88–89, file 1/1/11, GB165-0326, MECA.
103. "Report on the Kabul Mission, by Sir H. R. C. Dobbs, K.C.S.I., K.C.I.E", para. 12, N 1450/59/97, FO 371/8076, 1922, op. cit., TNA; 157-F, F&P, 1928, "Presentation to His Majesty the King of Afghanistan of motor car in which he toured England as a souvenir. Its free transit thorough India", NAI; Fraser-Tytler to Metcalfe, demi-official no. 1263, 9 February 1939, para. 4–5, N 908/144/97, FO 371/23628, 1939, "British position in Afghanistan", TNA. See also Nile Green, "The Road to Kabul: Automobiles and Afghan Internationalism, 1900–1940", in *Beyond Swat: History, Society and Economy Along the Afghanistan-Pakistan Frontier*, ed. Benjamin D. Hopkins and Magnus Marsden (London: Hurst, 2013), 77–92.
104. "Garage Standing Orders: Di[s]cipline", 41, IOR/R/12/200, op. cit., BL.

105. 513-F, F&P, 1933, "Outrage in His Majesty's Legation at Kabul. Murder of Mr. G. H. Stranger, Garage Superintendent, Irshad Hussein, Mir Munshi and Yakub, a wireman", NAI.
106. Maconachie to Simon, no. 120, 28 September 1933, no. 25, FO 402/16, 1933, op. cit., TNA.
107. "Garage Standing Orders: Di[s]cipline", 40–42, IOR/R/12/200, op. cit., BL.
108. Peter Mayne, *The Narrow Smile: A Journey Back to the North-West Frontier* (London: John Murray, 1955), 130–131; "Recollections of a political officer in India (1929–1947)", A. W. Redpath, 92–93, Mss Eur F226/24, "Redpath, Maj Alexander William (b 1909)", BL.
109. "Garage Standing Orders: Regulations for Mail Lorries", 34–39, IOR/R/12/200, op. cit., BL.
110. 24(3)-E, F&P, 1935, "Question of the extension of the appointment of Mr. C. D. Hewson as Second Clerk, British Legation, Kabul", NAI.
111. 314-A, EA, 1938, op. cit.; 315-F, EA, 1942, "Annual report of the Indian Trade Agent, Kabul for 1940–1941", NAI. From 1937 onwards, an Indian Trade Agent and two clerks resided in Kabul, who reported on economic relations by were not directly connected to the Legation.
112. Cynthia H. Enloe, *Bananas, Beaches and Bases: Making Feminist Sense of International Politics* (Berkeley: University of California Press, 2004).
113. Humphrys, telegram no. 182, 11 December 1923, no. 50, FO 402/2, 1923, "Further correspondence respecting Afghanistan: Part II", TNA.
114. Enloe, *Bananas, Beaches and Bases*, 93–123.
115. Mss Eur R152, "Lady Irene Mary Squire Papers", BL.
116. Ibid.
117. Mary A. Procida, *Married to the Empire: Gender, Politics and Imperialism in India, 1883–1947* (Manchester: Manchester University Press, 2002).
118. Enloe, *Bananas, Beaches and Bases*, 97.
119. Fraser-Tytler to his mother, 27 June 1935, no. 44–49, file 1/1/6, GB165-0326; Fraser-Tytler to his mother, 22 August 1935, no. 76–79, file 1/1/6, GB165-0326, MECA.
120. Humphrys, telegram no. 186, 12 December 1923, no. 52, FO 402/2, 1923, op. cit., TNA.
121. "The Kabul Legation: Safety of Women and Children: Taken to India by Air", *The Times*, 24 December 1928. Linda Colley, *Captives: Britain, Empire and the World, 1600–1850* (London: Jonathan Cape, 2002), 347–379. See also Chapter 5, note 77 and Chapter 6, note 91.
122. David Fairhall, "60 Years After, Raj Survivors Recall Our Own Kabul Airlift", *The Guardian*, 15 February 1989, 7.
123. Fraser-Tytler to his mother, 10–12 September 1936, no. 126–129, file 1/1/7, GB165-0326, MECA.

124. Fraser-Tytler to his mother, 20–21 March 1936, no. 46–49, file 1/1/7, GB165-0326, MECA.
125. Fraser-Tytler to his mother, 2–4 February 1939, no. 7–10, file 1/1/10, GB165-0326; Fraser-Tytler to his mother, 17–18 November 1939, no. 141–143, file 1/1/10, GB165-0326, MECA.
126. "Destruction of the Second British Legation in Kabul", 31 December 1926, file 9, GB165-0326, MECA.
127. "Kabul Legation Diary", 66, 68–69, file 8, GB165-0326, MECA.
128. See Amin Saikal, *Modern Afghanistan: A History of Struggle and Survival* (London: I.B. Tauris, 2012), 57–61.
129. "Kabul Legation Diary", 82, file 8, GB165-0326, MECA.
130. Ibid., 86.
131. Akbar S. Ahmed, "An Aspect of the Colonial Encounter in the North-West Frontier Province", *Asian Affairs* 9, no. 3 (1978): 319–327.
132. "Kabul Legation Diary", 86, file 8, GB165-0326, MECA.
133. Ibid., 65.
134. Metcalf, *Ideologies of the Raj*, 109.
135. Procida, *Married to the Empire*, 137.
136. I follow Gregorian's convention in referring to Habibullah Kalakani as "Bacha-i-Saqao": Vartan Gregorian, *The Emergence of Modern Afghanistan: Politics of Reform and Modernization, 1880–1946* (Stanford: Stanford University Press, 1969). See also Thomas Jefferson Barfield, *Afghanistan: A Cultural and Political History* (Princeton: Princeton University Press, 2010): "Bacha Saqao"; Saikal, *Modern Afghanistan*: "Bacha-ye Saqao".
137. Lorraine Gould to her mother, 19 December 1928, GB165-0407, MECA, emphasis added.
138. Ibid.; Humphrys, telegram no. 84, 23 January 1929, N 474/1/97, FO 371/13990, 1929, "Habibulla Khan", TNA; Best to Humphrys, 31 December 1928, N 562/1/97, FO 371/13990, 1929, "Afghan situation", TNA.
139. Ibid.
140. "Extract from Lady Humphrys' Diary of recent Events in Kabul", 29 January 1929, FO 371/13991, N 663/1/97, 1929, "Events in Kabul", TNA.
141. Ibid.
142. Fairhall, "60 Years After, Raj Survivors Recall Our Own Kabul Airlift".
143. Lorraine Gould to her mother, 19 December 1928, GB165-0407, MECA, emphasis in original.

CHAPTER 4

Biography and Imperial Governance

THE POWER OF DOCUMENTATION

In 1971, almost a quarter of a century after the independence of India and Pakistan in 1947, Terence Creagh Coen published an account of his former employer under the title *The Indian Political Service: A Study in Indirect Rule*. As a colonial administrator, who had turned to writing about his profession in postcolonial retirement, Coen was in good company. William Kerr Fraser-Tytler published his *Afghanistan* in 1950. Basil John Gould delivered his service autobiography, *The Jewel in the Lotus*, in 1957. In 2010, George Leslie Mallam's *Frogs in the Well*, also an autobiography, appeared. Many others, for whom the Legation in Kabul had been a station in their professional lives, deposited their recollections in the India Office Records at the British Library.[1] Unlike Fraser-Tytler, Gould and Mallam, Coen never was a member of the British Legation in Kabul during his career in the Indian Political Service, but he had been considered for a posting as First Secretary in 1941.[2] His book approached the Legation from the perspective of the colonial state's wider foreign and political network, and *The Indian Political Service* became a widely referenced text. In it, Coen dedicated merely three pages to India's relations with Afghanistan.[3] In line with his own, and his colleagues', determination to write their own history in a context that also celebrated the statecraft of the Raj, Coen stated that "[f]ew but distinguished have been the British representatives in Kabul since the establishment of normal diplomatic relations [after 1919]".[4] Within the

© The Author(s) 2019
M. Drephal, *Afghanistan and the Coloniality of Diplomacy*,
Cambridge Imperial and Post-Colonial Studies Series,
https://doi.org/10.1007/978-3-030-23960-2_4

117

limited space at his disposal, Coen focused on flattering his colleagues, who had served in Kabul. He also reinforced his own image as their equal, as he restricted his summary description of the Legation to positions predominantly held by European men. Coen named the five Ministers, but listed only the Counsellor, Secretary and Military Attaché. He omitted everyone else, together with the Indian Oriental Secretary and the European Legation Surgeon. As a member of the Indian Political Service, Coen applied mechanisms of differentiation and exclusion, whilst the Legation's subordinated staff were written out of his history. Coen's book illustrates the mindset of a European colonial-diplomatic elite from the inside out and from the top down in postcolonial time. As such, it also offers insights into the constitution of this elite at the Legation in Kabul and in a wider region through India's oceanic connections.

This chapter is part two of the Legation's collective biography. Chapter 3 showed that notions of race, class and gender formed powerful divisions that were translated into the hierarchies at the Legation. While it defined the Legation's subalterns through their absence from government publications such as the annual ministerial *Lists*, this chapter defines the Legation's elite according to its presence in them. Like subalternity, elite membership existed in several degrees. The discussion begins outside of Kabul at the two Consulates in Kandahar and Jalalabad, which throw further light on the Indian threads in the polyvalent fabric of 'British' diplomacy in Afghanistan. Returning to Kabul, the chapter follows the Legation's hierarchy from the bottom up, beginning with the Oriental Secretary, the Military Attaché and the medical practitioners before concluding with its senior positions, the Secretary, Counsellor and Minister.

In contrast to the Legation's subalterns, the colonial archive displays a remarkable variety and wealth in its commemoration of the few dozen elite individuals. The chapter rests on a rich collection of archival resources, including the annually published *Lists* of the Foreign Office, the India Office (until 1937) and the India and Burma Office (from 1938).[5] It also scoures regular monthly, quarterly and annual reports on Afghanistan, which document the Legation's personnel movements, in addition to the Military Attachés' and Secretaries' weekly, later fortnightly, *Intelligence Summaries* or *Diaries*.[6] Finally, the chapter uses biographical dictionaries, including service statements, application files and newspaper obituaries. Together, these materials allow the reconstruction of the Legation's colonial genealogies in networks of family and profession as well as the career geographies of its gazetted elite.[7] Considered collectively, this rich prosopography reveals the Legation in Kabul as an emerging unit in the colonial state's imperial apparatus spanning diplomatic missions, princely states, colonial districts, frontier posts and government secretariats from South Asia to the Arabian Peninsula.

The Legation's people were intricately connected to the colonial state in India and its empire. Their presence in Kabul ensured the Legation's pervasive coloniality. As transmitters of imperial governance, they were invested in the transfer of ideas that aligned diplomatic practice and colonial discourse in India, Afghanistan and elsewhere.[8] The chapter moves in two directions. In one direction, the chapter reconstructs the rationale, which informed the selection of certain individuals for a posting in Kabul. It, thus, reveals the fluidity and continuity of the local, regional, colonial and imperial geographical framework in which Kabul was conceptualised. In other words, it captures the collective of individual careers 'before Kabul' as an indicator of the Legation's identity. From this perspective, individual knowledge shaped the Legation. In the other direction, the chapter considers the institution's afterlife in individual lives 'after Kabul'. It assesses to what extent the British Legation in Kabul presented a model institution that was built on the export of the colonial state's technologies of rule as much as it shaped governmental and bureaucratic practices of other institutions in the Indian Empire and beyond.

THE CONSULATES IN JALALABAD AND KANDAHAR

Diplomatic relations between Afghanistan, India and the United Kingdom included two Consulates, which were mostly excluded from the political realm of those relations.[9] Situated along the main roads that connected Afghanistan to Peshawar and Chaman in India, the Consulates issued visas and "motor passes" to Afghans travelling to India.[10] The selection of the Consuls rested with the British Minister in Kabul. For different reasons, the first British Minister, the Foreign and Political Department in India, Foreign Office in London as well as the Afghan government were inclined against Indians becoming 'British' Consuls.[11] But, since Jalalabad and Kandahar allegedly presented dangers and discomfort to Europeans, staffing the Consulates with colonial officers was ruled out as being "impracticable".[12] As with many other questions concerning Indians, the Government of India misrepresented an unwanted outcome as a virtue, arguing that public opinion in India expected Indians to be represented in British diplomacy in Afghanistan. There were also very material considerations as diplomacy's Indian labourers weight lighter on the Raj's payrolls.[13] Between 1923 and 1926, the *Foreign Office List* confused the Consuls in Kandahar and Jalalabad, casting doubt on the importance attached to the adequate representation of Indians in India's imperial apparatus.

The chosen Consuls were high-ranking individuals, and the incumbents were recruited from the North-West Frontier Province in the beginning. Kandahar's first Consul, Khan Sahib Mahmud Khan, came highly recommended as a member of the Sadozai dynasty whose "loyalty is beyond question".[14] Ahmad Shah Abdali, or Durrani, had established the Sadozai dynasty in Afghanistan, whose last representative on the throne had been Shah Shuja, who had met Elphinstone. The Sadozai were replaced by the Muhammadzai Barakzai, whose first ruler was Dost Mohammed Khan. After 1818, Shah Shuja lived in Indian exile on an East India Company pension until the First Anglo-Afghan War, when the invading army reinstalled him on the throne of Afghanistan, only to be deposed again with the collapse of the occupation.[15] For Jalalabad, Khan Sahib Syed Mahmud Shah was Francis Henry Humphrys' first choice. His record spanned nineteen years of service in the North-West Frontier Province, which equipped him with the requisite "ability, tact and common sense and experience in dealing with Afghans".[16] He had also been involved in the preparatory talks for the Mussoorie Conference in 1920.[17] However, this did not ensure the success of Mahmud Shah's tenure as Consul. He cited "despondency over his failure" in a letter to Richard Roy Maconachie, the later Minister (1930–1935), before he committed suicide in Simla in 1924. His example points to the pressures of holding colonial office and its implications for mental health. Mahmud Shah's successor in Jalalabad was Muhammad Jehangir Khan, "a Sunni Muhammadan [who] takes religion very seriously – a bit of a Mullah in fact".[18] His English language skills counted in his favour, but he appeared "not as a man of outstanding ability".[19] Over time, Consuls were also recruited from Baluchistan. Khan Sahib Sher Zaman Shah, Consul in Kandahar from December 1936, was a member of the Baluchistan Provincial Service.[20]

The Consuls in Jalalabad and Kandahar enjoyed an elevated social status, which is indicated by their Islamic titles Mufti, Haji and Syed, the latter indicating direct descent from the Prophet Muhammad. A *mufti* was an interpreter of Islamic law, while a *haji* had completed a pilgrimage to Mecca (*haj*). It was "essential" that they were of Sunni faith.[21] Apart from Islamic markers of distinction, the Consuls were also recipients of colonial honours for the services they had rendered to the Raj. They held the titles Khan Sahib and Khan Bahadur, which also identified them as colonial subjects. Among the Consuls was also an officer of the Indian Army in the rank Risaldar Major (Cavalry Commander). This rank could only be held by Indians and was subordinate to European officers. Instead of perceiving them as members of 'British' diplomacy in Afghanistan, they were regarded as its others within. In 1940, Fraser-Tytler commented on the visit to Kabul of the two Consuls from Jalalabad and Kandahar: "They live in the Indian guest rooms, mainly because their bed room habits are not our habits, but eat with us and have the run of the house. A pleasant pair of people, but a little difficult to talk to for a week".[22]

As much as they were subordinated to Europeans, the Consuls headed diplomatic establishments that were entirely staffed by Indian personnel. Both Consulates included a dispensary operated by Indian Sub-Assistant Surgeons, who were also officers of the Indian Army, or private practitioners from India, as well as a hospital orderly. Jalalabad's Ministerial Clerk between 1940 and 1942 was Rahmat Khan.[23] There were also two Afghan guards (*mulki sowar*, sg.) and a gardener.[24] Parallel to the Legation's operative staff structure in Kabul, the Consulates in Jalalabad and Kandahar employed Indians under European supervision from Kabul, who themselves organised largely anonymous Indian and Afghan labourers. Whilst the Consuls were largely excluded from the interactions with the Afghan government, their presence underlined the multinational setup of Anglo-Afghan relations. The institutions of Anglo-Afghan diplomacy recreated imperial hierarchies in Afghanistan, turning Kabul into a 'centre', from where the representatives of the imperial government administered the subordinated Indian 'periphery' in the shape of the Consulates in Jalalabad and Kandahar. Geographically removed from Kabul, the Consulates represented the reality of India's international consular connections with Afghanistan. In 1940, the Consulate in Kandahar issued up to forty visas daily, indicating the outlines of the documented movement of people between India and Afghanistan.[25]

The "Oriental Secretaries"

The designation of the Oriental Secretary's position was an act of differentiation. The job was modelled on the intelligence offices at Indian Residencies, which catered to the need of collecting information on local conditions. In the Agency system, Indians collected, recorded and forwarded information on other Indians. Prior to 1919, the Government of

India's need for information from Kabul had been served by Newswriters. In 1918, India's Foreign Secretary described the ideal British Agent in Afghanistan as "a Muhammadan of somewhat notorious piety, of about the same age as the Amir and not too rabidly loyal to the British Government. I do not mean that we want a disloyal British Agent, but I mean that we do not want a pigheaded rampant loyalist".[26] Ideally, Newswriters would be socially acceptable to both employers, through loyalty, as well as to the people on whom they were sent to report, through their faith and tribal affiliation. Habibullah Khan referred to Hafiz Saifullah Khan as an "Afghan", thus turning the Pashtun into a perfect middleman for Indo-Afghan interaction.[27] The politics of the frontier, which divided and measured loyalty between Afghanistan and India, were consequently translated into the Anglo-Afghan encounter.

The description of the ideal Newswriter in Kabul also echoes the stereotypes applied to the Legation's other South Asian employees, who could never fulfil the expectations of their European rulers. Although the Newswriters in Kabul were the Government of India's eyes and ears in Kabul before 1919, they were never objectively rated. Coen considered the Newswriter to have been a "comparatively lowly Indian official who lived in Kabul and sent out such information as he could pick up – neither in quality nor in quantity did it seem usually to amount to much".[28] Nevertheless, by employing a Newswriter in Kabul, the Government of India effectively mimicked practices of intelligence gathering in precolonial South Asia.[29] From 1922, the Oriental Secretary's position at the Legation was designed as an intermediary between the Afghan public and the British Legation. He was tasked to fill the perceived gap between Afghan conditions and British diplomatic intentions, functioning as a translator in the widest sense:

> The Oriental Secretary should, if possible, be an Indian Musalman on the Indian Civil Service, or Political Department of the Government of India. He should be a man of exceptional scholarship in English and Persian, and should, if possible, know Pashtu [sic] as well, though this latter is not essential. He should receive a duty allowance [...] to enable him to provide cigarettes and light refreshments without stint to Afghan callers.[30]

The appointment of the Oriental Secretaries followed a rationale similar to that employed in the case of the Consuls. Unlike subordinated political officers at Indian Residencies, the Oriental Secretary was not recruited locally from Afghanistan. The frontier provided the most important training and recruiting ground, forging the requisite social, linguistic and cultural knowledge of Afghanistan.[31] The recruitment of socially elevated Pashtuns from the North-West Frontier Province as Consuls was replicated in the recruitment of Oriental Secretaries. The same rationale rated highly exposure to the frontier and its people in the recruitment of political staff. Like the Consuls, the Oriental Secretaries were highly decorated members of the colonial state. They, too, carried the colonial, quasi-indigenous titles Khan Bahadur, Nawab and Sheikh, the latter indicating membership in a ruling family or a religious official.[32] Their families belonged to the colonial state's "north-west frontier gentry".[33] In general, they were recruited from a frontier elite whose careers had benefited from close involvement with the Raj. Yet, like the few Indians who became Counsellors, the Oriental Secretaries were initially members of the lesser-ranked Provincial Civil Services of the Raj. Whilst they were comparatively high-ranking individuals in terms of their social status due to their intimate and long-running connections with the colonial state, the very titles that elevated them from the vast majority of colonial subjects restricted them to being recognisably Indian others of their European counterparts to whom they were subordinated.

A few individual life histories throw further light on the position. Nawab Muzaffar Khan had taken part in the talks in Rawalpindi in 1919 and was the Oriental Secretary of the Dobbs Mission in 1921. He stayed in Kabul after Henry Dobbs' departure and contributed to the establishment of the Legation in 1922. "[H]is knowledge of Afghan procedure of personalities" was deemed crucial in shaping the Legation according to Afghanistan's diplomatic practice.[34] He applied to join India's diplomatic service in February 1922 and was supported by Humphrys who wrote that "[t]he Nawab has been of the greatest assistance to me in every way and I parted from him with much regret. We were all new to Afghanistan and unfamiliar with Kabul etiquette and his advice has been most valuable".[35]

Mahbub Ali Khan Yusufzai replaced Muzaffar Khan in 1922.[36] He was a landlord in Sheikhan, a village in the Peshawar district of the North-West Frontier Province, and had joined the Provincial Civil Service in 1915.[37] Around that time he worked on the staff of the British Agent in Kabul. Between 1917 and 1922, Mahbub Ali Khan was Extra Assistant Commissioner in the North-West Frontier Province, but seems to have also spent some time in Kabul. He joined the Dobbs Mission as Sub-Assistant Surgeon, before returning to Kabul as the Legation's Oriental Secretary from 1922 until 1929.[38] In the final report on the Dobbs Mission, Mahbub Ali Khan received special mention, as his "previous knowledge was of the greatest help" in constructing the Legation.[39] The first two Oriental Secretaries forged vital personal links on whose foundations both Dobbs and Humphrys later established the Legation. In 1929, Mahbub Ali Khan was assigned to watch the movements of Nadir Khan, Shah Wali Khan and Hashim Khan on their journey into Afghanistan.[40] Muzaffar Khan joined India's diplomatic service in late 1929 as Assistant Commissioner in Peshawar. His application for the single Indian vacancy of that year was also supported by Humphrys: "His services [...] in Kabul have shown him to be a man of unusual acuteness of brain and profound knowledge both of tribal and of Afghan psychology. He has pleasing manners and has a broader outlook on life and is more a man of the world than other Indians of the N.W.F.P. with whom I am acquainted".[41] Humphrys' letter of recommendation indicates the qualities expected of prospective Indian members of India's diplomatic service, especially their ability of 'knowing' Afghans as well as their willingness to apply that knowledge for the good of frontier administration and Anglo-Afghan relations. At the same time, Humphrys played to the idea of Afghanistan as an "inward-looking society", isolated from the world at large, unable to produce capably intelligent offspring in substantial numbers.[42]

For these reasons, Mahbub Ali Khan's subsequent career posts crisscrossed the North-West Frontier Province, but he became Political Agent in Malakand only as late as 1946.[43] Sikandar Khan, the Oriental Secretary from 1930 to 1942, authored a specialist memorandum on judicial procedures in Afghanistan.[44] Michael Francis O'Dwyer described Nawabzada Muhammad Aslam Khan, of the North-West Frontier Province Civil Service and Oriental Secretary between 1942 and 1948, in terms that echoed the ideology of the 'martial races':

> The applicant belongs to one of the most loyal and martial tribes [of] the Awans in the North Punjab and his own family rendered excellent service during the War in supplying recruits and no less than 4 of his brothers actually joined up. [...] He is good type of the stalwart loyal mohammadan of the North Punjab.[45]

As the Governor of Punjab in 1919, O'Dwyer had been the host of the Rawalpindi conference. The alignment of Afghan independence and the violence of the Jallianwala Bagh killings of 1919 reverberated in London two decades later. In 1940, O'Dwyer was assassinated during a lecture given by Percy Sykes on "Afghanistan: the Present Position".[46] Among the attendants were Louis Dane and Audrey Mander, who, as Audrey Harris, wrote about her travels in Afghanistan.[47] Lawrence Dundas, the Secretary of State for India and Burma and former Governor of Bengal, was wounded by the shots, and Dane broke an arm.[48]

In 1947, both Mahbub Ali Khan and Muhammad Aslam Khan were among the only seventeen Indians on the Indian Political Service.[49] Oriental Secretaries provided a desirable divide between the Legation's European and its South Asian personnel. They existed in liminal conditions, removed as they were from both colonial masters and subjects alike. On a practical level, the Oriental Secretary managed the Legation's Indian employees by issuing green passes and passports.[50] Similar necessities for the Legation's European personnel were organised by Europeans. The racial divisions in the structure of the Legation's operative personnel were, thus, also visible among its gazetted officers. The Oriental Secretary's position, together with the few Indian incumbents amongst its Counsellors, illustrates a division that was pertinent in the colonial services as a whole. Although the European representatives of the colonial state relied heavily on the specialist knowledge of successive Oriental Secretaries, they also provided a useful argument against the employment of additional, unwanted Indians. Shielding the Indian Political Service from 'Indianisation' measures in the 1930s, Maconachie argued that "[a]n Indian is already a Secretary of the Legation [...] and therefore it seems to me that it would be difficult to make any a case for an increase of the Indian element in the superior staff of the Legation itself".[51]

MEDICAL PRACTITIONERS

The Legation maintained a medical unit, which employed a Sub-Assistant Surgeon, a compounder (pharmacist), a dresser and a nursing orderly, all of whom were recruited from India's medical services. The Legation's Sub-Assistant Surgeons carried the rank of Jemadar, which was only given to Indian officers in the Indian Army. As with the Legation structure as a whole, the majority of medical work was performed by Indians, yet the establishment was headed by a European colonial officer. The Surgeons received their medical training at universities 'at home' and then applied to the Indian Medical Service. The Indian Medical Service was part of the Indian Army setup, but also supplied the cadre of civilian doctors in India. Doctors of the Indian Medical Service, too, could apply for service under the Foreign and Political Department, which employed them for both medical and for political work.[52]

Most Surgeons' career geographies exposed them to the frontier prior to arriving in Kabul. They accumulated precious knowledge of tribal society in the medical encounter. Experience in particular locations came with knowledge of certain people. As ethnically conceptualised spaces, knowledge of the frontier prepared for service in Afghanistan. George MacGregor Millar had served in military campaigns in the North-West Frontier Province in 1908 and 1917.[53] Harold Hay Thorburn had served in Malakand, Khyber and Waziristan between 1907 and 1912. He became Agency Surgeon in Meshed in 1913 and was later tasked with military counteraction against the German mission to Afghanistan during World War I. According to his obituary, Thorburn "knew how to win the confidence of the tribesmen, and he was instrumental in raising the Hazara Levies, which he commanded and used for the important purpose of preventing armed parties of enemy emissaries entering Afghanistan from Persia".[54] During this time, he crossed paths with Sykes. Medical practitioners in Kabul combined several skill sets, of which medicine was only one. Thorburn became Civil Surgeon in Quetta in 1918, was Chief Medical Officer in Baluchistan between 1920 and 1924 and again in 1932, thereby adding to his portfolio "experience of work among Baluchi tribesmen".[55] For Millar and Thorburn, Kabul was a station along a career that moved from early postings in tribal administration to senior positions in India's medical services afterwards.[56] In similar fashion, Henry Hawes Elliot had served in the Waziristan Field Force in 1923 and 1924 and worked in Dera Ismail Khan from 1926. He first came to Kabul in 1930 and returned in August 1933 "at his own wish" after being confirmed in the Foreign and Political Department.[57] As later Surgeons to the Viceroy, Elliot and Thorburn provide a little recognised parallel to senior political officers who became Private Secretaries, their jobs bringing them into close physical contact with the very centre of power of colonial India.[58]

William Peat Hogg had one previous civilian posting in Quetta before coming to Kabul as a probationer.[59] By contrast, R. F. D. MacGregor was one of the most senior members of the Indian Medical Service establishment in 1943, both in terms of service as well as age, having been Chief Medical Officer in Baluchistan, Central India as well as Residency Surgeon in Hyderabad in addition to working in several princely states. Already in 1926, he was described as "by far the most suitable selection" for the post of Legation Surgeon.[60] In addition to the Surgeons' career backgrounds, other considerations played a role. Edward Stanley Sayer Lucas was in Kabul in between Elliot's two postings from August 1932 to August 1933.[61] In Maconachie's words, Lucas' superior officer in Kabul: "Normally, he is pleasant and cheerful company, and a 'good mixer', although his personality is not such as to impress Orientals on first acquaintance".[62] Maconachie implied that Lucas could do more to fully use his position as the Legation's medical officer to underline ideas of racial and cultural distance.

Ideas of race and its assumed social implications mattered, too. Henry William Farrell had worked in military hospitals in Rawalpindi and Peshawar and as Civil Surgeon in Bihar. He was in Kabul twice, briefly in 1934 and again as Elliot's successor.[63] Herbert Aubrey Francis Metcalfe, a former Counsellor in Kabul and then India's Foreign Secretary, remarked with regard to the job interview which he had conducted with Farrell:

> In the matter of intelligence and manners he seemed to be well to the average but there is no denying the fact that his speech betrays a somewhat lowly Irish origin. He tells me that his father was a country doctor in Queen's County & that he was educated entirely in Ireland, which is sufficient to account for his pronounced accent. Personally I should not seek to regard this as a disqualification for service in the Political Deptt. especially on the Frontier or in comparatively wild places, where energy, character & ability are more important than 'Oxford accent'. His speech might however be considered as a handicap, if he is to be employed on the Internal side.[64]

The Viceroy, too, considered Farrell's speech to be "a little odd", effectively juxtaposing India and a particular articulation of the English language on the one hand with an Irish dialect and the "wild places" of Afghanistan and Ireland on the other.[65] Rudyard Kipling's novel *Kim* was based on similar ethno-linguistic assumptions that posited an orphan of Irish extraction as an able frontier navigator and border crosser. Perhaps because of these stereotypes that likened Irish to tribal society, Farrell's medical and governmental performance was commented on positively. Maconachie "found him very keen on his work, pleasant to live with, and absolutely straight. He was popular with his fellow officers in the Legation, with the Afghan Sardars—especially the Prime Minister—and, in spite of being a good disciplinarian, with his own subordinates".[66] In other words, Farrell excelled where Lucas underperformed.

In terms of career geographies, Surgeons often moved from Baluchistan and the North-West Frontier Province to Kabul and on to India. William

Joseph Moody, who was in Kabul between 1938 and 1940, also connected the Legation to the Arabian Peninsula. He had been Medical Advisor to the Political Resident in the Gulf.[67] Moody's example from the 1930s and early 1940s indicates a widening of the geographical remit of colonial India's diplomatic relations. The Legation Surgeons after Moody, H. A. Ledgard, R. D. MacRae, Douglas Percy Dewe, are elusive in terms of information on their life histories and career biographies, but, like MacGregor, have remained visible as authors of annual medical reports on Afghanistan.[68]

THE MILITARY ATTACHÉS

As "sanctioned spies", the Military Attachés were primarily charged with the collection of military intelligence.[69] When the Legation was set up, a "military chargé d'affaires" was thought to be an "essential" position. It arose from considerations that foregrounded the physical defence of India in the aftermath of the Afghan War of Independence.[70] Like the Surgeon, the position was exclusively filled by Europeans. Events, persons of interest and observations on Afghanistan's military setup were reported in weekly *diaries* and *summaries*. The Military Attachés textual outputs also listed various other topics, such as accounts of Afghanistan's annual independence games, their military parades and implications for the physical abilities of the Afghan body politic.[71] Successive Military Attachés visited civilian and military installations, including barracks and hospitals.[72] They charted, mapped and measured Afghanistan's geology and mobility infrastructure, such as airfields and roads, counted aeroplanes and assessed its navigability, sending their accumulated information to the Army Headquarters in India. The post also liaised between the headquarters of the Indian Army and the Afghan state. At the Legation, the Military Attaché was also in charge of the guard.

Of the twelve Military Attachés in Kabul between 1922 and 1947, at least a quarter descended from former colonial officers. Two fathers had served as civilians in India (Claude Ernest Torin Erskine, Percy Charles Russell Dodd), and one in the Indian Army (Charles Hamilton Grant Hume Harvey-Kelly). Only two had no family relations in India (Alexander Boyes-Cooper, Alexander Stalker Lancaster). In other cases, fathers were attached to the Royal Army Military College in Sandhurst (William Archibald Kenneth Fraser, Alfred Noel Irvine Lilly).[73] One was a reverend (Harold Victor Lewis). Even if descent from Indian service families was absent, colonial genealogies extended beyond the biological. Robert MacGregor Macdonald "Rab"

4 BIOGRAPHY AND IMPERIAL GOVERNANCE 129

Lockhart (1893–1981), Military Attaché from 1934 to 1935, married Amy Margaret, the daughter of Robert Neil Campbell, a senior figure in the Medical Service.[74] Family relations also connected them by other means, as Lockhart's father was George Cunningham's headmaster.[75] Incidentally, Lockhart became Acting Governor of the North-West Frontier Province in 1947 in between Cunningham's two spells in the same post, although he seems to have never entered India's political service.

Alexander Stalker "the Duke" Lancaster served longer than any other Military Attaché, from 1935 to 1938 and again from 1940 to 1947.[76] In between his two postings, he took part in one of several military missions from India to discuss military assistance to Afghanistan in 1939 at a time of latent anxieties about a British 'loss of prestige' in the Muslim world during Germany's offences of the early Second World War.[77] On the one hand, Lancaster's example illustrates the meticulous collection of information on Afghanistan for the production of military knowledge. Lancaster toured Afghanistan intensively, measuring road distances and conditions, assessing their usability, as well as mapping, charting, surveying and photographing the country and people outside of Kabul.[78] On the other, Lancaster embodied the overlap of the personal and the political in the Military Attaché's diplomatic work. In 1948, Giles Frederick Squire credited Lancaster as having been a crucial connector in Anglo-Afghan military consultations:

> During his years in Kabul, Col. Lancaster has created a unique position for himself, and won a very high degree of confidence from Afghan officials. It is due to him in no small measure that we are even now, after our departure from India, so frequently consulted on military and air force matters by the Afghans.[79]

Lancaster's tenure as Military Attaché provides two fascinating insights into the study of Anglo-Afghan military relations in terms of space and time. As mobile military missions, Lancaster's tours increased the Legation's mobility and extended its reach far beyond Kabul up until 1947. After 1947, the metropolitan government in London continued to reap the benefits from the Anglo-Afghan military relationship created in paracolonial time.

The Indian Political Service and Colonial Networks of Family and Profession

Closing in on the top of the Legation's staff pyramid, the remainder of this chapter discusses the members of India's Foreign and Political Department. Reporting directly to the Viceroy, India's Foreign Secretary administered colonial India's external relations. A Political Secretary, or Political Advisor to the Crown Representative after 1937, supervised the central government's relations with the princely states. The Government of India Act of 1935 reorganised India's relations with the princely states, resulting in the reshaping of the Foreign and Political Department as the External Affairs Department in 1937. The cadre of colonial officers, who had previously worked under the Foreign and Political Department remained the same, but was then renamed the Indian Political Service.[80]

The Indian Political Service was a radically conservative cadre. Its ranks were shielded by patronage, seniority and the maintenance of a numbered list that expressed each member's position in its hierarchy. The service's personnel was recruited predominantly from the Indian Civil Service and the Indian Army, thus crafting India's diplomatic service as a supercolonial elite: a small community chosen from the colonial state's comparatively small European ruling class. Military entrants into the service were not allowed to married, had to be under twenty-six years of age and pass a promotion exam.[81] Any member of the Indian Civil Service with less than five years of service, who had passed his examination, was also eligible. There was an exact formula that regulated that four soldiers were taken in one year and five in the other; that there were two 'civilians' every year, but only one in the fifth. As a consequence, around seventy percent of the service came from the Indian Army and around thirty from the Indian Civil Service.[82] For the Legation in Kabul, the ratio in favour of military over civilian personnel was further extended if the Military Attachés and the Surgeons are counted as part of the Indian Army establishment. The Legation's political elite was almost predominantly in the hands of serving or former colonial military men. The preference for military officers over civilians was informed by aesthetic, cultural and economic notions. Stereotypes made soldiers appear physically more imposing than 'bookish' civilians: the former demanded respect from 'native' rulers on the basis of their rank, and they were cheaper to employ.[83]

After applying, candidates for India's diplomatic service underwent a series of interviews with senior members of the Government of India's establishment, including the Private Secretary of the Viceroy, the Foreign and the Political Secretaries, who decided if a candidate was more "frontier material" or rather destined for service in the princely states, a distinction already highlighted in Farrell's appointment as Surgeon.[84] Candidates were then invited to lunch with the Viceroy at the Viceregal Lodge in Delhi.[85] The Viceroy reserved absolute discretion in the selection of any officer.[86] The Indian Civil Service selected its members on a competitive basis provided by entry exams, which until the end of the Raj discriminated against Indians. By contrast, India's diplomatic service handpicked its candidates purely on the basis of autocratic patronage.[87] Through membership in the Indian Political Service, candidates gradually climbed to the mythical top of India's Olympian colonial elite. This perception helped to perpetuate an erroneous sense of achievement and administrative excellence, commonly assumed among the members of this *super*colonial entity. Coen encapsulated this mentality, as the discussion in this chapter's opening paragraph indicates.

After selection, a successful candidate underwent a three-year period of probation. In the first six months, the probationers were sent either to an Indian state or to a frontier district "for training in political or frontier work".[88] There was little formal training, as the probationers learned on the job.[89] At the end of their probation, candidates had to undergo oral and written examinations, which tested their "general knowledge of Indian History and Political subjects or frontier conditions". Alfred Lyall's *Rise and Expansion of the British Dominion* was standard reading for all candidates. Political candidates also had to be familiar with Aitchison's collection of treaties on Central India and Rajputana, frontier candidates with those relating to Afghanistan. In addition, candidates were expected to be familiar with other works, which instilled them with a sense of the colonial state's hagiography, romance and sense of purpose. A passage taken from the "[r]ules regulating the admission of junior members of the Indian Political Service to the Political Department of the Government of India" illustrates this well:

> Candidates will also be expected to have some knowledge of standard works bearing on the country in which they are serving; i.e. in the case of - *Native States*. – Tod's *Rajasthan*, Malcom's "Central India," Sleeman's "Rambles and Recollections," Lyall's "Asiatic Studies," and in the case of – *The Frontier*. – Edwards' "Year on the Punjab Frontier," Thornton's "Life of Sir Robert Sandeman," Chirol's "The Middle Eastern Question".[90]

All authors were former colonial servants who contributed to the accumulation of colonial knowledge of India, its frontiers and the places beyond, with the exception of Ignatius Valentine Chirol, a "blatant imperialist" nonetheless in Sumit Sarkar's words.[91] Former colonial officers trained future candidates both as administrators and scholars. Over time, candidates became "scholar-administrators" themselves, contributing to the collection and dissemination of colonial best practices by writing history handbooks, Coen and Fraser-Tytler for example, or by revising their own exam papers for future generations.[92] Fraser-Tytler, for instance, revised the introduction to the Afghanistan section for the 1933 edition of Aitchison's treaty collection.[93] Maconachie compiled the encyclopaedic *Précis on Afghan Affairs* for the perusal of the employees of the colonial state.[94]

These were not the only pathways by which members of the Indian Political Service accumulated and disseminated knowledge. Political candidates had to have family in India in order to be eligible for service. The result was an overlap of professional and private networks that resulted in the creation of a political elite by biological means.[95] In addition to safeguarding its ranks through a process of appointment, instead of examination, India's diplomatic service was also largely a family affair, a South Asian aristocracy of European descent. "A moderate dose of nepotism never did a cadre any harm, and most of those officers who had relations in the service stood out as certainly above the average in efficiency", wrote Coen in 1971.[96] Family relations in the service would ensure the efficient running of an administrative colonial bureaucracy, whose routines were handed down through generations and whose familial origins testified to an individual's "character" and ability.[97] Successful colonial servants of the past literally bred the colonial administrators of the future. Maconachie, for instance, referenced his father's example and joined the Indian Civil Service.[98]

The application files for the Foreign and Political Department of the Government of India explicitly reveal a candidate's overlapping private and professional networks like no other biographical record. The standardised questionnaires consisted of two parts, one of which had to be completed by the applicant himself and the other by his commanding officer. Among other things, the applicant was asked to reveal his education, language qualifications, family relations in India and whether any known relatives had served, or were serving, in India's governmental apparatus. The questionnaires also requested names of referees "who can testify to character and qualification" in support of the application, thereby providing important information on the applicant's professional networks.[99] By contrast, military records list an individual's next-of-kin, and biographical dictionaries, such as the *Who's Who & Who Was Who*, record only an entry's paternal line.[100] The King's India Cadetship records at the British Library reveal a candidate's paternal side because the father's history of colonial office was a prerequisite for the son's eligibility for a cadetship. The sons of "mutiny survivors" of 1857 scored particularly high marks in the application process for such cadetships.[101]

MINISTERS, COUNSELLORS, SECRETARIES AND COLONIAL GENEALOGY

The example of Francis Henry Humphrys, the Legation's first Minister in Kabul in 1922, indicates the extensive networks of family and profession, in his own time. His application file lists three family members who served in the Indian Army. His uncle, General Francis John Davies, held the highest rank, and there were also two cousins F. G. H. Davies and C. H. Davies.[102] Humphrys also listed Colonel W. B. Capper, who was married to another of Humphrys' cousins, as a referee. In October 1903, when Capper was Director of Military Education, he wrote personally to Dane to lobby on Humphrys' behalf. Dane was India's Foreign Secretary and about to lead a diplomatic mission to Kabul in 1904. Humphrys entered the Political Department in 1903 and spent his probation in the North-West Frontier Province, which had been created only two years before at the instigation of the George Nathaniel Curzon as Viceroy in 1901. From 1903 until 1917, Humphrys worked in various functions and districts on the frontier. In April 1905, he became Harold Deane's, the Chief Commissioner's, Personal Assistant.[103] Humphrys belonged to the first generation of administrators for whom the newly created province provided career prospects as well as family bonds. Humphrys married the Chief Commissioner's daughter, Gertrude Mary, in Peshawar in 1907.[104] Humphrys' oldest son, Arthur Francis Walter, born in Abbottabad, married Archibald and Lady Wavell's daughter, Pamela Eugène, in 1941. At one point, he was considered for the position of Military Secretary of the Viceroy Lord Wavell (1943–1947), but the job ultimately went to Evan Jenkins, the last Governor of Punjab, who was the godfather of one of Francis Henry Humphrys' grandchildren.[105] Humphrys' example illustrates the making and the extent of colonial genealogies among the Legation's diplomatic leadership as well as the interplay and overlap of private and professional networks, all of which intimately connected individuals with the administration of the colonial state.

Humphrys exemplifies the contemporary making of an elite invested in the colonial administration in and beyond the Indo-Afghan borderland in the early twentieth century. By contrast, Fraser-Tytler's example displays the historical depth of these networks. Before he became Minister in 1935, Fraser-Tytler had an expansive historical network of family in India, which included participants in the First and Second Anglo-Afghan Wars as well as contemporaneous serving officers. Fraser-Tytler named General Sir James Macleod Bannatyne Fraser-Tytler and Colonel Percy Clare Elliott-Lockhart in support of his application for the Political Department. James Macleod Bannatyne, William Kerr's paternal great uncle, was a soldier in the "army of retribution" under the command of General George Pollock, which in 1842 laid waste to Kabul's market and surrounding villages in response to the disastrous end to the British occupation force the year before. He participated in the Sikh War, which eventually saw the annexation of the Punjab and of Peshawar in 1849. His colonial service record was further distinguished by his "services in the Indian Mutiny" in 1857. Bannatyne was the brother of William Fraser-Tytler, also of the Bengal Army, who took part the First Anglo-Afghan War of 1839.[106] The other reference, Percy Clare Elliott-Lockhart, was the author of *A Frontier Campaign*, which documented events from the perspective Malakand and Buner Field Forces in 1897 during an uprising in India's Swat Valley. Incidentally, these operations also featured Humphrys' later father-in-law, Harold Deane, who had served on several military operations on the frontier at the turn of the century.[107] In addition to these two, Fraser-Tytler listed Colonel Robert Scott-Kerr as a professional referee. However, Scott-Kerr was also Fraser-Tytler's maternal uncle and an officer in the Royal Army with experience in warfare in Africa from the 1880s to the 1900s. Fraser-Tytler's other professional referees were the Governor of Bengal, Thomas Gibson-Carmichael, and M. H. Wheeler, Secretary in the Secret and Home Department of the Government of India.[108] Fraser-Tytler was well connected with Afghanistan through historical family connections even before he applied to the political service, which later made him Secretary, Counsellor and Minister in Kabul. A letter to his mother from 1936 further mentions an "Uncle Jim Hunter", who took part in Lord Roberts' "famous Kabul to Kandahar march" during the Second Anglo-Afghan War.[109] Fraser-Tytler's army service record lists his active service in East Africa from 1917 to 1918 as well as his participation in the Third Anglo-Afghan War. For Fraser-Tytler,

Afghanistan combined family history with colonial warfare that preceded his own diplomatic career.

Several Counsellors provide further varied colonial genealogies. Counsellor and Secretary in 1924, Arthur William Fagan's great-grandfather, Christopher Sullivan Fagan, had served in the Bengal infantry, and his grandfather, George Hickson Fagan, in the Indian Army.[110] Through his great-grandfather, Fagan was related to Patrick James Fagan, of the Indian Civil Service, who held several positions in Punjab.[111] The latter contributed two chapters on colonial administration to the sixth volume of *The Cambridge History of India* in 1932.[112] As a candidate for political work, Arthur William Fagan, thus, appeared to be "above the average".[113] George Cunningham's spell as Counsellor at the Legation in 1925 and 1926 left "no special mark" according to his biographer, who perceived of Kabul as little more than a career detour.[114] Cunningham was a great-nephew of Sir Robert Sandeman, who, like Cunningham himself, has been largely framed as one of the leading frontier administrators and whose biography was standard reading for candidates of the political service.[115] Edward Thomas Ruscombe Wickham was Counsellor in 1927.[116] His father, Colonel William James Richard Wickham, took part in the Second Anglo-Afghan War in 1879 and 1880 and on the Frontier in 1888.[117] Wickham mentioned his father's career in an application to a King's Cadetship, when applying to Sandhurst and again on his annual reviews as Indian Army officer, giving an idea of the permanence of his father's influence in terms of career progression.[118]

Crawford Cecil Lindsay Ryan, Counsellor in 1934, had a cousin in the Foreign and Political Department and a step-uncle in the Indian Army.[119] The latter actively intervened in Ryan's application process, explicitly drawing on his father's exploits as well as asking for advice on how to further Ryan's career options.[120] Moreover, Ryan's father, Perceval Cecil Hardinge Ryan, was a doctor at the Royal Military Academy College at Sandhurst. Philip Cotes Hailey, Counsellor from 1940 to 1942, was related to several colonial officers. His father, Hammet Reginald Clode Hailey, was a former Indian Civil Servant in the United Provinces.[121] He, too, contributed a chapter to the sixth volume of *The Cambridge History of India* in 1932 on India's finances.[122] Hammet's younger brother and Philip Cotes' uncle was William Malcolm Hailey, Finance Member of the Viceroy's Council, Governor of Punjab in 1924 and of the United Provinces in 1928, which was regarded as the highest posting in the Indian Civil Service.[123] The later Baron Hailey also wrote to India's Foreign Secretary between 1920 and

1930, Denys Bray, who reported directly to the Viceroy, to inquire about the status of his nephew's application for the Political Department.[124] This documents a striking overlap of family relations and professional connections. Lancelot Cecil Lepel Griffin, Counsellor after Hailey from 1942 to 1943, presents a similarly illustrious example. His father, Lepel Henry Griffin, was appointed Chief Political Officer in 1880 during the British occupation of Afghanistan and later became Agent to the Governor-General in Central India. In comparison to other scholar-administrators, his record of publications on topics related to India was extensive, and he co-founded the *Asiatic Quarterly Review*.[125] In 1927, this level of paternal accomplishment translated into Griffin's own "special claims" to joining the Political Department because of the "distinguished services of his father".[126] Coen dedicated his book to Griffin as "a great political officer and good friend". Perhaps it was Griffin's example that informed Coen's statement on the prevailing "nepotism" in the service on which he wrote.

Secretaries, too, illustrate a multiplicity of colonial genealogies. Alexander Alfred Russell, Secretary in 1925 and 1926, descended from a family of five generations of colonial officers. His father was an Indian Civil Servant, and there were several family members in the Indian Army. Russell first applied in 1923, his uncle in the Indian Army recommending him as being "good at games, popular in Regiment, and a keen shikari [hunter or gamesmen]".[127] Russell was not selected, but tried again in 1924, expressing his reluctance to use his familial relations in support of his application for the Political Department. He argued that "I could perhaps get some influencial [sic] backing but I would infinitely prefer to get in on my own merits".[128] Russell's example provides an interesting inside perspective on applicants to the diplomatic service, who strove to prove their skills independently of the safety of their familial heritage. The Legation also made families. Leslie William Hazlitt Duncan Best, Secretary in 1928 and 1929, became the son-in-law of Horatio Norman Bolton, a high-ranking member of the Indian Civil Service, whose offices included Chief Commissioner of the North-West Frontier Province and Deputy Secretary in the Foreign and Political Department of the Government of India. Best met his wife, Bolton's daughter Iris, when the Boltons came to visit their "old friends", the Humphrys, in Kabul in 1928.[129]

Arnold Crawshaw Galloway, Secretary from 1934 to 1936, and Patrick John Keen, Secretary in 1938 and 1939, present slightly different examples. There is little information on Galloway, but the existence of an application for a King's India Cadetship suggests that Galloway's father served in India.[130] By contrast, Keen was born in Simla, his father being a Lieutenant in the Indian Army with service in the Anglo-Afghan War of 1919, in Waziristan (1920–1921), on the frontier (1930–1931) and as Commander of the Kohat Brigade (1929–1932).[131] Keen's uncle, too, served in the war of 1919, became a member of the political department in 1901 and was officiating Chief Commissioner of the North-West Frontier Province from 1925 to 1926.[132] Keen's grandfather General Sir Frederick Keen had distinguished himself by his services during the "mutiny", on the frontier and in the Second Anglo-Afghan War.[133] The father of Guy Irvine Pettigrew, Secretary in 1943, worked for the Indo European Telegraph Company.[134] Finally, the father of Alexander William Redpath, Secretary from 1946, also served in India and was killed in Gallipoli.[135]

As an exercise in visualising the networks of family and profession of the Legation's colonial officers, the preceding paragraphs exemplify the Legation's deep and wide-ranging connections with the colonial state in India in the past and in its present. British diplomats in Kabul descended from vast colonial family networks, which bred them and supported their careers. Some were, quite literally, married to the colonial services and produced further generations of colonial administrators, officers and governors. Through the support of their patrons, who knew the ropes of colonial bureaucracy well, and its small cadre of decision-makers, the *protégés* of colonial India's political aristocracy were set up for careers in its diplomatic service, which laid the colonial Indian foundations of the British Legation in Kabul. In Kabul, this self-fashioned familial-professional community cemented hierarchies along the markers of difference discussed in Chapter 3, which elevated this elite above its subordinated others.

Ministers, Counsellors, Secretaries, Colonial Office and Career Geographies

Studies on the Indian Political Service have so far focused either on its frontier or its princely aspects, treating them as separate and formative systems, not least by means of the above-mentioned application process, and effectively sidelining a perspective on India's foreign relations.[136] In doing so, they have closely followed Harcourt Butler's assertion of 1910 as India's Foreign Secretary that "[w]e want lean and keen men on the Frontier, and fat and good-natured men in the States".[137] The existence of specific cadres for the North-West Frontier Province and Baluchistan on the one hand and the princely states on the other suggests that the Legation and other localities in the Indian Empire were mere appendages to the colonial system of "indirect rule".[138] This binarity does not sufficiently acknowledge the changing circumstances in South Asia's political landscape as a consequence of Afghan independence in 1919. This section enquires whether the Legation assisted the formation of a distinct 'Afghanistan cadre', which required particular governmental expertise but also served as a training ground. In other words, the Kabul Legation was both an expression as well as determinant of diplomacy as a form of colonial governance in the Indian Empire.

Each political position at the Legation required its own terms of experience. Ministerial tenures began as five-year terms, but these could be ended or extended. For Ministers, the Viceroy Lord Willingdon (1931–1936) defined the necessary qualifications in 1934:

> They are (a) recent knowledge of conditions, problems and personalities in Afghanistan, (b) familiarity with the working of the Government of India Secretariat and some acquaintance with the internal condition of India and India's probable constitutional future in so far as these affect the relations between his Majesty's Government and Afghanistan, (c) experience of the North-West Frontier particularly of tribal areas which will enable the Minister to realise and appreciate the point of view of the N.W.F. Administration when he is dealing with the minor problem of Frontier relations between the Afghan Government and the Government of India, (d) some knowledge of the Persian and French languages which will facilitate direct intercourse with the Afghans and with other Legations.[139]

According to this definition, the ideal British Minister's primary qualification had to be a solid grounding in affairs affecting Afghanistan as an international polity (a). But incumbents also had to combine features of high-level colonial service in India (b) with particular knowledge of India's frontier administration (c) in addition to mastering the languages of the Afghan (and former Mughal) court and of international diplomacy (d). With regard to career geographies, points (b) and (c) are of particular importance. Point (b) was usually dispensed with by means of a stint at the departmental headquarters in Delhi. Point (c) captured the long-standing antagonism between civilian and military means of colonial administration in the tribal areas.[140] In Kabul, the civilian dimension of frontier administration in India took on the shape of diplomatic interaction.

From the perspective of imperial administration in 1919, Afghanistan and the North-West Frontier Province appeared to be "intimately connected", requiring a "common policy for both".[141] According to

Gould, Counsellor between 1926 and 1929, "[t]en million Pathans live in a region which extends from Chitral to Kandahar and from Kabul to the Indus".[142] As Charles Lindholm has shown, colonial interaction with Pashtuns went through several stages since Mountstuart Elphinstone's mission to Peshawar at the beginning of the nineteenth century. Colonial officers met Pashtuns as emissaries and guests, as soldiers and administrators of 'indirect rule', "from the centralized kingdom of Afghanistan to the anarchic democracies of the hill tribes".[143] The "vacillations of colonial policy" prompted "particular historical colonial settings".[144] These, in turn, produced varied and contradictory descriptions of Pashtuns as "treacherous and greedy", "savage but honourable warriors" as well as "loyal and gentlemanly".[145] After 1919, these "images of the Pathan" jumped scale as they took on an international dimension and informed colonial approaches to Anglo-Afghan diplomatic relations.[146] In the beginning, the post in Kabul attracted colonial servants with particular knowledge of the Pashtun tribes that inhabited the Indo-Afghan borderland. Over time, the post developed its own logic of recruitment, which compartmentalised knowledge of the frontier alongside other job skills. By 1940, Fraser-Tytler warned that "[a]ny suggestion of paramountcy of alternatively that they are merely a glorified frontier tribe would be disastrous, and might sadly impair the Minister's influence here from the outset".[147] Future Ministers in Kabul had to have "*some* knowledge of the Frontier":

[A]n expert on frontier affairs is on the whole not required in this post, and may indeed find his expert knowledge a disadvantage. But a Minister should have a general knowledge of the Frontier, sufficient to enable him to distinguish between tribes and their peculiarities, and to understand their various problems and the manner in which they are being tackled.[148]

Ministers

Humphrys' colonial service record straddled the so-called settled districts and tribal areas of the North-West Frontier Province almost exclusively after entering the political service in 1903, apart from a short stint as Officiating Deputy Secretary in 1921.[149] He possessed "special knowledge" of "the most important" Afridi tribe in the Khyber district.[150] Despite this, Humphrys was not the first choice for the position in Kabul. Feeling "tired", Humphrys was close to retirement when he was proposed to become the British Minister to Afghanistan during home leave.[151] Amanullah Khan wanted Dobbs to become the first British Minister, but Dobbs needed long leave. In November 1921, Curzon gave instructions to prepare a letter of credence for Steuart Edmund Pears.[152] Two days later, Amanullah Khan informed Dobbs in Kabul that Pears' name had become associated with the "diplomatic rebuffs which [Mohammed] Wali had sustained in London" by Curzon.[153] As a member of Dobbs' entourage at the Indo-Afghan conference in Mussoorie in 1920, Pears had also accessed and reported on the correspondence between the Afghan delegation in Mussoorie and Kabul.[154] Amanullah Khan was clear that Pears' rejection "had nothing personal in it".[155] Dobbs drew up a fresh shortlist of candidates, which included Humphrys but not in first spot.[156] By the end of November, Humphrys emerged as the India Office's preferred, though most junior, candidate.[157] Like Dobbs and Pears, Humphrys had taken part in the Mussoorie talks.[158] In early December, Curzon agreed to Humphrys "or indeed to any office whom the I[ndia] O[ffice] recommend".[159] He also backtracked: "As long as I am at the F[oreign] O[ffice] I shall never dream of appointing anyone except in consultation with the I[ndia] O[ffice]".[160] Owing to the "special importance of appearances vis-à-vis of both Bolsheviks and Afghans", Humphrys was promoted from Major to Lieutenant-Colonel.[161] By 1926, "[Humphrys'] frontier experience and local knowledge equip[ped] him singularly well for the task of wearing down the Afghan Government in its attempts at intrigues with our tribesmen and of inducing it to adopt a more and more seemly attitude on the frontier".[162]

Maconachie's and Fraser-Tytler's service records came closer to Willingdon's ideal candidate, covering all of the Viceroy's four points. Maconachie owed his appointment as Minister to Kabul in 1930 to his familiarity with the Afghan government, which he acquired during his posting as the Legation's first ever Counsellor between 1922 and 1925. He was also Political Agent in the Kurram district, which he swapped for Kabul with Gould, when Nadir Khan captured Kabul after the uprising against Amanullah Khan in 1929.[163] According to Fraser-Tytler, "[t]he two men [Nadir Khan and Maconachie] met and talked, and from that meeting there developed a mutual confidence and respect for each other's integrity, which was to be of infinite value to themselves and their Governments in the years that followed".[164]

Maconachie's selection, thus, followed the colonial state's logic of governance on its frontier, according to which knowledge of outstanding individuals played a key role in the application of power. Like Maconachie,

Fraser-Tytler had been to Kabul before when he became Minister in 1935. Between 1922 and 1935 he occupied all of the Legation's political positions, being Secretary, twice Counsellor and Chargé d'Affaires.[165] His friendship with Hashim Khan, Afghanistan's Prime Minister, was regarded as "a great asset".[166] Together, Maconachie and Fraser-Tytler represented the 'Afghanistan cadre' of the Foreign and Political Department. Between 1922, Maconachie's appointment as Counsellor, and 1941, Fraser-Tytler's departure as Minister, they established the Legation's lasting practices.[167] Although Maconachie and Fraser-Tytler came to Kabul from the opposite ends of India's political service, the Indian Civil Service and the Indian Army, respectively, they also cultivated a personal and professional friendship.[168] Fraser-Tytler was intensely critical of the Government of India's military policy in the tribal areas of the North-West Frontier Province.[169] He acquired an intense familiarity with, as well as an equally strong sense of knowing, Afghanistan. This development of "partisanship" was not uncommon among political officers of the Government of India, but has not been established as a phenomenon outside of the colonial state in its external relations.[170] In 1932, Fraser-Tytler commented that "Roy and I seem to be the only people at present who *really understand* the Afghan problem".[171] In his words,

> the Minister's job is an amazingly difficult one in his efforts to reconcile two attitudes towards the problem [of the frontier] which seem poles apart. On one side the strict sort of policeman method, the insistence on the maintenance of prestige, 'the inexorable determination to punch' which seems the most salient feature of our frontier rule today. On the Afghan side a much looser method, of compromise & laissez faire, of live & let live, mingled with a little bribery & chicanery, typically Oriental but quite successful.[172]

Fraser-Tytler recognised two very different "frontier governmentalities".[173] In 1938, he complained that "the military tail is wagging the Government of India dog".[174] When the "world crisis" loomed in June 1939, Fraser-Tytler was retained in Kabul until November 1941.[175] He became eligible for retirement in December 1941. But, Fraser-Tytler's persistent critique accelerated discussions about his recall. His health and age became the frame of reference for this argument. In late 1940, Fraser-Tytler underwent an appendectomy. By March 1941, the Viceroy Lord Linlithgow (1936–1943) "thought that he had aged a good deal": "I would not regard him at any time has having been an outstanding or very decisive personality, but he has done us admirably in more quiet times. But I doubt his capacity to take a really definite line with the Afghans, and I think that he is rather too anxious to avoid trouble with them".[176] Fraser-Tytler "had lost the confidence of the Government of India".[177] He was opposed to the idea of a change in Ministers, arguing that "experience has shown that it takes from 4 to 6 months for the Afghans who are a primitive suspicious people to get used to the idea of such a change and about an equal time to give their confidence to the new incumbent, even when the latter is well known to them".[178] To his superiors, Fraser-Tytler appeared "more Afghan than the Afghans".[179] He also admitted to a "biassed [sic] way view of [Afghanistan's] inhabitants and their ways".[180] Fraser-Tytler argued that his Orientalist knowledge of Afghanistan made him the ideal candidate.

In the eyes of the Viceroy and his advisors, age and physical frailty had made Fraser-Tytler 'go soft' on Afghans. Leopold Amery, the Secretary of State for India, toned down Linlithgow's critique of Fraser-Tytler, but still agreed on the need for a change in personnel: "Incidentally, though Fraser-Tytler has never been so outstanding as his two predecessors, Sir Francis Humphrys and Sir Richard Maconachie, the Viceroy is perhaps a little hard on him (his recent deficiencies having been due, I think, to ill health and over fatigue rather than to lack of qualifications)".[181] In May 1941, Linlithgow wrote to Fraser-Tytler personally to inform him of his immediate replacement. The Viceroy also suggested that health would be the right frame to explain this change in order "to avoid sowing any suspicion in the Afghan mind".[182] The Viceroy then dictated to Fraser-Tytler the very terms by which he was to communicate this decision to the Afghan Prime Minister:

> [Y]ou should at once ask for an interview with Hashim Khan, and say that the length of your tenure in Kabul (which has already been prolonged for over a year) has had some effect on the state of your health, and that, with great regret, you have reached the conclusion that (since in any event your term was now drawing to a close) it was wiser for you to take no risks in the matter, and to ask His Majesty's Government to permit you to be relieved earlier than would otherwise have been the case. You could add that you have now heard from His Majesty's Government that with great reluctance they have agree to do so.

Fraser-Tytler rejected this reasoning, his health being "probably better than at any time in the last six years":

I did not think it advisable to stress very strongly the question of my health, which since my operation for appendicitis is probably better than at any time in the last six years. The Prime Minister is well aware of the fact that only last week I climbed to very near the top of the Paghman range, and that I am playing tennis and riding regularly. I felt that to dwell too strongly on my physical unfitness would in such circumstances have immediately given rise to suspicions, which we are anxious to avoid, that a change of incumbents at the present juncture meant something more than merely the replacement of a man who has finished his job by another.[183]

When Fraser-Tytler informed Hashim Khan of his impending departure, the latter thought it "a cardinal error" and "a fatal mistake".[184] In Kabul, Fraser-Tytler was considered "persona gratissima".[185] Given his "closest friendship" with Hashim Khan the change in personnel driven by Linlithgow would be "most regrettable".[186] R. T. Peel found Fraser-Tytler's reply to Linlithgow "[a] most dignified and convincing letter. [...] It is certainly not the writing of a man who has lost his grip".[187] G. E. Crombie noted that the change in Ministers "has been v[ery] badly bungled" by the Government of India headed by Linlithgow.[188]

Francis Verner Wylie's Ministership (1941–1943) during the Second World War signalled the gradual adjustment of recruiting strategies for the Foreign and Political Department's 'Afghanistan cadre'. The Second World War, in the words of Linlithgow, constituted "the end of a chapter, and the new chapter may need somewhat different handling".[189] Afghanistan had entered the Second World War as a neutral country. In 1940, Germany proposed von Werner Otto von Hentig as German Minister in Kabul. He was a member of the mission in 1915 that unsuccessfully attempted to convince Habibullah Khan to attack India. The British Legation pressured the government of Afghanistan to reject this "really dangerous man".[190] Wylie came to Kabul to force the removal of Germans and Italian 'Axis nationals' from Afghanistan.[191] This international intervention into Afghan sovereignty illustrated the qualified nature of Afghan independence. It also rested on a colonial precedent when in 1919 the colonial government of India had demanded the removal of "hostile foreigners" from Afghanistan.[192] The Viceroy justified Wylie's posting with the necessity to employ "the best possible men on the periphery rather than at the Centre".[193] As Governor of the Central Provinces and Berar between 1938 and 1940 and India's Political Secretary in late 1940, Wylie was a senior civil servant.[194] His experience fulfilled Willingdon's ideal with several years of service in the North-West Frontier Province and in the Secretariat. Linlithgow described him as having been "nurtured and reared on the North-West Frontier".[195]

The Legation's last Minister, Giles Frederick Squire, presents a career geography that contextualised Kabul in an even wider remit of the Indian Empire. Already in contention for Fraser-Tytler's succession in 1939, Squire had failed to make the cut then.[196] When he finally became Minister in Kabul in 1943, he differed from his predecessors because he had not served in the North-West Frontier Province, but several years in neighbouring Baluchistan. He had been Consul-General in Meshed in 1936 and Counsellor in Tehran in 1941.[197] Squire's appointment differed from the familiarity which all of his predecessors had with either Afghanistan or with the administration of the colonial state. In 1948, Squire became Ambassador, transitioning British diplomacy in Afghanistan from colonial rule into colonialism's diplomatic afterlives. Together, the Legation's five Ministers present diverse career geographies, which illustrate the colonial state's changing localisation of the Legation in India's imperial networks. Beginning with an exclusive focus on the North-West Frontier Province in 1922, the Ministers' careers eventually departed from that principle. Of the five Ministers in Kabul, only Wylie returned to India after Kabul. Humphrys became High Commissioner and later Ambassador in Iraq in succession of Dobbs, while for Maconachie, Fraser-Tytler and Squire Kabul became their last career posting in the colonial service. In 1943, Fraser-Tytler began working for the Red Cross.

Counsellors

The Counsellor's position complemented the Minister's expertise. When the Minister left Kabul on leave, for talks in India or on special deputation, the Counsellor stepped in to become temporary head of mission or Chargé d'Affaires in case of longer absences. Maconachie and Fraser-Tytler were the only two Counsellors who also became Ministers later on. But, several Counsellors were shortlisted for Ministerships, Cunningham for instance. Arthur Edward Broadbent Parsons, Counsellor in 1930, was ruled out of contention for the Ministership because he was unmarried, "a considerable handicap in the social work which has no small importance in Kabul".[198] Similarly, William Rupert Hay, Counsellor from 1934 to 1936, had "the right kind" of experience to be Minister, but "the Afghans do not like him".[199] Writing in 1947, Squire explained how the position of the Counsellor was defined against that of the Minister:

> It has always been considered essential that either the Minister himself or the Counsellor here should have an intimate knowledge of Indian frontier affairs as they are of the utmost importance whenever there is unrest on either side of the border [...]. The principle is sound and as I am not myself a Frontier 'expert' I must have a Counsellor who is.[200]

The North-West Frontier Province prepared British diplomats for service in Kabul like no other post. By comparison, Kashmir "was not an ideal preparation for Kabul".[201] Between 1922 and 1947, there were twenty individual Counsellors at the British Legation spreading over twenty-one incumbents, including Maconachie and Fraser-Tytler, the latter doing the job twice. According to their service records, fifteen of twenty-one Counsellors had some experience of colonial service in the North-West Frontier Province.[202] Reginald George Evelin William Alban and Wickham had held office in Baluchistan, including Quetta-Pishin, Sibi and Kalat. Fagan's record is incomplete, and statements for army officers generally do not reveal postings prior to joining the diplomatic service, potentially adding to the tally of colonial personnel with experience of the North-West Frontier Province. There were different degrees of exposure to the frontier in this group. Abdur Rahim Khan, Cunningham, Gerard Charles Lawrence Crichton, Hay, Metcalfe and Parsons are well-documented names in the history of India's north-western frontier. Cunningham had experience of diplomatic interaction with Afghan representatives, having also taken part in the Rawalpindi negotions in 1919.[203] Agha Saiyid Bad Shah, Fraser-Tytler, Gould, Maconachie and Mallam had three years or more on their record. The service records of three Counsellors (Fraser-Tytler, Arthur Ernest Henry Macann, Parsons) list their participation in the Third Anglo-Afghan War of 1919.[204] Five Counsellors (Fagan, Fraser-Tytler, Macann, Roderick Wallis Parkes, Wickham) had been Secretaries before. While they stood out in terms of their familiarity with Afghanistan, this did not necessarily qualify them for prolonged service. Despite serving a total of five years in connection with Afghanistan, Macann was found "not suited" as Fraser-Tytler's successor as Minister in Kabul.[205] The Counsellors came to Kabul from across the entire portfolio of the Foreign and Political Department from the Arabian Peninsula, through the North-West Frontier Province, Baluchistan, several Indian states and provinces to the Himalayan posts in

Kashmir, Sikkim, Tibet and Bhutan. Griffin is an exception to the rule, as his posting followed a purely Indian geography prior to Kabul.

In terms of career trajectories, the Counsellors came to Kabul from a posting in the North-West Frontier Province in almost half the cases (9/21). Another seven went to the North-West Frontier Province after Kabul. The rest were evenly spread across the diplomatic service's portfolio to the Secretariat (4), postings in India (2), and outside of India (2), as members of the Viceroy's personal staff (1) or to Baluchistan (1).[206] The Legation in Kabul became a colonial posting among many. Gould's career, for instance, eventually turned him into an "authority on Tibet".[207] Some of the Legation's employees reached the highest echelons of the colonial administration. Parsons and Cunningham became Governors of the North-West Frontier Province. Metcalfe was India's Foreign Secretary from 1932 to 1939. Griffin was India's last Political Secretary. Cunningham and Fraser-Tytler later became Private Secretaries to the Viceroy. Kabul was firmly embedded in India's network of colonial administration.

The twenty individual Counsellors were half Indian Civil Service, half Indian Army. The first five Counsellors had Indian Civil Service backgrounds. The other five were recruited over a stretch of twenty years thereafter and had little experience of the North-West Frontier Province with the exception of Crichton. As the Indian Civil Service struggled to recruit sufficient numbers of European candidates at the entry level for the Indian colonial services, it reluctantly turned to Indians to fill vacant positions formerly occupied by Europeans. The Foreign and Political Department, which continued to recruit Europeans from the Indian Civil Service, did not follow suit with the "Indianisation" of its cadres.[208] The resultant "paucity of candidates" of European origin diminished the pool of such candidates from the Indian Civil Service and was, thus, passed on to India's diplomatic service.[209] In 1947, the sanctioned size of the Indian Political Service was 170, but only 124 positions were filled. Of these only seventeen were Indians.[210] The "manpower shortage" led to accelerated training schedules and career progression.[211] The average age of Counsellors in Kabul between 1922 and 1947 was thirty-nine. Meredith Worth was only thirty-one years old, Parkes came to Kabul as Secretary at the age of twenty-seven and was still only twenty-nine when he became Counsellor. Keen was also only twenty-seven years of age when he succeeded Parkes as Secretary.

The Legation's last two Counsellors were also the Indian Political Service's first Indian Politicals.[212] The employment of Indians as the Legation's Counsellors mirrored the employment of Indians in the Legation's subordinated positions. In terms of India's covenanted services, so called for the covenant taken at the entry into colonial administration, Indians were initially restricted to judicial positions and did not hold any executive power.[213] Shah had exclusively served in the North-West Frontier Province and in Baluchistan and received good references throughout his career. His employment caused concern over his access to Foreign Office ciphers and codes.[214] In 1947, Squire denied Shah access to communication which did not involve the soon-to-be independent Government of India, locking such correspondence in a safe and entrusting the key not to him as the nominal Chargé d'Affaires, but to the European Military Attaché.[215] The Attaché was put in charge of cipher work, and the Secretary became head of the Chancery, effectively excising the then Indian Counsellor from the Legation's leadership. The racist misgivings articulated towards Shah's proximity to the Legation's communication are indicative of a "reluctant Indianization" of the colonial services.[216] Shah was appointed on the basis of his experience in the Government of India's Information and Broadcasting Department, but even his exceptional skills did not overcome Squire's doubts about the general suitability of Indians in India's diplomatic service.[217] As the Interim Government took office in India in 1946, the loyalties of India in colonial employ came under increasing scrutiny.

Shah was succeeded by Abdur Rahim Khan, who, in absolute terms, was the Legation's most experienced frontier officer.[218] Khan's and Shah's South Asian origins were balanced against their military record in the Indian Army, which suggested their identification with its "martial" traditions.[219] Both appointments were also justified in paternalistic tones, which reinterpreted the shortage of sought-after European members for the colonial elite as an attempt to gloss over the service's inbuilt conservatism. In 1944, Olaf Caroe advocated Shah's employment as a benevolent attempt to help the independent India of the future create its own diplomatic service.[220] Squire agreed to an Indian Counsellor in late 1946 as the "lesser of the two evils" to pre-empt Jawaharlal Nehru from "insisting on the immediate setting up of a separate Indian Legation".[221] Incidentally, Shah's recruitment as Counsellor in Kabul also overcame language barriers, as he "went down excellently with Afghan officials. He and his wife both speak excellent Persian".[222] Speaking no less than seven languages, Shah was one of the best linguists of India's political service.[223] Despite their outstanding skills, India's European diplomats never perceived of Indians as desirable equals.

Secretaries

The Secretary was the most junior of the three political positions at the Legation, both in terms of age and career experience. Originally styled as "British personal assistant", the position was designed to have "educative value for junior officers".[224] Changes in the recruitment of colonial service personnel were most tangible here. Among the nineteen incumbents, at least eight had experience of the North-West Frontier Province. In addition to those eight for who service in the North-West Frontier Province is documented, the Legation's last Secretary, Alexander William Redpath, "was familiar with the history of Afghanistan and knew something of Afghan attitudes to the north west frontier".[225] Both, Redpath and Keen were *aides-de-camp* with the government of the North-West Frontier Province.[226] Wickham was not among those with experience of the North-West Frontier Province, but his experience of Tehran was no less sought after.[227]

The Legation's first two Secretaries, Wickham and Fraser-Tytler, also became Counsellors. They entered the service on the same date, together with Parsons. In private correspondence, Fraser-Tytler referred to Wickham as his "rival".[228] Having been Secretary did not automatically qualify for a future posting as Counsellor. For instance, Caroe objected to Russell, who descended from several generations of colonial servants, and did "not recommend" him.[229] Edward Walter Fletcher was a very experienced Secretary, but Fraser-Tytler thought of him as "a really dreadful man, who has done a good deal of harm up here and of whom we would be well rid".[230]

In terms of career trajectories, eight Secretaries came to Kabul following a posting in the North-West Frontier Province. Five Secretaries went in the other direction from Kabul to the North-West Frontier Province. While the North-West Frontier Province provided an important point of reference for Kabul, India's larger imperial connections are equally tangible. As a collective, the Secretaries' careers cover the entire geographical spread of the Foreign and Political Department and the Indian Political Service, with five moving to postings outside of India after Kabul. The increase of service outsiders, notably of British origin, towards the end of the Raj points to a shortage of 'desirable' candidates for India's colonial services and underlines the reluctance to fill sensitive posts with Indian incumbents. Ten Secretaries came to the diplomatic service from the Indian Army, and six from the Indian Civil Service. Ronald Giles Daubeny joined the political service from the Indian Police, and William Richard Connor Green was deputed from the British diplomatic service. Green's appointment from the Foreign Office also indicates an integration between several systems of imperial governance during the Second World War.[231]

MEANINGS, IDENTITIES AND IMPLICATIONS OF DIPLOMACY IN COLONIAL CONTEXTS

In India's system of imperial rule, diplomacy had several meanings, and members of the Indian Political Service had several identities. By means of India's diplomatic service, Afghanistan was incorporated into a wider network of colonial administration. Its job descriptions required colonial officers in administered districts, governmental "advisors" in princely states, Political Agents in the frontier areas and diplomats outside of India.[232] But, there were significant overlaps between diplomatic and colonial practices, which eased the transition between them.[233] Different postings required and generated different governmental skills. In the North-West Frontier Province, Indian Politicals faced at least two different sets of tasks. On the one hand, the so-called settled districts of Hazara, Peshawar, Kohat, Bannu and Dera Ismail Khan rested on the foundations of a colonial bureaucracy. Here, political officers applied the colonial state's fiscal and judicial powers similar to Indian Civil Service officers and representatives of the colonial state employed in districts all over India.[234] On the other hand, these functions of the colonial state did not exist in the so-called tribal areas of the North-West Frontier Province where political officers were styled as Political Agents without the backing of statal bureaucracy. In the idiom of the colonial state's civilising intentions, "administered" districts bordered on "indigenous anarchy".[235] The boundaries between those different colonial and imperial spaces were only loosely defined at best. The Frontier Crimes Regulation treated all inhabitants as imperial objects as opposed to colonial subjects living in India's provinces.[236] The mentioning of certain tribes, of whom colonial officers had particular knowledge, is a reminder that the colonial space on the frontier was "ethnically delimited if not topographically demarcated".[237] The situation was yet more complex for the former Indian Civil Service officers among India's Politicals. They had been trained as judges and revenue collectors in colonial districts. But, at the princely courts, they *acted* as feudal representatives of the imperial monarch to local royalty. They perceived of themselves as standing behind the throne of a local ruler, paralleling privileged 'personal touch' with political access. Chapters 5 and 6 develop further the notions of performing diplomacy as well as its corporeal dimensions. While India's political service differentiated between "advising" and "ruling", service at the Legation in Kabul represented another dimension entirely. In Afghanistan, the political officer "*functioned* in a more traditional diplomatic manner".[238] The political officer's multiple tasks beg the question whether the requisite identities could actually be simply assumed in one place, shed and separated from others by means of moving from one job in one place to another somewhere else. Afghan independence in 1919 extended the roles of India's political officers—colonial servant, Political Agent, Resident, bureaucrat hitherto divided into the two cadres of the frontier and the princely states—to include yet another, namely international diplomacy in a host country, whose independence had been widely recognised. As a consequence, an individual political officer had to master diverging and graded colonial skills during his career. Indian political officers carried with them several colonial governmentalities from one posting to another, combining an array of identities produced by their service at any given point in time. The multitude of colonial identities among the Legation's diplomatic leadership informed its approach to the political relations with Afghanistan between 1922 and 1947. British diplomacy in Kabul was modelled on diplomatic practices already in use in India.

Colonial officers applied colonial precedents to Afghanistan and actively shaped South Asia's international landscape after 1919. Through the export of colonial technologies of rule into new forms of inter-state organisation, they ensured the practical continuation imperial overrule. Political officers in the princely states, in particular, saw themselves as keepers of a "real India", an "Indian India", which had to be enshrined and protected from the changes consequent to increasing democratisation in the wake of Indian nationalism. The courts of princely India exerted on them a 'special romance'.[239] The North-West Frontier Province and Baluchistan generated their own romantic appeal and attractive "spice of life".[240] As diplomats in Kabul, the same individuals were confronted with circumstances, which on paper required them to relinquish all previous experience of dispensing colonial rule. Yet, as district officers and Residents they had radically different and shifting ideas about the sovereignty of South Asian state formations.[241] This point has a larger significance for the book's overall argument, highlighting the inbuilt tensions carried into a global diplomatic system, in which European nations blurred the boundaries between colonialism and diplomacy by employing one and the same set of individuals to dispense colonial justice, sway native royalty, negotiate with tribal leaders and present themselves as exemplary diplomats to former subjects and newly independent states.

TRANSFERRING COLONIAL DIPLOMACY, CULTURES AND TECHNOLOGIES

During the Second World War, several positions were added to the Legation's structure. From 1940, there was an additional Secretary and an Attaché, the latter being tasked with intelligence work.[242] It emerged from the position of the Minister's Personal Assistant, a 'semi-official' post held previously by Esme Williams. From 1940, the incumbents were military officers of the British or Indian Army. Thomas Edward Brownsdon (1940) was a member of the Indian Political Service with Baluchistan experience. Peter Francis Cobham Nicholson (1941) was a probationer. Edward Jervoise Ferrand Scott (1942–1945) was an officer of the Royal Army who was seconded to the Foreign Office diplomatic service. There is no service record for A. W. Morgan, suggesting that published information on Attachés may have been purposely withheld.[243] From 1943 to 1947, Mirza Mumtaz Hasan Kizilbash held the newly created post of Commercial Secretary, which advised on trade relations between India and Afghanistan.[244]

This and the preceding chapter locate the British Legation in Kabul in the midst of extensive colonial networks of family and profession as well as the manifold careers geographies that colonial office in the Indian Empire entailed. The Legation emerges as a colonial institution *en miniature*, which funnelled diverse colonial experiences of governance within the colonial state in India and its empire at large. The Legation's political personnel were primarily drawn from India-wide colonial services. Legation Surgeons and Military Attachés connected it to the Indian Army, Oriental Secretaries and Consuls to the Provincial Services of the North-West Frontier Province and Baluchistan. Office staff originated from the Army Headquarters and the clerical services of India's north-western districts. A largely marginalised group of Indians and Afghans as local intermediaries and household staff created and maintained the material environment in which diplomacy could take place. A small European colonial elite, itself divided sharply by rank, class and gender, administered a much larger group of Indians and Afghans. Paralleling hierarchical asymmetries of colonial society in India, the political elite distanced Indians, included them only reluctantly or partially, subordinated them or barred them from office. On all levels, the Legation closely resembled the structure of colonial localities in India. Itself, it constituted a colonial enclave in the age of independence.

In terms of diplomatic relations, the Legation attracted the entire spectrum of experience of India's political or diplomatic and colonial services. This experience was always informed by colonially shaped ideas. The colonial state trained the Legation's diplomatic staff as colonial administrators, revenue collectors, district judges, political Agents and Residents. When they came to Kabul, all had some experience in exercising and practicing colonial governance. The career geographies revealed that frontier and Afghanistan 'experts' were most wanted for service in Kabul. This practice was installed in order to align colonial policy in the North-West Frontier Province with British diplomacy in Afghanistan, linking the defence of empire with the administration of India and likening India's north-western localities to the state of Afghanistan in terms of social structure, customs, politics and language. This overlap also ensured that British perceptions of Pashtun society informed British perceptions of Afghan politics, as India's frontier districts were framed as colonial representations of Afghanistan, which prepared for diplomatic service in Kabul. As colonial officers became diplomats, colonialism internationalised.

As the Indian likenesses of Afghan notables, the Legation recruited the South Asian members of its political staff from the North-West Frontier Province. The same area also provided the closest equivalent to local recruits. Pashtuns from the North-West Frontier Province were thought to 'understand' as well as fit into Afghanistan's tribal organisation, qualifying them singularly well for jobs, which involved a degree of interaction with Afghans or with fellow Indians at the Legation. In Kabul itself, glimpses of a specific cadre of colonial Afghanistan specialists could also been seen. The importance given to knowledge of local circumstances and important people is indicative of a colonial ambition to administer power rather than manage relations between equals. British diplomacy in Kabul was founded on the specific ethnographic and geographical knowledge of its practitioners. That knowledge was of colonial origin, predating the moment of Afghan independence in 1919 and outliving the end of colonial rule in 1947 as well as, parallel to that process, the Legation's transitioning into the British Embassy in 1948. As Afghanistan emerged from a colonial past, a conservative elite of colonial administrators ensured that the responses to political changes in South Asia were framed in the terms of that past.

Through their links to the colonial state, the Legation personnel were carriers of professional and private knowledge, mentalities and lifestyles, which, in their totality, exercised the colonial influence of the Raj in Afghanistan until and beyond 1947. As Kabul was incorporated into the network of colonial localities, colonial officers in Kabul became agents in the transfer and application of a colonial bureaucracy outside of colonialism's immediate remit. Conditions that had previously applied to institutions of colonial rule in India were now extended and applied to Kabul, the capital of independent Afghanistan. The Afghan polity was approached in the terms of colonial bureaucracy. Rather than witnessing a withdrawal of the colonial state after 1919, the very practice of employing British colonial officers on Afghan soil led to the colonial state's seeming expansion into Kabul. Knowledge, practices and assumptions flowed freely between colonial secretariats in India and Kabul. Moreover, the colonial archive, to which these diplomats contributed, ensured a particular perception of Afghanistan by generations of recruits to the Indian colonial services, in which the independent state was contextualised in terms of colonial administration and imperial defence. This laid the basis for the reaffirmation of commonly held notions of Afghans and Afghanistan and for a recycling of past patterns of history, behavioural conduct and expectations. In this respect, the institutional history of this diplomatic mission reveals the origins of diplomatic interaction in colonial asymmetries of power. The British Legation in Kabul borrowed heavily from the diverse Indian storehouse of colonial practices of power. Its collective biography establishes its pervasive coloniality.

With the transmitters of imperial and colonial technologies of rule in place, the following chapters turn to the practices they imported into Kabul. The next chapters, respectively, look at performative blueprints of encountering Afghans diplomatically (Chapter 5), at the roles of the body (Chapter 6) and at empire's material representations and its concomitant anxieties (Chapter 7).

Notes

1. Mss Eur F226/16, "Keen, Maj Patrick John (b 1910)", Mss Eur F226/24, "Redpath, Maj Alexander William (b 1909)", Mss Eur F226/34, "Worth, Meredith (b 1905), Mss Eur F226, "Memoirs of former members of the Indian Political Service or their wives"; Mss Eur F625, "Papers of Leslie Best (1896–1932) and Sir Norman Bolton (1875–1965)", BL.

2. Wylie to Caroe, 5 September 1941, IOR/R/1/4/997, "Certain changes made in the superior staff of the British Legation, Kabul during 1941–1942", BL.
3. Terence Creagh Coen, *The Indian Political Service: A Study in Indirect Rule* (London: Chatto & Windus, 1971), 237–239. For a more critical assessment see Ian Copland, "The Other Guardians: Ideology and Performance in the Indian Political Service", in *People, Princes and Paramount Power: Society and Politics in the Indian Princely States*, ed. Robert Jeffrey (Oxford: Oxford University Press, 1978), 275–305.
4. Coen, *The Indian Political Service*, 239.
5. See also Maximilian Drephal, "The British Legation in Kabul: The Coloniality of Diplomacy in Independent Afghanistan, 1922–1948" (PhD thesis, Loughborough University, 2015).
6. 747-F, EA, 1939, "Discontinuance of the printing of the Kabul Intelligence Summaries by Foreign Office London"; 969-G, EA, 1939, "Foreign Office Circular regarding the compilation of annual reports. Decision that War Annual reports should be suspended for the time and that only concise political reviews need be sent to the Foreign Office", NAI; Foreign Office circular, 4 November 1939, L 6851/842/405, FO 370/582, 1939, "Question of discontinuation of annual reports during wartime", TNA.
7. Elizabeth Buettner, *Empire Families: Britons and Late Imperial India* (Oxford: Oxford University Press, 2004); Desley Deacon, Penny Russell, and Angela Woollacott, *Transnational Lives: Biographies of Global Modernity, 1700–Present* (Basingstoke: Palgrave Macmillan, 2010); David Lambert and Alan Lester, eds., *Colonial Lives Across the British Empire: Imperial Careering in the Long Nineteenth Century* (Cambridge: Cambridge University Press, 2006).
8. For "imperial transmission", see Benjamin D. Hopkins' forthcoming work on *The Imperial Frontier*: "Frontier as Practice: Frontier Governmentality Along the Nineteenth Century Global Periphery", Unpublished paper, *Contested Borders? Practising Empire, Nation and Region in the Nineteenth and Twentieth Centuries*, German Historical Institute London, 28 April 2018.
9. "Afghanistan: Annual Report, 1935", para. 295, N 1831/1831/97, FO 371/20321, 1936, "Annual report on Afghanistan for 1935"; "Note on the Kandahar Consulate and of certain topics discussed", E 7900/86/97, FO 371/34921, 1943, "Situation at Kandahar", TNA; Squire to H. Weightman, No.44/45/F, 1 February 1946, IOR/L/PS/12/1914, "Coll 4/54(1) Future Diplomatic Representation in Kabul (British and Indian)", BL and E 1392/1392/97, FO 371/52290, 1946, "Afghan-Indian relations as regards Legation", TNA.

10. Squire to E. P. Donaldson, D.O.BLK/9/47, 23 August 1947, IOR/L/PS/12/1914, op. cit., BL.
11. W. Murray Hogben, "An Imperial Dilemma: The Reluctant Indianization of the Indian Political Service", *Modern Asian Studies* 15, no. 4 (1981): 757.
12. Memorandum by Humphrys, 3 March 1922, 68(7)-Est A, F&P, 1923, "1. Appointment of Khan Sahib Mahmud Khan as Consul at Kandahar and of K.S. Syed Muhammad Shah as Consul at Jalalabad. 2. Temporary appointment of Muhammad Khan as Consul at Jalalabad"; 252-E, F&P, 1929, "Question of filling the appointments of British Consuls in Afghanistan by European officers from the cadre of the Political Department of the Government of India", NAI.
13. Foreign and Political Department to Secretary of State for India, 22 June 1922, 68(7)-Est A, F&P, 1923, op. cit., NAI.
14. Memorandum by A. B. Dew, 20 April 1922, 68(7)-Est A, F&P, 1923, op. cit., NAI.
15. Christine Noelle, *State and Tribe in Nineteenth-Century Afghanistan: The Reign of Amir Dost Muhammad Khan, 1826–1863* (Richmond: Curzon Press, 1997), xiii-xiv.
16. Memorandum by Humphrys, 3 March 1922, 68(7)-Est A, F&P, 1923, op. cit., NAI.
17. Ludwig W. Adamec, *Afghanistan, 1900–1923: A Diplomatic History* (Berkeley: University of California Press, 1967), 149.
18. H. N. Bolton to Maconachie, 23 July 1924, 68(7)-Est A, F&P, 1923, op. cit., NAI.
19. Ibid.
20. "Afghanistan: Annual Report, 1936", para. 237, N 843/843/97, FO 371/21070, 1937, "Annual Report on Afghanistan for 1936", TNA.
21. Maconachie to H. N. Bolton, 5 July 1924, 68(7)-Est A, F&P, 1923, op. cit., NAI.
22. Fraser-Tytler to his mother, 23 August 1940, no. 104–107, file 1/1/11, GB165-0326, MECA.
23. He may be identical to the former caretaker of the Legation in Kabul: 313-A, F&P, 1932, "Budget estimates of the British Legation at Kabul for the year 1933–34"; 314-A, EA, 1940, "Budget estimates of the Kabul Legation for 1941–42"; 314-A, EA, 1942, "Budget estimates of the Kabul Legation for 1943–44", NAI.
24. 256-A, F&P, 1924, "Budget estimates of the British Legation Kabul for the year 1925–26"; 313-A, F&P, 1932, op. cit., NAI.
25. "Note on the Kandahar Consulate and of certain topics discussed", E 7900/86/97, FO 371/34921, 1943, op. cit., TNA.
26. Pros., February 1920, Nos. 22–76, "Return to India of the members of the British Agency Kabul", NAI.

27. Adamec, *Afghanistan, 1900–1923*, 91.
28. Coen, *The Indian Political Service*, 237. See also Shah Mahmoud Hanifi, *Connecting Histories in Afghanistan: Market Relations and State Formation on a Colonial Frontier* (Stanford: Stanford University Press, 2011), 154.
29. Michael H. Fisher, *Indirect Rule in India: Residents and the Residency System, 1764–1858* (Oxford: Oxford University Press, 1991), 352–357.
30. "Rough note on the proposal for a British Minister at Kabul", S. E. Pears, 24 November 1921, 2, 68(20)-Est, F&P, 1923, "Note by Mr S. E. Pears, C.S.I., C.I.E., on the proposed establishment of a British Legation at Kabul", NAI.
31. See also James Onley, *The Arabian Frontier of the British Raj: Merchants, Rulers, and the British in the Nineteenth-Century Gulf* (New York: Oxford University Press, 2007), 42–43. Contrary to the entry "dragoman" on page xxvi, the Oriental Secretaries in Kabul were of Indian origins until 1947.
32. Sana Haroon, *Frontier of Faith: Islam in the Indo-Afghan Borderland* (London: Hurst, 2007), 220; Onley, *The Arabian Frontier of the British Raj*, xxiii.
33. W. Murray Hogben, "British Civil-Military Relations on the North-West Frontier of India", in *Swords and Covenants*, ed. Adrian W. Preston and Peter Dennis (London: Croom Helm, 1976), 136; Murray Hogben, "An Imperial Dilemma", 753.
34. 68(8)-E, F&P, 1922, "Oriental Secretary for the Kabul Legation", NAI.
35. Letter by Humphrys, April 1922, IOR/R/1/4/1347, "Personal File of Khan Bahadur Nawab Muzaffar Khan, Late of the Political Department", BL.
36. See also Leon B. Poullada, *Reform and Rebellion in Afghanistan, 1919–1929: King Amanullah's Failure to Modernize a Tribal Society* (Ithaca: Cornell University Press, 1973), 266.
37. Basil John Gould, *The Jewel in the Lotus: Recollections of an Indian Political* (London: Chatto & Windus, 1957), 47, 105.
38. For the overlap of medical and political roles see "surgeon" in Onley, *The Arabian Frontier of the British Raj*, xxix.
39. "Report on the Kabul Mission, by Sir H. R. C. Dobbs, K.C.S.I., K.C.I.E", N 1450/59/97, FO 371/8076, 1922, "Negotiations conducted by British Mission in Kabul during 1921", TNA.
40. Shah Wali, *My Memoirs* (Kabul, 1970), 51.
41. 223-E, F&P, 1929, "Question of the appointment of P.C.S. officers to the Political Department. Selection of Khan Bhadur Mahabub [sic] Ali for appointment to the Political Department", NAI.
42. Louis Dupree, *Afghanistan* (Karachi: Oxford University Press, 1997), 248–251; Shah Mahmoud Hanifi, "The Pashtun Counter-Narrative", *Middle East Critique* 25, no. 4 (2016): 385–400.

43. "Mahbub Ali Khan, Khan Bahadur Shaikh, O.B.E. (b. Mar., 1894)", *India Office and Burma Office List for 1947*; "Mahbub Ali Khan, Khan Bahadur Shaikh, O.B.E. (b. Mar., 1894)", *India Office and Burma Office List for 1939*.
44. 12(5)-E, EA, 1940, "Further retention in the service of Khan Bahadur Sikandar Khan, as Oriental Secretary, British Legation, Kabul", NAI; "Memorandum of Judicial Procedure in Afghanistan", no. 4, FO 402/19, 1938, "Further correspondence respecting Afghanistan: Part XXI", TNA.
45. "Excerpt from letters of credentials regarding M. A. K. Malik from M. F. O'Dwyer, late Governor Punjab, dated 29 November 1925", 27(4)-E, F&P, 1929, "Applications for Employment in the Political Department", NAI. Coen, *The Indian Political Service*, 146–148; Murray Hogben, "An Imperial Dilemma", 766, n. 50; Intelligence summary no. 46, 7-F, EA, 1942, "Weekly Intelligence Summaries from British Legation, Kabul, for the Year 1942", NAI.
46. Percy Sykes, "Afghanistan: The Present Position", *Journal of The Royal Central Asian Society* 27, no. 2 (1940): 141–171.
47. Audrey Harris, "From Kabul to the Oxus I: Afghanistan by Lorry. Travels of an English Girl", *The Times*, 5 April 1937, 15; Audrey Harris, "From Kabul to the Oxus II: The Afghans. A Motor-Car Over a Mountain", *The Times*, 6 April 1937, 15; Audrey Harris, "From Kabul to the Oxus III: Amid the Bare Mountains: The Turkestan Horses", *The Times*, 7 April 1937, 17.
48. "Outrage at a London Meeting. Sir Michael O'Dwyer Shot Dead. Lord Zetland and Two Former Governors Wounded", *The Times*, 14 March 1940, 8.
49. Murray Hogben, "An Imperial Dilemma", 766, n. 50.
50. "2. Passports and Rahdaris – British Indian subjects – Legation employees", "3. Preparation of British Indian passports and green passes", 20, IOR/R/12/200, "British Legation, Kabul: Office Manual", BL.
51. Maconachie to Howell, 11 March 1930, 252-E, F&P, 1929, op. cit., NAI.
52. See also Thomas Jefferson Barfield, *Afghanistan: A Cultural and Political History* (Princeton: Princeton University Press, 2010), 128; Coen, *The Indian Political Service*, 57; Onley, *The Arabian Frontier of the British Raj*, xxix, 39.
53. "Millar, George MacGregor", Dirom Grey Crawford, *Roll of the Indian Medical Services 1615–1930* (London: Thacker, 1930); "Millar, George McGregor, O.B.E., M.B., Lt Col., I.M.S., Retd. (b. 12th Sept., 1880)", *India Office and Burma Office List for 1939*; "G. MacG. Millar, O.B.E., M.B., B.Ch.", *British Medical Journal* 1, no. 5287 (5 May 1962): 1281–1283.
54. "Colonel Thorburn: Adventures in India and Persia", *The Times*, 28 January 1937, 16.

55. Ibid.
56. "Thorburn, Harold Hay", Crawford, *Roll of the Indian Medical Services 1615–1930.*
57. 23(2)-E, F&P, 1929, "Appointment of Major H.H. Elliot, M.B.E. M.C., I.M.S., to officiate as an Agency Surgeon. 2. The services of Major H.H. Elliot, M.B.E. M.C., I.M.S., placed at the disposal of the Government of India, Department of Education Health and Lands"; 10(12)-E, F&P, 1930, "Appointment of Major H.H. Elliot, M.B.E. M.C., M.B., F.R.C.S.E., I.M.S. as Surgeon to the British Legation, Kabul", NAI; "Afghanistan: Annual Report, 1933", para. 284, N 2031/2031/97, FO 371/18259, 1934, "Annual report on Afghanistan", TNA.
58. "Elliot, Henry Hawes, M.B.E., M.C., M.B., F.R.C.S.E., Lt-Col., I.M.S. (surg. to Viceroy), (b. 22nd May, 1891)", *India Office and Burma Office List for 1939*; "Elliot, Henry Hawes", Crawford, *Roll of the Indian Medical Services 1615–1930*; "Elliot, Lt-Col Henry Hawes", *Who's Who & Who Was Who 7*, 1971–1980 (London: A & C Black, 1981); "Lieutenant-Colonel H. H. Elliot", *British Medical Journal* 2, no. 5804 (1 April 1972): 54–55; IOR/L/MIL/14/68688, "Elliot, Henry Hawes", BL.
59. "Hogg, William Peat", Crawford, *Roll of the Indian Medical Services 1615–1930*; "Hogg, William Peat, D.S.O., M.C., Lt.-Col., I.M.S. (resdy. Surg. Mewar) (b. 29th Feb., 1888)", *India Office and Burma Office List for 1939*; 117(4)-E, F&P, 1930, "Confirmation of Majors J.P. Huban, O.B.E., I.M.S., and W.P.Hogg, D.S.O., M.C., I.M.S., as Agency Surgeons under the Foreign and Political Department", NAI; IOR/L/MIL/14/11881, "William Peat Hogg", BL.
60. Note by Lothian, 25 November 1926, 2(56)-E, F&P, 1926, "Grant of leave to Lt. Col. H. Hay Thorburn, C.I.E., I.M.S., Agency Surgeon, Kabul, with effect from the 26th April 1927 and selection of Major W. P. Hogg as Agency Surgeon to officiate vice Lt. Col. H. Hay Thorburn", NAI; "MacGregor, Robert Forrester Douglas, M.C., M.B:, Lt.Col., I.M.S.", *India Office and Burma Office List for 1939*; "Obituary: R. F. D. MacGregor, C.I.E., M.C., M.B., Ch.B. M.R.C.P.Ed", *British Medical Journal* 2, no. 5205 (8 October 1960): 1098–1098; "Obituary: R. F. D. MacGregor, C.I.E., M.C., M.B., Ch.B. M.R.C.P.Ed", *British Medical Journal* 2, no. 5195 (30 July 1960): 395–395; "MacGregor, Robert Forrester Douglas", Crawford, *Roll of the Indian Medical Services 1615–1930*; "MacGregor, Lieut.-Colonel Robert Forrester Douglas, C.I.E.", *Who's Who & Who Was Who* 5, 1951–1960 (London: A & C Black, 1967).
61. "Lucas, Edmund Stanley Sayer", Crawford, *Roll of the Indian Medical Services 1615–1930*; "Lucas, E. S. S., Captain, I.M.S. (civ. Surg.) (b. 1st Nov., 1897)", *India Office and Burma Office List for 1939*; IOR/L/MIL/14/15538, "Lucas, Edmund Stanley Sayer", BL; 49(5)-

4 BIOGRAPHY AND IMPERIAL GOVERNANCE 159

Est, F&P, 1931, "Application from Capt. E. S. S. Lucas, I.M.S. for employment as Agency Surgeon under the F&P Dept.", NAI.
62. Report by Maconachie, 7 November 1933, IOR/L/MIL/14/15538, op. cit, BL.
63. "Colonel H W Farrell", *British Medical Journal* 291, no. 6491 (3 August 1985): 357–359; "Farrell, Henry William", Crawford, *Roll of the Indian Medical Services 1615–1930*.
64. Note by H. A. F. Metcalfe, 8 August 1932, IOR/R/1/4/923, "Application from Captain H.W. Farrell, I.M.S. for Medical Employment under the Foreign and Political Department", BL.
65. Note by E. Mieville, 12 August 1932, ibid.
66. Maconachie to Metcalfe, 27 July 1934, IOR/L/MIL/14/15451, "Annual Confidential Reports on Farrell, Henry William", BL.
67. Fraser-Tytler to his mother, 28 November 1940, no. 153–155, file 1/1/11, GB165-0326; Fraser-Tytler to his mother, 29 August 1940, no. 108–110, file 1/1/11, GB165-0326; Fraser-Tytler to his mother, 25 July 1940, no. 90–93, file 1/1/11, GB165-0326; Fraser-Tytler to his mother, 9 June 1939, no. 64–67, file 1/1/10, GB165-0326; Fraser-Tytler to his mother, 21 July 1939, no. 88–90, file 1/1/10, GB165-0326, MECA; "Obituary: Lieutenant Colonel William Joseph Moody", *British Medical Journal* 299, 5 August 1989, 387.
68. "Medical Affairs in Afghanistan", 13(13)-IA, EA, 1947, "Report by the Legation Surgeon on Medical Affairs in Afghanistan", NAI; "Ledgard, H. A.", *India Office and Burma Office List for 1947*. See also Chapter 6.
69. Maureen O'Connor Witter, "Sanctioned Spying: The Development of the Military Attaché in the Nineteenth Century", in *Intelligence and Statecraft: The Use and Limits of Intelligence in International Society*, ed. Peter Jackson and Jennifer Siegel (Westport, CT: Praeger, 2005), 87–108. See also James Louis Hevia, *The Imperial Security State: British Colonial Knowledge and Empire-Building in Asia* (Cambridge: Cambridge University Press, 2012), 107–151; Alfred Vagts, *Defense and Diplomacy: The Soldier and the Conduct of Foreign Relations* (New York: King's Crown Press, 1956); Alfred Vagts, *The Military Attaché* (Princeton: Princeton University Press, 1967).
70. "Rough note on the proposal for a British Minister at Kabul", S. E. Pears, 24 November 1921, 2, 68(20)-Est, F&P, 1923, op. cit., NAI.
71. Maximilian Drephal, "Contesting Independence: Colonial Cultures of Sport and Diplomacy in Afghanistan, 1919–1949", in *Sport and Diplomacy: Games Within Games*, ed. J. Simon Rofe (Manchester: Manchester University Press, 2018), 89–109.
72. Squire to Bevin, 3 August 1946, E 7972/66/97, FO 371/52277, 1946, "Independence Celebrations", TNA.

73. G. E. W., "Obituary: Major-General William Archibald Kenneth Fraser, C.B., C.B.E., D.S.O. and bar, M.V.O., M.C.", *Journal of The Royal Central Asian Society* 56, no. 2 (1969): 209–210.
74. "Lockhart, Gen. Sir Rob (MacGregor Macdonald)", *Who's Who & Who Was Who* 7, 1971–1980 (London: A & C Black, 1981).
75. Norval Mitchell, *Sir George Cunningham: A Memoir* (Edinburgh: William Blackwood, 1968), 15; Marsh and Tripodi follow him: Brandon Marsh, *Ramparts of Empire: British Imperialism and India's Afghan Frontier, 1918–1948* (Basingstoke: Palgrave Macmillan, 2015), 27; Christian Tripodi, *Edge of Empire: The British Political Officer and Tribal Administration on the North-West Frontier, 1877–1947* (Aldershot: Ashgate, 2011), 30.
76. IOR/L/MIL/9/488/37-45, "Lancaster, Alexander", BL: his father's professions are given as lead miner and farmer; Fraser-Tytler to his mother, 22 October 1936, no. 150–153, file 1/1/7, GB165-0326, MECA.
77. Milan Hauner, "The Soviet Threat to Afghanistan and India 1938–1940", *Modern Asian Studies* 15, no. 2 (1981): 302, 303, 306.
78. "Papers associated with Col Alexander Stalker Lancaster, 10th Gurkha Rifles, 1917–1956; relating principally to his tours of duty as Military Attache in Kabul, 1934–1935 and 1940–1948", NAM; 633-F, EA, 1943, "Tour of British Minister and Military Attaché, Kabul in North Afghanistan", NAI; "General Report on a Tour carried out by the Military Attaché, Kabul, in North-Eastern Afghanistan during September and October 1946", E 13387/13387/97, FO 371/52304, 1946, "Report of a Tour of North Eastern Afghanistan by the British Military Attaché at Kabul. Code 97 File 11387"; "General Report on a Tour carried out the Military Attaché Kabul in N.E. Afghanistan between 4th and 23rd June 1948", F 10799/167/97, FO 371/69454, 1948, "Tour by Colonel Lancaster of North Eastern Afghanistan"; "General Report on a tour carried out by the M.A. Kabul during the period 2nd – 9th October, 1948", F 15935/392/97, FO 371/69459, 1948, "Military Attaché's Report on a recent tour from Kabul to Kandahar, Quetta and Girishk", TNA.
79. Minutes on file cover, F 10799/167/97, FO 371/69454, 1948, op. cit., TNA.
80. On the "demi-official existence" of the term prior to 1937 see Coen, *The Indian Political Service*, 54–55; Fisher, *Indirect Rule in India*, 456; Onley, *The Arabian Frontier of the British Raj*, xx.
81. For the Secretariat as a "closed shop to the military cadre" cf. Copland, "The Other Guardians", 295.
82. Coen, *The Indian Political Service*, 5, 35; Fisher, *Indirect Rule in India*, 456.

83. Ian Copland, *The British Raj and the Indian Princes: Paramountcy in Western India, 1857–1930* (Bombay: Orient Longman, 1982), 69–87; Copland, "The Other Guardians", 286–289.
84. E.g. IOR/R/1/4/1006, "Confidential Report on Major W.K. Fraser-Tytler, M.C., of the Indian Political Service", BL.
85. For instance, J. P. Thompson to G. Cunningham, 11 May 1927, 428(2)-E, F&P, 1927, "Selection of I.C.S. Officers for the Political Department of the Government of India, 1927", NAI; letter by Humphrys, 20 October 1903, IOR/R/1/4/1334, "Personal file of Lieut. Colonel F.H. Humphrys, C.E.I., late of the Political Department", BL; 49(5)-Est, F&P, 1931, "Application from Capt. E. S. S. Lucas, I.M.S. for employment as Agency Surgeon under the F&P Dept.", NAI.
86. For recruits from the Indian Civil Service see IOR/R/1/4/1331, "Personal File of Mr A.W. Fagan, Late of the Political Department", BL; "Rules regulating the admission of junior military officers to the Political Department of the Government of India", 329, 39-Est, F&P, 1922–1923, "Applications from Indian Army Officers for admission to the Political Department (REJECTED)", NAI; The British diplomatic service held similar ideals. Ernest Satow, *A Guide to Diplomatic Practice*, vol. 1 (London: Longmans, Green and Co., 1917), 184.
87. Copland, "The Other Guardians", 290; Marsh, *Ramparts of Empire*, 28; Barbara N. Ramusack, *The Indian Princes and Their States* (Cambridge: Cambridge University Press, 2004), 103.
88. "Rules regulating the admission of junior military officers to the Political Department of the Government of India", 329, 39-Est, F&P, 1922–1923, op. cit., NAI; "Rules regulating the admission of junior members of the Indian Civil Service to the Political Department of the Government of India", IOR/R/1/4/1331, op. cit., BL.
89. E.g. Fisher, *Indirect Rule in India*, 456.
90. As transcribed from IOR/R/1/4/1331, op. cit., BL.
91. Sumit Sarkar, *Modern India, 1885–1947* (New York: Palgrave Macmillan, 1983), 6.
92. See also Ranajit Guha, "Dominance Without Hegemony and Its Historiography", in *Subaltern Studies VI: Writings on South Asian History and Society*, ed. Ranajit Guha (Delhi: Oxford University Press, 1992), 210–309; on "scholar-administrators" see Magnus Marsden and Benjamin D. Hopkins, *Fragments of the Afghan Frontier* (London: Hurst & Company, 2011), 1–22.
93. Fraser-Tytler to his mother, 19 December 1930, no. 23–24, file 1/1/3, GB165-0326; Fraser-Tytler to his mother, 16 January 1931, no. 4–5, file 1/1/4, GB165-0326, MECA.
94. IOR/L/PS/20/B285, "A Précis on Afghan Affairs from February 1919 to September 1927", BL; "Statement of Services of Mr. R. R. Maconachie,

C.I.E., I.C.S.", N 5646/5646/97, FO 371/14001, 1929, "Appointment of His Majesty's Minister to Kabul", TNA.
95. See also Purnima Bose, *Organizing Empire: Individualism, Collective Agency, and India* (Durham: Duke University Press, 2003), 186.
96. Coen, *The Indian Political Service*, 36. Cf. Copland, "The Other Guardians", 298–299; Christian Tripodi, "Peacemaking Through Bribes or Cultural Empathy? The Political Officer and Britain's Strategy Towards the North-West Frontier, 1901–1945", *Journal of Strategic Studies* 31, no. 1 (2008): 127–128.
97. Buettner, *Empire Families*; Ralph Crane and Radhika Mohanram, *Imperialism as Diaspora: Race, Sexuality, and History in Anglo-India* (Liverpool: Liverpool University Press, 2013); Lambert and Lester, *Colonial Lives Across the British Empire*.
98. William Kerr Fraser-Tytler, "In Memoriam", *Journal of The Royal Central Asian Society* 49, no. 2 (1962): 118–119; "Maconachie, James Robert", *India List and India Office List for 1920*; "Maconachie, Sir Richard (Roy)", *Who's Who 2011 & Who Was Who* (Oxford University Press, 2011).
99. See "Information to be supplied by a candidate for Political employ", IOR/R/1/4/1334, op. cit., BL. Nine application files could be traced and accessed, which spread evenly across the Legation's top ranks. They include two Ministers (Humphrys, Fraser-Tytler), four Counsellors (Fagan, again Fraser-Tytler, Ryan, Hailey), three Secretaries (again Fagan, again Fraser-Tytler, Russell) and three Surgeons (Elliot, Lucas, Farrell).
100. For instance those in the IOR/MIL/14 and IOR/MIL/7 series at the British Library.
101. See Dodd's application: IOR/L/MIL/7/13115, "Dodd, Percy Charles Russell", BL. Among those who appear in the records are a Counsellor (Wickham), three Secretaries (Pettigrew, Galloway, also Wickham) and three Military Attachés (Dodd, Erskine, Harvey-Kelly).
102. IOR/R/1/4/1334, op. cit., BL; "Humphrys, General Sir Francis John", *Who's Who & Who Was Who* 4, 1941–1950 (London: A & C Black, 1967).
103. For further reading on the "handsome and talented" (Winston Churchill) Harold Deane see Murray Hogben, "British Civil-Military Relations on the North-West Frontier of India", 134–137.
104. According to his granddaughter, Horatio Norman Bolton, who also worked with Harold Deane and George Roos Keppel in the North-West Frontier Province, had proposed to Gertrude Mary Deane, whilst Francis Henry Humphrys was rejected by Horatio Norman Bolton's later wife, Ethel Frances Mary Mansfield. Mss Eur F625/9, op. cit., BL.
105. Item 9g, IOR/L/PO/8/9a-9j, "Objection of Sir Guy Cooper to appointment of Major Humphrys as Military Secretary", BL; "Christenings", *The Times*, 8 July 1946, 7.

106. "Death of Sir James Fraser-Tytler", *The Times*, 4 February 1914, 11; Fraser-Tytler to his mother, 17 April 1931, no. 20–21, file 1/1/4, GB165-0326, MECA: Fraser-Tytler described the 1839 invasion of Afghanistan as a "very discreditable campaign"; Fraser-Tytler to his mother, 24 November 1936, no. 169–174, file 1/1/7, GB165-0326, MECA: Fraser-Tytler did not believe that his ancestor William of Aldourie planted the explosive charges which enabled the storming of the Fort at Ghazni.
107. The Viscount Fincastle and Percy Clare Elliott-Lockhart, *A Frontier Campaign. A Narrative of the Operations of the Malakand and Buner Field Forces, 1897–1898*.
108. Tripodi, *Edge of Empire*, 27 notes that Fraser-Tytler's career was supported by the Governor-General of Australia, Lord Denham.
109. Fraser-Tytler to his mother, 24 November 1936, no. 169–174, file 1/1/7, GB165-0326, MECA.
110. "Fagan, Christopher Sullivan (1781–1813)", "Fagan, George Hickson (1810–1876)", V. C. P. Hodson, *List of the Officers of the Bengal Army, 1758–1834* (London: Constable & Co, 1927–1947).
111. "Fagan, Sir Patrick James, K.C.I.E., C.S.I., Late Indian C.S.", *India Office and Burma Office List for 1939*; IOR/R/1/4/1331, op. cit., BL.
112. Sir Patrick Fagan, "District Administration in the United Provinces, Central Provinces, and the Panjab, 1818–1858", in *The Indian Empire, 1858–1918*, ed. H. H. Dodwell, vol. 6, *The Cambridge History of India* (Cambridge: Cambridge University Press, 1932), 75–94; Sir Patrick Fagan, "District Administration in the United Provinces, Central Provinces, and the Panjab, 1858–1918", in *The Indian Empire, 1858–1918*, ed. H. H. Dodwell, vol. 6, *The Cambridge History of India* (Cambridge: Cambridge University Press, 1932), 276–293.
113. Maconachie to Ogilvie, 3 October 1924, "Confirmation of probationers in the Political Dept. 1924 and 1925", 112-E, 1924, F&P, NAI.
114. Mitchell, *Sir George Cunningham*, 46.
115. Marsh, *Ramparts of Empire*, 27; Tripodi, *Edge of Empire*, 40. For Sandeman's impact on colonial administration see Marsden and Hopkins, *Fragments of the Afghan Frontier*, 49–74; Christian Tripodi, "'Good for One but Not the Other': The 'Sandeman System' of Pacification as Applied to Baluchistan and the North-West Frontier, 1877–1947", *The Journal of Military History* 73, no. 3 (2009): 767–802.
116. Gould, *The Jewel in the Lotus*, 99.
117. "Wickham, Colonel William James Richard", *Who's Who & Who Was Who* 3, 1929–1940 (London: A & C Black, 1967). Colonel Wickham's father was Major E. T. Wickham. His wife Mary was related to a former Surgeon-General.

118. IOR/L/MIL/9/301/44(7), "Wickham, Edward Thomas Ruscombe"; IOR/L/MIL/9/307-4, "Wickham, Edward Thomas Ruscombe", BL.
119. IOR/R/1/4/1005, "File 8(4)-E(S)/1943 Confidential Report on Major C.C.L. Ryan of the I.P. Service", BL.
120. Ibid. See also IOR/R/1/4/1298, "Personal File (Part II) of Captain C.C.L. Ryan, of the Political Department", BL.
121. IOR/L/MIL/14/16995, "Annual Confidential Reports on Hailey, P C, Lt, 18th Royal Garhwal Rifles", BL; "Hailey, Hammet Reginald Clode, C.I.E., C.B.E., B.A., Late Indian C.S. (United Provs.)", *India Office List for 1936*.
122. H. R. C. Hailey, "The Finances of India, 1858–1918", in *The Indian Empire, 1858–1918*, ed. H. H. Dodwell, vol. 6, *The Cambridge History of India* (Cambridge: Cambridge University Press, 1932), 314–34.
123. John W. Cell, "Hailey, (William) Malcolm, Baron Hailey (1872–1969), Administrator in India and Writer", *Oxford Dictionary of National Biography* (Oxford University Press, 2004).
124. IOR/R/1/4/1255, "Personal File (Part II) of Lieut. P.C. Hailey, of the Political Department", BL.
125. "Griffin, Sir Lepel Henry, K.C.S.I., Late Bengal C.S.", *India List and India Office List for 1900*; Katherine Prior, "Griffin, Sir Lepel Henry (1838–1908), Administrator in India", *Oxford Dictionary of National Biography* (Oxford University Press, 2004). See also Ramusack, *The Indian Princes and Their States*, 102.
126. 28-E, F&P, 1927, "Candidature of Mr. L.C.L. Griffin, I.C.S.(U.P.) for appointment to the Political Department of the Government of India. Protest of the U.P. Govt. against recruiting their European I.C.S. officers for Pol. Deptt."; Note by J. P. Thompson, 7 June 1927, 428(2)-E, F&P, 1927, op. cit., NAI.
127. Letter of recommendation, Lt. Col. K. Dunolly, 1 March 1923, IOR/R/1/4/1297, "Personal File (Part II) of Captain A.A. Russell, M.C., of the Political Department", BL.
128. Letter from A. A. Russell, 15 February 1924, ibid. See also Coen, *The Indian Political Service*, 35–36.
129. "Leslie William Haslett Duncan Best O.B.E. M.C.", Mss Eur F625/9, "Biographies and photographs", BL.
130. IOR/L/MIL/14/1202, "Galloway, Arnold Crawshaw", BL; Galloway features prominently in Rosita Forbes, *Forbidden Road: Kabul to Samarkand* (London: Cassill & Co, 1937).
131. Mss Eur F226/16, op. cit., BL.
132. Aurel Stein expressed his gratitude to William John Keen, Keen's uncle, for facilitating his passage along the North-West Frontier Province. The same book is dedicated to Harold Deane, in addition to mentioning Francis Henry Humphrys and his wife Gertrude in Kabul as well as Herbert

Aubrey Francis Metcalfe. Marc Aurel Stein, *On Alexander's Track to the Indus: Personal Narrative of Explorations on the North-West Frontier of India* (London: Macmillan, 1929).
133. Mss Eur F226/16, op. cit., BL; "Keen, Col. Sir Frederick John", *Who's Who & Who Was Who* 1, 1897–1915 (London: A & C Black, 1966); "Keen, Brigadier Patrick Houston", *Who's Who & Who Was Who* 5, 1951–1960 (London: A & C Black, 1967); "Keen, Patrick John", *Who's Who & Who Was Who* 8, 1981–1990 (London: A & C Black, 1991); "Keen, Lt.-Col. William John", *Who's Who & Who Was Who* 5, 1951–1960 (London: A & C Black, 1967). See also Tripodi, *Edge of Empire*, 30.
134. IOR/L/MIL/9/301/148(5), "Pettigrew, Guy Irvine", BL.
135. "Recollections of a political officer in India (1929–1947)", A. W. Redpath, 92–93, Mss Eur F226/24, op. cit., BL.
136. Copland, *The British Raj and the Indian Princes*, 69–87; Copland, "The Other Guardians"; Fisher, *Indirect Rule in India*, 70–212, 454–457; Michael H. Fisher, "Indirect Rule in the British Empire: The Foundations of the Residency System in India (1764–1858)", *Modern Asian Studies* 18, no. 3 (1984): 393–428; Murray Hogben, "British Civil-Military Relations on the North-West Frontier of India"; Murray Hogben, "An Imperial Dilemma"; Marsh, *Ramparts of Empire*, 22–30; Onley, *The Arabian Frontier of the British Raj*, 38–43; Ramusack, *The Indian Princes and Their States*, 98–105; Tripodi, *Edge of Empire*, 21–48.
137. As quoted in Coen, *The Indian Political Service*, 37. Also requoted from there in Marsh, *Ramparts of Empire*, 25; Tripodi, *Edge of Empire*, 25; "Butler, Sir Spencer Harcourt, G.C.S.I., G.C.I.E., Late Indian C.S.", *India Office List for 1936*.
138. Ann Laura Stoler, "On Degrees of Imperial Sovereignty", *Public Culture* 18, no. 1 (2006): 136.
139. "Extract from private letter from Lord Willingdon to Sir Samuel Hoare, dated 26th August, 1934", IOR/L/PS/12/1913, "Coll 4/54 British Legation: appointment of Lt Col Sir W Kerr Frazer-Tytler [sic], Sir Francis Wylie and Mr G F Squire", BL.
140. E.g. Murray Hogben, "British Civil-Military Relations on the North-West Frontier of India".
141. Arthur Hamilton Grant to Denys Bray, 3 September 1919, Pros., February 1920, Nos. 22–76, op. cit., NAI.
142. Gould, *The Jewel in the Lotus*, 93.
143. Charles Lindholm, "Images of the Pathan: The Usefulness of Colonial Ethnography", *European Journal of Sociology* 21, no. 2 (1980): 352.
144. Ibid., 357.
145. Ibid.
146. Nivi Manchanda has added another 'image of the Pathan' to the history of Anglo-American engagement in Afghanistan after 2001 in Nivi

Manchanda, "Queering the Pashtun: Afghan Sexuality in the Homo-Nationalist Imaginary", *Third World Quarterly* 36, no. 1 (2015): 130–146.
147. Fraser-Tytler to Caroe, 7 November 1940, IOR/L/PS/12/1913, op. cit., BL
148. Ibid.
149. "Humphrys, Sir Francis Henry, G.C.M.G., G.C.V.O., K.B.E., C.I.E., Lt.-Col., I.A.", *India Office List for 1936.*
150. Gould, *The Jewel in the Lotus*, 93.
151. Note by Arthur Hirtzel, 15 December 1921, no. 57, P. 5307, "British Minister at Kabul: offer of appointment to Major Humphrys", IOR/L/PS/10/957/2, "File 15/1921 Pt 4 Afghanistan: Kabul Mission 1921; Question of Consular Establishments; British Minister at Kabul; Afghan Objection to Mr S E Pears; Appointment of Major Humphrys", BL; Humphrys to Wakely, 26 Dec 1921, no. 45, P. 5584, "Afghanistan: appointment of Major Humphrys as British Minister", ibid.
152. Foreign Office to The Under Secretary of State, India Office, N 12236/25/97, 23 November 1921, no. 81, P. 5289, "Afghanistan: Question of appointment of British Minister: Govt. of India proposes Major Humphrys", ibid., BL.
153. "From Viceroy, Foreign and Political Department, 25 November 1921", no. 77, P. 5289, "Afghanistan: Question of appointment of British Minister: Govt. of India proposes Major Humphrys", ibid.
154. Adamec, *Afghanistan, 1900–1923*, 151.
155. "From Viceroy, Foreign and Political Department, 25 November 1921", no. 77, P. 5289, "Afghanistan: Question of appointment of British Minister: Govt. of India proposes Major Humphrys", IOR/L/PS/10/957/2, op. cit., BL.
156. Ibid.
157. Viceroy, Foreign and Political Dept., to Secretary of State for India, 30 November 1921, no. 73, P. 5289, "Afghanistan: Question of appointment of British Minister: Govt. of India proposes Major Humphrys", ibid. Other contenders in addition to Dobbs, Pears and Humphrys were Keyes, Dew and Pipon: Arthur Hirtzel, 30 November 1921, "Copy of notes on P. 5258", no. 69, P. 5307, "British Minister at Kabul: offer of appointment to Major Humphrys", ibid.
158. Adamec, *Afghanistan, 1900–1923*, 149.
159. Note by Curzon, 5 December 1921, no. 62, P. 5307, "British Minister at Kabul: offer of appointment to Major Humphrys", IOR/L/PS/10/957/2, op. cit., BL.
160. Ibid.
161. From Secretary of State to Viceroy, Foreign Department, 3rd January 1922, N 199/59/97, FO 371/8076, 1922, "Departure of Major

Humphrys to Afghanistan"; Copy of Telegram, Viceroy, Foreign & Political Dept to Secretary of State for India, 15 February 1922, N 1592/59/97, FO 371/8076, 1922, "Relations between Great Britain and Afghanistan", TNA.
162. Government of India, Foreign and Political Department, no. 9, 7 October 1926, para. 2, N 5344/1716/97, FO 371/11744, 1926, "Anglo-Afghan relations", TNA.
163. Gould, *The Jewel in the Lotus*, 109, 111. In 1929, Nadir Khan became Nadir Shah when he ascended the Afghan throne: Dupree, *Afghanistan*, 459.
164. Fraser-Tytler, "In Memoriam", 119. See also Poullada, *Reform and Rebellion in Afghanistan*, 265; "Maconachie, Sir Richard Roy, K.B.E., C.I.E, B.A., Late Indian C.S.", *India Office and Burma Office List for 1939*.
165. "Fraser-Tytler, William Kerr, C.M.G., M.C. Lt.-Col., Indian Political Service", *India Office and Burma Office List for 1939*; "Fraser-Tytler, Lt-Col Sir William Kerr", *Who's Who 2011 & Who Was Who* (Oxford University Press, 2011).
166. "Paragraph included in S/S's lr. to VR of 25.5.41", IOR/L/PS/12/1913, op. cit., BL.
167. See also Christian Tripodi, "'Politicals', Tribes and Musahibans: The Indian Political Service and Anglo-Afghan Relations 1929–39", *The International History Review* 34, no. 4 (2012): 865–886.
168. E.g. William Kerr Fraser-Tytler, *Afghanistan: A Study of Political Developments in Central and Southern Asia*, 2nd ed. (London: Oxford University Press, 1953), xii–xiv.
169. For further reading on the civilian (diplomatic, political) and military ideals of India's political service and their opposition to one another see Copland, *The British Raj and the Indian Princes*, 69–87; Copland, "The Other Guardians", 286–289; Murray Hogben, "British Civil-Military Relations on the North-West Frontier of India"; Tripodi, *Edge of Empire*, 39–47.
170. Copland, "The Other Guardians", 280–281, 294.
171. Fraser-Tytler to his mother, 13 May 1932, no. 32–33, file 1/1/5, GB165-0326, MECA, emphasis added.
172. Fraser-Tytler to his mother, 20 September 1935, no. 96–98, file 1/1/6, GB165-0326, MECA.
173. Benjamin D. Hopkins, "The Frontier Crimes Regulation and Frontier Governmentality", *The Journal of Asian Studies* 74, no. 2 (2015): 369–389.
174. Fraser-Tytler to his mother, 1 September 1938, no. 104–106, file 1/1/9, GB165-0326, MECA; 542-F, EA, 1938, "Objections raised by the Afghan government against the 'Forward Policy' of the Government of India", NAI.

175. Peel to Collier, draft letter, 15 June 1939, IOR/L/PS/12/1913, op. cit., BL
176. "Extract from private letter from Lord Linlithgow to Mr. Amery, dated 6th/8th March 1941", ibid.
177. "Note by Kerr Fraser-Tytler on the Situation in Afghanistan", 20 August 1941, file 7, GB165-0326, MECA.
178. Ibid.
179. Fraser-Tytler, unofficial letter no. 3, 1 January 1940, N 1612/26/97, FO 371/24766, 1940, "Kabul quarterly unofficial letter", TNA.
180. Ibid.
181. Draft paragraph "in reply to the Viceroy's para. 9", no date, IOR/L/PS/12/1913, op. cit., BL.
182. Linlithgow to Fraser-Tytler, 29 May 1941, ibid.
183. Fraser-Tytler to Linlithgow, 7 June 1941, ibid.
184. Ibid.
185. Note by H. J. Seymour, 11 June 1941, E 3099/1968/G, ibid.
186. Fraser-Tytler to Linlithgow, 7 June 1941, ibid.
187. Comments by "RP", 5 July 1941, ibid.
188. Comments by "G.E.C.", 5 July 1941, ibid.
189. "Extract from private letter from Linlithgow to Mr. Amery, dated 6th/8th March 1941", ibid.
190. Fraser-Tytler to his mother, 1 August 1941, no. 103–105, file 1/1/12, GB165-0326; "The Expulsion of Axis Nationals from Afghanistan", file 11, GB165-0326, MECA.
191. Coen, *The Indian Political Service*, 239.
192. Adamec, *Afghanistan, 1900–1923*, 123.
193. "Telegram from Viceroy dated 25th April 1941", IOR/L/PS/12/1913, op. cit., BL.
194. Copland, "The Other Guardians", 294; Ramusack, *The Indian Princes and Their States*, 104.
195. "Telegram from Viceroy dated 25th April 1941", IOR/L/PS/12/1913, op. cit., BL.
196. "Extract from private letter from Lord Linlithgow to Lord Zetland dated 5th May, 1939", ibid.
197. "Squire, Sir Giles Frederick, K.B.E., C.I.E.", *Foreign Office List for 1949*; "Squire, Giles Frederick, B.A. (Oxon), Indian C.S., Indian Political Service", *India Office and Burma Office List for 1939*.
198. "Extract from private letter from Lord Willingdon to Sir Samuel Hoare, dated 26th August, 1934", IOR/L/PS/12/1913, op. cit., BL.
199. Draft paragraph "in reply to the Viceroy's para. 9", no date, ibid.
200. Squire to C. W. Baxter, No.44/45/F, 20 February 1947, IOR/L/PS/12/1914, op. cit., BL.
201. Maconachie, 5 November 1934, IOR/R/1/4/1005, op. cit., BL.

4 BIOGRAPHY AND IMPERIAL GOVERNANCE   169

202. The remaining six include three Indian Civil Service officers (Alban, Fagan, Griffin) and three Indian Army officers (Macann, Ryan, Wickham). The count is based on the service statements excerpted from the *India Office* and *India Office and Burma Office Lists*.
203. Hamilton Grant, No. 108-P.C., Nathia Gali, 6 September 1919, para. 8, 7, IOR/L/PS/10/808, "File 1061/1919, Pt 1-2 Afghanistan", BL.
204. For further reading on Arthur Edward Broadbent "Bunch" Parsons see Coen, *The Indian Political Service*, 161; Marsh, *Ramparts of Empire*, 37; Tripodi, *Edge of Empire*, 37.
205. Caroe to Wylie, 5 September 1941, IOR/R/1/4/997, op. cit., BL.
206. There is no information regarding follow-up postings in the service statements for the remaining four Counsellors.
207. "Sir Basil Gould: Authority on Tibet", *The Times*, 28 December 1958, 9.
208. Murray Hogben, "An Imperial Dilemma"; Chandar S. Sundaram, "Grudging Concessions: The Officer Corps and Its Indianization, 1817–1940", in *A Military History of India and South Asia: From the East India Company to the Nuclear Era*, ed. Daniel Marston and Chandar S. Sundaram (Westport: Praeger, 2007), 88–101.
209. Note by J. P. Thompson, 7 June 1927, 428(2)-E, F&P, 1927, op. cit., NAI.
210. Coen, *The Indian Political Service*, 4; Fisher, *Indirect Rule in India*, 457; Ramusack, *The Indian Princes and Their States*, 103.
211. David C. Potter, "Manpower Shortage and the End of Colonialism The Case of the Indian Civil Service", *Modern Asian Studies* 7, no. 1 (1973): 47–73.
212. Murray Hogben, "An Imperial Dilemma", 766, n. 50.
213. Fisher, *Indirect Rule in India*, 457.
214. IOR/R/1/4/1301, "Personal File (Part II) of Lieut. A.S.B. Shah, of the Political Department", BL; 22(2)-E, F&P, 1930, "Selection of Indian Military Officers of the Indian Army holding the King's Commission for appointment to the Political Department of the Government of India", NAI; E 6047/5888/97, FO 371/39976, 1944, "Acting Counsellor for Legation at Kabul"; E 6784/5888/97, FO 371/39976, 1944, "Appointment of Major Shah as Acting Counsellor at Kabul Legation"; E 7528/5888/97, FO 371/39976, 1944, "Appointment of Major Shah as Acting Counsellor at Kabul Legation", TNA.
215. Squire to C. W. Baxter, No.44/45/F, 20 February 1947, IOR/L/PS/12/1914, op. cit., BL.
216. Murray Hogben, "An Imperial Dilemma", 767; Ramusack, *The Indian Princes and Their States*, 103.
217. Squire to H. Weightman, No.44/45/F, 1 February 1946, para. 8–9, IOR/L/PS/12/1914, op. cit., BL.

218. IOR/R/1/4/1185, 1924, "File 7 Con Est 1930 Personal File (Part II) of Capt. Abdur Rahim Khan of the Political Department"; IOR/L/MIL/14/72566, 1922, "Khan, Abdur Rahim"; "Recollections of a political officer in India (1929–1947)", A. W. Redpath, 86, Mss Eur F226/24, op. cit., BL.
219. Murray Hogben, "An Imperial Dilemma", 756.
220. "Recollections of a political officer in India (1929–1947)", A. W. Redpath, 84–97, Mss Eur F226/24, op. cit., BL.
221. Squire to E. P. Donaldson, private letter, 5 October 1946, IOR/L/PS/12/1914, op. cit., BL.
222. Caroe, telegram no. 12152, 18 September 1944, 6047/5888/97, FO 371/39976, 1944, op. cit., TNA.
223. IOR/R/1/4/1301, op. cit., BL.
224. "Rough note on the proposal for a British Minister at Kabul", S. E. Pears, 24 November 1921, 2, 68(20)-Est, F&P, 1923, op. cit., NAI.
225. "Recollections of a political officer in India (1929–1947)", A. W. Redpath, 84, Mss Eur F226/24, op. cit., BL.
226. Ibid.; Mss Eur F226/16, op. cit., BL.
227. 68(18)-E, F&P, 1923, "Selection of Captain Wickham as Second Secretary for Kabul Legation", NAI.
228. IOR/R/1/4/1316, "Personal File (Part II) of Major E.T.R. Wickham, M.V.O. of the Political Department", BL; Fraser-Tytler to his mother, 13 May 1932, no. 32–33, file 1/1/5, GB165-0326, MECA.
229. Caroe to Wylie, 5 September 1941, IOR/R/1/4/997, op. cit., BL.
230. Fraser-Tytler to his mother, 1 August 1941, no. 103–105, file 1/1/12, GB165-0326, MECA.
231. IOR/L/PS/12/699, "Ext 1165/42 Employment of Connor-Green in Kabul", BL.
232. Cf. Coen, *The Indian Political Service*, 260.
233. Michael H. Fisher, "Extraterritoriality: The Concept and Its Application in Princely India", *Indo-British Review: A Journal of History* XV, no. 2 (1988): 103–122; Satow, *A Guide to Diplomatic Practice*, vol. 1, 240–241.
234. Marsh, *Ramparts of Empire*, 24–25.
235. Coen, *The Indian Political Service*, 201–208.
236. Hopkins, "The Frontier Crimes Regulation and Frontier Governmentality".
237. Ibid., 383.
238. Marsh, *Ramparts of Empire*, 25, emphasis added.
239. In particular Murray Hogben, "An Imperial Dilemma", 768. See also Ian Copland, *The Princes of India in the Endgame of Empire, 1917–1947* (Cambridge: Cambridge University Press, 1997), 21–27.
240. Gould, *The Jewel in the Lotus*, 150; Thomas R. Metcalf, *Ideologies of the Raj* (Cambridge: Cambridge University Press, 1994), 145–148; George

Fletcher MacMunn, *The Romance of the Indian Frontiers* (London: Jonathan Cape, 1931).
241. See Fisher, *Indirect Rule in India*, for term "career biography".
242. 314-A, 1940, EA, op. cit., NAI.
243. Geoff R. Berridge, *Embassies in Armed Conflict* (New York: Continuum, 2012), 19, n. 58.
244. Intelligence summary no. 48, 7-F, EA, 1942, op. cit., NAI.

CHAPTER 5

Accreditation and Performance

ENACTING AND WRITING THE ENCOUNTER

Accreditation is the process that formalises diplomats' role as the representatives of their respective sovereigns. Diplomacy is a "ritualised form of cultural contact", and its accreditations are charged with symbolism of exceptionally high intensity.[1] In April 1935, William Kerr Fraser-Tytler wrote home one of his many weekly letters. He gave his mother an account of his accreditation as British Minister in Afghanistan:

> The chief event this week has been my audience with the King which took place yesterday. It was really a rather impressive little performance. At half past one - in our full dress - we drove to the Palace in three Government cars with an escort of red coated cavalry on grey ponies. We went very slowly & took half an hour to get there. At the door we had a guard of honour & were met by the Master of Ceremonies who conducted us upstairs where the Lord Chamberlain met us & took me in to the audience chamber, where we formed up, self in front & my staff behind. The King, in full dress, attended by the Foreign Minister came in - we bowed & I read my speech, in Persian. I then bowed again & handed him my letter of credence, the precious letter which begins 'Sir my Brother', & ends 'Your Majesty's good Brother, George R.I.'[.] The King then read his reply, we shook hands & I introduced my staff who bowed & withdrew to another room. Then the King & the Foreign Minister & I sat down at a little table, & after requesting permission to talk French I told the King of my visit to Sandringham & gave him the message from the King. He replied & after we chatted away for a bit in Persian again.

© The Author(s) 2019
M. Drephal, *Afghanistan and the Coloniality of Diplomacy*,
Cambridge Imperial and Post-Colonial Studies Series,
https://doi.org/10.1007/978-3-030-23960-2_5

173

I gather H[is] M[ajesty] [Zahir Shah] is getting a bit rusty in French - & he then got up & said goodbye, & we returned as we came. It was all fearfully formal of course, but well done in a quiet way.[2]

The process of accreditation began with inter-governmental exchanges about suitable candidates long before the actual arrival of a Minister in Kabul. Francis Henry Humphrys was appointed British Minister because other candidates were either unavailable or had been found wanting.[3] The very mechanics of this process gave Afghanistan a degree of agency. Accepting a particular person was one facet of the Afghan state's international sovereignty. This agency included the liberty to reject particular candidates, such as Steuart Edmund Pears, and declare them *persona non grata*. Once the governments had agreed on a candidate through existing channels of communication, accreditation meant the writing and signing of letters of credence by the British monarch for presentation to the Afghan monarch.[4] Until the presentation of a candidate's credentials in Kabul, the process of accreditation was incomplete.

This chapter provides a close-up of the encounter of Ministers-in-the-making and Afghan kings, which is enshrined in the written records produced by successive heads of mission on the occasion of their first accreditations.[5] In addition to the arrival of diplomats, accreditations were also prompted by the termination of monarchical reigns. Richard Roy Monachie was Minister when he presented his credentials to Zahir Shah in 1934 following the assassination of Nadir Shah in 1933. Fraser-Tytler renewed his credentials in Kabul in 1936 and 1937, following the death of George V and the abdication of Edward VIII (r. 1936). The chapter's focus lies on the accreditation that initiated a particular constellation in Anglo-Afghan relations. Its reading is contextualised in the broader history of Anglo-Afghan relations as well as against the backdrop of the international politics of the Indo-Afghan borderland. For the diplomats involved, accreditation was a process of becoming. But, as with many other instances of gradation, the destination of that process was open-ended. In Kabul, appointed colonial officers took part in a ceremony that outwardly turned them into accredited diplomats in an international setting. And yet, like the Legation as a whole, British Ministers existed in liminal temporal, spatial and ontological conditions. They never fully completed the transition from the authoritarianism of colonial governance to the reciprocity and equality of international diplomacy. Accreditation was also a process of conserving the identities of colonial rulers. According to

Victor Turner, "[c]eremony indicates, ritual transforms".[6] In other words, rituals change existing social and political orders and enact this change in their participants, while ceremonies are symbolically charged sequences of action, which merely represent a new order, but do not necessarily enact a status change in their participants.[7] The power of the accreditation ritual to transform varied.

British diplomats did not, in marked contrast to Kabul's *corps diplomatique*, regard themselves as diplomats "de carrière".[8] Their point of reference was the Indian Empire and its gradations of authoritarian rule. In their career, diplomacy was one of many other facets of ruling. Aspiring Politicals thought of diplomatic life in India as "an eternal round (or so it was assumed by the uninitiated) of palace festivities, *shikar* [hunting] expeditions, and ostentatious ritual".[9] Fraser-Tytler had similar perceptions of the proper diplomatic life of his fellow international colleagues in Kabul, writing that "one of the great disadvantages of the life of a diplomat de carriere must be the eternal party".[10] Between local traditions of diplomacy in India and international conventions in Kabul lay several meanings of diplomacy. Indian Politicals in Kabul differentiated themselves from Kabul's diplomatic community in their embodiment of imperial power. When the Legation was being drawn up in late 1921, Pears declared that the future British Minister in Kabul "as regards status will be not inferior to that of a Resident, 1st Class, in India and that his staff will be if possible superior to that of the Minister of any other Power at Kabul".[11] Princely politics inspired the Legation in Kabul. Colonial officers only temporarily *assumed* the roles of diplomats and the concomitant rules of international relations as based on reciprocity and equality. They remained colonially trained officers of the Government of India, displaying the ingrained coloniality of their training and socialisation as well as perpetuating colonial asymmetries of power in independent Afghanistan.

None of the Ministers had previously undergone the process of ministerial accreditation themselves before coming to Kabul, though some were present as witnesses on several occasions. Colonial officers were used to an entirely different form of ritual. As servants of the colonial state, they were part of a colonial social structure, which ranked a European colonial elite over Indians and dispersed titles to both alike as a "fountain of honour".[12] In Kabul, however, they were part of a system, which, on paper, was based on equality and reciprocity. In search of role models, British diplomats in Kabul turned to their colonial forebears who had encountered Afghans before. These previous encounters filled the "museum" of past and present Afghan rulers and equipped British Ministers-to-be with the requisite knowledge to guide them through their own encounter.[13] They took colonial principles of enacting and writing the encounter and enshrined them in the Legation's diplomatic practices. At the same time that British colonial officers in Kabul relied on their predecessors, their own accreditations also "generated, confirmed, and contested" authority in Anglo-Afghan relations afresh.[14] They archived best practices of observation and recording. These moments often arose from the self-referential and self-contained system of Anglo-Afghan relations whose repetitive performative nature assured the stability of the diplomatic order.

This chapter understands the performance of diplomacy in three distinct ways.[15] First, diplomacy's performances are premeditated, well-organised encounters of international parties. Accreditations are instances of "diplomacy as theatre".[16] British diplomats in Afghanistan merely performed their part in the encounter with Afghan kings as set out by Afghan state protocol. Their very participation in this ritual took place at the Afghan state's discretion. This performance took place in front of an audience of select courtiers, government officials and diplomatic staff. It also involved a public audience during the transport of the British Minister-to-be from the Legation premises to the place at which the accreditation actually took place.

Second, another diplomatic performance took place in the diplomat's office. The performance of diplomacy extended to the dimension of solidifying and perpetuating the first performance in writing. This second performance drew from the colonial archive instances of previous encounters in order to contribute to the archive a revised one. The reports written on these encounters are privileged textual performances of the actual encounter. By recording their accreditations in writing, British Ministers in Afghanistan *re*enacted and *re*performed the ritual in which they had taken part. In other words, British Ministers in Afghanistan became both characters in and chroniclers of a performance originally scripted by Afghans in charge of diplomatic protocol. As much as the Minister was a captive of an Afghan script before, the Afghan participants in the accreditation now became characters in the Minister's text. Reversing the roles of the accreditation itself, the diplomat now "talked back" at the king, who could be muted at the Minister's discretion.[17] Ministers selected and omitted facts of the original encounter in written form. Afghan roles were revised according to the British Minister's expectations and the colonial state's brief of how representatives of the Afghan state, and by extension that state itself, were supposed to act and behave. Definitions of Afghan statehood defined the roles of the Afghans in the Minister's report on his accreditation. They then delivered this performance-in-writing for reading, archiving and referencing to an audience well known to them, which included other colonial administrators in India, bureaucrats at the Foreign and the India Office in London as well as the British monarch.[18] Composing their account in the right tone and from familiar tropes, Ministers tried to impress their expectant colleagues, superiors and peers. The document was an end product, which had undergone the performance of solidifying a selective reality through writing. The act of writing reclaimed and reinscribed imperial sovereignty into an encounter with the chief representative on an independent state.

Third, as past encounters were partially reperformed, the written records also took on board new meanings and shed old ones. Each encounter of a British head of mission and an Afghan king established a precedent, which informed a future encounter. Previous performances became performative blueprints. As such, British Ministers always partially reperformed their predecessor's experiences while adding to them their own insights. Accreditation reports were both imitative as well as creative. Performances that borrowed from previous encounters with Afghan monarchs are as tangible as the role models provided by previous encounters in other colonial contexts, such as the Indian princely states. While reperforming their encounters and borrowing archival insights from historical predecessors, each head of mission in Kabul simultaneously added himself to the illustrious hagiography of previous British representatives in Afghanistan. Accreditations, thus, form a string of performances through the life history of the British Legation in Kabul that connects it to the broader history of Anglo-Afghan relations from the earliest such encounter at the beginning of the nineteenth century to the practices of encountering of the later Embassy. British diplomats in Kabul performed history as well as the colonial archive.

The chapter approaches diplomatic communication in its performative dimensions, which unsettle its seemingly obvious meanings. By doing so, it questions the creation of colonialist historiography at the very moment of its production. Diplomatic accounts are more than just the raw materials for the reconstruction of past realities. They are richly suggestive and densely written documents. The textual record of diplomatic communication is conventionally approached as the undisputed rendering of the past. The fact that diplomatic records relating to the history of Anglo-Afghan relations are today housed in national archives and state repositories, having been found important enough to survive, adds to the records' claims over the past.[19] Historians interested in British diplomacy in Afghanistan, therefore, have usually been faced with the problem of having too much, rather than too little, source material at their disposal. These diplomatic records can be read, quoted and scavenged for relevant facts in an effort to reconstruct histories of events. Yet, probing their claim over the past can be equally rewarding. Because diplomatic historiography is rich in descriptive reports, suggestive letters as well as personal insights and observations, diplomatic historians can productively reflect on the nature of their source material. The chapter determines the accreditation report as a particular genre of historical document at the centre of its attention. Accreditations break open the seams of diplomatic reality, because they involve diplomats as actors, authors, observers, recorders, reporters and *dramatis personae* in their own writings, all at the same time. This partially distorts events in which diplomats took part and which they recorded, leading also to omissions as well as additions. As documents that constitute attempts to make sense of the past, even if a very recent one, they are history. The framing of diplomatic correspondence as historical literature seems a worthwhile undertaking for one reason in particular: while a comparative dimension forged from both sides of the Anglo-Afghan encounter would establish several perspectives on these past events, focusing the critical lens on these accounts and their authors themselves has the added advantage of supplying a set of tools to unravel similar, authoritative accounts of past events as well as inform other readings and ways of writing diplomatic histories more generally.[20] Subjecting diplomatic history's primary source to a critical enquiry of this kind is an important undertaking in view of the continuing power of colonial knowledge.[21]

Diplomatic Authority and the Colonial Archive

A rough sketch of the proceedings, which surrounded the accreditations of successive British Ministers in Afghanistan, can be established from a reading of several accounts. They reveal remarkably similar sequences of events on different occasions. From 1937, the Ceremonial Code of the state of Afghanistan guided the practice of accreditations.[22] It divided the proceedings into two parts, regulating the arrival of foreign diplomats in Afghanistan as well as the proceedings on the day of the accreditation:

On their arrival [...] Ministers Plenipotentiary [will be received] by the Assistant Directors of the Reception Branch at Begrami [Bagrami] or some other place outside the city or the aerodrome. [...] Heads of Diplomatic Missions accredited to the Royal Court at Kabul will inform the Reception Branch of their arrival by means of a note in which application for their first interview with the Minister for Foreign Affairs will be made. At this interview Heads of Diplomatic Missions will request the honour of an audience with the King at the same time presenting to the Minister for Foreign Affairs a copy of their credentials together with a copy of the speech which they propose to deliver before his Majesty. The Minister for Foreign Affairs will obtain His Majesty's orders and inform Heads of Diplomatic Missions of the date and hour fixed for their audience through the Director of the Reception Branch.[23]

The second part laid the framework for the accreditation itself:

On the day fixed for the audience the Assistant Director of the Reception Branch will call at the residence of the Minister Plenipotentiary. The Minister will ride in a motor car with the Assistant Director of the Reception branch on his left. The Legation staff, Counsellors, First Secretaries, Secretaries and Military, Air and Commercial Attachés will follow in other cars which will be provided by the Ministry of Foreign Affairs. A detachment of the Guards Division will present arms in front of the Royal Palace. On arrival the Minister will be met in the hall by the Minister of Court, His Majesty's Chief Secretary, the Commandant of the Guards Division and the Chief Military A. D. C. [aide-de-camp.] The Minister of Court will conduct the Minister and his staff to the Audience Chamber and usher them into His Majesty's presence. The Minister for Foreign Affairs will also be present. The Minister will read his address to His Majesty and His Majesty will reply. The Minister Plenipotentiary will then present his credentials to His Majesty and request permission to introduce the members of his staff. He will introduce them in order of precedence and with them take leave of His Majesty. Similar ceremony will be observed on the return journey. Full official uniform with decorations will be worn at the presentation of credentials to His Majesty the King.[24]

Diplomatic protocol organised diplomatic interaction with representatives of the Afghan state and made Anglo-Afghan diplomatic relations comfortingly predictable. Accreditations took place at the Dilkusha Palace, which had been built by an architect named Finlayson during the reign of Habibullah Khan. The Ceremonial Code formalised the order of entries of the Afghan king and foreign diplomats in order to pre-empt protocolic challenges to Afghanistan's sovereignty and agency in its diplomatic relations. Prior to 1937, the records of accreditation point to the fact that the British Minister entered the audience hall before the king, thereby giving the impression that they received, instead of being received. After 1937, this order was reversed to symbolise the reception of foreign diplomats by Afghan kings. Despite its detailed nature, the outline left sizeable room for interpretation, observation and documentation. Over the years, there were also variations in the number of the state cars and the size of the guard of honour at the Dilkusha Palace.

The British Minister's role as a royal messenger between the British and Afghan heads of state framed the written account on the accreditation. Several elements of the accreditation were preformulated, such as the letters of credence and the Minister's speech. But, there was also an impromptu element in the shape of a conversation, which took place between diplomats and Afghan kings after the exchange of letters. This conversation and the process of writing the accreditation allowed British Ministers to assume agency on an occasion when there was little agency to gain and, arguably, very little to gain from that agency. British Ministers capitalised on the power of documentation when they returned to the Legation's quarters to write their accounts after the accreditation. Their despatches were addressed to the Secretary of State for Foreign Affairs. In London, officials at the Foreign Office, usually, perceived these reports as "interesting", but to be "not of much substance".[25] The file cover on Humphrys' despatch stated that he "seems to have *performed* his task in an admirable manner".[26] And yet, as Peter Burschel has shown, royal audiences are instances of "high semiotic sensitivity".[27] Nothing is meaningless, every minute detail is taken in, interpreted and recorded. Their very existence shows that reports on accreditations fulfilled a larger cultural role in the practice of diplomacy. Beyond merely documenting the setting into place of diplomatic agents, accreditation reports uncovered and compensated for anxieties and insecurities of a more fundamental nature that occurred during the 'end of empire' in South Asia's shifting international political landscape. Their seeming irrelevance reassured the diplomatic order of Anglo-Afghan relations.

The furnishing of written accounts on the presentation of their letters of credence became customary practice for British Ministers in Afghanistan, whose previous examples include George Nathaniel Curzon's meeting Abdur Rahman Khan.[28] Incidentally, as Secretary of State for Foreign Affairs in 1922, Curzon was also the recipient of Humphrys' first encounter with Amanullah Khan. As a result of inner-institutional referencing, the accounts resemble previous examples, but also took on individual tones.

As much as the practice was established during this time, it was also subject to change, as the written reports became shorter and less informative over time. Nevertheless, they continued to follow a similar structure composed of three main elements. The first part contained a description of the accreditation. Humphrys and Maconachie prefaced this with a detailed description of their journey into Afghanistan and their arrival in Kabul. All Ministers-to-be travelled from India to Kabul. Their departure from India was greeted in the fashion of princely politics in India, with a gun salute ranging from fifteen in 1922 to eleven in later years.[29] In comparison, twenty-one gun salutes were given to the maharajas of Baroda, Gwalior, Hyderabad and Berar, Jammu and Kashmir and Mysore. The number of gun salutes, ranging in uneven numbers from a minimum of nine, indicated a hierarchy among India's 'princes' from the perspective of the Government of India.[30] The gun salute formalised the journey into Afghanistan as an important stage in the process of becoming British head of mission. It also gave the authors of the reports an opportunity to closely survey the country and its people, which usually translated into intensely critical descriptions as colonial officers trained their gazes on Afghanistan. These descriptions added the necessary local colour to the Ministers' later accounts of their accreditations. The literary backdrop served as a writing device that distanced and enhanced Ministers' roles in the proceedings.

Following the travelogue and a description of the accreditation, a second part of the account recorded a conversation between the newly accredited heads of mission and Afghan kings. A third part commented on the proceedings. The second and third parts, especially, allowed for a degree of agency on the part of British Ministers. The record of the conversation enabled the Minister to render his perception of the accreditation and, thus, break free from the restrictions, which the protocol of a former dependent state had imposed on him, the representative of the colonial state's ruling class, during the ritual. The writing of the report on the accreditation was in this way turned into an occasion on which the British Minister detached himself from merely following a foreign script and to add his own observations and opinions to that foreign ritual.

The following discussion is organised in chronological fashion around six occasions on which British Ministers-to-be presented their diplomatic credentials to Afghan monarchs between 1922 and 1943, beginning with Humphrys as the first-ever British Minister in Afghanistan in 1922 to Giles Frederick Squire in 1943.[31] Rather than contextualising each accreditation as an individual anecdote, the chapter understands all six occasions as interconnected performances, which reveal the practical application of the Legation's colonial past in its contemporary paracolonial dimensions.[32]

Humphrys and Amanullah Khan, 1922

Humphrys gave a full report on his movements from London to Kabul, which took him via Marseille and Aden to Bombay and Delhi, acknowledging in particular that he left "Europe" through Marseille on 12 January 1922. On his way to the Indo-Afghan border, he travelled to Peshawar and Landi Kotal. Having crossed into Afghanistan, Humphrys immediately drew attention to the "newly-acquired territory" that Afghanistan had gained in the war of 1919. Afghan border officials appeared "friendly, though constrained and nervous".[33] Near Jalalabad, he visited the grave of Habibullah Khan:

> I and my staff were careful to show our respect for the memory of a ruler who, with all his shortcomings, had proved himself a staunch supporter of the British connection, but this demeanour was evidently lost on our hosts, who laughed and chatted among themselves within the mausoleum itself.

Humphrys' reference to Afghanistan's late *amir* echoed Louis Dane's comments on Abdur Rahman Khan, then also dead three years, to the young Habibullah Khan. The emissaries in 1904 and 1922 referred to the deceased as exemplary politicians worthy of emulation in their conduct of Indo-Afghan relations.[34] By contrast, Humphrys' Afghan hosts in the present of early 1922 evidently did not meet the colonial officer's expectations of good behaviour at a memorial site. Nor did his action have the desired effect on them. From the beginning of his report, Afghans appear as antithetical characters in Humphrys' text. Humphrys was also received by a *hakim*:

> His conversation consisted of set speeches, addressed as much to the representative of the [Afghan] Foreign Office as to myself, and, opening almost invariably with eulogies of the present Ameer [Amanullah Khan], closed with perorations on his own devotion to duty. In spite of a somewhat limited education, his views were definite and immutable. Education itself seemed to him of little value, since geography, for instance, taught that the world was round, while he knew for a fact that it was flat.

Resistance to scientific knowledge, especially, underlined stereotypes, according to which Afghan society was predominantly determined by emotions and religion. These notions were also expressed by Afghans themselves. Shah Wali Khan also references "parrot-like mullahs" and their repetitive, unresponsive set speeches in his memoirs.[35] Woven into Humphrys' travelogue are his disagreement with officials of Amanullah Khan's government and the material manifestation of that government's interpretation of the war of 1919 as a war of independence. Humphrys reached Kabul on 6 March 1922. Describing his journey from the Legation to the accreditation, Humphrys wrote that: "On the road to the palace we passed the monument erected to the 'Victory of Thal.' Surrounded by chained lions [...] it affords an apt illustration of the official Afghan attitude towards recent history".[36] It had been photographed a year before by Sydney Frederick Muspratt, who was a member of the Dobbs Mission, so Humphrys likely knew what to expect.[37] The reference to the British fort at Thal was a powerful reminder of recent Anglo-Afghan history. In 1919, Afghan forces besieged the British fort located on the Indian side of the Indo-Afghan border in the Kurram valley, thereby contributing materially to Afghan independence. This was far from the only symbolism that representatives of the Indian Empire found challenging. A garden gate in Amanullah Khan's place of birth, Paghman, took the form of Paris' Arc de Triomphe. From 1930 onwards, Afghan kings opened the annual independence celebrations with a speech at the Minar-i-Istiqlal, the Pillar of Independence. In view of the political changes of the recent past and their material inscriptions in Kabul's cityscape, the resistance to scientific knowledge expressed by the *hakim* consoled Humphrys' and his audience's ideas about the fundamentally unchanging, timeless nature of Afghan society.

During his accreditation, Humphrys met Amanullah Khan for the first time. Although he did not know Amanullah Khan personally, the colonial archive ensured that Humphrys was familiar with Amanullah Khan's "character" and with the process of observing and describing such formal occasions. Henry Dobbs had written a character sketch on the Afghan ruler in January 1922, only weeks before Humphrys wrote his account on 25 March 1922.[38] The colonial archive also supplied Humphrys with the account of his predecessor in Kabul, Pierre Louis Napoleon Cavagnari. In 1879, Cavagnari reported his arrival in Kabul, describing the countryside, his reception in camp outside of Kabul, his ride into town on an elephant and the Afghan failure to adequately intone "God save the Queen".[39] Finally, Humphrys' nominal superior in London, Curzon, had also left an account of Abdur Rahman Khan and, by extension, a blueprint for describing Afghan kings in general. As a consequence, Humphrys' account was constructed from colonial precedents as much as it also gave insight into his state of mind. Humphrys mixed acknowledgements of Afghan hospitality with complaints on the "uncomfortably small", "unhealthy and inadequate" nature of the house reserved for the Legation.[40] He expressed his "disappointment" that the Afghan Foreign Office had not ensured the receipt of the Legation's mail from India. Intended to reflect on the Afghan government and local conditions, Humphrys' rendering of his immediate environment also reveals his state of physical and emotional wellbeing as well as a sense of tension and anxiety of arriving in an unfamiliar place.

The accreditation took place a week later, on 13 March 1922. Humphrys noted that the delay was partially caused by the "inability" of the Afghan Foreign Office to translate his credentials and the absence of the Afghan Foreign Minister, Mahmud Tarzi. Up to the moment of the accreditation, Humphrys had focused his account exclusively on Afghan shortcomings. Humphrys and Amanullah Khan then exchanged preformulated speeches. Humphrys assured Amanullah Khan that "it will be my earnest endeavour to promote, as far as in me lies, the growth of amicable feelings between the two States". He thanked Amanullah Khan for his assistance and hospitality in the conduct of the mission from India to Kabul. Humphrys' caveats are unmistakable. Saying that good relations first had to grow, he suggested that they did not exist at the moment of writing. His own ability to influence Anglo-Afghan relations is qualified by the addition of "as far as in me lies". This could be an indication of diplomatic ability. It could also be read as an indication that Humphrys was unwilling to look beyond his own well-established cultural and political assumptions of Afghan behaviour. Amanullah Khan responded, in Humphrys' words, that

> It causes me much pleasure that relations with old friends have been established. We were friends in former days, and it was owing to misunderstandings that our friendship was interrupted, war resulted, and we became enemies. [...] I trust that [...] friendly feelings between our Government will increase. [...] Afghanistan desires to be on good terms with the whole world, and especially with her neighbours and old friends.

The reference to "friendly" feelings aimed at the nature of the Treaty of Kabul as a 'treaty of neighbourly relations', not as a 'treaty of friendship' that Amanullah Khan and Dobbs had preferred. Amanullah Khan's words appear to express the wish to reconfigure diplomatic relations less ambiguously, and the two men also handled the situation differently. Humphrys included an unflattering description of Amanullah Khan, "who appeared extremely nervous, then took his seat and read the letters of credence. [...] Tea was served when the formal speeches were over and the attitude of the Ameer became less constrained". The references to Amanullah Khan's emotional state in the above passages—"nervous", "constrained"—are noteworthy, because Humphrys' own feelings are not explicitly referenced. Afghan emotions and 'British' reason are applied as antitheses.[41] The very process of documentation, which burdened Afghan actions and appearance with Humphrys' opinions and observations, revealed its underlying perceptions. Humphrys suggested that formality did not suit emotional Afghans. Everyday activities, such as drinking tea, however, had a relaxing effect. Humphrys' subtext gave the impression that Amanullah Khan inevitably appeared out of his depth in following international diplomatic practice.[42] Afghans were distanced and othered, and Humphrys' focus on the Afghan participants also sought to cloak his own inexperience in such encounters. Humphrys did not conceal his contempt when he offered an explicitly racialised explanation for the behaviour of his Afghan opposites. The colonial officer, who had served about two decades on the Indo-Afghan border, wrote: "The natural uncouthness of the Afghan renders him awkward and ill at ease on such occasions, and details of the procedure prescribed might be freely criticised from the European standpoint".[43] Humphrys' approach intended to make it impossible for the readers of his despatch to accept the Afghan participants in the court ritual as reliable actors in international diplomacy.

Once the letters of credence had been presented and the formal speeches exchanged, Humphrys and Amanullah Khan engaged in conversation. Amanullah Khan suggested that "he looked forward to establishing [...] in this capacity close personal relations with the British Minister". As the Afghan king sought the company of the British Minister, Humphrys' importance in relation to Amanullah Khan was notably elevated. Amanullah Khan's wish chimed well with the monopoly of access that Residents enjoyed in India. The rest, according to Humphrys, was "half an hour's desultory conversation on a variety of topics". Humphrys' rendering of the conversation inverted the hierarchy on the occasion of his accreditation. His text does not include a reply to Amanullah Khan's expressed wish, casting the Afghan king as a petitioner whose words did not require acknowledgement. Conversation with the Afghan king beyond topics of

Afghanistan's international relations seemed pointless. Because the accreditation followed an Afghan script, the conversation's failure rested with the Afghan hosts. Humphrys' subtly, yet firmly, deflected responsibility.

Humphrys' impression of Amanullah Khan was informed to a large extent by Dobbs' observations and commentary. In the report on his mission, Dobbs had given an elaborate character sketch of Amanullah Khan. Dobbs' references to Amanullah Khan's "neurotic temperament", his dislike for "all ceremony", and his position as the most outstanding character were all echoed by Humphrys.[44] Courtly games, which to Dobbs appeared as "sheer horseplay", informed Amanullah Khan's "want of proper dignity".[45] In terms reminiscent of late medieval European monarchy, Amanullah Khan was described as *primus inter pares*.[46] Dobbs objected to what appeared as a flat hierarchy in Amanullah's dealings with his ministers and courtiers. A few weeks later, Humphrys got to know the king himself. Humphrys admitted that "[t]hough his glance was too quick and shifting to give an idea of much dignity or composure, he smiled at times with a sudden attractiveness".[47] The admission betrays Humphrys' determination to resist being carried away by the king's impression. Although Amanullah Khan was far from Humphrys' well-rounded idea of a king, he did contrast advantageously to other Afghan statesmen and notables: "He was certainly the most interesting figure in the room and a remarkable contrast to the elephantine imbecilities, his brother and his uncle, between whom he sat". Amanullah Khan, thus, also contrasted with those Afghans who Humphrys had described on his journey to Kabul. He was the most important person in Afghanistan, and members of the court were being cast in terms of irrelevance. This important admission confirmed that Humphrys only had eyes for Amanullah Khan. In accordance with concepts of "oriental despotism", the king mattered most.[48] Whilst Dobbs had indicated the quickly shifting constellation of advisors in Amanullah Khan's political entourage, Humphrys reproduced the seating arrangement, but did not comment on the presence of particular individuals nor on its inherent hierarchy. It appears that he left it to someone else for decoding. And yet, the international politics of monarchical relations and its fine-tuned gradations of difference were established in this accreditation. Humphrys addressed Amanullah Khan as 'His Majesty', but the latter only appeared as 'the Ameer' and not as 'King' for most of Humphrys' Ministership.

The final paragraph of Humphrys' report concluded that the arrival of the British Legation had been "adequate and not wanting in any manifestation of respect".[49] This was only a thin layer of praise covering an otherwise destructive commentary. Humphrys explicitly condemned that "[t]he tone of the Afghan's conversation was pathetic in its anxiety to convince themselves and their hearers that they had nothing to regret or feel ashamed of in the recent war, except the misunderstandings which led to it". Humphrys' record of the accreditation suggests his inability to come to terms with the changed international circumstances which had prompted the inception of the Legation in the first place. Peter Sluglett suggests that "Humphrys seems to have had some difficulty in adjusting to the fact that Afghanistan was no longer a dependency of British India".[50] In similar terms, Leon B. Poullada has argued that Humphrys' Ministership in Kabul was defined in terms of a personal "feud" and "vendetta" between Humphrys and Amanullah Khan.[51] The evidence extracted from Humphrys' written record of his first encounter with Amanullah Khan corroborates these observations. Until December 1923, the printed versions of Humphrys' despatches from Kabul referred to Afghan independence in inverted commas. Almost two decades later in 1942, Francis Verner Wylie reintroduced this practice of qualifying Afghan independence by means of scare quotes.

The tone of Humphrys' despatch and the approach to his Ministership were informed by the political circumstances of India's and Afghanistan's common border. The colonial state's perceptions of its neighbour produced the requisite character scripts for Humphrys' own behaviour and for his perception of the Afghan state and its representatives. The Durand Line entangled colonial policy and international diplomacy. Colonial perceptions of Afghanistan laid the behavioural foundations for later Ministers. They generated performative blueprints for encountering and recording Afghans. A few months after his accreditation in August 1922, Humphrys declared that the interests of Afghanistan and of India were "mainly identical", echoing the Government of India's comments on the Rawalpindi negotiations in 1919:

> The Ameer and his advisers are young men impatient of their rights and fanatically sensitive on the subject of their independence, which they are eager to advertise to the world at large. But the essential dependence of their country on the British Empire will come to be realised, not only through their terror of Russian penetration, but through a growing conviction that Great Britain alone among the nations is both able and willing to assist towards the free development of Afghanistan.[52]

Humphrys' accreditation performance followed a colonial script, which had been laid down in the years 1919–1921 by Hamilton Grant's and Dobbs' interactions with Afghan parties. Diplomacy in Kabul was guided by the rationale of the Indo-Afghan borderland. To Humphrys it seemed that Amanullah Khan was unwilling to accept the colonial boundary demarcated by the Durand Agreement in 1893. Indeed, Amanullah Khan sought to maintain and extend his patronage of tribal groups across the border into India.[53] The Durand Agreement had demarcated Afghanistan's borders with British India and since marked the eastern contours of the territory of the Afghan state. The Durand Line was drawn across the economic, familial and social realities of the Indo-Afghan borderland.[54] Although it originated in the idea of a 'scientific frontier', its "arbitrariness" as an international boundary was acknowledged by fellow colonial officers in official correspondence, for instance by Fraser-Tytler in 1940.[55] Afghanistan's international boundary from 1919 had originally been designated as a delimitation of the respective Afghan and Indian 'spheres of influence'. In 1919, it was turned into an international boundary whose origins were not determined by the allegiances and identities of the people living in its vicinity, but by strategic considerations of the imperial sovereign. The boundary was a manifestation of the colonial construction of Afghanistan as a heavily armed defensive 'buffer' against rival empires in Asia. The prehistory of that boundary dates back to the aftermath of the First Anglo-Afghan War. Since then, successive Afghan governments, who agreed to uphold this logic, received cash payments, cheap loans and shipments of arms and ammunition in return. In 1869, Sher Ali Khan (r. 1863–1879) received artillery batteries and 10,000 rifles. Under the terms of the Treaty of Gandamak, India would assist Afghanistan with money and arms in the event of an invasion. Abdur Rahman Khan's subsidy was increased by 50% upon his acknowledgement of the Durand Agreement. By 1908, Habibullah Khan declared that he could arm every Afghan adult.[56] In 1929, Nadir Shah received an interest-free loan and 10,000 rifles. In 1936, Afghanistan received 30,000 rifles and 8 aeroplanes. The colonial state intended to create a "strong and friendly", "strong and independent", "strong and prosperous" Afghanistan by monetising and weaponising its neighbour.[57] Controlling the flow of small arms equated to a degree of security.

From the perspective of the Government of India, Amanullah Khan's transborder relationships were not accepted as "good" "neighbourly" behaviour, but were generally labelled under the rubric of Afghan "intrigue".[58] If Afghanistan wanted to appear and be treated as "a civilised nation" it had to "conform to the decencies of the international comity" by accepting the Durand Line as an international boundary regardless of its divisive character.[59] The colonial state's attitude formed a crucial part of Humphrys' brief. It defined the rules for "good" Afghan behaviour. In 1924, Humphrys noted that, during a conversation, "[the] Amir's attitude was extremely friendly throughout and there were, for the first time, indications that he appreciated the point of view of His Majesty's Government".[60] Another conversation between Humphrys and Amanullah Khan in 1925 drove home the point: "I told [Amanullah Khan] that he could count on the friendship of the British Empire, whose interests were in reality identical with his own, if only he would contrive that Afghanistan should be a good and faithful neighbour".[61] Frontier practice became diplomatic practice, as colonial law was enforced and the Afghan polity bounded. In 1926, diplomatic relations appeared to show "a marked improvement" from British and Indian perspectives.[62]

The colonial state's vision of empire in South Asia envisaged Afghanistan to accede to its imperial formation sooner or later. Imperial overrule was an inescapable condition in Humphrys' worldview. Afghanistan's incorporation in the colonial state's administration by means of a common border policy seemed inevitable to the British Minister in Kabul. Afghanistan's transborder connections were, therefore, unacceptable. While there seemed to be an improvement in Anglo-Afghan relations from Humphrys' perspective, the Afghan Minister in London presented a complaint of his government to the British Foreign Secretary in 1927, which outlined Humphrys' "unfriendly attitude" and requested his recall from Kabul.[63]

When written by individuals with close links to the British state, through the Foreign Office or the former Government of India, the historiographical assessment of Amanullah Khan is constrained by a narrow frame of reference.[64] Poullada has pointed to the uniformity of the verdicts passed on Amanullah Khan's "character" by British diplomats in Kabul, among them William Archibald Kenneth Fraser and Fraser-Tytler.[65] According to Terence Creagh Coen, Amanullah Khan, "meant [to do] well, but he was a weak man and an ass".[66] Amanullah Khan's reform programme was nothing but "wind in the head".[67] Martin Ewans, who was Britain's Ambassador in Kabul between 1967 and 1970, describes Amanullah Khan in terms that suggest a problematic personality and lack of judgement: "Despite his many attractive qualities, he was arrogant, impatient and impulsive, and increasingly surrounded himself with incompetents and sycophants".[68] Colonial officers' initial assessment of Amanullah Khan was based on contested interpretations of a colonial border and Afghan statehood as well as qualifying limitations imposed on Afghanistan's independence and sovereignty. As the inheritors of colonial ideas, diplomats have carried that historical assessment into the postcolonial age.

Humphrys emphasised Afghan failures in his accreditation report, while suggesting that his own actions were entirely in line with what was expected of him. He borrowed aspects from earlier Anglo-Afghan encounters for his written performance, which constituted a performative sample for imitation by later Legation Ministers. Its central features consisted of cultural distancing, the inversion of hierarchy and a noticeable political edge. Humphrys' scepticism of Amanullah Khan and other Afghan statesmen was already well established at the very beginning of his Ministership. Amanullah Khan embodied the adversity which had marked the political relations between colonial India and Afghanistan in 1919. In Humphrys' accreditation report, we can see the ideas that informed his approach to diplomacy in the following decade, including the events which contributed to Amanullah Khan's abdication in 1929.

HABIBULLAH KALAKANI AND THE POLITICS OF ACCREDITATION AND LEGITIMACY, 1929

In 1929, Afghanistan was ruled by four kings. Inayatullah briefly succeeded his brother, Amanullah Khan, before Habibullah Kalikani seized the throne and the treasury. Before he captured Kabul, Habibullah Kalakani's advance took him past the Legation grounds, where he met Humphrys at the gates of the Legation in December 1928. Despite Habibullah Kalakani's assurances that the extraterritoriality of the Legation would be assured under his regime, Humphrys orchestrated the departure from Kabul in January 1929. In a telegram, he explained that there was "[d]anger of a sudden *débâcle* of an unrestrained mob and of a general (? loot) and massacre from which even foreign diplomats would not be exempt".[69] However, it was not the perception of a threat that made Humphrys decide in favour of a withdrawal. Rather, it was the

> Undignified and increasingly embarrassing position of a diplomatic mission which is officially warned that it is not safe to go far outside the Legation grounds, and which may at any time be wooed simultaneously by three of four different candidates for the throne. [The p]osition is all the more bizarre since the King, to whose court I am accredited, has fled from the capital, and

after a short abdication affects to reign in Kandahar, while the *de facto* ruler is an illiterate brigand who is being daily threatened by another powerful claimant in (? Jalalabad).[70]

Humphrys' argued that the Legation was specific to a particular person, the court of Amanullah Khan, not the Afghan state. Afghanistan's international relations with India as represented by the British Legation in Kabul were not based on the idea of sovereign statehood but on relations with Afghan rulers based on treaties with individuals.[71] Afghanistan's international relations were inherently discontinuous and, thus, subject to renegotiation at times of succession. Tellingly, the file discussing the question of diplomatic relations with Amanullah's successor was entitled "recognition of Kabul Government", restricting the Afghan polity spatially to the location of the court in the tradition of Mountstuart Elphinstone's *Account of the Kingdom of Caubul*.[72] Habibullah Kalakani was not recognised by the Government of India. The nineteenth-century practice of considering the legitimacy of individual Afghan royal contenders in the secretariats of the colonial state continued. From the early nineteenth to the twenty-first century, there were several moments in the history of Afghanistan when political legitimacy was renegotiated, every time with the support of imperial orders.[73] As much as these were moments of rupture, they also provided opportunities for intervention, readjustment and renegotiation. Habibullah Kalakani was not perceived as a legitimate contender or king, nationally or internationally. His "non-Pathan" ethnic origins constituted an insurmountable obstacle for political legitimacy and diplomatic recognition.[74] In the eyes of the colonial government, he did not qualify as a king of Afghanistan, which had been governed by Pashtun dynasties since 1747. Habibullah Kalakani was classified as a "non-Afghan", who upset the Afghan polity's ethnic hierarchies and its colonial conception as an extension of Pashtun tribal society.[75] As the 'water-carrier's son' and as an "illiterate" "Tajik" "brigand", Habibullah Kalakani's reign has been assessed in the idioms of illegitimacy, ethnicity and class.[76] A later "autobiography", *From Brigand to King*, has contributed to this perception.

The Legation departed, and the drama surrounding the withdrawal of women, children and the mission itself was captured in terms of the heroic and mythical at the time.[77] Humphrys' "coolness under fire became legendary", as he left Kabul on the last plane of the "pioneering airlift" with "the legation flag tucked under his arm".[78] Later that year, Nadir Khan took Kabul from Habibullah Kalikani with the help of an army consisting of 12,000 Wazir tribesmen from India. Colonial authorities in India issued strong protests, "threatening that if these people did not return to their homes in Waziristan immediately, the British planes would not hesitate to bombard their houses and families".[79] In Humphrys' words, the British government "refused to take any part in King-making; their policy was one of strict neutrality, and non-interference".[80] This, of course, was a rhetorical exercise, since the colonial state had materially contributed to the challenge of a contender, the very existence of which had justified the withdrawal of the Legation from Kabul in the previous year. Nadir Khan was Humphrys' preferred candidate for the Afghan throne.[81] Nadir Khan, the *Sipah Salah* or Commander-in-Chief of Afghan forces during the Third Anglo-Afghan War, and his brothers were at first denied visas by the British Consul in Nice and Ambassador in Paris before being allowed passage through India. In the Kurram Valley, Nadir Khan, Shah Wali Khan and Hashim Khan met Maconachie, who repeated to them India's stance of neutrality. At the same time, Maconachie expressed "deep sorrow", "great concern" and "anxiety" about the "likelihood of a general conflagration" in Afghanistan.[82] According to Shah Wali Khan's memoirs, Nadir Khan took the hint and responded "calmly":

> I appreciate your policy of neutrality and non-interference. It is a wise step. We hope you will stick to it to the end and will in no way interfere with our domestic affairs and with our efforts in liberating our motherland. Our people, who have achieved their independence at the cost of so much sacrifice and after many a hard and sanguinary battle, are not prepared to give it up easily and accept foreign domination in whatever form it may be.[83]

Maconachie, in no uncertain terms, expressed to the brothers that Afghanistan needed them. The political officer's assessment squared with what Shah Wali Khan later described as the brothers' drive to "liberate the people from tyranny".[84] The conversation hinged on the interpretation of the notion of 'non-interference', and Maconachie accepted the version of the Musahiban brothers. That interpretation was not defined by borderlines, but by notions of national identity, "blood" and kinship. Maconachie, like the governments that eventually issued visas that enabled the journey of the brothers from southern France to Afghanistan, chose to temporarily disarm the logic of the Indo-Afghan border when political circumstances appeared to call for it. This was a moment of exception, in which the colonial state's own rules were remade and reapplied.

When Nadir Khan assumed the rulership, he became Nadir Shah (r. 1929–1933), dropping the title of *amir* that all Afghan kings had adopted since Dost Mohammed Khan's decision against the Persian title of *shah* in 1826. Then, the Muhammadzai Barakzai of Dost Mohammed Khan had replaced the Sadozai of Shah Shuja. Now, the descendants of Dost Mohammed Khan, including Amanullah Khan, were replaced by the Musahiban, who included the five brothers Muhammad Aziz, Muhammad Nadir, Shah Wali, Muhammad Hashim and Shah Mahmud.[85] This dynastic line emerged from Dost Mohammed Khan's brother, Sultan Mohammad Khan, whose historical base was Peshawar. Nadir Khan was born in Dehra Dun, India. By adopting the title of *shah*, Nadir Shah distanced himself from Amanullah Khan.[86] He and his brothers asserted their authority over the country. Hashim Khan was named Prime Minister, Shah Wali Khan Minister of War and Shah Mahmud Minister of the Interior.[87] Habibullah Kalakani was executed. There was also a different approach to Afghanistan's international relations. Nadir Shah pronounced a course of neutrality, which promised that Afghanistan would not "interfere" with the Pashtun tribes in India.[88] As in the aftermath of the Second Anglo-Afghan War, when Abdur Rahman Khan had entered into an agreement with the colonial authorities that restricted Afghanistan's exercise of its sovereignty internationally for the next forty years, another future Afghan king accepted the demands of colonial officers with regard to Afghanistan's international conduct. The example of Abdur Rahman Khan was on the minds of colonial authorities in 1929.[89] Nadir Shah agreed to restrict the influence of the Afghan state to the territory located inside its borders, following the colonial state's delineation of Afghanistan's territorial sovereignty, rather than Pashtun relations of kinship which extended beyond state borders. The colonial state ultimately made Nadir Khan's challenge to the throne possible by allowing the later king and his soldiers passage. Once again, colonial India shaped Afghanistan according to its own ethnographic and dynastic perceptions.

MACONACHIE AND NADIR SHAH, 1930

In contrast to Humphrys and Amanullah Khan, Maconachie and Nadir Shah knew each other. This was also not their first encounter, neither was it Maconachie's first accreditation. He was present in 1922, having been Counsellor between February 1922 and December 1925. Maconachie had met Nadir Khan in person in 1924 and 1929. The meeting in 1929 took place just before Nadir Khan and his brothers entered Afghanistan.[90] In the spring of 1930, the British Legation returned to Kabul.[91] On 22 May 1930, Maconachie wrote to the Secretary of State for Foreign Affairs about his arrival in Kabul. Following the precedent set by his predecessor, Maconachie began his account with a travelogue. The journey from home to Kabul represented a ritual of becoming British Minister in Kabul. Unlike Humphrys, Maconachie gave the travelogue more importance by dedicating it to a separate despatch.[92]

Maconachie made large parts of the journey in an aircraft, stopping in Cairo and Baghdad, where he met Humphrys, then British High Commissioner in Iraq. Like Dobbs had informed Humphrys in 1922, Humphrys now passed on "much valuable advice" to Maconachie, ensuring the transmission of diplomatic knowledge among colonial servants. His next stop was Delhi, where he stayed with India's Foreign Secretary, Evelyn Berkeley Howell, and discussed "current Afghan problems" with the Viceroy. From Delhi, Maconachie and his staff travelled to Peshawar, where their journey was held up by "disturbances".[93] The Legation studied the "situation on the Frontier" in a tour "through Waziristan, visiting Miranshah, Razmak, Jandola, Wana, Tank, and Dera Ismail Khan" together with Horatio Norman Bolton, the Chief Commissioner of the province.[94] Importantly, the Legation staff "were placed informally at the disposal of the local Administration, whose hands were over full" as a consequence of the frontier uprising. Thus, the process of becoming accredited diplomats of international stature merged with the needs of the colonial state. Maconachie's journey from Europe to Afghanistan maps the colonial dimension of doing diplomatic service in Afghanistan, as he met his predecessor in Iraq, the Viceroy and the Foreign Secretary of India at the centre of the colonial state in addition to an inspection of the North-West Frontier Province.

Maconachie followed Humphrys' writing strategy to a large extent, reserving his judgment and descriptions of events and people for the Afghan side of the border. The Afghan border guard was conducted "less successfully" than the Indian one, their "physique was poor and appearance slovenly". By contrast, the military escort, which accompanied the British mission into Kabul, seemed "of good physique and friendly manners". Maconachie "spent half an hour in a fly-blown shed during the examination of our passports by the frontier officer, whose attitude was courteous and apologetic". Maconachie relayed to his readership comments of the Afghan border agent in inverted commas. "'All in ruins', he remarked". The use of quotation marks intended to raise the truthfulness of Maconachie's account. According to Maconachie, "the recent revolution has done much to cure the Afghan official of the self-assertive rudeness towards foreigners which too often characterised him in the time of Amanullah Khan". Maconachie perceived of violent destruction as a successful way to reform Afghan political behaviour.

A stay in Jalalabad enabled Maconachie to introduce 'typical' Afghan characters. Maconachie questioned Muhammad Gul Khan, the Home Minister, how he could "carry out his duties as a member of the Cabinet at a place 125 miles distant from Kabul, with which it is at present unconnected by either telegraph or telephone". Meeting Abdul Qaiyum Khan, the Governor of the Eastern Province, Maconachie noted that "[h]is manners had improved greatly since I first made his acquaintance, possibly owing to the fact that he had spent four years of the interval in jail". Maconachie glossed over these comments with a diplomatic tone of mediation by expressing that the Afghan officials "were courteous *enough*", but suggested that they were not trustworthy.[95] "[E]vidently acting on instructions received, [they] harped on the necessity of close friendship and cooperation between their country and ours". Afghan officials were not believable, and their opinions were not their own. Modelled on Humphrys' report of 1922, Maconachie's subsequent "visit of respect" to Habibullah Khan was effectively balanced with living Afghan contemporaries, who were undeserving of trust.

In contrast to Afghan notables, Maconachie seemed particularly caring of Afghan landscapes:

> Jalalabad has suffered more than any other place we saw from the revolution, but its gardens have not been damaged, and the distinctive charm of its fine trees, seen against the snow ranges of Kunar to the north and the Sufed Koh to the south, is unimpaired. Next day, May 10th, we looked in at Nimla, 25 miles from Jalalabad, and were glad to find that the cypresses, reputed to have been planted by Shah Jehan [sic], had survived yet another dynasty, and that the famous garden, though neglected, was as beautiful as ever.

Maconachie's interest in outdoor activities resonates in this passage.[96] On the way to Kabul, the Legation spent another night in a "grove of trees" in Kulali.[97] These stops along the way were familiar waymarkers that had been documented in photographs by colonial officers before.[98] Maconachie's attention to the horticultural achievements of the Mughal period is striking, particularly as it is counterbalanced with a report on the destruction suffered by the British Consulate in Jalalabad during the rebellion against Amanullah Khan.[99] Maconachie's focus on historical items and personae is indicative of the power which historical knowledge played in Maconachie's perception of contemporary Afghans and Afghanistan. While living people did not invite trust, the past and nature both were romantic and reliable places. The recorded experiences of his diplomatic predecessors bolstered Maconachie's own travels.

Maconachie concluded his travel account with diplomatic formulae, which acknowledged Afghan hospitality but came with qualifications. For instance, "the attitude of all the Afghan officials with whom we had to do was *remarkably* cordial".[100] Yet, there was also an element of surprise and unexpectedness. Seen as a whole, Maconachie's despatch concentrated on Afghan shortcomings. It confirmed and reinforced perceptions of Afghan statesmen already established by Humphrys. In Maconachie's written performance, Europe and India figured as places of technological advancement, order as well as diplomatic and colonial knowledge, while Afghanistan appeared as a place of natural beauty yet marred by political disorder and malfunction.

Maconachie's accreditation took place on 17 May 1930 (Fig. 5.1). His report is packed with multiple registers expressing difference. The escort "compared unfavourably, as regards both horse and man, with the old Shahi Risala of Amanullah Khan's time".[101] Drawing attention to its "scraggy ponies", this observation established Maconachie's attention to detail. Kabul appeared as an uninviting place, and Maconachie measured Afghans according to notions of time and punctuality:

> Our cars proceeded, wrapped in clouds of dust, at a very slow pace, which was only quickened when it became evident that we were *likely* to be late. The dust then grew even denser, and the deficiencies in the springing of our cars more noticeable.[102]

Maconachie suggested Afghan tardiness, but did not substantiate it. He challenged Afghan time-keeping, and that challenge was not withdrawn later. Finally, the material equipment of the Afghan state cars was revealed as being insufficiently comfortable, echoing Cavagnari's descriptions of his elephant ride into Kabul in 1879. In essence, Maconachie established the backdrop for his upcoming accreditation, from which he stood out owing to his self-ascribed ability for observation.

5 ACCREDITATION AND PERFORMANCE   197

Fig. 5.1 An accreditation scene, 1930: Arthur Ernest Henry Macann (Secretary), Richard Roy Maconachie (Minister), Sikander Khan (Oriental Secretary), Henry Hawes Elliot (Surgeon), Arthur Edward Broadbent Parsons (Counsellor) (*Credit* Photo 667/2(373), Parsons Collection, BL)

Maconachie borrowed and extended Humphrys' performative template for writing the encounter by adding an explicitly political dimension to his accreditation:

> King Nadir Shah entered almost immediately wearing scarlet military uniform, without any decorations, and I pronounced a Persian rendering of the speech [...]. At the point where I mentioned the inference I had drawn from my previous conversations with him he made a slight bow in confirmation.

This "inference", which Maconachie drew attention to, was a particularly important political statement:

> I have gained the impression that your Majesty is fully convinced of the essential identity of interest existing between our two countries, and it is this fact which encourages me to count upon the support of your Majesty in the discharge of my duties.[103]

The logic of the Durand Line divided India and Afghanistan as territorially delineated states, but also joined them in the governance of frontier tribes. As Fraser-Tytler put it in 1939, "the tribes should be looked on, not as a defensive barrier between themselves and India, but as a menace, far greater to themselves than to India, which constantly threatens their economic and dynastic stability".[104] The frontier held Afghanistan's rulers in check. The Durand Line was an instrument of imperial control. Maconachie sought to employ Nadir Shah as a partner in the colonial state's frontier governance. The absence of Afghan "subjects" from the frontier rising of 1930 was interpreted as the new Afghan government's good intentions.[105] Maconachie's accreditation was politically conditioned. By assuming that British and Afghan interests were "identical", it also established a form of patronage commonly applied in India's system of 'indirect rule', particularly in connection with the princely states. The declaration moulded Afghan agency according to British colonial policy, a reality which Nadir Shah's "slight bow" acknowledged. Maconachie now ventured to incorporate Afghanistan in the achievement of the colonial state's objectives, a significant departure from the antithetical perceptions colonial officers had entertained of Amanullah Khan's independent Afghanistan. In London, Afghan cooperation in British border management was received as the inevitable outcome of British purpose: "There is little reason to doubt that Nadir Shah himself is genuinely friendly, *as indeed it is in his interest to be*".[106] Maconachie's authoritative rendering of the text excluded the possibility that Nadir Shah's bow meant anything but approval. In the long run, Maconachie's positive acknowledgment of the Afghan king's identification with imperial interests contributed to Nadir Shah's perception as a "puppet" ruler.[107] The speeches at Maconachie's accreditation were published in the Afghan press. In 1931, the Government of India also published details of a grant given to Nadir Shah in return for his acquiescence to the terms of his accession. It included a loan of £175,000 free of interest, 10,000 .303 rifles and ammunition. This form of material assistance, far from uncommon in the history of Afghanistan's international relations, reinforced existing political resentment of Nadir Shah.[108] The Afghan Ceremonial Code, which regulated state occasions from 1937, for instance, demanded that speeches by prospective British Minsters would have to be preapproved on future occasions. The adverse reactions to Nadir Shah's cooperation with colonial India raise doubts over Maconachie's interpretation of Nadir Shah's bow as approval. Maconachie did not acknowledge the possibility that the incorporation of Afghanistan into India's frontier governance undermined the king's authority in the politics of Afghanistan. Maconachie continued his narrative of the accreditation:

> His Majesty read his reply in rather a formal and lifeless tone. His whole manner changed however as he came forward and shook hands with me, making personal enquiries, and laughing at his recollection of an incident which had occurred at our last meeting.[109]

Maconachie's rendering of Nadir Shah mimicked Humphrys' impressions of Amanullah Khan. Based purely on suggestive phrases, Maconachie split the personality of the king into two. As king, Nadir Shah's words and the manner of their presentation did not fully square up, but the person Nadir Shah was outgoing and pleasing. Humphrys' suggestion of Afghan discomfort in formal situations echoes here. Ultimately, this subverted Maconachie's narrative and the reception of Nadir Shah. Even though Nadir Shah "greeted very cordially" all members of the British Legation, the ineptitude of the Afghan monarch resonates in ink, as Maconachie's suspicions subtly flowed into his narrative. The record of conversation between Maconachie and Nadir Shah is built on this tension whilst also offering comparisons to Amanullah Khan's reign. For the benefit of King George V, who was among the recipients of Maconachie's despatch, Maconachie noted that Nadir Shah received the royal message "with every mark of respect and gratification", saying that it compared favourably to that given to Amanullah Khan. Maconachie also pointed to Nadir Shah's "pleasure" at his own appointment.

> [H]e remarked how advantageous it was from his stand-point that I was already acquainted with his country and its problems. [...] I would help him in bringing about real friendship between the two Governments, and the first requisite for success in this direction was the removal of any suspicion which either might have in regard to the other's actions and motives.

Following the positive references to himself, Maconachie offered his version of the conversation with Nadir Shah:

> I suggested in reply that the best means of removing suspicion was frank discussions, and said that, if there was ever anything in the policy of my Government which caused him anxiety or doubt, I hoped he would instruct his Foreign Minister to ask me directly for the explanation which I would always be ready to give. King Nadir Shah expressed his cordial agreement, and said he was sure that he and I would be as frank with each other in the future as we have been in the past.

In essence a description of the working of diplomatic business, the passage also establishes the potential for diverging interpretations. Whereas Maconachie conducted diplomatic business rationally, Afghans were prone to "suspicion", "doubt" and "anxiety". As Andrew Rotter has shown, frank discussions often meant sharp disagreement.[110] The wording closely resembled the terms that Dobbs had adopted in his reporting on the Indo-Afghan conferences between 1919 and 1921. In particular, Dobbs had advocated meeting Afghan delegates in India in 1920 in order "to create an opportunity for the frank discussion of our differences" with Amanullah Khan.[111]

Having given his rendering of the conversation with Nadir Shah, Maconachie indicates that he "withdrew" from the audience chamber.[112] In writing, Maconachie inverted the hierarchy at the accreditation by assuming a degree of agency, which did not necessarily seem to have been his in actuality, even more so because the British mission was escorted back to the Legation premises in Afghan state cars and not in its own. It seems plausible that Nadir Shah ended the meeting. Maconachie suggested to his readership that the British Minister in Afghanistan had ready solutions to Indo-Afghan diplomatic questions as much as he timed royal receptions.

In the last part of his report, Maconachie volunteered his comments on the proceedings. The person of Nadir Shah was at the forefront of Maconachie's attention. In contrast to Amanullah Khan, Nadir Shah and his policies appeared in a pleasing light. He was a capable ruler of Afghans themselves marked by "innate savagery".[113] The readers of Maconachie's despatch noted that "[i]t is fortunate that our fears [...] have been unfounded".[114] The end of Amanullah Khan, the reign of Habibullah Kalakani and the installation of a new dynasty of rulers in quick succession had left its mark on imperial administrators. Maconachie's own literary descriptions qualify these impressions to some extent:

> King Nadir Shah has a well-known talent for giving conventional courtesies an air of reality; but, even so, the whole atmosphere of this function impressed all of us as being noticeably friendly, and such shortcomings as might have been found in externals were certainly not due to any lack of goodwill on the part of the King or his Minister.

Maconachie appeared to be sceptical of Afghan court ritual in general, as he distinguished "reality" and "conventional courtesies". His attempt to highlight the "noticeably friendly" atmosphere of the encounter is undermined by the context in which it is presented. For instance, Nadir Shah's ability to evoke an emotional response from Maconachie stands in contrast to the latter's earlier comment on the "lifelessness" of Nadir Shah's speech. And, the very reference to "shortcomings" ends up reinforcing the previously established notion of Afghan discomfort in the execution of diplomatic performances. Capitalising on the uncertainties established by his own writing strategy, Maconachie elevated himself and his relationship with Nadir Shah. "[T]he King" and "*his* Minister" arose as the personalised relationship that steadied Anglo-Afghan relations.[115] Owing to his familiarity with Afghanistan's 'problems', Maconachie transgressed his brief as a diplomatic representative and turned himself into an advisor by invitation. Maconachie's report was riddled with ambiguity, but he packaged Afghan deficiencies into a well-organised despatch. Since the execution of Afghan ritual was wanting, Maconachie's own written performance had to stand out in contrast to it. It was designed to give the impression that its author was up to the task of structuring Anglo-Afghan relations.

Maconachie's accreditation offers an important and largely overlooked ambiguity in the historiographical reception of Nadir Shah. Previous commentators, Fraser-Tytler and Poullada for instance, have pointed out that the political relationship between Maconachie and Nadir Shah impacted positively on Anglo-Afghan relations.[116] Recent studies, too, have underlined Maconachie's "immediate liking" of Nadir Shah and that the period of Nadir Shah's reign differed distinctly "in substance and tone" from Amanullah Khan's reign.[117] Maconachie certainly contributed to this assessment of Nadir Shah, but there is also another argument to be made. Since 1919, Nadir Shah had been viewed as the "arch-intriguer among the tribes on the Indian frontier", having commanded Afghan troops successfully in the Third Anglo-Afghan War of 1919.[118] In 1920, Dobbs had characterised him as "the truculent and ambitious Nadir Khan".[119] Both Humphrys and Maconachie were outspoken critics of Nadir Khan in 1924, shortly before the latter left Afghanistan to become Afghan Minister in Paris. Humphrys referred to Nadir Khan's "insincere flattery", his "honeyed subservience" and "servile adulation" towards Amanullah Khan. In terms of the politics of the Indo-Afghan borderland, Humphrys described Nadir Khan as a 'two-faced' character:

> Nadir Khan's attitude towards me had been one of almost cringing civility, but the mask appeared to drop from his face for an instant when he added bitterly: 'You have achieved success, it is true, but at what a cost to myself and to Afghan influence with the frontier tribes!'[120]

In contrast to Amanullah Khan, Nadir Khan appeared to be even less manageable. He was the primary Afghan 'troublemaker'. Maconachie, Counsellor in 1924, chimed in unreservedly:

> I warned him [Nadir Khan] very frankly that, in view of his reputation in India, his behaviour while there would be regarded with suspicion, and that it was to the interests of Afghanistan that he should do nothing to confirm this. [...] I regard Nadir Khan's assurances in themselves as *worthless*.[121]

Maconachie's previously expressed opinions explain the ambivalence of the report of his accreditation. The file cover of Maconachie's accreditation report suggests that Nadir Khan's "attitude" only changed as a result of an audience given by the British monarch to the Afghan Minister in London.[122]

Maconachie displayed yet another register in his perception of Nadir Shah shortly after the king's assassination in 1933. He wrote an "appreciation of Nadir Shah's character", which attempted to straighten out the archival record. Maconachie actively revised an image of the Afghan king which he had shaped himself. For instance, in 1930, Maconachie had described Habibullah Kalakani's execution at the hands of Nadir Shah as a "thinly-disguised piece of trickery" because of the latter's vow on the Koran to spare Habibullah Kalakani's life.[123] This was an acknowledgement of Nadir Shah's capacity for brutality and violence. Yet, in 1933, Maconachie argued that the execution had been inconsequential since others "would have certainly have lynched the Bacha themselves".[124] Nadir Shah's rule was allegedly marked by "clemency".[125] As Nick Cullather has written, Nadir Shah "established a monarchy based on Pasthun nationalism with overtones of scientific racism".[126] Maconachie attempted to support his doubtful claim by citing superior knowledge and familiarity with Nadir Shah:

> The fact was, while at the close of the third Afghan war he had regarded the maintenance of Afghan influence among the Indian tribes as essential for the defence of his country against the possibility of British aggression, he had realised, by the time he became King, that the danger to Afghanistan lay in the north, not the east, and that, British and Afghan interests being essentially identical, he would service his country best by scrupulous fulfilment of his obligations to His Majesty's Government.[127]

The statement is more than a realisation of Nadir Shah's nationalist history: it was a benevolent obituary to a lost friend. No matter how brutal Nadir Shah's reign, Maconachie was at pains to convince colleagues in New Delhi and London that Nadir Shah's policy was in striking contrast to Amanullah Khan's "'irredentist' attitude" and that there was "no reason to doubt its sincerity".[128] Apart from confessing friendship, Maconachie's approach may also have been informed by the Afghan government's wish to have Humphrys' withdrawn in 1927, a charge that Maconachie did not want to see levelled against himself. By 1933, Maconachie seems to have interpreted his role less as a representative of the colonial state and more of a commentator of Afghanistan. Although Nadir Shah's rule, like Amanullah Khan's, was marked by a "genuine—almost fanatical—patriotism", Maconachie attempted to differentiate between the two kings.[129] In essence, Nadir Shah's attractiveness existed in his perceived willingness to model the behaviour of the Afghan state towards India along lines prescribed by the colonial state and its representative in Kabul. The suggestion of a growing intimacy between the two men, both inspired by authoritarian ideals, paralleled the perceived alignment of their interests and of their adherence to the same notions of normative statal behaviour within the delineated territories of colonial India and Afghanistan. This normativity showed itself in Nadir Shah's adherence to the imperial interpretation of "common sense".[130] Moreover, in his obituary Maconachie eventually reunified the figure of the Afghan king and the person of Nadir Shah, which he had split his accreditation report three years before:

> He would open a private audience with an expression of relief at being able to drop 'this King business,' as he called it, for a couple of hours, and to talk as to an old friend. For the British character he seemed to have a genuine regard, probably as the result of his own and his brother's happy experiences in Europe and in acknowledging a courtesy shown him at the time of his deepest humiliation he made the memorable remark: 'No one but an Englishman would have done that'.[131]

Maconachie's ambiguous perception of the king and of the person dissipated by 1933. Instead, the king's policy was rendered exclusively in personal terms, which also offered a reassessment of Maconachie's accreditation in 1930:

> It was his humour which made conversation with him so entertaining; but it deserted him entirely when [...] he began to speak of the needs of Afghanistan, and of himself as nothing but the instrument chosen by God for the service of his country and people. On this topic he would hold forth with a fluency which was tedious to Western ears, and would have been intolerable but for the *obvious sincerity of the speaker*.[132]

Maconachie effectively mixed his own attraction for the late king with the latter's pleasing adherence to the colonial state's objectives. At the time of his accreditation in 1930, the reign of Amanullah Khan had informed the ambiguities which Maconachie harboured against Nadir Shah, rendering the latter's development partially unbelievable. The resultant ambiguity seeped into the script for the king's character in Maconachie's written report. While Amanullah Khan had been described as an interesting character, his political outlook brought him into conflict with Humphrys' observations and exposed him to later commentators. At the time of Maconachie's accreditation in 1930, a degree of uncertainty persisted about Nadir Shah's character. In 1933, Maconachie revised his assessment, acknowledging Nadir Shah's "real success, perhaps even greatness".[133]

Maconachie's successor, Fraser-Tytler endorsed descriptions of Nadir Shah as a "great administrator".[134] "Amanullah Khan was a man of few qualities. He lacked stability of purpose, balance and statesmanship, he squandered money on palaces and unfinished roads while at the same time starving his army".[135] Nadir Shah, by contrast 'built' Afghanistan's great north road, a "masterpiece of policy".[136] Like other "great statesmen" of the world in the 1930s as well as numerous apologists of the Raj after 1947, Nadir Shah was measured against the creation of infrastructure.

Fraser-Tytler continued to impress on the Government of India and the Foreign Office the cooperative character of Afghan frontier policy since 1929.[137] Both, Maconachie and Fraser-Tytler repeated Afghan concerns to their superiors rather than impressing onto Afghan statesmen those of the colonial state.[138] This reversal of diplomatic roles, which merged with the personal, almost emotional, attachment expressed by Maconachie towards Nadir Shah, is reminiscent of similar patterns of behaviour of political officers in the princely states in India. Maconachie divided the person from the office, establishing intimacy with the person first and only then with the office holder. While the office of the Afghan king remained ambiguous, as indeed was the case with regard to Afghanistan entirely, Maconachie sought to convince his readership of Nadir Shah's humane characteristics. His accreditation stands at the interpretive crossroads of Nadir Shah. By offering an endearing account only posthumously Maconachie indirectly cemented suspicions of living Afghan statesmen and people. Historical distance generated the romanticisation of past events and people.

MACONACHIE AND ZAHIR SHAH, 1934

In the politics of princely India, the departure of a ruler, usually owing to death, resulted in serious concern on the part of colonal administrators, especially when the loyalty of an heir or a successor could not be assured. The assassination of Nadir Shah in 1933 prompted the renewed presentation of Maconachie's credentials to Nadir's Shah's successor and son, Zahir Shah. Maconachie voiced doubts about the strength of the government left behind by Nadir Shah:

> The peaceful succession of his son, which has falsified the expectations of most observers, including myself, is a hopeful sign, but it remains to be seen whether the new King and his uncles will be able, now that the moderating

influence of Nadir Shah has been withdrawn, to sink their mutual jealousies in a common effort for the good of their country.[139]

While the members of the ruling family struggled for leadership, Maconachie's kept sight of Afghanistan as a whole. Similar to his first accreditation record, Maconachie again introduced a moment of doubt with regard to a new Afghan king. Zahir Shah was resigned to the bounds of failure even before he assumed rulership, as per Maconachie's own admission. His young age, nineteen years at the start of his reign, contributed to a lifelong impression that Zahir Shah's reign was ever youthful, even childlike.[140] Zahir Shah appeared as an under-age king in need of political guidance by his elders and the Indian colonial officer. Maconachie suggested that this Afghan king was, in comparison to his predecessors, of diminishing importance in Afghan politics. Consequently, Maconachie quickly established the repetitive character of the accreditation, noting it was "generally the same" as in 1930 and underlining the performative templates which he followed.[141] Maconachie still gave an account, of the three cars that picked up his staff and himself before going "through the bazaar, presumably in order to make the proceedings more impressive". He drew attention to the different route to the Dilkusha Palace, interpreting the bazaar as a public place, which provided an audience for the staging of diplomacy's theatrics. Maconachie took his readership straight into the audience hall, which "King Zahir Shah entered in scarlet uniform". He then reported that he gave a speech in Persian, delivered a letter of George V and presented his staff. When Legation staff had departed afterwards, Maconachie stressed that his conversation with the king descended into almost immediate disorganisation due to the latter's unfamiliarity with the accreditation procedure:

> His Majesty, being evidently at a loss what to do next, glanced enquiringly at Sardar Faiz Muhammad [the Afghan Foreign Minister]. The latter thereupon launched into a lengthy eulogy of myself, to which his hearers listened with feelings ranging from ill-concealed ennui to acute discomfort. In reply, I expressed my acknowledgments, and alluded briefly to my personal relations with the late King. His Majesty was good enough to say that his father had often mentioned me to him, and that he himself had deeply appreciated the sincerity of my sympathy in his recent bereavement.

This being the third accreditation participated in, Maconachie sought to distinguish himself from the young king. Adding to Maconachie's earlier statement on the future of Afghanistan, the age difference as well as his knowledge of the ritual served to underline Maconachie's diplomatic 'seniority'. Maconachie's text suggests that he perceived Zahir Shah's lack of experience by interpreting the Afghan king's look, illustrating his attention to and understanding of detail to authoritatively read the king's "glances" correctly as a non-verbal royal order. As regards the response to Faiz Muhammad's eulogy, it is not clear if Maconachie indicates his own feelings. The author of the despatch disappears into the community of "hearers". However, Maconachie's observation skills make out "ill-concealed ennui" as an Afghan response, while "acute discomfort" could only have been experienced by Maconachie himself. The brief conversation is relayed in terms of staged diplomatic humility, but Maconachie's sense of personal loss as a consequence of the late Afghan king's assassination comes through strongly in the "sincerity of my sympathy", of which only Maconachie could have been the best judge.

In terms of structure, the account followed previously established patterns and was also repetitive of well-established Afghan characteristics. Afghan nervousness and the king's appearance, his physique and friendliness continued to be benchmarks of writing the encounter. In keeping with former accounts on accreditations, Maconachie commented that:

> King Zahir Shah was a very presentable figure, and in spite of occasional signs of nervousness carried himself with leisurely dignity. In externals the proceedings were an improvement on those of May 1930. The escort on this occasion was better turned out, and the cars, besides being better sprung, were more imposing in appearance. The whole ceremony, however, was a very lifeless one, and the impression of sincerity which the personality of the late King lent to functions of this kind was noticeably lacking.

The passage indicates both changes and continuities. As regards continuity, the theme of Afghan behaviour in formal situations was, by then, well established. This accreditation appeared "very lifeless", a more than ambiguous expression, considering that it had been necessitated by the death of Nadir Shah. The brevity of Maconachie's descriptions points to his own failure in striking a personal chord with the young king, suggesting his difficulty in generating benevolent perceptions of contemporary Afghans, who were not well known to him. Zahir Shah's comparison to Nadir Shah, for instance, does not go in the young king's favour. Zahir Shah was a "very presentable figure" head. As regards changes in writing the encounter, the only physical references to the young king underline his "nervousness" but little else. Descriptions of Zahir Shah's body are absent from the narrative, in striking contrast to existing stock traits and detailed textual portraits of Nadir Shah, Amanullah Khan and other Afghan kings.[142] Unlike them, Zahir Shah's body was not representative of a larger body politic and disappeared from view. Removed from government office, the king's ritual body was not burdened by his predecessors' constraints and, therefore, appeared to move with "leisurely dignity" in Maconachie's view. The following Chapter 6 discusses the role of the body in Anglo-Afghan relations in greater detail.

Maconachie's descriptions of the escort as having been "better turned out" and the state cars as having been "more imposing in appearance" again echo his own report of 1930.[143] Noting differences in the quality of the material representations of the accreditations over the years, these perceptions further refined Maconachie's portrayal of himself as a sharp observer. While the accreditation's materiality improved, "sincerity" was lacking. British diplomats in Kabul were critical of Afghan displays of material wealth, because it obscured more than it revealed. Anglo-Afghan relations actually needed physical closeness and the application of a "personal touch".[144] Maconachie intended to show his distinction by looking beyond the improved material facade of the proceedings. A keen observer of the king's body language, Maconachie's diplomatic self was not to be misled into trusting the new Afghan leadership by the fact that things felt and looked better. According to Maconachie, Zahir Shah appreciated the "sincerity of my sympathy" while Maconachie seemed to doubt even the "impression of sincerity" of Zahir Shah.[145] As a result, Maconachie reinforced an ambiguity of both Nadir and Zahir, while furthering his own authority over the text and its audience. The accredited diplomat Maconachie had been made in 1930. The occasion of 1934 constituted a refinement of his previous performances.

Maconachie's report of 1934 established that there was no personal connection with the king. Maconachie could not co-opt a personal relationship for the benefit of international political relations. Government was in the hands of the king's uncles, shielding Zahir Shah from the political influence of the colonial officer. Between 1933 and 1946, Hashim Khan governed Afghanistan as Prime Minister. This left Maconachie unable to get his political point across in private conversation with the king. Added to the realisation that he did not have the king's ear was the suggestion that the king did not matter much any longer in Anglo-Afghan relations.

In comparison to the relationship between Maconachie and Nadir Shah, Zahir Shah represented Maconachie's loss of access to one aspect of the Afghan leadership. Zahir Shah's junior role seemingly gave credence to his quietness and his state-averse, inconsequential personal conversations. The portrayal of Zahir Shah as a marginal king has had a significant effect on the writing of the encounter, as the following sections show. This image persisted among future diplomatic commentators.[146] For the late 1950s and early 1960s, however, Nicholas Barrington argued that the king's alleged passivity was misleading because he "did actually operate a collective leadership with other senior members".[147] Maconachie's accreditation report established a character sketch of Zahir Shah. It became a staple of repeat performances.

Fraser-Tytler and Zahir Shah, 1935

Fraser-Tytler succeeded Maconachie. Having served in all political positions at the Legation, Fraser-Tytler was familiar with its diplomatic practices. Fraser-Tytler continued the process of thinning out the written performance. Whereas Humphrys and Maconachie had provided their itineraries from Europe to Afghanistan in official despatches, Fraser-Tytler presented a considerably shorter version, which followed Maconachie's second accreditation in terms of style. As a consequence, Fraser-Tytler did not commit to official paper the ritual of travel, through which his two predecessors had become Ministers in Kabul. Nevertheless, Fraser-Tytler did perceive the travelogue as an important part in the process of becoming head of mission and left an account of his passage from Europe to Kabul in a series of no less than five private letters to his mother.[148] The existence of a short official rendering of the proceedings and an extended private account allows insights into Fraser-Tytler's professional and private selves.[149] According to his private documents, becoming British Minister in Afghanistan still involved meeting the predecessor and being "tackled [...] at once on the Afghan problem" by the Viceroy. The letters indicate a sense of estrangement with the Government of India with regard to its administration in the North-West Frontier Province as Fraser-Tytler showed himself "appalled at Government's present attitude towards the Afghan problem".[150] He was more forthcoming in private about his diplomatic life than he was in official capacity. The audience itself "was really a rather impressive little performance", drawing a far more positive and emotional response in comparison to his predecessors.[151] The expression of personal feelings carries a larger significance for diplomatic historiography. In private letters, diplomats expressed aspects of their occupation, which did not necessarily find their way into professional transactions. The process of selecting information for a particular audience and omitting it in communication with another is indicative of the performative aspects of diplomatic correspondence more generally. Privacy is not easily defined but rests primarily on the exclusion of particular audiences from accessing information. In this way, Poullada referred to the "privacy of official correspondence", including the assessments of Afghan statesmen and kings discussed here, who did not have access to that correspondence.[152] As a result of selecting audiences and information accordingly, Fraser-Tytler emerges as an official and a private self from the archival record.[153]

His official report closely followed Maconachie's example of 1934. After a brief narrative of the three state cars, the reception at the Dilkusha Palace and the inspection of the guard of honour, Fraser-Tytler focused on the "private audience", which followed the exchange of speeches. He delivered a message from the British monarch:

> The King listened with the closest attention and with evident gratification. At the close of the audience he asked me to convey to His Majesty his warm thanks for his gracious message and desired to reaffirm his determination to follow by every means in his power the policy of his father in his relations with His Majesty's Government.[154]

The exchange of royal messages between the monarchs began in Maconachie's farewell audience when Zahir Shah used similar assurances to adhere to his father's foreign policy on the occasion of Maconachie's recall.[155] This section gives the impression of the Afghan king's political obligation to the British monarch. Fraser-Tytler's account describes the king in terms of able observation and diplomatic tact. His own role as the bearer of a royal message takes up half of the textual rendering of the conversation. The brief description intends to display Fraser-Tytler's ability to simultaneously discharge his diplomatic responsibility and to observe the Afghan king's concentrated response. In private, however, Fraser-Tytler confessed that the procedure was "fearfully formal".[156] Ministers' reactions to the accreditations are usually absent from the commentary. By contrast, every Afghan action and reaction, however small, was recorded and interpreted. Contrary to the image generated in his official capacity, Fraser-Tytler indicated the emotional challenges of participating in Afghan state ritual. It effectively unravels the notion that Fraser-Tytler was fully in control of himself or of the events unfolding around him. The admission of a degree of discomfort in correspondence with his mother again illustrates the process of performative selection. It reveals the unarticulated subtext of these and similar official diplomatic reports. In order to maintain his authority over the text, Fraser-Tytler resorted to a careful selection of information in his official report. Its brevity excludes a reference to his difficulty with talking Persian with the Afghan king while a letter reveals that the conversation was held in French at Fraser-Tytler's own request. When the conversation returned to Persian, Fraser-Tytler suggested in his official report that "H.M. is getting a bit rusty in French", glossing over the inadequacy of his own language skills entirely.[157]

In the official account, Fraser-Tytler continued the tradition of focusing on the external appearance of the Afghan king:

> The King, whom I had met on several occasions in 1932, appeared to be in good health and spirits. He referred in cordial terms to our previous acquaintance, and spoke warmly of the manner in which my predecessor, Sir Richard Maconachie, had maintained and strengthened the relations between our two countries. I was struck by the friendliness of his manner, which seems to have lost none of that quiet courtesy which was his most attractive characteristic when we last met.[158]

Fraser-Tytler's surprise at the Afghan's king's friendliness repeated previous admissions of this kind. Despite many years of service, it suggested that expectations of contrary sentiments were still commonly held among colonial officers and diplomats. Zahir Shah's "warm" words for Maconachie do not only indicate Fraser-Tytler's perceptiveness and the beginning of a bond. They also reinforce the high professional regard which Fraser-Tytler himself maintained for Maconachie's ability, references to which are spread widely across his private and official writings. In 1931, for instance, Fraser-Tytler commented to his mother that "Roy has established such excellent relations with the Afghan Government that one can discuss things freely and easily in a way that one never could before".[159] The insertion, therefore, may have been an adequate representation of Zahir Shah's words, but it also served to confirm Maconachie's standing with the Afghan government for Fraser-Tytler's official audience. Zahir Shah's "quiet courtesy" resonates with Maconachie's description of Zahir Shah as conducting himself with "leisurely dignity", a flattering observation, which also indicated a degree of powerlessness in terms of ruling the Afghan state. In Maconachie's descriptions of Nadir Shah, "quietism" also circumscribed Afghan policy towards the Indo-Afghan borderland.[160] The King's personal appearance paralleled the state's behaviour. Fraser-Tytler picked up the theme established by Maconachie before him in his *Afghanistan* in 1950:

> At the time of his accession Zahir Shah was a youth of nineteen who had been brought up in France and educated in Paris. He returned to Afghanistan in 1930 and though little was heard of him he was known to be engaged in military and other studies befitting the heir-apparent to the throne. He was at this time a young man with a pleasant courteous manner who was known to be a fine horseman and a keen shot. He had also latent in him something of his father's quiet authority and natural dignity. But in 1933 he was as yet too young to assume active control of so difficult a country, and it was obvious that for some time to come his uncles would have to shoulder the responsibility for the affairs of the Government.[161]

Zahir Shah's behaviour pleased Fraser-Tytler's expectations, but the passage restricted the king, who would reign until 1973, to a state of perpetual adolescence. Other members of the Legation, such as the Military Attaché Lancaster, also referred to Zahir Shah in terms of learning rather than leading: "King Zahir Shah is said to be continuing to take an interest in current affairs".[162] Accreditation ceremonies did not just capture the process of becoming British Minister in Afghanistan, they also displayed Afghanistan and its kings in a state of developmental limbo.

Wylie and Zahir Shah, 1941

In 1941, Wylie presented his credentials simultaneously with Fraser-Tytler's letter of recall.[163] He did not leave a travel document. While Maconachie had been granted a farewell audience, Fraser-Tytler was unceremoniously withdrawn.[164] Wylie's accreditation was the first to follow the Afghan Ceremonial Code established in 1937. The protocol now included a visit to the tomb of Nadir Shah, replacing the visit to the memorial of Habibullah Khan, which Humphrys and Maconachie had undertaken in 1922 and 1930, respectively, to honour his 'pro-British leanings'. In contrast to Amanullah, Habibullah Khan and Nadir Shah appeared as "good" kings. The politics of the dead were a continuing presence in the accreditation ritual. Colonial India and Afghanistan agreed on Nadir Shah as an agreeable role model for future kings.

Another change concerned the order of entries into the audience hall. On the four occasions prior to 1937, British Ministers had received the king in the audience chamber. The record of Wylie's accreditation in 1941, the first occasion after the change was implemented, does not reveal any particular reaction on Wylie's part. But it is conceivable that Zahir Shah's government introduced the change in order to highlight the king's guiding role in the event. The order sought to reclaim the king's centrality in the proceedings by illustrating that it was he who received the British Minister who himself was "ushered" into "His Majesty's presence".[165]

Wylie's written despatch followed Fraser-Tytler's example of 1935 to a large extent. It did not include a travelogue. Wylie travelled from India, not Europe, on becoming Minister in Kabul. As a high-ranking Indian Civil Service officer who identified closely with the Government of India and had no previous experience of diplomatic service in Afghanistan, Wylie's appointment differed from his two predecessors. Owing to the circumstances of the Second World War, it also took place at "an exceedingly delicate time".[166] Following Maconachie's and Fraser-Tytler's examples, Wylie's report provided only a brief summary of events. On arrival at the Dilkusha Palace, Wylie inspected the guard of honour and met the Minister of Court in the ante-room. Wylie's description of the Afghan king followed previous performances but added caveats: "He displayed, *I thought*, a quiet dignity, showed no signs of nervousness, and read his speech with, *at any rate*, all *outward* appearance of sincerity and goodwill".[167] Zahir Shah's "quiet dignity" and "nervousness" echo well-established characteristics. G. E. Crombie alluded to the repetitiveness of Wylie's textual rendering, noting that others had described Zahir Shah in exactly the same terms before Wylie. Instead of realising the performative blueprint that the colonial archive provided, Crombie took self-referential and repetitive techniques of observation as confirmation of the young king's 'character': "While he would appear to be more than a mere cypher, he has not apparently shown signs of any great strength of character".[168] While the king did not appear nervous, it was still important to make a note of it. But, Wylie seemed unsure of his own observations, adding "I thought" and "at any rate" to his borrowings from previous encounters. Like them, Wylie was immediately sceptical of the words spoken by the Afghan king, suggesting that there might have been another dimension hidden behind the "*outward* appearance of sincerity and goodwill".[169] Wylie covered his own insecurities in taking in the details of the king's appearance by questioning the king's integrity.

Wylie then pronounced his speech to Zahir Shah in Pashto, although this was usually done in Persian. Zahir Shah congratulated Wylie on becoming the first British Minister to do so, but:

> The Minister for Foreign Affairs at this stage rather anxiously explained that had His Majesty known that I was going to speak in Pushtu he would have replied in the same tongue. Actually, I understand that, although it is now an order in Afghanistan that all Ministers and officials shall learn Pushtu on pain of the direst penalties, and although His Majesty has himself, in order to set an example, applied himself to a study of this language, he is not yet able to express himself in what is – for Afghanistan – a politically important medium.[170]

Hence, Wylie assumed that Pashto must, therefore, also be spoken amongst Afghanistan's leadership, although it was acknowledged even in India that Persian was the official language of the Afghan state.[171] The Military Attaché's *intelligence summaries* reported regularly on the Afghan state's initiatives to establish a national curriculum for Pashto.[172] The rationale of Indian colonial administrators captured Afghanistan as a linguistic and ethnic extension of Pashtun society, despite Nadir Shah's own recourse to the Persianate origins of the Sadozai dynasty.[173] To Wylie, Pashto was an authentic linguistic marker of Afghanistan. In his address, Wylie committed what his predecessor in Kabul, Fraser-Tytler, had warned would be major transgressions of colonial and diplomatic etiquette, namely suggestions of paramountcy and of the Afghan government as being a "glorified frontier tribe".[174] Wylie achieved both in his first encounter. In addition, Viceroy Linlithgow, who had pushed for Fraser-Tytler's replacement by Wylie, was wary that Wylie's association with the Indian States "might even incline the Afghans to view his appointment askance".[175] Wylie's approach to Anglo-Afghan relations appeared to turn back the clock to 1919.

Wylie used the confusion to convince his readership of his own grasp of the country. The king's alleged inability to express himself and the Foreign Minister's anxiety offer an important foil to Wylie's own decisiveness. Wylie explained Zahir Shah's reluctance to respond in Pashto in terms of ridicule. The same technique of covering transgressions and shortcomings was applied by Fraser-Tytler. In terms of writing the encounter, Wylie's authoritative rendering of his accreditation displays a significant gap between self-perception and reality. Although he was following Afghan protocol, Wylie wrote as if he was in charge, even to the extent of breaking protocol again by exiting at his own instigation: "This conversation having presently exhausted itself, I left the Audience Chamber".[176] According to the Ceremonial Code and to Fraser-Tytler's private account, the agency of parting lay with the Afghan king, but Maconachie had introduced a tendency among British Ministers to assume this agency in their official accounts.[177] Although Wylie referred to the Ceremonial Code several times, his actions suggest that he did not pay much attention to its guidelines. His previous experience as Governor in India informed Wylie's approach in dealing with Afghan state protocol. Conspicuously, before and after his Ministership in Kabul, Wylie held the post of Political Adviser to the Crown Representative, making him the highest-ranking colonial servant in India's relations with the princely states under the Viceroy. This offers an explanation for his authoritarian approach to the diplomatic encounter with the young Afghan king. Wylie performed the asymmetries of Indian princely politics in Kabul. He had been briefed to replace Fraser-Tytler in order to force the expulsion of 'Axis nationals', a significant transgression of Afghanistan's declared war-time neutrality as well as its international sovereignty: "[O]ut of consideration for Afghan sovereignty the German and Italian Legations were to remain open".[178]

The symbolic importance of laying a wreath at Nadir Shah's tomb seems to have escaped Wylie altogether. Yet, this contrasts starkly with Humphrys' observations of allegedly inappropriate Afghan behaviour at the tomb of Habibullah Khan in 1922. Wylie did, however, point out that: "The tomb itself is on the top of the Siah Sang Hill overlooking the capital, and like so many other buildings in Kabul is still under construction".[179] Wylie capitalised on Afghan shortcomings in an attempt to stamp his authority on the text. More importantly, however, his report was informed by a colonial hierarchy which ranked European administrators over South Asian 'princes'. There is no record that Wylie met Fraser-Tytler in preparation for his posting to Kabul, explaining Wylie's unfamiliarity of, or unwillingness to engage with, conditions and practices in Kabul. But this ignorance also guarded him against interpreting the Ministership as a messenger of the Afghan government in Anglo-Afghan relations, as Maconachie and Fraser-Tytler had. Wylie's recall only two years later suggests that his appointment was never designed to complete its five-year term. In contrast to Maconachie and Fraser-Tytler, Afghanistan did not signify the climax of Wylie's colonial career. Wylie's perceptions of Afghanistan and its representatives render his accreditation almost exclusively in terms of the meaningless. Unwilling to go through a repeat performance of writing the encounter, Wylie's report was comparably brief. According to his superiors, his "eccentricities" made him "his own worst enemy".[180] He exasperated them by losing the 'close personal touch', which his predecessors in Kabul had established with successive Afghan representatives. For Wylie, Zahir Shah was but a figure king. Executive power rested with Hashim Khan, and the colonial state demanded the Afghan Prime Minister's attention: "We do not wish to give up the principle that our Minister can have access to the Prime Minister when necessary. Our position in India entitles us to this and it may come in very useful in future. The parallel with Reza Shah in Persia is a sound one", wrote I. T. M. Pink.[181] "It is [...] important in countries run by dictators for H.M. Representative to see the dictator fairly often".[182] The Second World War exacerbated the already existing imbalances in Anglo-Afghan relations in a wider regional context that saw the occupation of neighbouring Persia. Wylie left Kabul in 1943. He was replaced by Squire, whose career geography fittingly included postings west of Afghanistan.

Squire and Zahir Shah, 1943

Squire presented both his credentials as well as his predecessor's letter of recall on the occasion of his accreditation. He considered himself an outsider to India's colonial services. Like Wylie, Squire was new to Afghanistan. Squire did not meet Wylie in person, but they exchanged opinions on the protocol to be followed upon Squire's arrival.[183] Squire's accreditation redirected the trajectory of the Legation's institutional memory in a double sense. On the one hand, he had no practical experience of diplomacy in Afghanistan; on the other, this was accentuated by the fact that his predecessor had already broken with many of his predecessors' writing strategies. As a result, Squire's report on his accreditation in 1943 is almost wholly devoid of the characteristic patterns established by previous Ministers in Kabul. The practices of writing the encounter established since 1922 by Humphrys, Maconachie and Fraser-Tytler, witnessed by and also passed on amongst them, were not reproduced as extensively. The application of diplomacy's practical knowledge depended on the biographical and geographical movement of the transmitters of that knowledge. The performative archive of diplomacy in Kabul was subject to individual pathways. The Legation's cultural origins of writing the encounter receded into the background, several other elements set in place by Wylie kept the Legation's overall colonial and imperial framework in place. The similarity of Wylie's and Squire's accreditations is testament to the fundamental rupture that

Linlithgow had intended in opening a 'new chapter' in Anglo-Afghan relations by recalling Fraser-Tytler in 1941. As a result, the colonial templates of performing diplomacy in Kabul found different highlights.

Above all stood the notion that King Zahir Shah was a marginal figure in the politics of Afghanistan and yet the recipient of royal messages and letters of credence that admitted colonial officers into diplomatic office in Kabul. Squire followed Wylie's example in several instances. To begin with, Squire did not include an account of his journey into Afghanistan. Like Wylie's, Squire's report was also comparatively brief. Squire noted that the ritual differed only slightly from his predecessor's accreditation, noting the reassuring repetitiveness of the performance. The brevity of Squire's report as well as its contents represent Squire's alignment to Wylie's observations. Because this king did not matter much in this reading, Squire did not initiate conversation of a political nature that conditioned his appointment. Unlike Humphrys and Amanullah, Maconachie and Nadir Shah, policy was decided elsewhere. Squire portrayed Zahir Shah in more active and inquisitive terms, describing him as being "most affable and quite informal".[184] The accreditation became an occasion on which what Humphrys had referred to as 'desultory conversation' now took centre stage. In conversation, Zahir Shah asked Squire where he had learned Persian. Squire admitted in writing that he had "cheated in this matter by having had the translation checked and corrected by a Persian friend". This explanation, noted by Squire in brackets, gives the comment the air of a dramatic aside. While he did not make obvious his 'cheating' to the king, Squire instead boasted that he had studied Persian at Oxford together with the British Foreign Secretary, Anthony Eden. The bracketing is indicative of a double layer that kept Squire's two performances, the actual encounter and the written one, separate from one another. Noting that "the King expressed much interest", Squire achieved his objective. As the politics of Anglo-Afghan relations lost their performative value, Squire seemed to think that he had managed to impress the king as well as flatter his long-term acquaintance.

As an outcome of this shift in the dynamics of Legation accreditations, and contrary to previous literary portraits, Zahir Shah appears as an incisive thinker and engaging sovereign. Continuing their conversation, Zahir Shah asked Squire whether he had any previous connections with India. Squire delivered the king's question with an exclamation mark. Squire recognised its political importance and maybe also expressed his own surprise about its articulation. Zahir Shah's question displayed his political awareness of colonial India's role in Anglo-Afghan relations. The government of Afghanistan objected to the practice of employing Indian colonial officers in posts at the British Legation.[185] Since 1919, it had sought to attract career diplomats from the Foreign Office as a 'true' expression of Afghan independence from the colonial government of India and its egalitarian treatment as a sovereign state on a par with the metropolitan government in London. Zahir Shah's question aimed at the Legation's deliberate diplomatic asymmetry. In this respect, it is noteworthy that Zahir Shah enquired about Fraser-Tytler, but disregarded Wylie. This damning silence was not commented on by Squire, but it is a powerful indicator of Zahir Shah's opinion on Wylie's Ministership. In this case, it suggests both a sense of opposition to the Indian practice of employing colonial officers as diplomats in Kabul as well as to Anglo-Afghan relations as personified by Wylie and inspired by Linlithgow. Unlike previous Ministers, who had authoritatively handled their accreditations and connected it to the politics of Anglo-Afghan diplomacy, Squire had left an opening for the king to talk back.

Performing Coloniality

The writing of the encounter was a performance, during which British Ministers in Kabul reclaimed authority over a ritual, in which they had almost none. Accreditations generated multiple performances. First, there was the accreditation itself. Then, there was the writing of a report. Finally, the reports generated a culture of writing the encounter, on the basis of which later accreditations performed previous encounters. The Afghan state's ritual display during the series of accreditations provided an occasion to inspect the state of Afghanistan in a double sense. Accreditations provided close-ups of Afghan sovereigns and occasions for textual portraits, which both defined a monarch and a Minister-to-be, who as authors strove to present themselves in the best possible light. Consequently, the diplomatic ritual was overburdened with meaning. Accreditations served the purpose of formalising diplomatic relations, but contributed little towards their qualitative improvement. This display, however, was judged by successive British Ministers on the basis of its external appearances. The more efficient and ostentatious they seemed, the less friendly the terms in which they were recorded. According to Fraser-Tytler, for instance, the display was seen to exist in a paradoxical relationship with the conduct of Anglo-Afghan relations. If the display impressed, it was almost certainly rendered suspicious.[186] This equation runs contrary to assumptions, according to which 'Oriental splendour' was an important ruling device. If the display did not impress, the accounts noted that the Afghan ritual appeared inferior to European standards. This rationale enshrined the state of Afghanistan in a state of lack.

The writing process enabled British Ministers in Kabul to break out of the confines of an Afghan script, which had initially reduced them to characters, and to render their own observations, opinions and assessments. While writing the encounter, they became its first chroniclers, exercising absolute authority over the text production process and over Afghans ruler as absolutist characters in it. The authority was occasionally undermined by uncertainty. The resulting written accounts contained significant biases and contradictions, creating unflattering descriptions of Afghanistan and its people, which supplanted the diplomat's own passivity. They tended to highlight shortcomings instead of positives and aimed to distinguish their authors as sharp, rational observers. Dipesh Chakrabarty has argued that "the themes of 'failure,' 'lack,' and 'inadequacy' […] so ubiquitously characterize the speaking subject of 'Indian' history".[187] British diplomats in Kabul applied the very same techniques in describing their encounters with Afghan kings, thereby subjecting Afghanistan and its representatives to the burdens of a colonialist historiography in the making.

Accreditations prompted lengthy and detailed reports and several long-lasting impressions. The written performances decreased in quantity over time, ending in Squire's largely pragmatic despatch of 1943. The performative aspects of becoming a diplomat in Afghanistan disappeared, as the silences and repetitions increased. This has an important bearing on reading diplomatic texts in general, as they reveal individual perceptions. As such, they are only partially reliable with regard to the representation of events and people. Arguably, they offer scope for the enquiry of their authors' 'states of mind'.[188] But, the accreditation report was more than "a commentary on itself".[189] It showed its author's brief as well as his approach to Anglo-Afghan relations. Diplomatic records have been read as representations of past reality when, in fact, they are also projections of past fictions, biases and distortions. The authors were not just diplomats. They were colonial officers, who performed a diplomatic ritual, with which they were familiar to varying degrees. In addition, they wrote for a particular audience of colleagues, officials and British monarchs. This led them to demonstrate a variety of diplomatic skills through writing the encounter—such as writing itself, observation and negotiation—as confirmations of their appointment. In contrast, their personal views only surfaced in silences or other documents entirely. Writing the encounter was an inherently selective performance.

As much as they are unreliable, however, diplomatic reports were also highly suggestive. British Ministers' perceptions of successive Afghan kings were burdened with emotional observations and insights, which were not based on material evidence. For instance, Zahir Shah's "quiet dignity" or "quiet authority" were never fully explained. Its meanings can only be partially reconstructed. Yet, they constituted highly suggestive references to an audience well versed in generations of Afghan kings. Maconachie even revised his opinion on Nadir Shah, further undermining his earlier observations and recording. The opinions expressed about Afghan kings by successive British Ministers have played significant, long-lasting roles. The almost collective condemnation of Amanullah Khan, the ambiguity surrounding Nadir Shah and the marginalisation of Zahir Shah have been repeated, but new meaning has hardly ever been added. Diplomatic practice of the present borrowed from its past instances. The emotional state of Afghan kings, too, was an important and repetitive object of concern. Their alleged 'nervousness' indicated discomfort while undergoing a severely regulated procedure of international diplomacy. This focus waned at times but carried on even after the end of the colonial state itself. The focus on Afghan kings also effectively reflected the silence in which British diplomats clothed their own discomfort on these occasions. The above, then, has brought out clearly the repetitiveness of British diplomatic reporting in Afghanistan and has shown the power of the colonial archive, which provided stock characters and ensured the survival of these records even across the postcolonial threshold. The chapter shows the colonial archive in action and in the process of constant reconfiguration.

The chapter underlines the coloniality of British diplomacy in several ways. In order to become British Ministers, all five British heads of mission travelled to Kabul via or from India. In order to become diplomats, they had to be colonial officers first. Although not all travelogues are forthcoming, some give an account of their travels from Europe or India into Afghanistan. Strikingly, descriptions of travel events, places and people increase in depth only on the approach to the Afghan border. Knowledge of Indian places and people was set aside because they were assumed to be well known among the audience of the reports. In contrast, Afghanistan was a place worth describing, adding to the idea of it being uncharted, uncivilised, uncolonised. Passing through India, Ministers-to-be met with high-ranking Indian political officers and discussed Indian and Afghan 'problems' in terms of colonial law, order and rule. This process of passing on institutional knowledge ensured the perpetuation of particular habits of observation and reporting in Kabul. Maconachie's example makes the interplay between frontier policy and Afghan politics particularly visible. Later instances include a written exchange between Wylie and Squire. Moreover, Afghanistan appears as a place of incompletion, densely populated with dysfunctional characters. The Afghan state and its representatives were described in terms of shortcomings and oddities, which loom even larger in view of the authority which British Ministers imposed on their written accounts. Similar to colonial histories of colonised spaces and people, the written accounts on accreditations never achieve a fully representative state. Its people are less than perfect masters of diplomatic ritual. The occasional visibility of hierarchical inversions, textual and actual, adds to this imbalance. The three distinct performances, thus, are indicative of the asymmetry of power in Anglo-Afghan relations, locking Afghanistan in a subordinated position in the international diplomatic system according to the representatives of the colonial state in India.

Notes

1. Peter Burschel, "Einleitung", in *Die Audienz: ritualisierter Kulturkontakt in der Frühen Neuzeit*, ed. Peter Burschel and Christine Vogel (Köln: Böhlau, 2014), 7–8.
2. Fraser-Tytler to his mother, 11 April 1935, no. 10–12, file 1/1/6, GB165-0326, MECA.
3. See Chapter 4.
4. See "accreditation" and "persona non grata" in Berridge, James, and Lloyd, *The Palgrave Macmillan Dictionary of Diplomacy*; "Persona grata", Ernest Satow, *A Guide to Diplomatic Practice*, vol. 1 (London: Longmans, Green and Co., 1917), 188–199.
5. For a summary of the "performative turn" and its implications for the study of history see Bachmann-Medick, *Cultural Turns*, 104–143; Peter Burke, "Performing History: The Importance of Occasions", *Rethinking History* 9, no. 1 (2005): 35–52.
6. Victor Turner, *From Ritual to Theatre: The Human Seriousness of Play* (New York: Performing Arts Journal Publications, 1982), 80. For the idea of context as part of the interpretation of ceremony see David Cannadine, "The Context, Performance and Meaning of Ritual: The British Monarchy and the 'Invention of Tradition'", c. 1820–1977", in *The Invention of Tradition*, ed. Eric J. Hobsbawm and T. O. Ranger (Cambridge: Cambridge University Press, 2013), 105.

7. Burschel, "Einleitung", 7, n. 4.
8. Fraser-Tytler to his mother, 18 July 1935, no. 56–59, file 1/1/6, GB165-0326; Fraser-Tytler to his mother, 21 February 1936, no. 31–33, file 1/1/7, GB165-0326; Fraser-Tytler to his mother, 19 March 1937, no. 39–41, file 1/1/8, GB165-0326, MECA; Basil John Gould, *The Jewel in the Lotus: Recollections of an Indian Political* (London: Chatto & Windus, 1957), 96.
9. Ian Copland, "The Other Guardians: Ideology and Performance in the Indian Political Service", in *People, Princes and Paramount Power: Society and Politics in the Indian Princely States*, ed. Robert Jeffrey (Oxford: Oxford University Press, 1978), 288.
10. Fraser-Tytler to his mother, 19 March 1937, no. 39–41, file 1/1/8, GB165-0326, MECA.
11. "Rough note on the proposal for a British Minister at Kabul", S. E. Pears, 24 November 1921, 1, 68(20)-Est, F&P, 1923, "Note by Mr S. E. Pears, C.S.I., C.I.E., on the proposed establishment of a British Legation at Kabul", NAI.
12. Bernard S. Cohn, "Representing Authority in Victorian India", in *The Invention of Tradition*, ed. Eric J. Hobsbawm and T. O. Ranger (Cambridge: Cambridge University Press, 2013), 171, 181. See also Thomas R. Metcalf, *Ideologies of the Raj* (Cambridge: Cambridge University Press, 1994), 194–196.
13. For further reading on the "museum aspect" of princely India see Nicholas B. Dirks, *The Hollow Crown: Ethnohistory of an Indian Kingdom*, 2nd ed. (Ann Arbor: University of Michigan Press, 1993), 384–400.
14. Edwards S. Haynes, "Imperial Ritual in a Local Setting: The Ceremonial Order in Surat, 1890–1939", *Modern Asian Studies* 24, no. 3 (1990): 494.
15. Burschel, "Einleitung"; Johannes Paulmann, *Pomp und Politik: Monarchenbegegnungen in Europa zwischen Ancien Régime und Erstem Weltkrieg* (Paderborn: Ferdinand Schöningh Verlag, 2000). See also Daniëlle de Vooght, *The King Invites: Performing Power at a Courtly Dining Table (Belgium, 1831–1909)* (Brussels: Peter Lang, 2011); Iver B. Neumann, *Diplomatic Sites: A Critical Enquiry* (London: Hurst, 2013).
16. Naoko Shimazu, "Diplomacy as Theatre: Staging the Bandung Conference of 1955", *Modern Asian Studies* 48, no. 1 (2013): 225–252.
17. For the idea of writing as "talking back" see Anshu Malhotra and Siobhan Lambert-Hurley, eds., "Introduction: Gender, Performance, and Autobiography in South Asia", in *Speaking of the Self: Gender, Performances and Autobiography in South Asia* (Durham: Duke University Press, 2015), 1–32; Gayatri Chakravorty Spivak, "Can the Subaltern Speak?", in *Marxism and the Interpretation of Culture*, ed. Cary Nelson and Lawrence Grossberg (Basingstoke: Macmillan Education, 1988), 271–313.

18. See Malhotra and Lambert-Hurley, "Introduction: Gender, Performance, and Autobiography in South Asia", 24.
19. See also David Cannadine, "Introduction: Divine Rites of Kings", in *Rituals of Royalty: Power and Ceremonial in Traditional Societies*, ed. David Cannadine and S. R. F. Price (Cambridge: Cambridge University Press, 1992), 2.
20. Contemporary Early Modern History is particularly innovative in new approaches to diplomatic history: Peter Burschel and Christine Vogel, eds., *Die Audienz: ritualisierter Kulturkontakt in der Frühen Neuzeit* (Köln: Böhlau, 2014), and, in particular, Antje Flüchter, "Den Herrscher grüßen? Grußpratiken bei Audienzen am Mogulhof im europäischen Diskurs der Frühen Neuzeit", ibid., 17–56.
21. See also Ranajit Guha, "On Some Aspects of the Historiography of Colonial India", in *Subaltern Studies I: Writings on South Asian History and Society*, ed. Ranajit Guha (Delhi: Oxford University Press, 1982), 37–44.
22. IOR/L/PS/12/1925, "Coll 4/61 Ceremonial Code: Ceremonies to Be Observed for Reception and Audiences of Ambassadors and Ministers", BL.
23. Ibid.
24. Ibid.
25. Humphrys to Curzon, no. 3, 25 March 1922, N 3667/59/97, FO 371/8077, 1922, "Movements of Lieutenant-Colonel Humphrys" and no. 2, FO 402/1, 1922, "Correspondence respecting Afghanistan: Part I", TNA.
26. Ibid., emphasis added.
27. Burschel, "Einleitung", 11.
28. George Nathaniel Curzon, *Tales of Travel* (London: Century, 1988), 39–84.
29. *India Office and Burma Office List for 1947*, 44. 182-F, F&P, 1935, "Ceremonials observed on the occasion of the passage of His Majesty's Minister (Colonel W. K. Fraser-Tytler) in Afghanistan through Peshawar and Khyber Pass to Kabul", NAI.
30. Cohn, "Representing Authority in Victorian India". For a list see Terence Creagh Coen, *The Indian Political Service: A Study in Indirect Rule* (London: Chatto & Windus, 1971), 262–265.
31. The two occasions, on which Humphrys and Fraser-Tytler presented their diplomatic credentials afresh in 1927 and 1940, are not considered here. Squire's accreditation as Britain's first Ambassador in 1948 is discussed in Chapter 8.
32. Humphrys to Curzon, no. 3, 25 March 1922, N 3667/59/97, FO 371/8077, 1922, op. cit.; Maconachie to Henderson, no. 5, 22 May 1930, N 4006/6/97, FO 371/14786, 1930, "Return of His Majesty's

Mission to Kabul" and no. 75, FO 402/12, 1930, "Further correspondence respecting Afghanistan: Part XII"; Maconachie to Henderson, no. 6, 23 May 1930, N 4007/6/97, FO 371/14786, 1930, "Presentation of credentials by His Majesty's Minister to Afghanistan" and no. 76, FO 402/12, 1930, op. cit.; Maconachie to Simon, no. 11, 22 January 1934, no. 3, FO 402/16, 1934, "Further correspondence respecting Afghanistan: Part XVII"; Fraser-Tytler to Simon, no. 47 Confidential, 12 April 1935, no. 6, FO 402/16, 1935, "Further correspondence respecting Afghanistan: Part XVIII"; Wylie to Eden, no. 59, 18 September 1941, IOR/L/PS/12/1913, "Coll 4/54 British Legation: appointment of Lt Col Sir W Kerr Frazer-Tytler [sic], Sir Francis Wylie and Mr G F Squire", BL and no. 5, FO 402/22, 1941, "Further correspondence respecting Afghanistan: Part XXIV", TNA; 4(2)-F, EA, 1943, "Appointment of Mr. G. F. Squire, CIE, as H.M.'s Minister at Kabul and ceremonial observed on the occasion of his passage through Peshawar and Khyber Pass & Kabul. His audience with H. M. the King of Afghanistan", NAI.

33. Humphrys to Curzon, no. 3, 25 March 1922, N 3667/59/97, FO 371/8077, 1922, op. cit., TNA. All following quotations are taken from this file unless specified otherwise.
34. Ludwig W. Adamec, *Afghanistan, 1900–1923: A Diplomatic History* (Berkeley: University of California Press, 1967), 49.
35. Shah Wali, *My Memoirs* (Kabul, 1970), 63.
36. Ibid., 24.
37. "'Victory' Memorial, Kabul", Mss Eur F223/115(16)-(17), "Papers of General Sir Sydney Muspratt, Indian Army 1898–1941", BL.
38. "Report on the Kabul Mission, by Sir H. R. C. Dobbs, K.C.S.I., K.C.I.E", para. 12–15, N 1450/59/97, FO 371/8076, 1922, "Negotiations conducted by British Mission in Kabul during 1921", TNA; Leon B. Poullada, *Reform and Rebellion in Afghanistan, 1919–1929: King Amanullah's Failure to Modernize a Tribal Society* (Ithaca: Cornell University Press, 1973), 60–61.
39. From Sir Louis Cavagnari to Lord Lytton, Kabul, 24 July 1879, Elizabeth Edith Balfour Countess of, *The History of Lord Lytton's Indian Administration, 1876 to 1880: Compiled from Letters and Official Papers* (London: Longmans & Co, 1899), 342–344.
40. Humphrys to Curzon, no. 3, 25 March 1922, N 3667/59/97, FO 371/8077, 1922, op. cit., TNA. All following quotations are taken from this file unless specified otherwise.
41. See also Burschel's term "kulturelle Distanzerfahrung", or "experience of cultural distance" Burschel, "Einleitung", 1.
42. See also Metcalf, *Ideologies of the Raj*, 66–112; Neumann, *Diplomatic Sites*, 45–72.

43. Humphrys to Curzon, no. 3, 25 March 1922, N 3667/59/97, FO 371/8077, 1922, op. cit., TNA. All following quotations are taken from this file unless specified otherwise.
44. "Report on the Kabul Mission, by Sir H. R. C. Dobbs, K.C.S.I., K.C.I.E", para. 12, N 1450/59/97, FO 371/8076, 1922, op. cit., TNA.
45. Ibid., para. 12; David B. Edwards, *Before Taliban: Genealogies of the Afghan Jihad* (Berkeley: University of California Press, 2002), 1–24.
46. "Report on the Kabul Mission, by Sir H. R. C. Dobbs, K.C.S.I., K.C.I.E", para. 12, N 1450/59/97, FO 371/8076, 1922, op. cit., TNA.
47. Humphrys to Curzon, no. 3, 25 March 1922, N 3667/59/97, FO 371/8077, 1922, op. cit., TNA. All following quotations are taken from this file unless specified otherwise.
48. See also "India and 'Oriental Despotism'", Metcalf, *Ideologies of the Raj*, 6–15.
49. Humphrys to Curzon, no. 3, 25 March 1922, N 3667/59/97, FO 371/8077, 1922, op. cit., TNA.
50. Peter Sluglett, "Humphrys, Sir Francis Henry (1879–1971), Colonial Administrator and Diplomatist", *The Oxford Dictionary of National Biography* (Oxford: Oxford University Press, 2004).
51. Poullada, *Reform and Rebellion in Afghanistan*, 252.
52. Humphrys to Curzon, no. 11, 20 September 1922, para. 3 & 9, no. 5, FO 402/1, 1922, op. cit. and N 8664/59/97, FO 371/8077, 1922, "Situation in, and British policy towards, Afghanistan", TNA; Government of India, Foreign and Political Department, no. 73, 2 October 1919, para. 6, IOR/L/PS/10/808, "File 1061/1919, Pt 1-2 Afghanistan", BL.
53. Sana Haroon, *Frontier of Faith: Islam in the Indo-Afghan Borderland* (London: Hurst, 2007), 91–124.
54. Shah Mahmoud Hanifi, *Connecting Histories in Afghanistan: Market Relations and State Formation on a Colonial Frontier* (Stanford: Stanford University Press, 2011); Marsden and Hopkins, *Fragments of the Afghan Frontier*; Bijan Omrani, "The Durand Line: History and Problems of the Afghan-Pakistan Border", *Asian Affairs* 40, no. 2 (2009): 177–195.
55. Fraser-Tytler to Viscount Halifax, no. 3, 10 January 1940, para. 5, no. 18, FO 402/21, 1940, "Further correspondence respecting Afghanistan: Part XXIII", TNA; Among many other examples: William Kerr Fraser-Tytler, *Afghanistan: A Study of Political Developments in Central and Southern Asia*, 2nd ed. (London: Oxford University Press, 1953), 300; Omrani, "The Durand Line", 186.
56. Adamec, *Afghanistan, 1900–1923*, 72.
57. Ibid., 185; "A survey of Anglo-Afghan relations", 4, 17, 19, 29, F 1161/108/97, FO 371/69451, 1948, "Corrections to the Foreign Office Research Department memorandum on Anglo-Afghan relations from 1747 to the present day", TNA.

58. Government of India, Foreign and Political Department, no. 9, 7 October 1926, para. 2, N 5344/1716/97, FO 371/11744, 1926, "Anglo-Afghan relations", TNA. See also 240-F, F&P, 1926, "Afghan interference with British tribesmen", NAI.
59. Government of India, Foreign and Political Department, no. 9, 7 October 1926, para. 2, N 5344/1716/97, FO 371/11744, 1926, op. cit., TNA.
60. Humphrys, telegram no. 80, 4 April 1924, N 3100/4/97, FO 371/10393, 1924, "Demands from His Majesty's Government from Afghan Government" and no. 58, FO 402/3, 1924, "Further correspondence regarding Afghanistan: Part III", TNA.
61. Humphrys to Chamberlain, no. 75, 5 September 1925, no. 47, FO 402/5, 1925, "Further correspondence respecting Afghanistan: Part V", TNA.
62. Government of India, Foreign and Political Department, no. 9, 7 October 1926, para. 3, N 5344/1716/97, FO 371/11744, 1926, op. cit., TNA.
63. Chamberlain to Gould, no. 27, 30 May 1927, no. 3, FO 402/7, 1927, "Further correspondence respecting Afghanistan: Part VII", TNA; Ludwig W. Adamec, *Afghanistan's Foreign Affairs to the Mid-Twentieth Century: Relations with the U.S.S.R., Germany, and Britain* (Tucson: University of Arizona Press, 1974), 98. See also Chapter 7 below.
64. Fraser-Tytler, *Afghanistan*, 200; Amin Saikal, *Modern Afghanistan: A History of Struggle and Survival* (London: I.B. Tauris, 2012), 313.
65. Poullada, *Reform and Rebellion in Afghanistan*, 54ff.
66. Coen, *The Indian Political Service*, 237.
67. Ibid., 238.
68. Martin Ewans, *Afghanistan: A New History* (Richmond: Curzon, 2000), 97. See also Arnold Fletcher, *Afghanistan: Highway of Conquest* (Ithaca: Cornell University Press, 1965), 186.
69. Humphrys, telegram no. 129, 1 February 1929, N 699/1/97, FO 371/13991, 1929, "Withdrawal of His Majesty's Legation from Kabul", TNA.
70. Ibid.
71. At the conclusion of Dane's mission in 1905, Habibullah Khan had attempted to give the agreed treaty a "national rather than personal" character, according to Adamec, *Afghanistan, 1900–1923*, 61.
72. N 4424/1/97, FO 371/13999, 1929, "Nadir Khan and recognition of Kabul Government", TNA.
73. Thomas Jefferson Barfield, "Problems in Establishing Legitimacy in Afghanistan", *Iranian Studies* 37, no. 2 (2004): 263–293.
74. "Afghanistan: Question of recognition of Habibullah", N 4424/1/97, FO 371/13999, 1929, op. cit., TNA.
75. Notes on file cover, N 474/1/97, FO 371/13990, 1929, "Habibulla Khan", TNA.

76. "Afghanistan: Question of recognition of Habibullah", N 4424/1/97, FO 371/13999, 1929, op. cit.; Humphrys, telegram no. 129, 1 February 1929, N 699/1/97, FO 371/13991, 1929, op. cit., TNA.
77. For instance, "Perseus Crosses the Khyber", *The Times*, 24 December 1928; "The Rescues from Kabul. Women's Ordeal. Rebel Snipers Active", *The Times*, 28 December 1928; "First Photographs from Kabul. The Knight Volant", *The Times*, 22 January 1929; "A Great Deliverance", *The Times*, 21 February 1929; "Withdrawal from Kabul", *The Times*, 25 February 1929; "Kabul. Airmen's Final Voyage. A Magnificent Record. Over 500 Persons Rescued", *The Times*, 27 February 1929. See also Anne Baker and Ronald Ivelaw-Chapman, *Wings Over Kabul: The First Airlift* (London: Kimber, 1975). See Chapter 3, note 121 and Chapter 6, note 91.
78. David Fairhall, "60 Years After, Raj Survivors Recall Our Own Kabul Airlift", *The Guardian*, 15 February 1989, 7.
79. Shah Wali, *My Memoirs*, 93
80. "Interview between Sir F. Humphrys and Nadir Khan", N 1404/1/97, FO 371/13994, 1929, "Interview between Sir F. Humphrys and Nadir Khan", TNA.
81. Poullada, *Reform and Rebellion in Afghanistan*, 254.
82. Shah Wali, *My Memoirs*, 51.
83. Ibid.
84. Ibid., 47.
85. Saikal, *Modern Afghanistan*, 106.
86. Thomas Jefferson Barfield, *Afghanistan: A Cultural and Political History* (Princeton: Princeton University Press, 2010), 188–197, 206–210; Saikal, *Modern Afghanistan*, 33, 99.
87. Gould, *The Jewel in the Lotus*, 101.
88. See Barfield, *Afghanistan*, 206; Louis Dupree, *Afghanistan* (Karachi: Oxford University Press, 1997), 459; Saikal, *Modern Afghanistan*, 102.
89. "Afghanistan: Question of recognition of Habibullah", N 4424/1/97, FO 371/13999, 1929, op. cit., TNA.
90. William Kerr Fraser-Tytler, "In Memoriam", *Journal of the Royal Central Asian Society* 49, no. 2 (1962): 118–119.
91. See Adamec, *Afghanistan's Foreign Affairs to the Mid-Twentieth Century*, 183–188 for a narrative of events on the resumption of diplomatic relations.
92. Maconachie to Henderson, no. 5, 22 May 1930, N 4006/6/97, FO 371/14786, 1930, op. cit., TNA. All following quotations refer to this file unless specified otherwise.
93. For an account of the "Peshawar disturbances" see Brandon Marsh, *Ramparts of Empire: British Imperialism and India's Afghan Frontier, 1918–1948* (Basingstoke: Palgrave Macmillan, 2015), 59–114.

94. Maconachie to Henderson, no. 5, 22 May 1930, N 4006/6/97, FO 371/14786, 1930, op. cit., TNA. All following quotations are taken from this file unless specified otherwise.
95. Emphasis added.
96. Fraser-Tytler, "In Memoriam".
97. Maconachie to Henderson, no. 6, 23 May 1930, N 4007/6/97, FO 371/14786, 1930, op. cit., TNA.
98. "'Nimla'", Mss Eur F223/115(6), "Papers of General Sir Sydney Muspratt, Indian Army 1898–1941", BL.
99. Humphrys, telegram no. 285, 28 March 1929, N 1786/1/97, FO 371/13995, 1929, "Attack on His Majesty's Consulate at Jalalabad", TNA.
100. Maconachie to Henderson, no. 5, 22 May 1930, N 4006/6/97, FO 371/14786, 1930, op. cit., TNA, emphasis added.
101. Maconachie to Henderson, no. 6, 23 May 1930, N 4007/6/97, FO 371/14786, 1930, op. cit., TNA. All following quotations are taken from this file unless specified otherwise.
102. Emphasis added.
103. Enclosure, ibid.
104. Fraser-Tytler, unofficial letter no. 1, 1 July 1939, IOR/L/PS/12/1765, "Coll 3/166 Indo-Afghan frontier: measures to give British frontier officials a better understanding of Afghanistan; A)issues of quarterly unofficial letter by British Legation Kabul; B)proposed mutual exchange of visits by British and Afghan frontier officials", BL.
105. See comments on file cover, N 4007/6/97, FO 371/14786, 1930, op. cit., TNA; Marsh, *Ramparts of Empire*, 175–176.
106. See comments on file cover, N 4007/6/97, FO 371/14786, 1930, op. cit., TNA, emphasis added.
107. Fletcher, *Afghanistan*, 231.
108. "A survey of Anglo-Afghan relations", 17, F 1161/108/97, FO 371/69451, 1948, op. cit., TNA.
109. Maconachie to Henderson, no. 6, 23 May 1930, N 4007/6/97, FO 371/14786, 1930, op. cit., TNA. All following quotations are taken from this file unless specified otherwise.
110. Andrew J. Rotter, "Culture", in *Palgrave Advances in International History*, ed. Patrick Finney, *Palgrave Advances in International History* (Basingstoke: Palgrave Macmillan, 2005), 268.
111. Dobbs, No. 178-M.C., 6 August 1920, para. 9, 3, N 127/127/97, FO 371/5381, 1920, "Proceedings of the British-Afghan Conference at Mussoorie, 1920", TNA.
112. Maconachie to Henderson, no. 6, 23 May 1930, N 4007/6/97, FO 371/14786, 1930, op. cit., TNA. All following quotations are taken from this file unless specified otherwise.

5 ACCREDITATION AND PERFORMANCE   229

113. Maconachie to Simon, no. 153, 29 November 1933, para. 8, no. 23, FO 402/16, 1933, "Further correspondence respecting Afghanistan: Part XVI", TNA.
114. See minutes on file cover N 4007/6/97, FO 371/14786, 1930, op. cit., TNA. All following quotations are taken from this file unless specified otherwise.
115. Emphasis added.
116. Fraser-Tytler, "In Memoriam", 119; Poullada, *Reform and Rebellion in Afghanistan*, 264–265.
117. Marsh, *Ramparts of Empire*, 175; Christian Tripodi, '"Politicals", Tribes and Musahibans: The Indian Political Service and Anglo-Afghan Relations 1929–39', *The International History Review* 34, no. 4 (2012): 866.
118. Maconachie to Simon, no. 153, 29 November 1933, para. 5, no. 23, FO 402/16, 1933, op. cit., TNA.
119. Dobbs, No. 178-M.C., 6 August 1920, para. 29, 12, N 127/127/97, FO 371/5381, 1920, op. cit., TNA.
120. Humphrys, telegram no. 81, 9 April 1924, N 3224/4/97, FO 371/10393, 1924, "Activities of Nadir Khan", TNA; "Note of a conversation held on April 4 between His Majesty's Minister, Kabul, and Serdar Nadir Khan, Afghan Minister of War", 13 May 1924, N 4076/3320/97, FO 371/10408, 1924, "Nadir Khan" and no. 84, FO 402/3, 1924, op. cit., TNA.
121. Maconachie, telegram no. 134, 9 July 1924, N 5763/3320/97, FO 371/10408, 1924, "Appointment of Nadir Khan as Afghan Minister in Paris", TNA, emphasis added.
122. See minutes on file cover N 4007/6/97, FO 371/14786, 1930, op. cit., TNA.
123. "Afghanistan: Annual Report, 1930", para. 6, N 760/760/97, FO 371/15550, 1931, "Annual report on Afghanistan", TNA.
124. Maconachie to Simon, no. 153, 29 November 1933, para. 3, no. 23, FO 402/16, 1933, op. cit., TNA.
125. Ibid., para. 2.
126. Nick Cullather, "Damming Afghanistan: Modernization in a Buffer State", *The Journal of American History* 89, no. 2 (2002): 518.
127. Ibid., para. 5.
128. "Afghanistan: Annual Report, 1930", para. 112, N 760/760/97, FO 371/15550, 1931, op. cit., TNA. See also Marsh, *Ramparts of Empire*, 174–180.
129. Maconachie to Simon, no. 153, 29 November 1933, para. 5, no. 23, FO 402/16, 1933, op. cit., TNA.
130. "Afghanistan: Annual Report, 1930", para. 112, N 760/760/97, FO 371/15550, 1931, op. cit., TNA.

131. Maconachie to Simon, no. 153, 29 November 1933, para. 9, no. 23, FO 402/16, 1933, op. cit., TNA.
132. Ibid., para. 7, emphasis added.
133. Ibid., para. 11.
134. Fraser-Tytler, *Afghanistan*, 243.
135. Fraser-Tytler, unofficial letter no. 1, 1 July 1939, IOR/L/PS/12/1765, op. cit., BL.
136. Ibid.
137. Fraser-Tytler, *Afghanistan*, 236–237.
138. Further see Tripodi, "'Politicals', Tribes and Musahibans".
139. Maconachie to Simon, no. 153, 29 November 1933, para. 11, no. 23, FO 402/16, 1933, op. cit., TNA.
140. E.g. Fletcher, *Afghanistan*, 235. See also Adamec, *Afghanistan's Foreign Affairs to the Mid-Twentieth Century*, 198, n. 21; Barfield, *Afghanistan*, 19.
141. Maconachie to Simon, no. 11, 22 January 1934, no. 3, FO 402/16, 1934, op. cit., TNA. All following quotations are taken from this file unless specified otherwise.
142. See also Mrinalini Sinha, *Colonial Masculinity: The "Manly Englishman" and the "Effeminate Bengali" in the Late Nineteenth Century* (Manchester: Manchester University Press, 1995).
143. Maconachie to Simon, no. 11, 22 January 1934, no. 3, FO 402/16, 1934, op. cit., TNA.
144. Fraser-Tytler, *Afghanistan*, 131–132, 209, 236. See also Dobbs, No. 178-M.C., 6 August 1920, para. 9, 3, N 127/127/97, FO 371/5381, 1920, op. cit., TNA.
145. Maconachie to Simon, no. 11, 22 January 1934, no. 3, FO 402/16, 1934, op. cit., TNA. All following quotations are taken from this file unless specified otherwise.
146. E.g. Dupree, *Afghanistan*, 477–499; Ewans, *Afghanistan*, 104; Angelo Rasanayagam, *Afghanistan: A Modern History* (London: I.B. Tauris, 2003), 25.
147. Nicholas Barrington, *Envoy: A Diplomatic Journey* (London: I.B. Tauris, 2014), 26.
148. Fraser-Tytler to his mother, 3 March 1935, no. 1–3, file 1/1/6, GB165-0326; Fraser-Tytler to his mother, 13 March 1935, no. 4–5, file 1/1/6, GB165-0326; Fraser-Tytler to his mother, 24 March 1935, no. 6, file 1/1/6, GB165-0326; Fraser-Tytler to his mother, 4 April 1935, no. 7–9, file 1/1/6, GB165-0326; Fraser-Tytler to his mother, 11 April 1935, no. 10–12, file 1/1/6, GB165-0326, MECA.
149. For writing the self see Roy Porter, "Introduction", in *Rewriting the Self: Histories from the Renaissance to the Present*, ed. Roy Porter (London and New York: Routledge, 1997), 1–14; Winfried Schulze, ed.,

Ego-Dokumente: Annäherung an den Menschen in der Geschichte (Berlin: Akademie-Verlag, 1996); Sidonie Smith, *Reading Autobiography: A Guide for Interpreting Life Narratives* (Minnesota: University of Minnesota Press, 2001).

150. Fraser-Tytler to his mother, 24 March 1935, no. 6, file 1/1/6, GB165-0326, MECA.
151. Fraser-Tytler to his mother, 11 April 1935, no. 10–12, file 1/1/6, GB165-0326, MECA.
152. Poullada, *Reform and Rebellion in Afghanistan*, 55.
153. See also Malhotra and Lambert-Hurley, "Introduction: Gender, Performance, and Autobiography in South Asia".
154. Fraser-Tytler to Simon, no. 47 Confidential, 12 April 1935, no. 6, FO 402/16, 1935, op. cit., TNA.
155. Maconachie to Simon, no. 25, 27 February 1935, N 1509/11/97, FO 371/19403, 1935, "Departure of Sir R. Maconachie from Kabul", TNA.
156. Fraser-Tytler to his mother, 11 April 1935, no. 10–12, file 1/1/6, GB165-0326, MECA.
157. Ibid.
158. Fraser-Tytler to Simon, no. 47 Confidential, 12 April 1935, no. 6, FO 402/16, 1935, op. cit., TNA.
159. Fraser-Tytler to his mother, 24 September 1931, no. 45–47, file 1/1/4, GB165-0326, MECA.
160. "Afghanistan: Annual Report, 1930", para. 112, N 760/760/97, FO 371/15550, 1931, op. cit., TNA.
161. Fraser-Tytler, *Afghanistan*, 243–244.
162. "Intelligence Summary No. 27 for the Week ending July 3, 1936", no. 67, FO 402/17, 1936, "Further correspondence respecting Afghanistan and Nepal: Part XIX", TNA.
163. Wylie to Eden, no. 59, 18 September 1941, IOR/L/PS/12/1913, op. cit., BL and no. 5, FO 402/22, 1941, op. cit., TNA.
164. Maconachie to Simon, no. 25, 27 February 1935, N 1509/11/97, FO 371/19403, 1935, op. cit., TNA. See also Chapter 4.
165. IOR/L/PS/12/1925, op. cit., BL.
166. Wylie to Eden, no. 59, 18 September 1941, IOR/L/PS/12/1913, op. cit., BL. All following quotations are taken from this file unless specified otherwise.
167. Ibid., emphasis added.
168. Comments by G. E. Crombie, 19 November 1941, ibid.
169. Emphasis added.
170. Ibid.
171. E.g. 582-F, F&P, 1935, "Printing and distribution of a pamphlet 'Afghanistan - hints for visitors and motorists' compiled by Captain A. C. Galloway", NAI: "Persian is the official language of Afghanistan, and

is also the vernacular to the north and west of the Helmand river. Pushto is also spoken, but only in the east, and some Turki in the north".
172. "Intelligence Summary No. 46 for the week ending 18th November, 1938", para. 7, IOR/L/PS/12/1842, "Coll 4/3(7) British Legation: Diaries of Military Attache, 1938–1939", BL.
173. E.g. Barfield, *Afghanistan*, 24. See also Shah Mahmoud Hanifi, "A History of Linguistic Boundary Crossing Within and Around Pashto", in *Beyond Swat: History, Society and Economy Along the Afghanistan-Pakistan Frontier*, ed. Benjamin D. Hopkins and Magnus Marsden (London: Hurst, 2013), 1–16.
174. Fraser-Tytler to Caroe, 7 November 1940, para. 4, 2, IOR/L/PS/12/1913, op. cit., BL.
175. Linlithgow to Fraser-Tytler, 29 May 1941, ibid.
176. Wylie to Eden, no. 59, 18 September 1941, IOR/L/PS/12/1913, op. cit., BL.
177. Fraser-Tytler to his mother, 11 April 1935, no. 10–12, file 1/1/6, GB165-0326, MECA.
178. "The Expulsion of Axis Nationals from Afghanistan", file 11, GB165-0326, MECA.
179. Wylie to Eden, no. 59, 18 September 1941, IOR/L/PS/12/1913, op. cit., BL.
180. Minutes by Pink, 25 March 1943, E 1595/86/97, FO 371/34920, 1943, "Interview between Sir F. Wylie and the Afghan Prime Minister", TNA.
181. Ibid.
182. Minutes by Rumbold, 18 March 1943, ibid., and 536-F, EA, 1943, "H.M.'s Minister, Kabul's interviews with the Prime Minister of Afghanistan", NAI.
183. Correspondence between Squire and Wylie, 4(2)-F, EA, 1943, op. cit., NAI.
184. Squire to Eden, no. 42, 6 August 1943, ibid. All following quotations are taken from this file unless specified otherwise.
185. IOR/L/PS/12/1729, "Coll 3/139 British Legation at Kabul: Attitude of Afghan government regarding members of the Indian Civil Service being appointed to posts at British Legation", BL.
186. Fraser-Tytler, *Afghanistan*, 228–229.
187. Dipesh Chakrabarty, "Postcoloniality and the Artifice of History: Who Speaks for 'Indian' Pasts?", *Representations* 37, special issue: *Imperial Fantasies and Postcolonial Histories* (1992): 8.
188. Ranajit Guha, "On Some Aspects of the Historiography of Colonial India", in *Subaltern Studies I: Writings on South Asian History and Society*, ed. Ranajit Guha (Delhi: Oxford University Press, 1982), 38–39.
189. Charles Lindholm, "Images of the Pathan: The Usefulness of Colonial Ethnography", *European Journal of Sociology* 21, no. 2 (1980): 360.

CHAPTER 6

Diplomatic Bodies

DIPLOMATIC GAZES

When Francis Henry Humphrys laid eyes on Amanullah Khan in the course of his accreditation in 1922, it prompted him to sketch a bodily portrait of the Afghan ruler: "My first impression of the Ameer suggested a good-looking and intelligent young man, a little too soft physically and mentally somewhat highly strung. Though his glance was too quick and shifting to give an idea of much dignity or composure, he smiled at times with a sudden attractiveness".[1] Humphrys captured the king and, in capturing the king, revealed his own reactions to the king's bodily condition and actions. From the king's external appearance, Humphrys also deducted his intelligence and reliability. It mattered how this Afghan ruler looked and behaved. Anglo-Afghan relations depended on it. At the same time, British diplomats' own bodies had to be fit and fully functioning. William Kerr Fraser-Tytler's age and bodily health became reference points in the decision of his recall from Kabul in 1941.[2] He was "in no sense an athlete", but considered himself "both active and able-bodied".[3] Whereas Humphrys' exposure to the frontier had 'hardened' him in the eyes of his superiors, Fraser-Tytler had gone "soft" in Afghanistan.

Bodies were on the minds of British diplomats in Kabul. And, the body played a central role in Anglo-Afghan diplomatic relations. Afghanistan was feminised, sexualised and infantalised. She had "aspirations".[4] According to Henry Dobbs in 1922, the more Afghanistan "exposes herself to

© The Author(s) 2019
M. Drephal, *Afghanistan and the Coloniality of Diplomacy*,
Cambridge Imperial and Post-Colonial Studies Series,
https://doi.org/10.1007/978-3-030-23960-2_6

the steadying influence of education and the public opinion of civilisation, the less chance of *her* ignorance, vanity and fanaticism tempting *her* into aggression".[5] Her "desires" prompted "overtures" that would "attract" international suitors.[6] These in turn, put her at risk of "penetration" by Russia in the 1920s and Germany in the 1930s.[7] Eventually, colonial administrators thought, Afghanistan would experience the "indifference with which they as a whole regard her".[8] Independence would demonstrate "her slow advance in education", allowing Afghanistan to find "her proper level".[9] Upon "learning her impotence" intellectually, Afghanistan would realise the "might of Great Britain" and "her dependence on India not merely economically but also for her free intercourse with the civilised world".[10] In contrast to the patriarchal gendering of Afghanistan, Amanullah Khan appeared in hypermasculine terms. According to Dobbs, he had "a ruling passion for expansion".[11] Unless it was diverted towards Central Asia, the "gaze of the Amir" would "inevitably be fixed upon India" in order to "satisfy" it: "India is in herself the most attractive [...] because of her riches".[12]

In addition to the performative blueprints of encountering Afghans discussed in the previous chapter, the Indian colonial officers who became accredited diplomats in Kabul also exported bodily practices out of India, into Afghanistan and through the Indian Empire at large. The history of the British Legation in Kabul offers a rich array of evidence for an exploration of diplomatic history's corporeal dimensions. As much as they forged Anglo-Afghan relations, the imperial transmitters also shaped embodied thinking about Afghanistan's international relations and the Legation's quotidian practices. Bodies were at the heart of colonial ambitions in Kabul, and bodily practices lay bare the tensions in the diplomatic-colonial relations existing between the British mission in Kabul and the Afghan state. In order to further reveal both these tensions and ambitions, the chapter first develops the concept of the diplomatic body as an analytical category.

SPACE, LANGUAGE, MEDICINE AND THE DIPLOMATIC BODY

The *corps diplomatique* usually describes the community of diplomatic agents accredited to a particular government.[13] Exploiting the ambiguity of the term, this chapter understands it, quite literally, as the diplomatic body. This offers a fresh perspective on diplomatic history, as Robert Dean has shown:

[I]t seems fair to characterize much 'traditional' diplomatic history as focused on the construction of narratives designed to reconcile the presumed imperatives of 'national interests' (however construed), with a relatively *disembodied* policy-making process (i.e., minds at work, employing a rational strategic calculus). Statesmen, in this vision, are rarely depicted as driven by emotions of lust, anger, fear, disgust, loneliness, desire for intimacy, jealousy, or the burdens of physical frailty, at least as part of a systematic analysis of historical outcomes.[14]

This marked criticism of the constructions of conventional diplomatic history indicates that writing new diplomatic history can give us "a better understanding of the intersections between elements of identity formation, the individual actor in all his or her complexity, and the outcomes of political practice".[15] The historiography of diplomacy and international relations has fruitfully harvested the results of a number of turns in the social sciences, which are discussed in Chapter 1.[16] The product is an innovative array of useful frameworks that read archival materials in "new and interesting ways".[17] The chapter follows the lead of body historians, who have already read the body as the "body politic" in the context of the history of medicine as well as in terms of international relations.[18] In the medical history of colonial India, the body has been interpreted "as a site of colonizing power and of contestation between the colonized and the colonizers" and as an "imperial body".[19] The chapter captures "the body of the diplomat" and other diplomatic bodies. Chapters 3 and 4 show how bodies were organised into hierarchies at the Legation along, which endowed them with meaning and organised them according to gradations of power. This chapter explores the ubiquity of the body in the Legation's everyday routines.[20]

Diplomats, being observers, commentators, collectors and disseminators of information, reporters and interpreters, documented pieces of everyday life in abundance even if they were only vaguely related to diplomatic business. Diplomatic texts, ranging from the private to the official, reveal a significant amount of corporeal detail, because the diplomats in question, consciously or otherwise, attached great importance to their own bodies. Colonial officers focused on the impact on their bodies of administering colonial rule in order to justify colonial rule's means and ends.[21] The physical strains caused by living and working amongst strange people, in foreign places and unbearable climates attempted to make the heavy duty of the "white man's burden" in colonial circumstances relatable.[22] In this sense, the body was part of a lived experience that turned into a rhetorical device.

This chapter excavates the diplomatic body from between the lines of diplomatic reporting and recording.

In Kabul, the body of the diplomat was inscribed with imperial sovereignty. It was a vessel of state power. The bodies of British-Indian diplomats represented a complex configuration of power, including an imperial government as well as the colonial state. As Chapter 5 shows, all Ministers enacted ideas of Afghanistan's position within the Indian Empire. Embodied representations of power reveal themselves in a wide array of physical registers in diplomats' writing strategies. Diplomatic correspondence relating to Anglo-Afghan relations was written in rich 'body language'. In their accreditation reports, British Ministers in Kabul assessed the physique and mental state of Afghan kings, in addition to a variety of other characters, basing also their assessment of royal abilities on these observations. As a consequence, Afghan, Indian and British bodies were written into the archival record. No less obviously, Humphrys elicited a brief moment of attraction to Amanullah Khan in the quotation opening this chapter. Moreover, he displayed anxieties dressed in complaints when arriving in Kabul for the first time as seen in Chapter 5.

Against this backdrop, the chapter embraces several meanings of the diplomatic body. It employs the diplomatic body in its perhaps most common form as a descriptor for the collective of diplomatic agents. Moving beyond this conventional understanding, it uses the concept in reference to the body of an individual engaged in diplomacy and international relations on the one hand and to a body charged with diplomatic significance and purpose on the other. An overview over the chapter's main argument illustrates this. The body is conceptualised as a contact zone, which allows for the exploration of the three distinct, yet interrelated bodily themes of space, language and medicine.[23] The diplomats of the British Legation in Kabul assessed the Afghan diplomatic space in relation to the physical reactions it excited. Their own bodies were fundamentally important requirements to conduct diplomacy in the assigned spatial conditions. As Chapter 3 shows, certain spaces were only accessible to women. The violent history of Anglo-Afghan relations ensured that Afghanistan and Kabul were considered in terms of bodily security and insecurity. British diplomats also employed a wide spread of physical and emotional registers in their textual recordings of the Afghan representatives with whom they interacted. Renderings of Afghan space and people captured the body both as a means of communication, contact and interaction. The body was a gauge with which to assess, not just record, Afghan bodily qualities as well as describe the newly independent state of Afghanistan and its representatives.[24] It highlighted perceived political and civilisational differences by feeding off well-established colonial categories created during the formation of the Afghan state in the nineteenth-century.[25] In order to maintain their own bodies in Afghanistan as well as in order to enhance their political influence among Afghan bodies, the Legation employed medicine on a large scale by means of its medical unit. It sought to exploit medical care for political ends by drawing on the healthcare resources of colonial India and expanding them into Afghanistan. Anglo-Afghan relations were built around diplomatic bodies that were both frail and fit. The analysis focuses on representations of the body in diplomatic communication and literature, on the physical and emotional aspects of experiencing Afghanistan as well as on the employment of colonial healthcare. Far from being an instance of 'indirect' colonial rule, the Legation's diplomats came into close and direct contact with Afghan bodies, unleashing colonial concepts of the body onto the political relations with independent Afghanistan. The body plays a central role in British diplomacy's colonising tendencies.

"CONDITIONS IN KABUL ARE PECULIAR"[26]

Before they joined the colonial services, Indian Politicals were educated in public schools and universities, which provided a wide array of physical and competitive cultures.[27] Physical education and health were central aspects of British curricula especially since the middle of the nineteenth century.[28] Sport, in particular, was much more than a pastime. Games provided and encapsulated key concepts of imperialism. According to James Mangan's concept of the "games ethic",

> [T]he public schoolboy supposedly learnt inter alia the basic tools of imperial command: courage, endurance, control and self-control. However, there was a further and important dimension to the later concept of 'manliness': its relevance to both dominance and deference. It was widely believed, of course, that its inculcation promoted not simply initiative and self-reliance but also loyalty and obedience. It was, therefore, a useful instrument of colonial purpose. At one and the same time it helped create the confidence to lead and the compulsion to follow.[29]

First, public schooling perpetuated an imperial culture of sport and sought to 'diffuse' its ideals across the empire through its pupils. Then, universities sported their own physical cultures and led an individual to the colonial entrance exams and potentially into the colonial services. The body was a core selection criterion for "political employ" in colonial India and, therefore, also for the diplomatic post in Kabul. The colonial services routinely checked the physical and emotional fitness of their officers.[30] This practice enjoyed wide circulation outside of the colonial services. Writing on the ideal diplomat, Ernest Satow defined "[g]ood temper, good health and good looks" as "necessary qualifications for the diplomatic career".[31] Consequently, exercise and contest comprised all administrative layers from subaltern soldiers to the upper echelons including Governors-General and Viceroys. Not only in India, but across the British Empire, sport encapsulated a "badge of office" in its own right amongst imperial administrators.[32] An excessive focus on athletics and games even contributed to allegations of the "intellectual mediocrity" of India's diplomatic service.[33] Sport was a key element of colonial culture, which sought to prolong the physical fitness of its members and display key concepts associated with imperial power.[34] Elizabeth Collingham has argued that "[l]ate nineteenth-century anthropology conceived of the body as the physical outer map of the moral inner man":

> Indulging in an evening game of polo, squash, or tennis before a bath and dinner, the athletic civilian displayed his possession of an appropriate physique while simultaneously demonstrating his possession of the essential qualities of the ruling race: the ability to observe rules, loyalty and comradeship towards his team members, fair play to the other side – in other words, honesty, uprightness, courage and endurance.[35]

By the time a candidate joined the Indian Political Service, he had already been equipped with and trained in several instances of sport. Applications to the Indian Political Service asked for a candidate's general health, a history of field sports and the quality of his horsemanship, making athletic exploits part of the selection process of potential colonial officers. Referees were asked if a respective applicant was "of active habits and proficient in field sports".[36] In response, Humphrys was described as "a good all-round athlete" and as a "[v]ery good" horseman.[37] He had captained the cricket team at Shrewsbury School.[38] His hobbies included cricket, shooting and fishing.[39] Henry Hawes Elliot was found to be "fond of tennis & hockey". Asked if he was "a good, bad, or indifferent horseman", the referee replied: "Good".[40] Edmund Stanley Sayer Lucas "rides, shoots, swims & plays squash".[41] Squire played tennis and golf.[42] Richard Roy Maconachie's decision to apply for the Indian Civil Service in the first place was partly due to the fact that "life in India was preferable to life in London for anyone who loved the open air and all field sports".[43] Several of the Legation members were sportsmen of international stature. For instance, Arthur William Fagan represented Britain in fencing at the Olympic Games in Stockholm in 1912.[44] George Cunningham played international rugby for Scotland.[45] The diplomats who arrived in Kabul in early 1922 to set up the Legation emerged from a colonial system whose various physical cultures were immensely pronounced and finely tuned through decades of attention to the colonial servant's bodily qualities. They came to Kabul after experiencing the "corporality of colonialism in India" during many years of service.[46] Due to their cultural and political involvement in the colonial services in India, they exercised plenty in a variety of games, sometimes to the point of physical injury. Playing tennis, Humphrys "sprained his ankle rather badly".[47] In another game over a decade later, Fraser-Tytler "ruptured a tendon in his leg".[48] He also fell off a horse, which led to hearing loss in one of his ears later on.[49] These personal and private hobbies and activities were also transferred to the larger institution of the British Legation, which kept a running fishing record and hunting diary until the 1960s.[50] Physical and mental health played a key role in the recruitment of elite colonial officers. These aspects of health could fail, as the example of Mahmud Shah, the Consul in Jalalabad, shows in Chapter 3. In another instance, William Peat Hogg, the Surgeon, himself suffered from malaria and dysentery during his career in India, his treatment minutely evidenced in a service file.[51] Ill-health could also be figuratively attested if it served political ends; in a list of many reasons for Fraser-Tytler's withdrawal from Kabul in 1941 the first suggested that he had suffered "owing to the strain of his long service in Afghanistan, and on account of his health".[52]

As a result of these multiple layers of physical education, former colonial officers introduced colonial notions of physicality and racial difference into their relations with Afghan representatives and statesmen. They became agents in the transfer of colonialism's physical cultures as they applied to Afghanistan the lessons learned in the process of colonial encounters and bodily practices in India.[53] That transfer included the insecurities and anxieties experienced by colonial rulers at the prospect of losing control.[54] The body performed a key role in the way Afghanistan was experienced, perceived and recorded. Kabul's environmental, political and social conditions prompted definitions of an ideal diplomatic body, which was always male and of robust physical strength. The British diplomat's colonially trained body provided the primary point of reference for the experience of Kabul's spatial conditions in the early 1920s. Afghanistan was regularly cast in anti-Indian terms spatially, meteorologically and with regard to physical comforts, hygiene and civilisational chronology. It was not understood in absolute terms, but existed in reference to colonial India. In order to become British diplomats in Kabul colonial servants had to first cross the perceived civilisational threshold demarcated by the Khyber Pass. In Fraser-Tytler's collection of private letters to his mother, the very first is a travelogue from India to Afghanistan.[55] The North-West Frontier Province itself came close to an extra-colonial, inter-imperial space located between the colonial state in India and independent Afghanistan. On their way to Kabul, British diplomats, therefore, entered a passage from the colonial state through an extra-colonial corridor into an imperial space. As such an imperial space, Afghanistan was likened to the more familiar conditions on India's frontier and in India itself. Colonial conditions, thus, generated the norm by which Afghanistan's physicality came to be measured.

When British diplomats reached Kabul in early 1922, they were faced with the problem of accommodation. A residence, let alone an 'impressive' one, did not yet exist. Afghanistan in general and Kabul in particular constituted largely unfamiliar territory in terms of personal experiences.[56] At the same time, the colonial archive offered a multitude of blueprints in this regard, but the experience of the Dobbs Mission of 1921 provided the single most important reference for the Legation's setup. Its physical experience of Kabul's sensory stimuli directly informed the housing arrangements for the British Legation in Kabul. In late 1921, only days after the Dobbs Mission had concluded in the signing of the Anglo-Afghan Treaty, long-serving Indian Politicals drew up a plan for the establishment of a permanent British Legation in Kabul. The outline for a Legation touched upon the "unfavourabl[e]" accommodation which had confronted the Dobbs Mission in Kabul. It was quartered "next door to some infantry barracks[,] and [...] life in it was rendered almost unbearable owing to the plague of flies".[57] Henry Dobbs wrote of the "depressing and harassing conditions" in Kabul, which had contributed to the death of Khan Bahadur Ghulam Murtaza Khan, a member of his mission. The personnel was "crowded into a fairly restricted space[,] and sanitary arrangements were exceedingly difficult".[58] The plan for the establishment of a British Legation in Kabul concluded that "it would be preferable for the residence of a British Minister to be at some distance from the more densely populated part of Kabul

City", so as to render it "habitable according to European standards".[59] The physical separation of European and Afghan bodies in the process of the Legation's localisation ran parallel to ideas which underpinned the racial ordering of urban areas in colonial India, including India's new capital, New Delhi.[60]

Kabul was both unfamiliar and relatable. The Legation was at first accommodated in Bagrami on the eastern outskirts of Kabul near the road from Jalalabad.[61] In March 1922, only weeks after arriving in Kabul, Humphrys uttered a "cry from the heart: [...] [w]e are very uncomfortable and likely to remain so until the new Legation is built".[62] The spatial conditions inside the mission quarters did not suit the average British colonial diplomat. Afghan and European bodies alike were too close for comfort. In the summer of 1922, the Legation moved to two *serais* (courtyards), which were historically significant owing to the fact that the Durand Agreement of 1893 had been signed there.[63] Apart from representing a locality befitting the management of Anglo-Afghan relations, the *serais* also offered more space to the Legation staff, but still did not entirely correspond with the Legation's physical needs: "The approaches to them are mean, and the surroundings insanitary. As a residence for Europeans in so notoriously unhealthy a city as Kabul during the hot weather, they can only be regarded as a doubtful but inevitable expedient".[64]

Outside of the mission quarters, Kabul appeared as a health hazard, was allegedly infectious and overcrowded with Afghans, who preferred "dirty water" from streams and drains to the tap water coming from nearby hills.[65] George MacGregor Millar, the Surgeon, was called upon to assess the sanitary and hygienic conditions in Kabul in order to define suitable housing arrangements for a permanent British diplomatic mission. The Afghan summer of 1922, then at its peak, has left its mark on Millar's report. The Legation Surgeon urged that occupation of "the present *insanitary residence* by the British Legation should be as brief as possible".[66] In particular, Millar referred to Kabul's water supply, which consisted of local wells and a pipe originating in the Paghman Hills close to Kabul and running past the royal palace and the houses of Afghan officials.[67] The water was of good quality, but came in small quantities. According to Millar this impacted directly on the conditions of hygiene prevailing in Kabul:

> The method of sewage disposal is crude in the extreme [...]. Enteric fever seems to be fairly common in Kabul and its neighbourhood, but undoubtedly the great epidemic source is cholera [...]. The sickness among the members

of the Kabul Mission in 1921 was considerable[.] [...] [T]he immediate surroundings and neighbourhood of the very confined area of the Legation are insanitary to such a degree as to baffle description in ordinary language.[68]

Kabul was also liable to "attack by epidemic disease of the most serious and deadly order".[69] The report casts the Kabul of 1922 as a dirty and unhealthy place on the verge of being uninhabitable for European bodies. The absence of water purification promoted "agriculture rather than hygiene".[70] The existence of cholera epidemics in India became a civilisational marker of difference between the familiar colonial notions of progress and backwardness.[71] Similarly, Kabul constituted a place which could throw the British body into crisis, a common phenomenon in colonial contexts.[72] Hyperbole in reports from Kabul—"there is *no* sanitation in Kabul City"—and the claim regarding the indescribability of Afghan conditions are cases in point.[73]

In India, several rumours circulated regarding Kabul's other perceived disadvantages, which were largely based on a lack of experience with its conditions. One of these criticised the "notoriety" of Kabul's climate, which actually compared positively to India, as later diplomats testified.[74] R. F. D. MacGregor, the Legation Surgeon in 1944, wrote that "[t]here are four distinct seasons in Kabul; Spring is delightful, Summer not too hot, autumn beautiful, and winter the least pleasant (to me) season of the year. Taking it all round Kabul is a healthy place".[75] Kabul's climate attracted considerable attention because the colonial discourse on the environment conceived of tropical heat as a marker of health in its own right whose detrimental impact "sapped the strength" of even the most "virile" civilisations and, therefore, also posed a potential risk for colonial rulers in India.[76]

While Kabul's climate was increasingly regarded as being beneficial, healthy and even desirable in comparison to India, Afghanistan did not compare quite so favourably in other instances.[77] A posting in Kabul came with a range of amenities, such as free quarters, free transport between Afghanistan and India, exemption from Indian customs duty on imports from outside India, free electricity, free supply of fuel during winter months and free water. These amenities were designed to compensate to some extent and in differing degrees for Kabul's perceived lack of physical comforts in comparison to India.[78] Serving in Afghanistan was not a very popular thought "to the Indian mind", although there was a sizeable Indian community.[79] It was depicted by British diplomats in similar and, at times, even more extreme notions of overcrowding and unhealthiness than those pertaining, allegedly, to colonial India.[80] When Humphrys reported to George Nathaniel Curzon in London his journey to Kabul in 1922 he stressed that he and his personnel had been "more fortunate than could have been expected in withstanding the rigours of our journey and of Oriental cookery".[81]

In addition to health hazards, overcrowding and discomfort, the diplomatic job in Kabul also involved a significant amount of risk of violent injury or death, quite understandable in light of the killings of previous diplomatic envoys in Kabul in 1841 and 1879. The deaths of Alexander Burnes and William MacNaghten in 1841 circulated in various versions, all containing details of physical dismemberment.[82] Acutely aware of historical precedents, Britain's past encounters with Afghanistan cast a shadow on the minds of the new arrivals, who expected their effort to take place at the risk of their corporeal integrity.[83] Fraser-Tytler wrote in a letter to his mother that "[Humphrys] told me the other night that when he left for Kabul, [King] George V interviewed him before departure & expressed the hope that he would not match the example of previous envoys to the Afghan Court! They had a dinner the night they outlived [Pierre Louis Napoleon] Cavagnari, who only lasted 6 weeks [in 1879], & I think that we must have outlived MacNaghten now".[84] Judging from an entry in the *Kabul Legation Diary*, Maconachie, Counsellor in 1922, was aware of the fact that his date of birth overlapped with Cavagnari's date of death, 3 September.[85] History was at hand when events in the present appeared threateningly similar to those of the past. In an album of photographs by William Hazlitt Duncan Best, the Secretary, the meeting of armies near the Legation in 1928/1929 is labelled as a "siege", suggesting that representatives of empire, as on the occasions of the First and Second Anglo-Afghan Wars, were once again the primary target by Afghan fighters.[86]

The Legation's institutional memory of physical hazards suffered at the hands of diplomats in Afghanistan was restricted along lines of race. No one remembered Hafiz Saifullah Khan. The bodies of Indians were imperfect vessels for the sovereignty of the Raj although they enjoyed the immunity of consular law. Since the 1880s, India's Agents and Newswriters in Kabul were isolated from the centres of power and information. The British Agency had a hospital, and its workers acted as informers.[87] During the war of 1919, the British Agent was prevented from leaving Kabul for India despite the catastrophic deterioration of diplomatic relations between India and Afghanistan. Whilst the Afghan envoy in India returned to Afghanistan, the British Agency was placed under virtual house arrest. The British Agency and its staff, comprising horse-keepers, a *dhobi* and tailor, were prohibited from interaction with the outside world, including its arrangements regarding the supply of daily necessities for people and animals. Communication with India was cut off, and Khan Bahadur Hafiz Saifullah Khan's experiences survive in a diary that spans four months well beyond the conclusion of the treaty of peace concluded at Rawalpindi. In addition to isolation, the Agency suffered "captivity, public insult and injury", "curses, spittings, nick-names, and abuses of indescribable nature levelled at me and my Government".[88] Hafiz Saifullah Khan made several personal protests to Mahmud Tarzi and Amanullah Khan, all of which went unheeded. Nor did the Government of India initiate rescue. Unlike the women and children who were evacuated from Kabul in 1928/1929, Hafiz Saifullah Khan and the people in his charge were left to their own devices. The British Agent pondered the reasons for this inactivity:

> We are at a loss to know as to why no effective or strong measure have yet been taken by our own Government to liberate us from the distress and afflictions we are put under by the savage Afghan Government, which seems to be due to either our Goverment being unaware of our true condition which has been misrepresented to them by the Afghan deputation or to the fact that we are Indians and not the English.[89]

Despite the litany of physical and psychological violence to which the British Agency was subjected, its experiences were not widely circulated. Hafiz Saifullah Khan's body was not a vessel of sovereignty; its injuries could not prompt a political reaction. The language of the handwritten minutes on the file cover, tellingly, lends credence to Hafiz Saifullah Khan's own suggestion behind his captivity: "The Agent *not unnaturally* felt acutely his abandonment by his Gov[ernment] & attributes it partly to the fact that he is *only* an Indian".[90]

European fears for life and limb never fully disappeared. As a matter of last resort, the Legation secretly stored a case of "bombs" and rifles. Several events affected the Legation's sense of security, particularly during the winter of 1928/1929 and again in 1933. Both events were also widely reported on.[91] During the rebellion against Amanullah Khan in the winter of 1928/1929, the Legation found itself on the frontline between Habibullah Kalikani's and Amanullah Khan's soldiers. Fighting took place across the Legation grounds. In a letter to Austen Chamberlain after the event, Humphrys described events from his perspective:

The Legation has passed through a time of extreme peril without any serious casualties to British subjects, but very extensive material damage to buildings which were struck by sixty-six shells and thousands of bullets. I have to deplore the loss of two faithful Afghan servants, who were shot dead in the performance of their duty, while two others were wounded. Another shell passed through a car in the garage. The members of my staff behaved the greatest gallantry and many had hairbreadth escapes. One was shot through the fleshy part of the thigh, another had his face cut by splinters from a bullet, another was struck by a piece of a shell, while several had bullets through their clothes. A great variety of outside duties, such as laying out of signals for aeroplanes on the lawn, where cheerfully performed under a dangerous cross fire. The ladies of the Legation [...] splendidly upheld the proud traditions of their race.[92]

A handwritten addition continues in the margins: "and several Indian members of my staff were conspicuous for their bravery".[93] Humphrys had a narrow escape when a bullet broke his shaving glass and singed his moustache as Afghanistan's dangers imprinted themselves on his body in the process.[94]

The rebellion against Amanullah Khan was followed by a period of dynastic uncertainty that contributed to several violent incidents until 1933. In his ambition to quell opposition Nadir Shah arrested Ghulam Nabi Charkhi, a former general of Habibullah Khan's army, and an advocate of Amanullah Khan, in 1932. Ghulam Nabi Charkhi was executed on 8 November 1932. In June 1933, the Afghan Minister in Berlin, Muhammad Aziz Khan, Nadir Shah's half-brother was assassinated in an escalation of the domestic struggle for power fought between the former king in Italian exile and Nadir Shah. Exactly a year after the execution of Ghulam Nabi Charkhi, Nadir Shah was assassinated by a student with connections to Ghulam Nabi Charkhi's family. Two months before, in September 1933, Muhammad Azim, a teacher at the German school in Kabul, in his attempt to assassinate one of the Legation's diplomats, shot the Garage Superintendent Geoffrey Herbert Stranger, the Mir Munshi Syed Irshad Husain, and an Afghan employee named Yakub on the Legation grounds.[95] "Death was instantaneous in both cases: Mr. Stranger being shot through the brain, and Yakub through the heart".[96] As an embodiment of the colonial government, the British diplomatic body was targeted for political reasons. The violence was directed at the Legation as an imperial representation. This "outrage" was interpreted as an expression of resentment of imperial influence in Afghanistan.[97] In Fraser-Tytler's words, "[t]hey are still a very primitive people with a fanatical hatred of foreign domination".[98] The British Legation found itself in the middle of a dynastic struggle for Afghanistan, in which the party of the former king sought to break the "subservience of [the] present Government to British interests and their co-operation with [the] Government of India in crushing [the] independence of frontier, particularly [of the] Mohmand tribes".[99]

The events of 1928–1933 resonate in the context of continued attacks Kabul's diplomatic quarter since 2001. Kabul was a trying place in terms of physical and mental health, safety and comfort. As a consequence, reporting from Kabul, as instanced by the diplomats attached to the British Legation, cast Afghan space in terms of a masculine physique. As a "post of high and anxious responsibility" Kabul's was "no place for people with nerves and temperaments and such like things".[100] Male diplomats in possession of fit bodies and good mental health authored reports from Kabul, which suggested that only those male bodies could conduct diplomacy in Afghanistan successfully. Kabul was barely inhabitable for men and for most parts locked to women, whose movements were also closely monitored. When the first group of British diplomats travelled from Peshawar across the Khyber Pass, into Jalalabad and on to Kabul, they did so without their female partners, as, in the words of the Secretary of State for India, "it would not be wise for [the Minister] to take his wife to Kabul with him".[101] A sense of risk pervaded the instruction. Single men required fewer transport facilities and were more mobile in comparison to being with a partner.[102] They also occupied less space than couples, a not unimportant consideration particularly prior to the occupation of the permanent Legation premises in 1926. Restrictions on female travelling from India into Afghanistan could be tightened and loosened at will. In this respect, Afghanistan resembled a geographical extension of the masculinity of the North-West Frontier Province. Like the North-West Frontier Province, Kabul was at first considered "a 'no families' area for officials".[103] While restrictions on female travelling on and beyond the Indo-Afghan border were in place, importance was attached in Government of India circles to the provision to British officers of "alleviation" from the stresses of service on the frontier and beyond.[104] It is open to speculation whether this alleviation was restricted to the psychological sense of the word or whether it extended into a physical dimension. As Dane Kennedy has shown in reference to comparable colonial enclaves, women could prevent the onset of boredom in Kabul and guard against "loneliness, alcoholism and sexual deviancy".[105] In the early 1950s, diplomatic candidates for a posting to Kabul factored into their decision the argument that "there would be no women".[106] Over time, the restrictions imposed on wives and partners were lifted, as the walls of the permanent Legation premises later sheltered a family friendly abode from the danger and adversity lurking in Kabul. The next chapter discusses this aspect further (Chapter 7).

The Legation disciplined women according to the representational needs of the institution. If they failed to order the Legation's domestic realm and displayed "hysterias", they were threatened with departure, especially if "[t]hey let down the whole show badly, and all the Indians are talking about it, and probably all the Afghans too".[107] As the discussion in Chapter 3 shows, men sexualised women in their writings. At the same time, the presence of deviant women appeared to drive homosocial imaginings of a diplomatic utopia in Kabul: "The Legation is full of women, I would they were at once removed! Why is it that women are so much more troublesome than men?", Fraser-Tytler voiced his gynophobia to his mother.[108] In the absence of this utopia, the sexual relations of Legation employees were instead circumscribed. Male and female bodies were subjected to sexual regulation along patriarchal ideals. In another long letter to his mother, Fraser-Tytler articulated the idea in great detail:

> I have had a row with a member of my staff and a lady on whom he had set his eye. There [sic] conduct was so flagrantly indiscreet that it had developed into a public scandal and I had to remind him rather forcibly that as a temporary member of that most discreet body, the British diplomatic service, he must take a pull. He seemed unable to do so, and I was obliged to tell him that unless he did I should be obliged to ask for his replacement. He then confessed that he had every intention of marrying the lady, who has a husband, as soon as he could get rid of his own wife. As all of these people are unhappy and as the two who are the subject of this present tale would probably do very well together, I told him in somewhat modified terms that I sympathised with his attitude, but that he could not maintain it here, at any rate in war time when everyone is out to catch on to anything which may serve as a stick with which to beat the British. [...] So as they did not seem to know right from wrong, so far as public behaviour went, at any rate, I wrote down a few rules indicating what I meant by discreet behaviour.

a. Do not hold her hand in public places. (Remember she has a husband and he a wife, both here.)
b. Do not kiss her in the garden in daylight. (He'd done this.)

c. Do not isolate yourself from the rest of the community on all public occasions.
d. Do not gaze into each other's eyes like a pair of lovesick idiots of eighteen. (They are both well in the thirties.)
e. If you wish to go to the Italian Legation to play poker, take on occasions your respective wives and husbands with you. It looks better.
f. If you must spend hours in each other's company, don't park your car always outside her house, because it is on the main road, but part it round the corner, or send it down to the bazaar to buy something.[109]

Against this backdrop, Kabul required a particular kind of diplomatic body. In 1944, MacGregor, the Legation Surgeon in 1944, defined the "type of man [who] will do well in Kabul":

> He should be young, physically fit, preferably married, he should have no history of previous tropical disease; he should be fond of games and of a standard of intelligence which will enable him to take up such a hobby as language study. There is nothing 'romantic' about Kabul; the new recruit should be told so, also that hard work is the best preventive of what I must call tropical neurasthenia, and that a hobby is essential. It may be a language, it may be carpentry or photography; it must not be local tittle-tattle.[110]

Once again, Kabul appeared in contrast to India's 'romantic' places, first and foremost the "Indian India" of the princely states on the one hand and of the frontier on the other, both of which were administered by the same pool of people who also supplied Kabul's colonial diplomats. When MacGregor defined the ideal British diplomatic body for Kabul in 1944, the main risk for that body was psychological in nature and seemed to originate from living remotely among an alien people. MacGregor's use of "tropical neurasthenia" is particularly revealing, as it included an unspecified set of symptoms, which predominantly befell European colonial elites.[111] The British Legation in Kabul was conceptualised in the same terms as other colonial enclaves as its diplomatic bodies were subjected to the medical knowledge of other colonial contexts.

The Body and Diplomatic Language

The colonial services' physical routines trained and socialised the colonial diplomat and equipped him with the ability to perceive of and qualitatively label surrounding bodies. Physical appearance and bodily demeanour were central elements of colonial spectacle in South Asia.[112] The preceding Chapter 5 on accreditations indicates that notions of physicality adjoined the process of becoming a British diplomat in Afghanistan. In this chapter's opening paragraph, Humphrys describes an 'attractive', "good-looking and intelligent young", Amanullah Khan, who was also "a little too soft physically and mentally somewhat highly strung" and whose "glance was too quick and shifting to give an idea of much dignity or composure".[113] With almost twenty years of frontier experience, Humphrys seemed unable to appreciate Amanullah Khan physically as well as politically. As Leon B. Poullada has argued, "[l]ack of cultural empathy with Afghanistan, distaste for its nationalist policies, and personal antipathy toward Amanullah Khan were all united in Sir Francis Humphrys, the man chosen to be the first British minister to independent Afghanistan".[114] Humphrys' physical assessment of Amanullah Khan foreshadowed the antagonistic political relationship between the two men. The body, then, was a crucial register in Anglo-Afghan relations.

Ernst Kantorowicz' *The King's Two Bodies* differentiated royalty's body natural and its body politic, dividing the human being from the ruler.[115] In their descriptions of Afghan bodies, British Ministers combined both of these kingly bodies whose natural appearance was representative of the larger Afghan body politic. Describing the Afghan king's body was a well-established trope in diplomatic correspondence, and the colonial archive provided several textual role models. Peter Lumsden had described Dost Mohammed Khan as "tall, of fine physical development, and he truly looked a king".[116] Lepel Henry Griffin, who was in Kabul in 1880, described Abdur Rahman Khan as "a man of about forty, of middle height and rather stout. He has an exceedingly intelligent face, brown eyes, and a pleasant smile and a frank courteous manner".[117] Curzon's descriptions of Abdur Rahman Khan's "external appearance and mien" framed the narrative on the Afghan king's "most interesting traits of his shrewd untutored intellect": "In this strange and almost incredible amalgam of the jester and the cynic, the statesman and the savage, I think that a passion for cruelty was one his most inveterate instincts".[118] In *Leaves from an Afghan Scrapbook*, a copy of which was included in the Legation library, Annie and Ernest Thornton quoted Habibullah Khan as confessing that "'I eat very lot! Too much I eat!'".[119] Textual portraits of Afghan rulers showed their physical appearance, which revealed their inner character and ability to rule. Fraser-Tytler commented in 1953 on Griffin's rendering of Abdur Rahman Khan that, depending on their physical features, Afghan rulers could appear "just the type of man for the task in hand" or evoke doubts on that note.[120] As the previous Chapter 5 shows, Maconachie and Nadir Shah, established closer diplomatic relations, partly because Nadir Shah was seemingly co-opted into India's frontier governance. Maconachie, too, gave a detailed description of Nadir Shah's body:

> It was a pleasant surprise to find [Nadir Shah] looking in better health than I had ever seen. His eyes were bright and his movements brisk, without any appearance of fatigue or illness. He seemed to have put on weight since we had last met just over a year before, and [...] has actually gained 13 lb. since his entry into Kabul [in 1929].[121]

Maconachie's description of Nadir Shah's body is almost intimate, offering opportunities for the application of a "personal touch" to Anglo-Afghan relations: "The value of personal contact in oriental diplomacy is of first importance, and among Orientals it is nowhere more important than in dealing with Afghans".[122] The pleasing political outlook of the king went hand in hand with the positive representation of his body. No other Afghan notable received such positive, almost clinical, feedback on his physical appearance. Maconachie's readership in London found it "comforting that King Nadir Shah's health, upon which so much depends, is good".[123] In contrast to Amanullah Khan, Nadir Shah appeared strong, despite evidence to the contrary, paralleling hopes with regard to the agreeable ambitions of his reign.[124] British Ministers projected the expectations of Anglo-Afghan political relations onto the bodies of Afghan kings.

Observing the health of Afghan rulers went far beyond a personal expression of relief. Its resilience was synonymous with Afghanistan's 'stability', an important piece in the puzzle of the defence of India and in frontier governance. British diplomats perceived a close connection between the health of the Afghan ruling elite and the health of Afghanistan's larger body politic. The ruling family's physical health and its outdoor activities in pursuit of it were listed in great detail in the *annual reports* on Afghanistan.[125] Health was as important as political events because it was central to conducting diplomacy as much as it was key to the establishment of diplomatic routine. Afghan kings, too, customarily inquired after the health of British monarchs in conversation with British diplomats, signalling the close connection between the sovereigns' bodies, the health of the state and of diplomatic relations existing between the two.[126] Proximity in political outlook reflected positively on British representations of Afghan bodies, which in turn carried the weight of the entire Afghan state. Especially after Nadir Shah's assassination in 1933, Afghanistan's stability seemed to hinge entirely on Hashim Khan, Nadir Shah's brother and Zahir Shah's uncle.[127] Hashim Khan's rule of Afghanistan as its "autocratic" Prime Minister between 1933 and 1946 earned him the attributes "great man" and "dictator of this country".[128] The physical strength and good health of Afghanistan's leadership did not only indicate its ability to rule, but defined the country's fate. Illness caused "acute anxiety".[129] Hashim Khan's health, in particular, was closely monitored, especially when he suffered a heart attack in 1944 and gave up government office two years later.[130] In contrast to this strongman, Zahir Shah always appeared youthful with shoulders too slim to carry the burden of ruling Afghanistan.[131] In his farewell despatch from Kabul, Squire noted that a condition of the king's left eye was "causing much anxiety in court circles".[132] Contrary to these low expectations, Zahir Shah continued to rule Afghanistan until 1973, when a coup by his cousin, Mohammed Daoud Khan, the son of the Afghan Minister killed in Berlin, forced him into exile. Incidentally, the coup had taken place as Zahir Shah was undergoing treatment on his eyes in Italy.[133] After the fall of the Taliban, he returned to Afghanistan in 2002.

The Afghan body provided a foil for Anglo-Afghan relations and the projection of various political meanings and judgements. It prompted diverse responses, such as attraction, concern and disapproval, which indicated political cohesion and closeness or opposition and disagreement. The Afghan body was intimately assessed, but also expressed extreme estrangement. In his report on the peace negotiations in Rawalpindi, Hamilton Grant had laid down a behavioural code of conduct closely akin to a manual for the future diplomatic interactions with Afghans:

> It is difficult at first to realise, when one is confronted with a number of fine-looking, comparatively fair-skinned gentlemen, in frock coats or resplendent uniforms, that they are, beneath a thin veneer of civilisation, really very barbarous, very uncontrolled and very childish. Like children, they respond amazingly to the treatment accorded them. But they are high-spirited, wilful, rather naughty children, who are not to be cowed by hard words or threats. Kindliness, patience and candour alone can win them to see reason. They will accept the refusal of their most cherished desire if it is put to them in temperate, friendly words and the reasons for the refusal honestly explained.

But any attempt to browbeat them, and still more any attempt to trick them, is doomed to instant failure. They are proud as the proverbial Highlander, and hard words will drive them to hard answers, which they may afterwards regret, but which they will never admit that they regret. They are very clever, with the cunning of the barbarian, and deeply suspicious of cleverness in others. Hence it is much better to be frank with them and put the cards on the table, than to attempt to best them by diplomatic wiles. They have a great sense of humour, and an opportune jest will often take the edge off an acrimonious situation. They are credulous and will believe the most preposterous story especially if it is to the discredit of their adversary: but their wild beliefs are not to be broken down by sneers. Take them seriously: explain the facts quietly and logically – and they will in the end accept them. But with it all they are shrewd and sensible within the narrow limits of their experience.[134]

If Afghan statesmen did not correspond to colonial expectations of reasonable political behaviour, the Afghan body could be dehumanised in order to give expression to the colonial notion of civilisation, which placed the Afghan and Indian political orders into different stages of development. Reporting on the impact of Amanullah Khan's ambitious reform project in 1928, Humphrys likened Amanullah Khan to a horse: "I am reluctantly forced to the conclusion that King Amanulla[h] has temporarily taken the bit between his teeth and bolted. When he returns to the stable I shall use my best endeavors to curb his petulance and prevent another outbreak".[135] Humphrys suggested to his superiors in London that Amanullah Khan's political actions were animalistic, exceeding even the more common notions of Oriental irrationality. The Afghan king appeared in need of being reined in politically by the colonial officer. The political officer's core competence of horsemanship is also visible in Humphrys' description of Afghans as an "unbridled people".[136] Even if applied only metaphorically, the analogy suggests Humphrys' urge to order Amanullah Khan's nationalist and revolutionary politics. For colonial administrators in India and British diplomats in Kabul, Amanullah Khan remained a problematic figure long after his abdication in 1929. During his time in Kabul, Humphrys had already given him the nickname "Percy".[137] In 1939, Fraser-Tytler referred to "that unworthy object Amanullah Khan", removing him "beyond humanity" altogether.[138] Even if British diplomats maintained good personal relations with Afghan statesmen in Kabul throughout the 1930s, this did not guard against excesses of diplomatic reporting. In the early 1940s, Fraser-Tytler suggested that Afghan rulers suffered from "oriental fatalism [...] short-sightedness and narrowness of outlook":

> I have found that in dealing with Afghans it is not a bad thing to apply such knowledge as one possesses of dealing with horses and dogs particularly young ones. In both cases one wants an infinity of patience, and while a beating at times is necessary it is very unwise to lose one's temper with either. Afghans, even the oldest and wisest of them are very young in mind. They are like young animals or children, delightful people in many ways, courteous, friendly and yet at times pigheaded, unreasonable and petulant to a degree which is sometimes infuriating. It is often very hard when one meets them in society to realise how thin is the veneer of civilisation and how easy it is to scratch its surface and come on the savage beneath, with all the suspicious fears and circumscribed outlook of the primitive man or animal.[139]

Fraser-Tytler's comments echo Grant's of 1919, showing a discursive continuity informed by racism that placed Afghanistan in the realm of 'barbarity'. The body was employed to highlight Afghan difference. British diplomats gendered and infantilised, bestialised and Orientalised Afghan bodies in diplomatic reports by means of metaphors, which cast Afghan statesmen as children, animals, savages and early humans. They sought to express Afghanistan's lack of civilisational progress.[140] The body was the point of reference for the reporting of the imagined gap of development, which justified the colonial order.

HEALTH AND MEDICINE

British diplomatic bodies reacted to Kabul's spatial conditions, and the bodies of Afghanistan's ruling elite were intimately assessed. Both points illustrate that healthy bodies provided the initial requirement to conduct Anglo-Afghan diplomacy and that the functioning of the Afghan state depended on the health of its leadership. Medical knowledge had been developed into a diplomatic technology and applied in Anglo-Afghan relations since the nineteenth century. "There is nothing in which European surgery produces a stronger impression on the minds of Asiatics than in operations on the eye, a branch of the science of which they are altogether ignorant", wrote Percival B. Lord in the 1830s.[141] In 1862, Henry Walter Bellew's *Journal of a Political Mission to Afghanistan* broadened Afghanistan into a medical *terra nullius*: "These people have no regular doctors of their own, and are but seldom visited by any from other countries".[142] Afghanistan was constructed as a medical market in geopolitical terms, whose lack of competitive technologies demanded foreign medical intervention. Colonial governance developed humanitarian techniques that sought to exploit, not remedy, the condition of Afghanistan's healthcare. Unlike diplomats, "[a] doctor is practically always safe, even among the most fanatical tribes beyond our border-line", wrote Angus Hamilton in 1906.[143] During the reigns of Abdur Rahman Khan and Habibullah Khan, several European medical practitioners settled the humanitarianism that accompanied the travelling diplomacy of Anglo-Afghan relations in Kabul. Among these medical practitioners were dentists, surgeons, physicians to the *amir* and "medical attendants attached to the harem".[144] The physicians, especially, were tasked with safeguarding the health of Afghan *amirs* as part of a wider strategy to 'stabilise' the rulership of Afghanistan and, consequently, also the defence of India.[145] Medical officers were diplomatic agents, and sometimes both at the same time: Mahbub Ali Khan accompanied the Dobbs Mission as Sub-Assistant Surgeon before becoming Oriental Secretary. Tasked with writing up an account of "Medical affairs in Afghanistan" in 1942, H. A. Ledgard turned to the Legation's library, where he found Walter Bellew's *Journal of a Political Mission to Afghanistan* and John Alfred Gray's *At the Court of the Amir*, an account of Gray's time as Abdur Rahman Khan's physician.[146] Ledgard borrowed medical anecdotes from both, introducing travelling as well as settled medical interventions into the Legation's diplomatic framework.

Given the historical continuity ensured by colonial medical officers' borrowings from the colonial archive, Afghanistan was constructed as a healthcare void. 'Adequate' healthcare in colonial India was more than a day's journey away under perfect travel conditions. Looking from India, Kabul was a remote place. With Afghanistan's "national sanitary efficiency" in doubt and "uncertain medical help in time of need", a quick medical response on the spot proved vital.[147] The diplomat's body was cared for by the Legation Surgeon and the Legation's medical unit. Fraser-Tytler underwent a successful appendectomy in the 1940, while the Military Attaché Alfred Noel Irvine Lilly did not recover in 1924.[148] The reports on Kabul's environment reinforced the need to provide diplomatic bodies with the necessary immunity against Kabul's allegedly adverse hygienic and medical conditions.[149] Afghan and British bodies seemed to have identical needs, which could be met by the provision of healthcare from colonial India's medical services. The provision of medical autarchy to the Legation was the guiding principle behind the establishment of its medical unit, but it constituted only a minor share of the Legation's medical activities, as the Legation staff accounted for only a fraction of the cases which were treated there.[150] Rather, the Legation's medical establishment addressed Afghan bodies in need of healthcare on a large scale for diplomatic purposes.[151] In doing so, British diplomacy in Afghanistan revealed larger ambitions, which it disguised in humanitarian terms. The hospital was justified by "[t]he good feeling engendered by altruistic efforts to give medical aid to the inhabitants who, lacking as they do such help, are frequently attacked by disease".[152]

The idea to employ medical care for diplomatic ends was articulated very early during the planning stages of the Legation, as a "good hospital under a British medical officer would undoubtedly do much towards establishing good relations with the Afghans".[153] Although ambitions of this magnitude were not realised, Denys Bray, India's Foreign Secretary, underlined the "great political value" of a dispensary, a combined day-time practice and pharmacy.[154] Consequently, the Legation established an outpatient dispensary, which was open to all, approval of the Afghan government permitting. Most of the dispensary's medical work was undertaken by an Indian Sub-Assistant Surgeon, a pharmacist, a dresser and a full-time nurse. The Legation also featured a small-scale hospital, which provided medical care in urgent cases, particularly surgeries and confinements, "who cannot be moved from Kabul".[155] Its use was primarily reserved for the Legation's staff, Kabul's Indian community and other foreigners in emergencies, who needed stationary care. The Legation's hospital did not treat Afghans, who were referred to Kabul's public hospitals. The provision of medical care was structurally integrated into the British Legation's diplomatic setup from the very beginning. Even before the Legation moved into its purpose-built houses with its separate hospital compound in 1926, it already maintained a dispensary at its temporary accommodation in the historic *serais* of the Durand Agreement. It also provided, by and large, a cheap option to meet political ends: the costs for the medical unit were allocated at Rs. 100,000, while the construction of the Minister's residence alone consumed around Rs. 200,000.

The Legation dispensary became almost immediately popular with the Afghan population "in the absence of any clinic in this country in which Afghans put any faith".[156] In 1926, the dispensary registered about 26,000 annual cases. These figures rose to over 40,000 in 1938 and even 60,000 in 1941.[157] By comparison, estimates show that Kabul's population grew from 60,000 in 1916, to 120,000 in 1936 and 250,000 in 1959.[158]

Not surprisingly in light of these large numbers of patients, the dispensary provided "one of our most valuable political assets", according to Humphrys.[159] In order to underline that status, Humphrys requested the shipment of an X-ray machine, because no such machine was in operating order in Kabul in 1926.[160] When Kabul's only other X-ray machine broke down in 1931, the British Legation de facto became part of the state-run public health organisation of Afghanistan, simply by providing resources that were otherwise unavailable.[161] The Legation expanded into Afghanistan's medical market.

The Legation's medical unit provided several points of diplomatic contact. In addition to the public outpatient dispensary, the Legation Surgeon attended personally to the private circles of the royal family and to members of the court.[162] Amanullah Khan's "evident terror of disease" provided a point of entry for British medical officers to establish themselves as figures of authority in court circles.[163] The influence of the Legation Surgeon amongst Afghans was usually compounded by a sense of urgency, which provided him with an opportunity to stake out his work more clearly against that of other international doctors operating in Kabul. The Legation Surgeon became a diplomatic agent in his own right, as successive British Ministers highlighted the importance of his work for political reasons. Legation Surgeons "succeeded in winning the confidence and affection of Afghans of all classes", including the king's gratitude for providing him with a pair of glasses.[164] The resultant popularity of Legation Surgeons with high-ranking Afghan statesmen was often noted in diplomatic reports.[165]

In general, there was more medical work than the Legation could handle. Humphrys commented in 1925 that the number of patients at the dispensary was "inconveniently large", indicating that the Legation did not have sufficient personnel to satisfy Afghan demand.[166] As a consequence, the female partners of the British Legation staff took over nursing duties at the hospital.[167] A nurse from the Lord Minto Indian Nursing Association from Calcutta assisted Queen Soraya in the birth of her second son in 1923, expanding the points of contact between the Legation and the Afghan population otherwise closed to male diplomats. For a short time, Gertrude Humphrys, the British Minister's wife, had been considered to act as a midwife, providing a significant example of the overlap of the physical and the political.[168] Afghan women were visited at their homes. The Legation later established the post of a full-time nurse and even discussed the appointment of a "lady doctor" as well as a dentist.[169]

The Afghan body could be made dependent on Western medical care. It provided a political opportunity, which was not to be missed. The Legation's medical establishment—a dispensary for the public, a small-scale hospital for emergencies among the Legation personnel and foreigners living in Afghanistan, doctors and nurses—set it apart from other diplomatic missions in Kabul. The provision of Western medicine was applied to overcome the Legation's political status as the "most unpopular institution in Asia" in the early 1920s.[170] Humphrys' assessment of the Legation's reputation was balanced by the assumption of the Legation's medical unit being "[t]he only efficient, and by far the most popular medical institution in Afghanistan".[171] The reports written on the dispensary, hospital and the activities of the Legation Surgeon praised their various successes. Legation Surgeons likened their role to that of a "chairman" and "authority of appeal" of doctors in Kabul, without whose decision no important case could be concluded.[172] From the perspective of the British Legation in Kabul, public healthcare in Afghanistan seemed "crude and inadequate".[173] This assessment was fuelled and perpetuated by the popularity which the Legation's medical unit generated. As a result, the Legation sought to foster its influence in the Afghan medical sector. Both the inefficiency of Afghan institutions and the productivity of the Legation dispensary were continually advertised. H. A. Ledgard, Legation Surgeon in 1942, even suggested that the arrival of the British Legation in Kabul was coincidental with the "dawn of medicine in Afghanistan".[174] Given this situation, the spread of Western medicine appeared as a powerful tool for British diplomacy. Diplomatic medical care in Kabul displayed "hegemonic attributes and ambitions", which have been established for colonial medicine in India.[175] Once more, colonial India appeared as a point of comparison to the British Legation in Kabul. In India, medicine was initially employed as a "tool of empire", but had to adapt in order to fit Indian circumstances.[176] As in other colonial contexts, the British-Indian engagement in several areas of the Afghan medical and healthcare sector generated Afghan resistances. As early as 1925, the dispensary's popularity conflicted with the monopoly given to the medical department of the Afghan state. The close interaction of British and Afghan bodies at the dispensary seemed discomforting to the Afghan government for reasons of "undesirable activities" as much as for the "personal danger to the Legation staff".[177] Until early 1926, the Afghan government discouraged the treatment of Afghans at the dispensary, but Humphrys convinced Mahmud Tarzi, the Afghan Foreign Minister, to lift these restrictions for the male Afghan public.[178]

Afghan women were not allowed to seek medical help "in view of popular prejudice on the subject", but diplomatic reports indicate that Afghan women still sought treatment at the dispensary.[179]

Afghan attendance at the Legation dispensary was a recurring theme in Anglo-Afghan relations. In the summer of 1942, the Afghan government again prohibited the use of the Legation dispensary by the Afghan public. The ban was enforced by stationing police officers at the gates to the Legation's hospital compound.[180] The contingent and enclosed nature of the Legation eased its surveillance. The Afghan government acted in accordance with its policy of neutrality during the Second World War, while resistance to the British activities and ambitions displayed in the field of medical care may have also played a role. Francis Verner Wylie interpreted the restrictions placed on Afghan attendance at the British Legation as an effort by the Afghan government to maintain its monopoly on healthcare and to guard its independence. As the embodiment of the Afghan state's sovereignty, Afghan bodies was guarded against colonial medicine, even against their own wishes at times. The Legation, according to Wylie, had overstepped the initial need to establish a medical unit as he criticised the thinking underlying the maintenance of the dispensary for the Afghan population as "rank bad psychology".[181] The British Legation's medical facilities illustrated to a wide Afghan public the inadequacy of Afghanistan's own institutions.

> I am myself certain that it is the wrong approach and that all such activities here should be abated as gracefully as may be. The field for humanitarian activity in Afghanistan is of course practically unlimited and that Legation Surgeons should view it with constant impatience and with an ardent desire to be labouring in it is quite natural. The country is however administered by the Afghan Government and not by us. [...] There can be few foreign countries nowadays where the independence motif is so much in evidence as it is in Afghanistan while in connection with this obsession the foreign power which is always thought of as threatening Afghan independence is the British. It behoves the British Legation therefore to walk warily and neither by word nor by deed to suggest that we are here for any purposes other than diplomatic representation of the Government we serve.[182]

Like it did in his accreditation ceremony, Wylie's approach also differed here. To him, the challenges inherent in the Legation's medical humanitarianism were unnecessary distractions to the mission's diplomatic brief. Because the links between imperial power and healthcare provision were becoming increasingly evident, Wylie advised his superiors that the ban should not be challenged. Between 1944 and 1948 attendance at the walk-in dispensary did not exceed 10,000 cases per year, including Afghan patients, who circumvented the official ban.[183] With Afghan attendance reduced, the Legation provided healthcare on a smaller scale primarily to Kabul's international community. The Legation also facilitated the passage of Afghans to India and Europe for medical treatment, as it increasingly focused its efforts on select individuals.[184] Nevertheless, the political potential for the provision of medical care continued to be underlined by later Legation Surgeons as well as by Giles Frederick Squire, Wylie's successor.[185] Afghan bodies were determined to be in need of medical attention and care, establishing points of contact for British diplomacy. The body was a political asset to British diplomacy in Afghanistan, which could be exploited by technological means provided from India or by personal examination in Kabul.

British ambitions to exploit the Afghan body in need of medical attention led to resistance by the Afghan government, which tried to prevent British contact with the wider Afghan population. Afghan responses to the Legation's medical care were not uniform. The dispensary continued to be popular with both Afghan men and women, but the larger public was disallowed from profiting from medical measures while a selected few individuals were attended by the Legation Surgeon or afforded treatment in India or even further abroad.

RE-EMBODYING DIPLOMACY

Having explored several avenues of the Legation's body history, the evidence assembled in this chapter shows ways to read the history of diplomatic relations in bodily dimensions in contrast to conventional reconstructions of diplomacy's political aspects. Official and private texts alike show the potential for the study of the body as a significant element of diplomacy and international relations. The discussion of the various *corps diplomatiques* redresses the largely disembodied nature of diplomatic and international historiography. The prismatic effect of the exploration brings to the fore the ubiquity of the body in diplomatic history. It was significant in sickness and in health, on British and Afghan sides and across the sexes. Its ubiquity represents encompassing colonial ambitions of British interest in Afghanistan. The *corps diplomatique* was a mode of perception and expression. Its proximity could be an indicator of good relations. Its 'softness' could be read as political incongruity. The body offered a canvas for the projection of physical values and represented a channel of communication. Deciphering the body language of diplomatic texts bears out the governmental ambitions of the British Legation in Kabul. Perceptions of opposite numbers, their physical appearance, dress and habits carried political meaning. The presence of body language in diplomatic reporting—understood both as the richness of physical references in diplomatic language as well as physical interaction—is best explained by the fact that the diplomatic encounter was—and still is—a widely physical affair. The references to physical activities and conditions in diplomatic reports have generally been regarded as expressions of minor importance in comparison to the supposedly plain political content of the written word. But, as this chapter argues, the body was not only the garnishing on political reports and more than just a metaphor: it presents a central theme in its own right.

Whilst acknowledging that this chapter's understanding of body history is largely shaped by those records which have survived archival selection, the record for the period prior to 1947 establishes a variety of bodily themes in diplomatic understandings of Afghanistan. By acknowledging the centrality of the body in diplomatic relations, it is possible to extend the study of diplomatic history to a physical realm, which proves both innovative and rewarding. With regard to the British Legation in Kabul, the discussion of the different *corps diplomatiques* reveals the coloniality of British diplomacy in Afghanistan between 1922 and 1947. The British Legation was to a large extent a colonial enclave, which employed colonial power and knowledge, rather than a mere 'outpost of empire'.[186] Although Afghanistan was never formally colonised, the British Legation signified an extension of the Indian colonial state through its personnel and its technologies. The Legation's colonial personnel transported ideas of colonial and Afghan bodies into Afghanistan and relayed their experiences in Kabul through colonially shaped lenses. Legation diplomats assessed people and places according to their physical appearances, which were themselves informed by their colonial experiences in India. Kabul appeared in relation and comparison to descriptions of European settlements in India. The colonial archive and its textual portraits brought historical bodies into diplomacy's present. The power-laden perceptions of the colonial encounter in India further enriched Anglo-Afghan relations, leading to the othering of Kabul, the treatment of Afghan bodies as political assets, as well as the dehumanisation of Afghan heads of state in political reports. The colonial officers who became diplomats were agents in the transfer of a wide-ranging Anglo-Indian physical culture to Kabul. Formulae developed 'at home', in India and during the historical Anglo-Afghan encounter, which shaped, trained and maintained the colonisers' bodies and civilised the colonised, ensured that even after 1919 Afghanistan continued to be framed in a colonial context and not as part of an early postcolonial world. The British Legation in Kabul projected colonial ambitions of controlling and ordering Afghan bodies to differing degrees through the various shapes of the *corps diplomatique*, which had been formed in the colonial encounter in South Asia. The Legation's use of the diplomatic body was colonial in character and outlook. The colonial officers doubling as British diplomats minutely observed and assessed Afghanistan's diplomatic engagement with other internationally recognised independent states. But, they carved out for themselves spaces of diplomatic exception, trespassing against Afghan sovereignty by means of the Legation's access to Afghan bodies. They attentively monitored and crafted a narrative on Afghanistan's acceptance of Western concepts of diplomacy as an internationally accepted code of interaction between 'civilised states', whilst they themselves created transgressive norms of diplomatic practice that originated in colonial asymmetries of power. The British diplomats of the Legation in Kabul did not shed their colonial identities in favour of the diplomatic ideals of equality and reciprocity. This qualifies our understanding of diplomacy and colonialism alike at the end of empire; to the same extent that the diplomatic body in Kabul masked its colonial characteristics, colonialism itself existed in various shapes even outside established colonial orders, for instance as colonially inspired and sourced diplomacy and its concomitant means. The British Legation's history illustrates that the transition from the colonial to the postcolonial was a lengthy, fragmented and incomplete process. Its approach to Afghan bodies built an institutional and ideational bridge that connected nineteenth-century medical interventions and the twentieth-century "humanitarian invasion" of Afghanistan.[187]

Notes

1. Humphrys to Curzon, no. 3, 25 March 1922, N 3667/59/97, FO 371/8077, 1922, "Movements of Lieutenant-Colonel Humphrys" and no. 2, FO 402/1, 1922, "Correspondence respecting Afghanistan: Part I", TNA.
2. See Chapter 4.

3. "Note by Kerr Fraser-Tytler on the Situation in Afghanistan", 20 August 1941, file 10, GB165-0326, MECA.
4. Humphrys to Chamberlain, no. 87, 14 September 1926, para. 7, FO 371/11738, N 4556/1716/97, "Conversation between Sir F. Humphrys and the King of Afghanistan", TNA. See also Chapter 2, notes 85–88.
5. Government of India to India Office, 23 March 1922, para. 6., N 3998/59/97, FO 371/8077, 1922, "Sir H. Dobb's [Dobbs] report on his mission to Kabul", TNA, emphasis added.
6. Ibid.
7. Government of India, Foreign and Political Department, no. 9, 7 October 1926, para. 16, N 5344/1716/97, FO 371/11744, 1926, "Anglo-Afghan relations", TNA. See also FO 371/22257, N 3722/2706/97, "German Penetration in Afghanistan", TNA.
8. Government of India to India Office, 23 March 1922, para. 6, N 3998/59/97, FO 371/8077, 1922, op. cit., TNA.
9. Ibid.
10. Ibid.
11. "Report on the Kabul Mission, by Sir H. R. C. Dobbs, K.C.S.I., K.C.I.E.", para. 32, 18, N 1450/59/97, FO 371/8076, 1922, "Negotiations conducted by British Mission in Kabul during 1921", TNA.
12. Ibid. See full quote Chapter 2, note 81.
13. Keith Hamilton and Richard Langhorne, *The Practice of Diplomacy: Its Evolution, Theory, and Administration*, 2nd ed. (London: Routledge, 2011), 76; Iver B. Neumann, *Diplomatic Sites: A Critical Enquiry* (London: Hurst, 2013), 27; Ernest Satow, *A Guide to Diplomatic Practice*, vol. 1 (London: Longmans, Green and Co., 1917), 3.
14. Robert Dean, "The Personal and the Political: Gender and Sexuality in Diplomatic History", *Diplomatic History* 36, no. 4 (2012): 763, emphasis added.
15. Ibid., 764.
16. See for instance Patrick Finney, ed., *Palgrave Advances in International History*, Palgrave Advances (Basingstoke: Palgrave Macmillan, 2005); Jessica C. E. Gienow-Hecht and Frank Schumacher, eds., *Culture and International History* (New York: Berghahn Books, 2003); Michael J. Hogan and Thomas G. Paterson, eds., *Explaining the History of American Foreign Relations*, 2nd ed. (Cambridge: Cambridge University Press, 2004); Wilfried Loth and Jürgen Osterhammel, eds., *Internationale Geschichte: Themen, Ergebnisse, Aussichten* (München: Oldenbourg, 2000).
17. Tony Ballantyne and Antoinette M. Burton, "Introduction: Bodies, Empires, and World Histories", in *Bodies in Contact: Rethinking Colonial Encounters in World History*, ed. Tony Ballantyne and Antoinette M. Burton (Durham: Duke University Press, 2005), 12–13.

18. Among many others see Iver B. Neumann, "The Body of the Diplomat", *European Journal of International Relations* 14, no. 4 (2008): 671–695; Emily S. Rosenberg and Shanon Fitzpatrick, eds., *Body and Nation: The Global Realm of U.S. Body Politics in the Twentieth Century* (Durham: Duke University Press, 2014); Lauren B. Wilcox, *Bodies of Violence: Theorizing Embodied Subjects in International Relations* (Oxford: Oxford University Press, 2015).
19. David Arnold, *Colonizing the Body: State Medicine and Epidemic Disease in Nineteenth-Century India* (Berkeley: University of California Press, 1993), 7; Elizabeth M. Collingham, *Imperial Bodies: The Physical Experience of the Raj, c. 1800–1947* (Cambridge: Polity Press, 2001); Timothy Mitchell, *Colonising Egypt* (Cambridge: Cambridge University Press, 1988), 95–127; Roy Porter, *Bodies Politic: Disease, Death and Doctors in Britain, 1650–1900* (London: Reaktion, 2001); Emily S. Rosenberg and Shanon Fitzpatrick, "Introduction", in *Body and Nation: The Global Realm of U.S. Body Politics in the Twentieth Century*, ed. Emily S. Rosenberg and Shanon Fitzpatrick (Durham: Duke University Press, 2014), 1–15.
20. Roy Porter, "History of the Body", in *New Perspectives on Historical Writing*, ed. Peter Burke (Cambridge: Polity, 1991), 206–232; Angela Woollacott, *Gender and Empire* (Basingstoke: Palgrave Macmillan, 2006), 81–103.
21. Purnima Bose, *Organizing Empire: Individualism, Collective Agency, and India* (Durham: Duke University Press, 2003), 179–188.
22. See also ibid., 169–221.
23. Tony Ballantyne and Antoinette M. Burton, "Postscript: Bodies, Genders, Empires: Reimagining World Histories", in *Bodies in Contact: Rethinking Colonial Encounters in World History*, ed. Tony Ballantyne and Antoinette M. Burton (Durham: Duke University Press, 2005), 405–423; Kathleen Canning, "The Body as Method? Reflections on the Place of the Body in Gender History", *Gender and History* 11, no. 3 (1999): 499–513; Mary Louise Pratt, *Imperial Eyes: Studies in Travel Writing and Transculturation* (London: Routledge, 1992).
24. Frank Costigliola, "'Unceasing Pressure for Penetration': Gender, Pathology, and Emotion in George Kennan's Formation of the Cold War", *The Journal of American History* 83, no. 4 (1997): 1309–1339; Andrew J. Rotter, "Culture", in *Palgrave Advances in International History*, ed. Patrick Finney, *Palgrave Advances in International History* (Basingstoke: Palgrave Macmillan, 2005), 267–299.
25. Benjamin D. Hopkins, *The Making of Modern Afghanistan* (Basingstoke: Palgrave Macmillan, 2008), 11–33.
26. Note by W. M. Hailey, 13 October 1922, 212-F, F&P, 1922, "Construction of British Legation Buildings at Kabul", NAI.

27. Akbar S. Ahmed, "An Aspect of the Colonial Encounter in the North-West Frontier Province", *Asian Affairs* 9, no. 3 (1978): 323–325.
28. James Anthony Mangan, *Athleticism in the Victorian and Edwardian Public School: The Emergence and Consolidation of an Educational Ideology*, 3rd ed. (London: Frank Cass, 2000).
29. James Anthony Mangan, *The Games Ethic and Imperialism: Aspects of the Diffusion of an Ideal* (Harmondsworth: Viking, 1986). Mangan's argument is limited by its focus on the imperial 'diffusion' of sports.
30. "Information to be supplied by the Officer Commanding 25th Cavalry 77 Regiment respecting Lieutenant Fraser-Tytler, an applicant for political employ", Bannu, 28 March 1914, IOR/R/1/4/1006, "Confidential Report on Major W.K. Fraser-Tytler, M.C., of the Indian Political Service", BL.
31. Satow, *A Guide to Diplomatic Practice*, vol. 1, 183, para. 224.
32. Anthony Kirk-Greene, "Badge of Office: Sport and His Excellency in the British Empire", in *The Cultural Bond: Sport, Empire, Society*, ed. James Anthony Mangan (London: Frank Cass, 1992), 178–200.
33. Ian Copland, "The Other Guardians: Ideology and Performance in the Indian Political Service", in *People, Princes and Paramount Power: Society and Politics in the Indian Princely States*, ed. Robert Jeffrey (Oxford: Oxford University Press, 1978), 275–305.
34. James Anthony Mangan, "Britain's Chief Spiritual Export: Imperial Sport as Moral Metaphor, Political Symbol and Cultural Bond", in *The Cultural Bond: Sport, Empire, Society*, ed. James Anthony Mangan (London: Frank Cass, 1992), 1–10.
35. Collingham, *Imperial Bodies*, 121, 124.
36. IOR/R/1/4/1334, "Personal file of Lieut. Colonel F.H. Humphrys, C.E.I., late of the Political Department", BL.
37. Ibid.
38. Peter Sluglett, "Humphrys, Sir Francis Henry (1879–1971), Colonial Administrator and Diplomatist", in *The Oxford Dictionary of National Biography* (Oxford: Oxford University Press, 2004).
39. "Humphrys, Francis Henry", *Who's Who & Who Was Who* 7, 1971–1980 (A & C Black, 1981).
40. 4(12)-E, F&P, 1926, "Application from Captain H. H. Elliot, I.M.S., for medical employment under the Foreign and Political Department", NAI.
41. 49(5)-Est, F&P, op. cit., 1931, NAI.
42. "Squire, Giles Frederick", *Who's Who 2011 & Who Was Who* (Oxford University Press, 2011).
43. William Kerr Fraser-Tytler, "In Memoriam", *Journal of the Royal Central Asian Society* 49, no. 2 (1962): 118.
44. IOR/R/1/4/1331, "Personal File of Mr A.W. Fagan, Late of the Political Department", BL.

45. Ian Talbot, "Cunningham, Sir George (1888–1963), Administrator in India", in *The Oxford Dictionary of National Biography* (Oxford: Oxford University Press, 2004).
46. Arnold, *Colonizing the Body*, 7–8.
47. "Kabul Legation Diary", 32–33, file 8, GB165-0326, MECA.
48. Fraser-Tytler to his mother, 27–28 May 1937, no. 74–76, file 1/1/8, GB165-0326, MECA.
49. Fraser-Tytler to his mother, 24 July 1935, no. 60–63, file 1/1/6, GB165-0326, MECA.
50. IOR/R/12/LIB/11, "British Legation Kabul Fishing Record"; IOR/R/12/LIB/10, "British Legation Kabul Game Book", BL.
51. IOR/L/MIL/14/11881, "William Peat Hogg", BL.
52. "Note by Kerr Fraser-Tytler on the Situation in Afghanistan", 20 August 1941, file 10, GB165-0326, MECA.
53. Maximilian Drephal, "Corps Diplomatique: The Body, British Diplomacy, and Independent Afghanistan, 1922–47", *Modern Asian Studies* 51, no. 4 (2017): 956–990.
54. Jon Wilson, *India Conquered: Britain's Raj and the Chaos of Empire* (London: Simon and Schuster, 2016).
55. Fraser-Tytler to his mother, 7 April 1923, no. 1, file 1/1/1, GB165-0326; Fraser-Tytler to his mother, 12 April 1923, no. 2–4, file 1/1/1, GB165-0326, MECA.
56. Humphrys, no. 298, 20 May 1924, 1093(3)-A, F&P, 1923, "Kabul Legation Budget estimates for 1922–23 and 1923–24", NAI.
57. "Rough note on the proposal for a British Minister at Kabul", S. E. Pears, 24 November 1921, 4, 68(20)-Est, F&P, 1923, "Note by Mr S. E. Pears, C.S.I., C.I.E., on the proposed establishment of a British Legation at Kabul", NAI.
58. "Report on the Kabul Mission, by Sir H. R. C. Dobbs, K.C.S.I., K.C.I.E", para. 12, N 1450/59/97, FO 371/8076, 1922, op. cit., TNA.
59. "Rough note on the proposal for a British Minister at Kabul", S. E. Pears, 24 November 1921, 4, 68(20)-Est, F&P, 1923, op. cit., NAI.
60. Collingham, *Imperial Bodies*, 165; Dane Keith Kennedy, *The Magic Mountains: Hill Stations and the British Raj* (Berkeley: University of California Press, 1996), 175–201.
61. Humphrys, memorandum no. 12, 25 March 1922, N 6381/59/97, FO 371/8077, 1922, "Accommodation for British Legation at Kabul", TNA and 68(1)-E, F&P, 1922, "Equipment of the British Legation Kabul", NAI.
62. Humphrys to the Foreign Secretary to the Government of India in the Foreign and Political Department, 25 March 1922, 212-F, F&P, 1922, op. cit., NAI.

63. "Destruction of the Second British Legation in Kabul", 31 December 1926, 9, GB165-0326, MECA; "The Legation Fire in Kabul: Help from Neighbours", *The Times*, 31 December 1926, 9.
64. Humphrys to Curzon, no. 6, 3 June 1922, N 6381/59/97, FO 371/8077, 1922, op. cit., TNA and 68(1)-E, F&P, 1922, op. cit., NAI.
65. "Afghanistan: Annual Report, 1930", N 760/760/97, FO 371/15550, 1931, "Annual report on Afghanistan", TNA.
66. "Note on Sanitation in connection with the new British Legation", G. M. Millar, 26 July 1922, Appendix B, no. 26, 212-F, F&P, 1922, op. cit., NAI, emphasis added.
67. "Afghanistan: Annual Report, 1933", para. 159, N 2031/2031/97, FO 371/18259, 1934, "Annual report on Afghanistan", TNA; "Account of medical affairs in Afghanistan", 8 July 1942, 12, no. 167–181, IOR/L/PS/12/1733, "Coll 3/143 Medical arrangements in Afghanistan. Visit of Dr Rifki Bey to UK", BL.
68. "Note on Sanitation in connection with the new British Legation", G. M. Millar, 26 July 1922, Appendix B, no. 26, 212-F, F&P, 1922, op. cit., NAI.
69. Ibid.
70. "Afghanistan: Annual Report, 1933", para. 159, N 2031/2031/97, FO 371/18259, 1934, op. cit., TNA.
71. Arnold, *Colonizing the Body*, 199. See also David Arnold, "Cholera and Colonialism in British India", *Past & Present* 113, no. 1 (1986): 118–151.
72. See, e.g., Ballantyne and Burton, "Introduction", 7.
73. "Rough note on the proposal for a British Minister at Kabul", S. E. Pears, 24 November 1921, 4, 68(20)-Est, F&P, 1923, op. cit., NAI, emphasis added.
74. Memorandum by P. G. Loch, 14 January 1922, 1093(3)-A, F&P, 1923, op. cit., NAI; Fraser-Tytler to his mother, 12 April 1923, no. 2–4, file 1/1/1, GB165-0326, MECA: "It is a wonderful climate, cold & clear & still, [...] but I fancy it will be rather trying in the long winter months"; "Recollections of a political officer in India (1929–1947)", A. W. Redpath, 84, Mss Eur F226/24, "Redpath, Maj Alexander William (b 1909)", BL: "As I was familiar with the history of Afghanistan and knew something of Afghan attitudes to the north west frontier, the idea of going to Kabul appealed to me. Its invigorating climate, compared with that of Calcutta, was an added attraction".
75. "Medical Affairs in Afghanistan", 1944, 17, no. 76–98, IOR/L/PS/12/1733, op. cit., BL; William Kerr Fraser-Tytler, *Afghanistan: A Study of Political Developments in Central and Southern Asia*, 2nd ed. (London: Oxford University Press, 1953), 12.
76. Fraser-Tytler, *Afghanistan*, 285–296; Dane Keith Kennedy, "The Perils of the Midday Sun: Climatic Anxieties in the Colonial Tropics", in

Imperialism and the Natural World, ed. John Macdonald MacKenzie (Manchester: Manchester University Press, 1990), 118–140.
77. See also Corinne Fowler, *Chasing Tales Travel Writing, Journalism and the History of British Ideas About Afghanistan* (Amsterdam: Rodopi, 2007), 27–34.
78. Correspondence between R. W. Parkes and W. R. Hay, 55-F.O., EA, 1939, "Staff for the British Legation Kabul", NAI.
79. "Rough note on the proposal for a British Minister at Kabul", S. E. Pears, 24 November 1921, 8, 68(20)-Est, F&P, 1923, op. cit., NAI.
80. Kennedy, *The Magic Mountains*, 19–38.
81. Humphrys to Curzon, no. 3, 25 March 1922, N 3667/59/97, FO 371/8077, 1922, op. cit., TNA.
82. William Dalrymple, *The Return of a King: The Battle for Afghanistan, 1839–1842* (London: Bloomsbury), 294–354.
83. Fraser-Tytler, *Afghanistan*.
84. Fraser-Tytler to his mother, 31 January 1924, no. 30–32, file 1/1/1, GB165-0326, MECA.
85. "Kabul Legation Diary", 50, file 8, GB165-0326, MECA.
86. "The siege of the British Legation in Kabul", Mss Eur F625/2, "Leslie Best's photograph albums", BL.
87. Ludwig W. Adamec, *Afghanistan, 1900–1923: A Diplomatic History* (Berkeley: University of California Press, 1967), 21, 72, 76–78.
88. "Diary of the British Agent at Kabul for the period 9th May to 22nd September 1919", 3, file 1061/1919, pt 6, IOR/L/PS/10/809, "File 1061/1919 Pt 3-4, 6-7, 10 Afghan War", BL.
89. Ibid., "30th June 1919", 15.
90. Ibid., emphasis added.
91. "The Afghan Troubles. Legations Safe. Attitude of the Army", *The Times*, 19 December 1928, 12; "Isolation of Kabul. Message from Legation. Aeroplane in Touch", *The Times*, 20 December 1928, 14; "At the British Legation", *The Times*, 21 December 1928, 14; "Position at Kabul. Flight over Legation. British Machine Hit", *The Times*, 21 December 1928, 14; "The British Legation", *The Times*, 22 December 1928, 10; "The Kabul Legation. Safety of Women and Children. Taken to India by Air", *The Times*, 24 December 1928, 10; "The Crisis in Afghanistan. The British Legation at Kabul", *The Times*, 27 December 1928, 16; "The Fighting in Kabul. Casualties Among Employees at British Legation", *The Times*, 29 December 1928; "Kabul Legation Outrage: Three Persons Killed", *The Times*, 9 September 1933, 10. See also Chapter 3, note 121 and Chapter 5, note 77.
92. Humphrys to Chamberlain, no. 4, 5 January 1929, N 562/1/97, FO 371/13990, 1929, "Afghan situation", TNA.
93. Ibid.

94. Humphrys to Oliphant, no. 1, 9 January 1929, N 657/1/97, FO 371/13991, 1929, "Situation in Kabul", TNA.
95. Macoachie to Simon, no. 120, 28 September 1933, no. 25, FO 402/16, 1933, "Further correspondence respecting Afghanistan: Part XVI", TNA.
96. Ibid.
97. Ludwig W. Adamec, *Afghanistan's Foreign Affairs to the Mid-Twentieth Century: Relations with the U.S.S.R., Germany, and Britain* (Tucson: University of Arizona Press, 1974), 197.
98. Fraser-Tytler, unofficial letter no. 3, 1 January 1940, N 1612/26/97, FO 371/24766, 1940, "Kabul quarterly unofficial letter", TNA.
99. Maconachie, telegram no. 141, 18 September 1933, no. 8, FO 402/16, 1933, op. cit., TNA.
100. Fraser-Tytler to his mother, 16 March 1940, no. 26–29, file 1/1/11, GB165-0326, MECA; Bray to Ross, 9 July 1923, IOR/R/1/4/1173, "File Est Con 29 1926 Personal file of Mr. P.J.G. Pipon, C.M.G., C.I.E., of the Political Department", BL. See also Ann Laura Stoler, *Carnal Knowledge and Imperial Power: Race and the Intimate in Colonial Rule* (Berkeley: University of California Press, 2002), 1–2.
101. Handwritten note, no date, 98-F, F&P, 1922, "Grant of permission to the wives of members of the British Legation proceeding to Kabul", NAI.
102. Humphrys to Bray, 7 August 1924, 60(1)-E, F&P, 1924, "1. Selection of a successor to Major W.A.K. Fraser, as Military Attaché, British Legation, Kabul. 2. Death of Major A.N.I. Lilly, Mily Attaché British Legation, Kabul on 15th December 1924", NAI.
103. Ahmed, "An Aspect of the Colonial Encounter in the North-West Frontier Province", 325.
104. Note by C. E. Bruce, 8 November 1926, 24-F, F&P, 1924, "Revised rules regulating the visits of European ladies to places on or beyond the North-West Frontier", NAI.
105. Dane Keith Kennedy, "Diagnosing the Colonial Dilemma: Tropical Neurasthenia and the Alienated Briton", in *Decentring Empire: Britain, India, and the Transcolonial World*, ed. Durba Ghosh and Dane Keith Kennedy (Hyderabad: Orient Longman, 2006), 169.
106. Transcript of interview of Hugh Michael Carless, 23 February 2002, 5, https://www.chu.cam.ac.uk/media/uploads/files/Carless.pdf [accessed: 26 May 2018].
107. Fraser-Tytler to his mother, 5–6 May 1939, no. 43–46, file 1/1/10, GB165-0326; Fraser-Tytler to his mother, 16 March 1940, no. 26–29, file 1/1/11, GB165-0326, MECA.
108. Fraser-Tytler to his mother, 26 May 1939, no. 57–59, file 1/1/10, GB165-0326, MECA.
109. Fraser-Tytler to his mother, 7 December 1939, no. 151–154, file 1/1/10, GB165-0326, MECA. See also Ann Laura Stoler, *Race and the Education*

of Desire: Foucault's "History of Sexuality" and the Colonial Order of Things (Durham: Duke University Press, 1995).
110. "Medical Affairs in Afghanistan", 1944, 17, no. 76–98, IOR/L/PS/12/1733, op. cit., BL.
111. Kennedy, "Diagnosing the Colonial Dilemma: Tropical Neurasthenia and the Alienated Briton".
112. E.g. Bernard S. Cohn, "Representing Authority in Victorian India", in *The Invention of Tradition*, ed. Eric J. Hobsbawm and T. O. Ranger (Cambridge: Cambridge University Press, 2013), 165–209. See also Collingham, *Imperial Bodies*, 117–149. Collingham traces the relationship of the Anglo-Indian official's body and British rule in India.
113. Humphrys to Curzon, no. 3, 25 March 1922, N 3667/59/97, FO 371/8077, 1922, op. cit., TNA.
114. Leon B. Poullada, *Reform and Rebellion in Afghanistan, 1919–1929: King Amanullah's Failure to Modernize a Tribal Society* (Ithaca: Cornell University Press, 1973), 252.
115. Ernst Hartwig Kantorowicz, *The King's Two Bodies: A Study in Mediaeval Political Theology* (Princeton: Princeton University Press, 1997).
116. General Sir Peter S. Lumsden and George R. Elsmie, *Lumsden of the Guides: A Sketch of the Life of Lieut.-Gen. Sir Harry Burnett Lumsden, K.C.S.I., C.B., with Selections from His Correspondence and Occasional Papers* (London: John Murray, 1899), 137; Fraser-Tytler, *Afghanistan*, 127.
117. As quoted in Fraser-Tytler, *Afghanistan*, 151.
118. George Nathaniel Curzon, *Tales of Travel* (London: Century, 1988), 48–51.
119. Ernest Thornton and Annie Thornton, *Leaves from an Afghan Scrapbook: The Experiences of an English Official and His Wife in Kabul* (London: John Murray, 1910), 90. IOR/R/12/LIB/139, BL.
120. Fraser-Tytler, *Afghanistan*, 151.
121. Maconachie to Henderson, no. 6, 23 May 1930, N 4007/6/97, FO 371/14786, 1930, "Presentation of credentials by His Majesty's Minister to Afghanistan" and no. 76, FO 402/12, 1930, "Further correspondence respecting Afghanistan: Part XII", TNA.
122. Fraser-Tytler, *Afghanistan*, 236.
123. See comments on file cover N 4007/6/97, FO 371/14786, 1930, op. cit., TNA.
124. Maconachie to Simon, no. 153, 29 November 1933, para. 8, no. 23, FO 402/16, 1933, op. cit., TNA; Arnold Fletcher, *Afghanistan: Highway of Conquest* (Ithaca: Cornell University Press, 1965). See also "Note of a conversation held on April 4 between His Majesty's Minister, Kabul, and Serdar Nadir Khan, Afghan Minister of War", enclosure in Humphrys to MacDonald, no. 12, 17 April 1924, N 4076/3320/97, FO 371/10408,

1924, "Nadir Khan" and no. 84, FO 402/3, 1924, "Further correspondence regarding Afghanistan: Part III", TNA.
125. For example "Afghanistan: Annual Report, 1930", para. 108–111, N 760/760/97, FO 371/15550, 1931, op. cit.; "Afghanistan: Annual Report, 1931", para. 140–147, N 969/969/97, FO 371/16278, 1932, "Annual report on Afghanistan"; "Afghanistan: Annual Report, 1932", para. 170–173, N 1626/1626/97, FO 371/17198, 1933, "Annual Report on Afghanistan"; "Afghanistan: Annual Report, 1933", para. 184, N 2031/2031/97, FO 371/18259, 1934, op. cit.; "Afghanistan: Annual Report, 1935", para. 189–192, N 1831/1831/97, FO 371/20321, 1936, "Annual report on Afghanistan for 1935"; "Afghanistan: Annual Report, 1936", para. 160–164, N 843/843/97, FO 371/21070, 1937, "Annual Report on Afghanistan for 1936"; "Afghanistan: Annual Report, 1937", para. 115–119, N 768/768/97, FO 371/22254, 1938, "Annual Report on Afghanistan for 1937"; "Afghanistan: Annual Report, 1938", para. 122–125, N 783/783/97, FO 371/23630, 1939, "Annual Report on Afghanistan for 1938", TNA.
126. Wylie to Eden, no. 59, 18 September 1941, IOR/L/PS/12/1913, "Coll 4/54 British Legation: appointment of Lt Col Sir W Kerr Frazer-Tytler [sic], Sir Francis Wylie and Mr G F Squire", BL and no. 5, FO 402/22, 1941, "Further correspondence respecting Afghanistan: Part XXIV", TNA.
127. "Note by Kerr Fraser-Tytler on the Situation in Afghanistan", 20 August 1941, file 10, GB165-0326, MECA.
128. Fraser-Tytler to Eden, no. 146, 21 October 1936, no. 18, FO 402/17, 1936, "Further correspondence respecting Afghanistan and Nepal: Part XIX", TNA; Fraser-Tytler, unofficial letter no. 8, 1 April 1941, IOR/L/PS/12/1765, "Coll 3/166 Indo-Afghan frontier: measures to give British frontier officials a better understanding of Afghanistan; A) issues of quarterly unofficial letter by British Legation Kabul; B) proposed mutual exchange of visits by British and Afghan frontier officials", BL; Wylie to Peterson, demi-official no.C-22/41, 12 June 1943, 536-F, EA, 1943, "H.M.'s Minister, Kabul's interviews with the Prime Minister of Afghanistan", NAI.
129. "Political Review for 1943", para. 9, N 951/951/97, FO 371/39964, 1944, "Political Review of Afghanistan", TNA.
130. Squire to Eden, no. 59, 29 June 1945, para. 2, E 5095/5095/97, FO 371/45229, 1945, "Political situation in Afghanistan"; "Annual report on Afghanistan, 1946", para. 6, no. 2, FO 402/23, "Correspondence respecting Afghanistan: Part 1" and E 1164/1164/97, FO 371/61480, 1947, "Political Review of Events for the year 1946", TNA.
131. Fraser-Tytler, *Afghanistan*, 243–244.

132. Squire to Bevin, no. 99, 27 August 1949, F 13553/1894/97, FO 371/75652, 1949, "Farewell visit of Sir G. Squire to the King of Afghanistan on 26th Aug. 1949", TNA.
133. "Interview of Sir John Birch by Virginia Crowe", 10, British Diplomatic Oral History Programme, https://www.chu.cam.ac.uk/media/uploads/files/Birch.pdf [accessed: 26 May 2018].
134. Hamilton Grant, No. 108-P.C., Nathia Gali, 6 September 1919, para. 7, 6, IOR/L/PS/10/808, "File 1061/1919, Pt 1-2 Afghanistan", BL.
135. Humphrys to Cushendun, no. 107, 31 October 1928, para. 6, no. 44, FO 402/9, "Further correspondence respecting Afghanistan: Part IX" and N 5527/4401/97, FO 371/13289, 1928, "Social reforms in Afghanistan", TNA; Rotter, "Culture", 269–270.
136. Mark Jacobsen, "The Great Game Resumed: Afghanistan and the Defense of India, 1919–1939", in *Rediscovering the British Empire*, ed. Barry J. Ward (Malabar: Krieger Publishing Company, 2002), 92.
137. Humphrys to Bolton, 21 June 1928, Mss Eur 625/4, "Letters from Sir Francis Humphrys to H N Bolton", BL.
138. Fraser-Tytler to Metcalfe, demi-official no. 1263, 9 February 1939, para. 6, N 908/144/97, FO 371/23628, 1939, "British position in Afghanistan", TNA; Rosenberg and Fitzpatrick, "Introduction", 7.
139. Fraser-Tytler, unofficial letter no. 8, 1 April 1941, IOR/L/PS/12/1765, op. cit., BL.
140. Hopkins, *The Making of Modern Afghanistan*, 11–33.
141. Alexander Burnes, *Cabool: A Personal Narrative of a Journey To, and Residence in That City, in the Years 1836, 7, and 8*, 2nd ed. (Philadelphia: Carey & Hart, 1843), 22.
142. Henry Walter Bellew, *Journal of a Political Mission to Afghanistan, in 1857, Under Major (Now Colonel) Lumsden; with an Account of the Country and People* (London: Smith, Elder and Co., 1862), 125.
143. Angus Hamilton, *Afghanistan* (London: William Heinemann, 1906), 395.
144. Ibid., 389–395.
145. Jonathan Lee, "'Abd Al-Raḥmān Khān and the 'Maraẓ Ul-Mulūk'", *Journal of the Royal Asiatic Society* 1, no. 2 (1991): 209–242.
146. "Medical affairs in Afghanistan", 1943, no. 114–140, IOR/L/PS/12/1733, op. cit., BL. John Alfred Gray, *At the Court of the Amir: A Narrative* (London: Bentley, 1895). IOR/R/12/LIB/81 and IOR/R/12/LIB/102, BL.
147. "Medical Affairs in Afghanistan", 13(13)-IA, EA, 1947, "Report by the Legation Surgeon on Medical Affairs in Afghanistan", NAI.
148. Fraser-Tytler to his mother, 27 December 1940, no. 158–160, file 1/1/11, GB165-0326, MECA; Humphrys, telegram no. 204, 15

December 1924, N 9210/9210/97, FO 371/10410, 1924, "Death of Major Lilly", TNA.
149. I am grateful to David Arnold for raising this point.
150. In 1935, the Legation personnel accounted for 1830 in comparison to a total of 26,467 cases in that year. In 1936, the Legation personnel accounted for 2140 cases, while the Legation dispensary counted a total of 39,832 attendances: "Afghanistan: Annual Report, 1935", para. 168, 178, N 1831/1831/97, FO 371/20321, 1936, op. cit.; "Afghanistan: Annual Report, 1936", para. 142, 147, N 843/843/97, FO 371/21070, 1937, op. cit., TNA.
151. The literature on the interrelationship of the body, medicine and colonialism is rich. The case of India is particularly well represented. For example Arnold, *Colonizing the Body*; Pratik Chakrabarti, *Medicine and Empire, 1600–1960* (Basingstoke: Palgrave Macmillan, 2014); Deepak Kumar and Raj Sekhar Basu, eds., *Medical Encounters in British India* (New Delhi: Oxford University Press, 2013); Biswamoy Pati and Mark Harrison, eds., *Health, Medicine and Empire: Perspectives on Colonial India* (Hyderabad: Orient Longman, 2001); Biswamoy Pati and Mark Harrison, eds., *The Social History of Health and Medicine in Colonial India* (London: Routledge, 2009); Samiksha Sehrawat, *Colonial Medical Care in North India: Gender, State, and Society, c. 1840–1920* (New Delhi: Oxford University Press, 2013).
152. "Report on the proposed buildings for His Britannic Majesty's Legation in Kabul, Afghanistan", B. M. Sullivan, 27 September 1922, no. 29, 212-F, F&P, 1922, op. cit., NAI.
153. Note by E. B. Howell, 9 October 1922, 212-F, F&P, 1922, op. cit., NAI.
154. Note by D. Bray, 9 October 1922, 212-F, F&P, 1922, op. cit., NAI.
155. Fraser-Tytler to Collier, semi-official no. 339, 18 May 1938, para. 3, N 2911/2911/97, FO 371/22257, 1938, "Use of British Legation Hospital by Germans in Kabul", TNA.
156. "Medical Affairs in Afghanistan", 13(13)-IA, EA, 1947, op. cit., NAI.
157. "Afghanistan: Annual Report, 1938", para. 188, N 783/783/97, FO 371/23630, 1939, op. cit., TNA; "Legation Hospital and Consulate Dispensaries", Humphrys, 30 October 1925, 256(2)-A, F&P, 1925, "Budget estimates of the British Legation Kabul for the year 1926–1927", NAI; "Account of medical matters in Afghanistan", 8 July 1942, no. 180, IOR/L/PS/12/1733, op. cit., BL.
158. Helmut Hahn, "Die Stadt Kabul (Afghanistan) und ihr Umland", *Bonner Geographische Abhandlungen* 34, no. 1 (1964): 45.
159. Humphrys, no. 373/4, 9 January 1926, 256(2)-A, F&P, 1925, op. cit., NAI.

160. "Kabul Legation Budget, 1927–28: Annexure 3", 15 October 1926, 165-A, F&P, 1926, "Budget estimates of the British Legation Kabul for the year 1927–1928", NAI.
161. "Afghanistan: Annual Report, 1931", para. 124, N 969/969/97, FO 371/16278, 1932, op. cit., TNA.
162. "Summary of the Course and Tendency of Events during the Period May 15 to August 22, 1925", para. 7, no. 44, FO 402/5, 1925, "Further correspondence respecting Afghanistan: Part V", TNA.
163. "Report on the Kabul Mission, by Sir H. R. C. Dobbs, K.C.S.I., K.C.I.E", para. 34, N 1450/59/97, FO 371/8076, 1922, op. cit., TNA.
164. Annual confidential report on George MacGregor Millar for 1922, Humphrys, 29 November 1922, IOR/L/MIL/14/15591, "Millar, George MacGregor", BL; "Kabul Legation Diary", 66, file 8, GB165-0326, MECA; "Summary of the Course and Tendency of Afghan Internal Events during the Period January 16, 1926, to October 15, 1926", para. 3, no. 46, FO 402/6, 1926, "Further correspondence respecting Afghanistan: Part VI", TNA.
165. "Summary of Events in Afghanistan from August 17 to December 31, 1922", no. 1, FO 402/2, 1923, "Further correspondence respecting Afghanistan: Part II" and N 920/920/97, FO 371/9292, 1923, "Situation in Afghanistan", TNA; Maconachie to Metcalfe, 27 July 1934, IOR/L/MIL/14/15451, "Annual Confidential Reports on Farrell, Henry William", BL.
166. "Summary of the Course and Tendency of Events during the Period May 15 to August 22, 1925", para. 7, no. 44, FO 402/5, 1925, op. cit., TNA.
167. "Medical Affairs in Afghanistan", 1943, 19–20, no. 114–140, IOR/L/PS/12/1733, op. cit., BL.
168. Humphrys to Bray, 23 July 1923, 657-F, F&P, 1923, "Despatch to Kabul of an English nurse in connection with Her Majesty the Queen of Afghanistan's confinement. Question of sending a message of congratulation to Amir on the birth of a son", NAI.
169. Ibid.; "Account of medical affairs in Afghanistan", 8 July 1942, 14, no. 167–181, IOR/L/PS/12/1733, op. cit., BL; 392-F, EA, 1941, "Question of Introducing an English Dentist and a British Lady Doctor into Kabul", NAI.
170. "Kabul Legation Diary", 117–118, file 8, GB165-0326, MECA.
171. "Summary of the Course and Tendency of Events during the Period April 1, 1926, to June 30, 1926", para. 3, no. 40, FO 402/6, 1926, op. cit., TNA.
172. "Medical Affairs in Afghanistan", 1943, 13, no. 114–140, IOR/L/PS/12/1733, op. cit., BL; "Medical Affairs in Afghanistan", Squire to Bevin, no. 4, 19 January 1946, 435-F, EA, 1946, "Report by the Legation Surgeon on Medical Affairs in Afghanistan", NAI.

173. Wylie to Eden, no. 10, 2 March 1943, para. 8, IOR/L/PS/12/1733, op. cit., BL. See also Vartan Gregorian, *The Emergence of Modern Afghanistan: Politics of Reform and Modernization, 1880–1946* (Stanford: Stanford University Press, 1969), 246–247, 311–314.
174. "Account of medical affairs in Afghanistan", 8 July 1942, 1, no. 167–181, IOR/L/PS/12/1733, op. cit., BL; Prakash, "Introduction", 11.
175. Arnold, *Colonizing the Body*, 242.
176. Daniel R. Headrick, *The Tools of Empire: Technology and European Imperialism in the Nineteenth Century* (New York: Oxford University Press, 1981). Headrick's approach has been discussed extensively: David Arnold, "Introduction: Disease, Medicine and Empire", in *Imperial Medicine and Indigenous Societies*, ed. David Arnold (Manchester: Manchester University Press, 1988), 1–26; Arnold, *Colonizing the Body*; Biswamoy Pati and Mark Harrison, "Introduction: Health, Medicine and Empire: Perspectives on Colonial India", in *Health, Medicine and Empire: Perspectives on Colonial India*, ed. Biswamoy Pati and Mark Harrison (Hyderabad: Orient Longman, 2001), 1–36.
177. "Summary of the Course and Tendency of Events in Afghanistan during the Period February 16 to May 15, 1925", no. 7, FO 402/5, 1925, op. cit. and N 3409/533/97, FO 371/10986, 1925, "Afghan foreign relations", TNA.
178. Humphrys, no. 373/4, 9 January 1926, 256(2)-A, F&P, 1925, op. cit., NAI.
179. "Account of medical affairs in Afghanistan", 8 July 1942, 14, no. 167–181, IOR/L/PS/12/1733, op. cit., BL; Ronald Hyam suggests that "the deep-seated hostility of the Afghan people towards the British may well have been due to their resentment of the undisciplined lust with which British soldiers fell upon the women of Kabul in [1841]". Ronald Hyam, *Empire and Sexuality: The British Experience* (Manchester: Manchester University Press, 1990), 2; "Afghanistan: Annual Report, 1936", para. 141, N 843/843/97, FO 371/21070, 1937, op. cit., TNA.
180. Wylie to Eden, no. 10, 2 March 1943, para. 6, IOR/L/PS/12/1733, op. cit., BL.
181. Wylie, telegram no. 176, 11 September 1942, para. 4, IOR/L/PS/12/1934, "Affairs of the Legation Dispensary", BL.
182. Humphrys, no. 373/4, 9 January 1926, 256(2)-A, F&P, 1925, op. cit., NAI; Wylie to Eden, no. 10, 2 March 1943, para. 8, IOR/L/PS/12/1733, op. cit., BL.
183. "Medical Affairs in Afghanistan, 1947", no. 23, IOR/L/PS/12/1733, op. cit.; "Report on Medical Affairs, Afghanistan, 1948", no. 11, ibid.
184. Squire to Bevin, no. 12, 28 February 1946, para. 3, E 2578/66/97, FO 371/52275, 1946, "Review of events in Afghanistan", TNA.

185. Squire to Bevin, no. 9, 27 January 1948, IOR/L/PS/12/1733, op. cit., BL.
186. See also Arnold, *Colonizing the Body*, 61–115; Kennedy, *The Magic Mountains*, 8.
187. Timothy Nunan, *Humanitarian Invasion: Global Development in Cold War Afghanistan* (Cambridge: Cambridge University Press, 2016).

CHAPTER 7

Architecture

CURZON IN KABUL

On the eve of his departure for Kabul, Francis Henry Humphrys met George Nathaniel Curzon in London. Britain's Foreign Secretary had a special task for the Minister-to-be. A few months later, Humphrys dutifully reported on his progress in a despatch from Kabul: "In accordance with your Lordship's oral instructions, I have borne in mind the necessity of securing as soon as possible suitable accommodation for this Legation".[1] Between 1922 and 1926, the Legation was located in several places in and around Kabul. It first settled in Bagrami in early 1922. Later that year, it moved to two rented *serais*. But, renting accommodation was not what Curzon had had in mind; Curzon had given Humphrys a lesson in the imperial politics of monuments. According to William Kerr Fraser-Tytler, Curzon had advised Humphrys "to be the 'best housed man in Central Asia'".[2] Monuments and representation mattered to Curzon. He showed an interest in the looks of the Legation's guard, and Humphrys mentioned to him the memorial of chained lions that symbolised the taming of the Raj in the war of 1919 in his accreditation report. During his Viceroyalty of India, Curzon had attempted to mould Afghanistan into the Indian Empire. After 1919, material manifestations of Afghan independence in Kabul prompted material manifestations of empire. The architectural symbolism of Afghan independence in Kabul demanded an imperial monument that overshadowed that independence. Empires did not rent; they

© The Author(s) 2019
M. Drephal, *Afghanistan and the Coloniality of Diplomacy,*
Cambridge Imperial and Post-Colonial Studies Series,
https://doi.org/10.1007/978-3-030-23960-2_7

occupied and built. Well known for his autocratic, divisive and aggressive politics, Curzon instructed Humphrys to create the semblance of imperial sovereignty that covered the cracks in Britain's empire. A separate compound was found and populated between 1924 and 1927. The Minister's residence in white paint became its centrepiece and a "landmark".[3] The Raj came to life in Kabul. The compound was occupied by the Legation from 1926 and by the later Embassy until the end of the Soviet occupation.

Curzon's dictum has assumed a life of its own, undergoing distortions and reinterpretations over time. Francis Verner Wylie thought that Curzon's instructions were "apocryphal", and that Humphrys had instead been told "by high authority in India".[4] Giles Frederick Squire dated the meeting to 1920.[5] Sherard Cowper-Coles, writing on his experiences as British Ambassador in Kabul in the early twenty-first century, repeated this date.[6] In *Room for Diplomacy*, Mark Bertram follows Wylie and pushes the story to the realm of the legendary.[7] He also extended the meaning of Curzon's instructions to include all of Asia rather than only Central Asia.[8] George Leslie Mallam, Counsellor at the British Legation between 1932 and 1933, claimed that the Legation was "built by Curzon".[9] Nicholas Barrington, Oriental Secretary in Kabul from June 1959, describes the building of the Legation as "Curzonesque".[10] Recently, William Dalrymple referred to the "Curzon-era British Embassy".[11] According to Alexander Redpath, Secretary at the Legation, "[t]he Legation situated in 25 acres of beautiful walled grounds, was by far the most prestigious Mission in Kabul. Lord Curzon [...] had insisted that this was what it should be and plans for it had been made accordingly".[12] However vague the undocumented anecdote, Curzon arises as a pivotal authority in the Legation's material history.[13] Even the land on which the Legation was situated was said to have been "deliberately selected by Curzon".[14] Curzon appears similar to the "providential patriarchs" of the Indian hill stations, who were equally elusive, almost legendary figures as Dane Kennedy has shown.[15] Their visionary foresight guaranteed larger-than-life influence for themselves as much as it ensured the creation of abodes for generations of India's ruling elite. The memory of those who defined the requirements of the Legation, such as Henry Dobbs and Steuart Edmund Pears, or the architects who drew up its plans, or the scores of labourers, who physically built it, pales in comparison. According to Fraser-Tytler, Humphrys "literally carried out" Curzon's instructions.[16] Curzon shaped the Legation; everyone else became his conduit. Curzon's presence in the history of the Legation is remarkable, not least because he died in 1925 before it was finished. It is possible to recognise in this making of Curzon's legend in Kabul, the deployment of architecture as a device that was crafted against the backdrop of Curzon's own history in Anglo-Afghan relations. His Viceroyalty had witnessed diplomatic defeat during the Dane Mission. Curzon's idea for the Legation in Kabul, which he never saw with his own eyes, sought to enshrine and perpetuate imagined imperial power. It was meant to represent imperial might, to project it as well as gloss over its limitations. Since Afghanistan's independence was measured in economic terms, this mission traded in the terms of wealth and extravagance. It had to shield the tangible insecurities and anxieties that were prompted by Afghan independence. In this sense, architecture worked in two directions. It carried messages for those on the outside as much as it sought conserve the existing social, political, cultural and economic realities of the imperial and colonial orders that governed those within.

Diplomatic Reification and Its Audiences

The literature on architecture in the Indian Empire is rich.[17] Several examples have focused on the implementation of colonial and imperial architecture into foreign landscapes. Thomas R. Metcalf's *An Imperial Vision* argued that "it was essential always to make visible Britain's imperial position as ruler, for these structures were charged with the explicit purpose of representing empire itself".[18] According to Jan Morris, the British Empire "imposed [its] styles and purposes upon the rest of mankind".[19] Architecture represented, and the representational aspects of 'prestigious' imperial buildings have been at the forefront of scholarly attention. Diplomatic structures appear as intentionally awe-inspiring, but this only testifies to the longevity of their creators' ideas.[20] Curzon employed architecture as a means to effect an emotional response. Architecture sought to regulate the relationship between colonial and imperial, subjects and citizens toward government. The Indo-Saracenic style that shaped the buildings of the Raj from the mid-nineteenth to the early twentieth century purposely blended several South Asian architectural themes. It embodied the colonial state's claim to forge India's unity whilst the Raj simultaneously exacerbated communal and political division. The colonial government attempted to 'make sense' of India's pasts and cultures by offering its own interpretation, which redefined "Britain's empire in Indian terms" and also drew on the Mughal Empire through architectural reinscription.[21] Colonial rule claimed and communicated political legitimacy through architecture. This practice found application in imperial spaces across the Indian

Ocean. Here, comparable endeavours of imperial representation had been manifested themselves in the nineteenth century, such as the Legation in Tehran, which Curzon knew and where Mortimer Durand had been Minister. During the 'end of empire', ideas of imperial projection circulated globally. Edwin Lutyens built the British Embassy in Washington in the 1920s, and the British Embassy in Rio de Janeiro in the late 1940s invited the characterisation as a "death mask of imperial prestige".[22] The Legation in Kabul created its own eclectic style and was the result of a specific act of architectural distancing that was rooted in a deep history of Anglo-Afghan relations, but it was also representative of a broader materialisation of empire in governmental structures.[23]

To see the Legation through the eyes of those who documented their personal visual experience limits our understanding of what went on behind its deliberately 'magnificent' façade. Structures consciously "exemplified and epitomized", making imperial ambitions "physically apparent".[24] As magnificent structures, they literally "made empire great". Outside of the context of colonial governance, empire and its discourses also began shaping diplomatic representations in the context of European and American politics during the nineteenth century as Jakob Hort shows.[25] But, it is imperative to also consider them beyond a public diplomacy framework. As much as these structures projected might, they also invited people into its private spaces. At the same time, the outward façade and the accessible spaces within also shielded from view. The inside lives of imperial, colonial or diplomatic institutions have only rarely been contextualised, although the hidden relationships between people bounded by imperial and colonial architecture as well as its underlying power structures, racial and Orientalist predispositions speak to colonialism's lived experiences as well as its physical representations.[26] Crucially, architecture provided for more than just "room for diplomacy".[27]

Curzon's frame of reference was empire. It inspired the most visible blueprint for an architectural performance in Anglo-Afghan relations. As the echo of an imperial governing technology that ran through the colonial archive, the repetitive iconographic reproduction of the Minister's residence in and on many books, including the front cover of this present one, speaks to the self-referential system of knowledge that constructed and continues to inform Anglo-Afghan diplomatic relations. Building on the preceding chapters that explore people, performances, practices and show the ideational construction of the Legation of British diplomacy in Kabul, this chapter captures the complex set of ideas that made the Legation specific and unique as well as reflective of more general trends. It considers the incorporation of the Legation's colonial and imperial inspirations, bringing into one framework the considerations that drove its construction for exterior as well as interior audiences. As a reification of the Raj's coloniality, the Legation entombed both colonial India's imperial ambitions as well as its social realities. As a place, it settled and bounded diplomacy and empire. It elicited instances of resistance that utilised imperial diplomacy's bounded nature for its own ends. Although Curzon tried to create imperial permanence by, quite literally, setting in stone imperial objectives and colonial realities, the meanings attached to diplomacy's material manifestations changed over time together with political circumstances, such as dynastic change in Afghanistan in 1929, global war or the independence of India and Pakistan in 1947. Through its life history, the Legation's materiality was layered with new meaning. Its structures were subject to reinterpretation and renegotiation of past, present and future ambitions. On the inside, the Legation's layout, the arrangement of its houses, structures and elements ordered its people. In these avenues of enquiry that interlock the unique and the general, the external and the internal through time, the architectural evidence of the British Legation in Kabul and the correspondence surrounding its creation and later maintenance uncover the underlying rationale which inspired and guided British diplomacy in Afghanistan from 1922 until the end of the Raj and beyond.

In Kabul, the British Legation was only one of many other foreign missions. Because of this, the Legation's architectural structures spoke to several international audiences, including the Soviet Union, Britain's imperial rival in Central Asia, Kabul's growing international diplomatic society as well as Afghan and colonial Indian publics. This growing multinational, colonial and imperial audience conditioned the Raj's architectural performance at a time of imperial transformation following 1919. The Legation became British diplomacy's public face, its external image. In 1921, Denys Bray, India's Foreign Secretary, pointed to "the very real political necessity that our Legation in Kabul should stand out as the most imposing".[28] There was a necessity of "keeping up appearances" during Afghanistan's accelerating 'internationalisation'.[29] More specifically, architecture performed a key role in the next incarnation of the imperial contest in Central Asia, the Great Game. Humphrys urged that money should be spent in order to keep up with "the Bolsheviks", referring to the arrival of the Soviet Legation in 1921.[30] The shift from the imperial competition between 'Britain' and 'Russia' to an ideological contest between the 'British Empire' and 'Bolshevism' was fleeting. Russia, the Soviet Union and Bolshevism were synonymous. As the Russian imperial formation changed in the eyes of concerned Indian colonial officers, so the British Legation came to embody itself an imperial transformation of the Indian colonial state. In addition to this competition between "two great Asiatic powers", the architecture of the Legation also addressed Kabul's international diplomatic audience, including French, German, Italian, Persian and Turkish, later Japanese and US American missions as well as a Chinese delegation.[31] Ultimately, the structures created by British diplomacy were also directed at Afghanistan, including representatives of the state, Afghans as well as Kabul's inhabitants. The Legation's material representations provide important political, cultural and even scientific markers in a web of multiple recipients. The planners of the Legation were aware of the fact that the different audiences also required different, converging and at times conflicting architectural messages, all of which found their way into the Legation's larger physical manifestation.

The Legation was also a habitat whose structure reflected the various "forms of knowledge" connected with the everyday needs and lifestyles of its inhabitants. Chapter 6 evaluates the effects of Afghan space on colonial bodies. Since Afghan space was far from ideal, colonial bodies attempted to mould it according to their needs. British diplomats built houses, offices and spaces, where bodies could feel at home, work comfortably, safely and efficiently and where recreation was possible while maintaining a healthy distance between themselves, the Legation's "menial establishment", as well as a strange land and strange people.[32] In this respect, the internal construction of the British Legation in Kabul was focused on the needs of European bodies. In order to accommodate those needs, British architecture in Kabul borrowed from familiar colonial and metropolitan examples. As a result, the Legation's architectural diplomacy combined the three distinct, yet entangled objectives of imperial representation, colonial realities and metropolitan life styles. The Legation's material manifestations, which attempted to harness the multiple colonial and imperial identities of British diplomacy in Afghanistan, also exposed its inherent contradictions.

Colonial Construction in Kabul

Kabul was captured in the discursive terms of imperial competition, hygiene and security.[33] In June 1922, Humphrys felt reminded of "the necessity of securing as soon as possible suitable accommodation for this Legation".[34]

There was a shortage of "houses built on European lines".[35] Several arriving diplomatic missions competed for accommodation, and Amanullah Khan rented out royal palaces and buildings.[36] Following the principle of diplomatic equality, rent for the arriving British Legation was equivalent to the rent of the Afghan Legation in London.[37] The Soviet Legation had managed to "appropriate" the British Legation's preferred summer residence in the vicinity of Kabul before Humphrys' arrival. The Soviet Union was also quicker in accepting Afghanistan's international status and in exchanging mutual diplomatic missions between Moscow and Kabul.[38] This was fallout from the imperial procrastination of the years immediately following Afghan independence. Housing had to be 'adequate' and, ideally, more adequate housing than one's competitor's. Humphrys was granted the financial powers equivalent to that of a "minor local government in India" in order to acquire land and effect the building of a "permanent" Legation.[39] India provided the precedents for the Legation's financial structuring, likening Kabul to Indian Residencies. Humphrys' financial powers also explain the richness of the archival record that documents the architect's progress in annual reports. According to India's Finance Department, the Legation was to be treated "liberally" when it came to making available the necessary funds: "Of course, there is *no real analogy* between this Legation, the expenses of which are to some extent determined by the Home Foreign Office methods in dealing with their legations and also by the need of making some impressive display in Kabul, and the Residencies in India".[40] Still, the material representation of colonial rule in India informed the material embodiment of diplomacy in Kabul.

While British diplomats explored patches of land in and around Kabul, the British Legation was at first housed in a "shooting box" in Bagrami, east of Kabul. A few months later, in the summer of 1922, the British Legation moved to two *serais*, which had witnessed the signing of the Durand Agreement in 1893, its history befitting the purpose of managing Anglo-Afghan relations. The area also housed high-ranking Afghan officials as well as non-diplomatic foreigners, indicating a preference for socially elevated Afghans and non-Afghan groups as neighbours. According to Basil John Gould, Counsellor in Kabul from 1926 to 1929: "The British Legation was established in mud-walled single-storied buildings, set round two courtyards, which had formerly been the residence of the ladies of the Harem of Amir Habibullah".[41] The two *serais* had originally been built in 1884 as a "leather factory" by Abdur Rahman Khan, the so-called Iron Amir. His son, Habibullah Khan, "felt the need for sexual stimulants" and got two doctors, Allah Jawaya and Imam Din, to provide him with "potent excitant medicines".[42] As Orientalist prurience personified, Habibullah Khan developed a reputation for being "libidinous" owing to his polygamic marriage practices.[43] The *serais* were used as a *garam khana*, or *harem*, for some of his four wives and concubines.[44] When the British Legation moved in, three hundred women were turned out of the "lair".[45] George Kirkbride, Secretary at the Legation from late 1926 until 1928, noted in 1926 that "[s]trange it is to think that such a place was chosen in which to sign, thirty-two years ago that famous agreement drawn up by Mortimer Durand and resolutely imposed on a half-savage and wholly reluctant people".[46] To Kirkbride the occupation of the premises by the British Legation from 1922 seemed "by far the most respectable phase of its chequered life".[47] The walls of the temporary Legation premises breathed international history, as much as they reminded Kirkbride of Oxford and Cambridge colleges. By contrast, the Afghan occupation of the premises appeared less palatable. The Legation reconnected the *serais* to a tradition in which it had been possible to "resolutely impose" Afghanistan's territorial boundaries and conduct its international relations. The *serais*, thus, figured as a potent and melancholy reminder of a time gone by. Their occupation by the British Legation imposed a pleasing master narrative on the interpretation of their history. Yet, the temporary Legation was too small. Fraser-Tytler, Secretary in 1924, noted that he was not allowed to bring his wife to Kabul due to restrictions in space.[48] Humphrys, too, had reservations about the *serais*: "although more commodious and accessible than 'Baghrami', these serais are on political, as on other grounds entirely unsuitable for the purposes of a Legation".[49] Contemporary sources point to the "insanitary surroundings" and the "prison like exterior" of the "Ulya [Hazrat's] Serai".[50] Humphrys concluded that "no suitable house exists in Kabul, and nothing better can be obtained until new buildings are constructed".[51]

A fire made the *serais* uninhabitable in December 1926.[52] It burned through the wood and plaster ceiling, eventually collapsing the roof made of corrugated iron.[53] During the fire, Humphrys commended the actions of the Governor of Kabul who "set an excellent example at the start by felling to the ground, with his hunting crop, several Afghans who were seen to be making off with stolen property".[54] The episode made tangible a threat that seemed to emanate from the Legation's neighbourhood. It reinforced the need for protection, which flowed into the structural layout of the later Legation buildings. Humphrys justified the Governor's violent intervention because "when a building catches fire, the mob rushes in and loots everything within its grasp".[55] When walls failed, violence shielded Europeans from Afghans, and Humphrys resolutely supported what Ranajit Guha called "the idiom of Order".[56] Offering a balancing account of the fire, "there was little or no looting", according to Kirkbride: "The Minister perceived an Afghan of humble birth making off with what he fondly imagined to be a bottle of Johnny Walker, but which in reality was eau de quinine. We are now on the look-out for a hairy Afghan gorilla on whom to fasten the crime".[57] In Kirkbride's account, Afghans, who commit insubstantial thefts, are harmless beasts. Humphrys' view perceived Afghans as emanating danger, regardless of whether their objectives were of a material or a political nature. Afghan crowds unsettled. The panic during the evacuation from the fire brought into the open colonial officers' anxieties of exposure. By contrast, the presence of Europeans and Afghan state representatives, who provided active help and protection, had a soothing effect. Italian diplomats, Gino Cecchi, Doctor Marini and Signor Pennachio, a German Baron von Kaltenborn-Stachau in the employ of the Afghan War Office as well as the Governor Kabul and Amanullah Khan were commended by Humphrys in his report on the fire to the Austen Chamberlain.[58]

Humphrys' insecurities were given weight in the planning of the permanent Legation buildings: "I consider it essential, on grounds of security, that the main building should be defensible for a short period from a mob attack, and, in order to effect this, I suggest that the roof should be flat with a parapet all round and a stairway leading up to it.[59] In addition to adding a defensive quality, "this type of roof will not be inharmonious with the surroundings".[60] Humphrys accommodated both the Legation's securitisation and an existing architectural style in its vicinity, blending the mission's militarisation into the aesthetic background of its neighbourhood. Plans for the evacuation of the British Legation were under constant review, before and after the airlifts during the civil war of 1928/1929.[61] Based on the Anglo-Afghan encounter of the past, the need to remove a British mission from Kabul in times of crisis was a constant presence. Even as it 'settled' into its new environment, the Legation was ready to leave at a moment's notice for the safety of India.

Owing to the destruction of the *serais*, the British Legation moved into its new, yet only partially finished premises. Planning and construction on the purpose-built Legation compound outside Kabul had already begun in 1922. Eight different sites were visited and assessed on the basis of ground water levels and their distance "to some neighbouring villages".[62] The

Legation's Oriental Secretary, Sheikh Mahbub Ali Khan, purchased several plots of land on behalf of the British government. The main reasons for his participation in the transactions were his Persian language skills and his knowledge of Afghan court proceedings. He was also well versed in the details of land ownership, being a landlord in his home village, Sheikhan in the Peshawar district.[63] Under Afghan law, no foreigner was otherwise allowed to own land, but an exception was entered into the treaty of 1921, which exempted the British Legation from this clause.[64] According to the sale deeds, there were twelve separate plots of land, amounting to between 24 and 27 acres.[65] The acquisition process took place in stages between April/May 1923 and September/October 1925. The Treaty of Kabul had originally limited the acreage of the Legation to only fifteen. Twelve acres of land were acquired from Sardar Aminullah in May 1923, selling the land against the wishes of his nephew Amanullah Khan, who wanted Humphrys to build the Legation in Dar-ul-Aman, a suburban development project on the outskirts of Kabul.[66] At first, Humphrys seemed intent on making the Legation part of Dar-ul-Aman urging the Government of India in August 1922 that: "Politically it will show that the British Government are determined to take root in Afghanistan, and will be regarded as a sign of stability and strength. [...] On political, social and financial grounds it is of the utmost importance that the British Government should be first in the field, and that no time should be lost in making a start with the construction".[67] Later on, Humphrys declined on "general grounds", and his planning staff agreed "owing to the proximity of the subsoil water".[68]

Aminullah's "Turks Garden" provided the biggest single plot of land of the later Legation. Despite the disadvantageous reception of Aminullah in diplomatic privacy—"[h]e certainly has more than a screw loose"—his plot provided a substantial part of the Legation's land.[69] The acquisition of further plots in addition decreased "a congestion which I [Humphrys] did not consider justifiable".[70] Several patches of land appear as "agricultural land," a "garden plot," a "fruit garden" and access to *juis* (irrigation canals) in the English translation of the sale deeds.[71] At the foot of Asmai Hill, later claimed and renamed as "Legation Hill", the fertile land was in the countryside surrounded by fields (Fig. 7.1).[72] The plots were located at a noticeable distance from Kabul's urban centre at the time of its acquisition.[73] Removed from public access, the remote location accommodated both hygienic and defensive lines of argument.[74] Creating a European dwelling at a distance from indigenous populations was a standard feature of "European quarters" in colonial contexts in order to implement regimes of racial segregation in

Fig. 7.1 The British Legation compound, 1933 (*Credit* Photo 667/3(176), Parsons Collection, BL)

urban areas.[75] In 1955, Peter Mayne commented on the "atmosphere of insulated calm" at the then British Embassy.[76] As Kabul's urbanisation increased, the city eventually engulfed the mission.

In Kabul, the Indian colonial state distributed large sums for a "prestigious" object in suburban space. The first estimate of costs for the British Legation in Kabul accumulated an estimated sum of Rs. 21 lakh (Rs. 2,103,900), which was later brought down to Rs. 1,645,420.[77] "Judged by the standards of buildings put up in India, the Legation itself and the attached residences for officers are by no means expansive [sic]. [...] I dislike the idea of having to spend this money in our present difficulties, but [...] I believe that the expenditure is likely to be fruitful", wrote William Malcolm Hailey, the uncle of a later Counsellor.[78] As the Finance Member of the Viceroy's Council, Hailey was well acquainted with the politics of architecture that founded New Delhi. The financial considerations underlying the construction of the imperial capital now flowed into the planning of the Legation.[79] The colonial state sought to make the Legation "in every way worthy of the Empire whose representative it will accommodate".[80] But, the actual 'worth' of this empire based on the extraction of colonial funds was far from durable or beyond doubt. In the 1930s, the Legation's presence "afforded a valuable corrective to the ideas which [Afghan Ministers] form from notices in the press regarding the financial position of the Government of India".[81]

The acquired land provided a large territory for the application of architectural knowledge from colonial India.[82] India provided a swathe of blueprints on how to shield Europeans from the dangers and diversions of living in a foreign land among foreign people. This knowledge now travelled to Kabul. The city's inadequate water supply, its lack of housing, its "dirty" crowds; all added colour and depth to Curzon's instructions. Conceptualising Afghanistan as a princely state and the Legation as another colonial Residency, India delivered the knowledge which turned Afghan gardens into sites of imperial government and colonial residential areas. Colonial funds, which enabled the Legation's political tasks and its housing, were not the only aspect that was imported from India. Many of the Legation's materials, labour and ideas came entirely from Indian resources. Architects, engineers and construction-related contractors brought with them specific, colonially sourced knowledge. According to Wylie, "[i]deas which are suitable e.g. for the headquarters of a frontier political agency, have been extended to the residence of a diplomatic representative".[83]

Basil Martin Sullivan, who had been employed by the government of Punjab as an architect since 1913, embodied this transfer of colonial knowledge.[84] Humphrys had originally put forward Herbert Baker to draw up the plans for the new Legation owing to the latter's "New Delhi fame", a description that pointed to his contribution to the design of India's new capital.[85] Humphrys and Baker did not just share similar architectural visions; they were also connected by family bonds. Humphrys' daughter married Baker's son in 1941.[86] The Legation resembled New Delhi's 'classicism'. It was as good a stage as New Delhi when it came to putting up an imperial display. New Delhi had been chosen because it was an 'empty' space, in the colonial understanding of empty places; away from the political opposition generated by Indian nationalism at the turn of the twentieth century, but still close enough to evoke the symbolism of legitimacy generated by proximity to the Mughal court.[87] Sullivan followed a similar approach in order to wall in imperial glory. The Legation was to impose order, but its location outside and away from Afghanistan's political centre also undermined its marginal grasp on power. Leon Williamson Amps "of Khartoum", formerly Garrison Engineer in Peshawar, became the Legation's first Resident Engineer.[88] Several successive Resident Engineers from India, including Amps, A. Foster-Josephs, Robert Wilson and M. H. Jefferis, oversaw the construction and maintenance of the Legation buildings and also brought further clerks with them.[89] Owing to their professional backgrounds, the architect and the Resident Engineers were well versed with the contemporary aspects of colonial architecture and urban planning as well as with the organisation of colonial labour.

Amps visited Kabul in July 1922 and wrote a survey on existing architectural structures, building materials and labour rates. He noted that "all the best buildings" functioned as palaces for the Afghan king or as government offices.[90] Materials for those buildings were imported from India, while Afghan dwellings consisted of materials resourced in Afghanistan itself. Amps advised the use of burnt bricks "according to aesthetic requirements", while exercising economy on the "subsidiary buildings, such as stables and servants quarters", using sun-dried bricks. For structural support, Amps recommended the use of poplar. In terms of roofs, he argued against following Afghan practice, which adopted "galvanised corrugated iron", and opted for the application of burnt tiles in order to provide better shielding from the cold. Humphrys preferred wooden floorings "on account of the greater warmth, cleanliness and [...] economy", effectively mixing practicality with a colonial discourse of hygiene. For "special floors", Amps recommended importing teak. Exploring further potential materials, Amps minutely listed Afghan resources, including white marble, green marble, limestone and clay for bricks, tiles from Jalalabad, sand, *surkhi* (lime mortar), wood ashes, mortar, plaster and timber. These could be transported using camels, donkeys, bullocks and ponies or even Amanullah Khan's elephants. Everything else had to be imported from India, using cars, lorries, horse-drawn tongas and camel caravans. The items needed from India included "[r]olled steel joists; galvanised iron; and all other iron work; cement glazing; paints; door furniture; and electric light fittings; picks and shovels; and all other tools; oil, petrol stoves, etc., etc." According to Amps' observations, Afghanistan provided only cheap raw materials, while processed goods were exclusively sourced from India. The same economic principle informed the imperial model which linked India to Britain, in which the former was the market for the latter's manufactured goods. Afghanistan appeared to exist in a similar, yet supercolonial, relationship with India.

A gigantic labour force was employed during the construction process of the Legation. In preparation for the initial plans, Sullivan required a European engineer, a computor, a draughtsman, a head clerk, two assistant clerks, an accountant, a European sub-divisional officer, two overseers, another two clerks, four mechanics, an Indian sub-divisional officer "in charge of supply and stores", and two storekeepers.[91] The actual construction process required around 700 Indian labourers, 1000 Afghans and 25 Europeans.[92] In terms of local labour, Amps singled out Hazara men as being particularly productive. He described them as "a body of men who are strong, energetic and by far the best workers available".[93] It helped the implementation of colonial labour regimes that they also belonged to one of Afghanistan's vulnerable communities. The projection of specific qualities of productivity to individual ethnic groups imitated similar constructions of colonial knowledge with regard to Indian communities.[94] Seasonal migration during harvest brought about shortages in labour, but Amps discounted the possibility of attracting Indian contractors "to work in a strange country and under somewhat uncertain conditions without making a fairly high provision in their tender for unforeseen emergencies".[95] In light of this, Amps proposed to offer Afghan contractors "regular employment and good pay". In particular, building the Legation required a mason, plasterer, carpenter, painter, blacksmith, several water-carriers (*bhisti*, sg.), and carriers (*cooli*, sg.) and a surprising inclusion in this list of indigenous human labour: donkeys. As a reflection of the colonial hierarchies at work, an "Engineer-in-charge (Eurasian)" supervised the organisation of labour in addition to the construction of the water and electricity systems. Further, there was need for drivers, a wireman, a *cooli* for "cleaning and greasing", an overseer and three more mechanics. Amps pointed out that Persian was an essential prerequisite for communicating in Kabul as Pashto was spoken only in the provinces.

In terms of imported labour, Indian brick moulders were made to train "the more promising Afghans up to their standard", resulting in migrant labour between India and Afghanistan. An example from 1926 indicates that twenty brick burners went to Kabul, while Muslim Ahmedis were returned to India "on account of the persecution of this sect by the Afghans".[96] Charles Drace-Francis contends that "a special brick-making apparatus had to be dragged up to Kabul by elephant through the Khyber Pass".[97] Afghanistan was not only a place of raw materials, but also of 'unskilled' labour. India, by contrast provided technical expertise in the shape of European architects, engineers, professionals of many kinds as well as efficient organisation implemented by Indian draftsmen and storekeepers. Amps aligned Indians as the former trainees of Europeans, who now trained Afghans in Afghanistan in another colonial transfer of ideas. The employment of Indian labourers at the construction site of the British Legation in Kabul was justified twofold. On the one hand, it appeared "natural" that British subjects should also build a British mission in Afghanistan. On the other, Afghans were to a large extent considered unreliable labourers. Afghans "have to be watched very carefully or they will infallibly commit some b[ê]tise or other", thought Fraser-Tytler.[98] The resultant share of Indians in Kabul formed part of a complaint presented by the Afghan Minister in London to Chamberlain in 1927. According to the Afghan Minister, there was plenty of local labour, offering an important balance to colonial observations to the contrary.[99]

REPRESENTATING EMPIRE, RECREATING COLONY AND HOME

Inside the Legation compound, the Minister's residence has attracted most attention as its *pars pro toto*. Bertram, for instance, calls it "the Kabul legation house".[100] More expansively, Barrington describes it as "an imposing structure with portico, large dining and drawing rooms to left and right, and a ballroom behind stretching out into a series of terraces leading to lawns full of roses and flowering shrubs. It contained a fine library, full of early editions concentrating on the Great Game".[101] As Chapter 1 shows, the history of Afghanistan has often been written by diplomats and for diplomats as representatives of shifting British-Indian imperial formations. The library reinforced approaches to understanding the history of Afghanistan as an actor with limited agency in the power struggles of neighbouring empires. As such, it also revealed to any visitor the imperial identity of the Legation and later Embassy. The plan of the residence indicates that the large room to the right of the main entrance was originally labelled as a billiard room.[102] The Legation was designed to accommodate the head of the British mission and to impress and entertain visitors in a variety of social functions. Adjacent to it was the Minister's office and another drawing room, through which the greenhouse could be reached. This conservatory, in particular, was the result of an interpretation of Afghan architecture. It was placed in the vicinity of the Minister's office because it was deemed to be a requirement in the socially elevated circles of Kabul's society. Evelyn Berkeley Howell, temporary Foreign Secretary of India, pointed out the political role of the *gul khana*:

The 'Gul Khana' is a very distinctive feature of domestic architecture at Kabul. It consists of a glassed-in veranda and is the place where every one sits, where visitors come and where, as often as not, business is transacted. The Durand Agreement for example was signed in the Gul Khana of the old British Legation, now destroyed by fire. It is absolutely essential that the new Legation should have a fine spacious Gul Khana. It will be seen by visitors ten times for every time that they enter the state rooms on occasions of ceremony.[103]

As a "feature common to every Afghan house of distinction in Kabul", the *gul khana* also ensured a safe supply of flowers and warmth for the Minister's house during Kabul's colder seasons.[104] The Minister's house was partially designed according to British observations on Afghan social life and their relevance to diplomatic relations. Together, they informed designs which aimed at providing facilities for hosting diplomatic guests, parties and receptions. As Hailey pointed out: "It is necessary that this building should have adequate accommodation for entertaining, for this is likely to be a very powerful solvent of their suspicious minds. Indeed without being optimistic, I feel myself that the establishment of decent social relationships with Afghan Nobles and Ministers will be worth more to us in the long run than an increase of military armaments".[105]

Even the smallest detail of Afghan social life informed the interior planning. Dobbs set up a meticulous inventory, ranging from large items, such as buildings, to individual pieces of cutlery, crockery, dishes and even the size of curtains. He advised that more than the usual amount of spoons should be supplied to the Legation in Kabul, because "these play a large part in Afghan feeding arrangements".[106] There should be "extra tumblers", as Afghans enjoyed "fizzy water".[107] Since "Afghans admire English carpets much more than their own", Dobbs advised that only "the best pattern be brought out".[108] Afghan requirements, in fact, dictated the size of the original layout of the Minister's residence, as "[t]he size of the main building will have to be regulated by the number of guests to be entertained, and by the dignity appropriate to His Majesty's representative in a country where outward appearances count for much".[109] Accordingly, Anglo-Afghan relations required a lavish display of British imperial identity. As Chapter 4 shows that identity was an amalgam of imperial, colonial and metropolitan elements and was itself in the process of being fashioned along the Legation's life history. In addition, as the discussion of Chapter 5 concludes, British diplomats were themselves critically disposed towards Afghan presentations of material wealth. Accordingly, Humphrys estimated dinners for "50-60" guests and garden parties in the vicinity of "300-400".[110] The importance of physical intimacy translated directly into the structuring of social spaces for Anglo-Afghan diplomatic engagement: "Our influence in Kabul will rest largely in keeping close personal touch with Afghan notables and officials, which can only be done in the course of social meetings, and I understand that much of our information is obtained at dinners", noted P. G. Loch.[111]

The Legation's material arrangements provided the requisite space to also translate these specific ambitions into practice. In addition to reflecting colonial observations of Afghan social life, the Legation compound designed by Sullivan also followed more general design patterns. The Legation emerged from blueprints that informed the building of enclaves for rulers in the colonial world at large. Like the "colonial bungalow-compound complex", the Legation was surrounded by a wall and was accessible only through one gate. According to Anthony King, "the kitchen, as well as servants' quarters, stabling and room for carriage or car, are separate from and placed at the rear of the bungalow. [...] The complex is situated in [...] a rural, often isolated or semi-isolated site, far removed from other members of the colonial community".[112] A 1948 "site plan" counted fourteen houses, of which five were residences, four quarters, the Chancery, the stable compound and the garage (Fig. 7.2).[113] Each was a small household in itself, including also quarters for 'servants' and cooks. The residences were reserved for the Minister, the Counsellor, the Secretary and the Surgeon, the Military Attaché and the Office Superintendent. There was one block for three single British clerks, for the Garage Superintendent and European clerks, for married European clerks as well as for household staff. The Chancery was the professional hub of the Legation and contained the majority of offices. The Minister, Counsellor, Secretary and the Surgeon had offices in their residences. The type of dwellings inside the Legation compound followed a hierarchy even in their denomination: there were *residences* for the political officers and the Office Superintendent as well as *quarters* for clerks and "servants". In order of diplomatic precedence, other residences and quarters cost less than a quarter of the Minister's residence. Houses for Europeans cost more in terms of construction than houses for Indians. The buildings, where Europeans worked and lived, ranged from Rs. 24,500 to Rs. 52,000. Buildings for Indians ranged from Rs. 4800 to 35,000.[114] The hierarchical organisation also translated into the size of the dwellings, decreasing in size per occupant from the Minister's residence downwards. The Minister's and the Military Attaché's

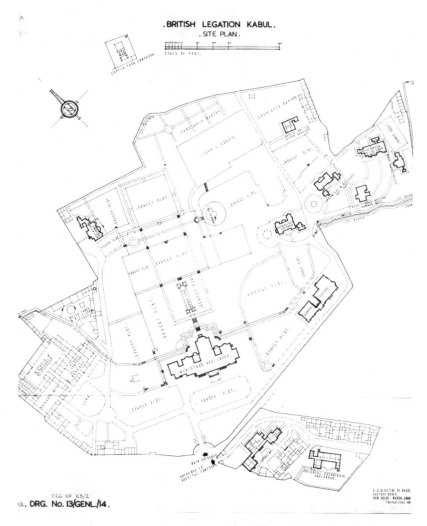

Fig. 7.2 British Legation Kabul, site plan, 1948 (*Credit* https://webarchive.nationalarchives.gov.uk/20120817042531/http://www.fco.gov.uk/en/about-us/our-history/historic-views-kabul/building-plans/)

residences measured three floors in total. The residences of the Secretary and Surgeon, the Office Superintendent as well as the economically sized quarters shared by the Garage Superintendent and the European clerks measured two. Those buildings located outside of the Legation compound, the Oriental Secretary's residence and the hospital, were the only single-storey buildings.

The Legation's hierarchy also informed the compound's spatial structuring. The Minister's residence was situated close to the Legation's gates and provided the first impression for any visitor entering the grounds. The Counsellor and the Military Attaché had their own residence, while the Secretary and the Surgeon shared one. The Oriental Secretary's house was located outside the compound, indicating a racialised division of Legation society. Although crucial to the diplomatic mission, his position did not warrant inclusion in the compound. Instead, he lived and worked in the direct neighbourhood of the hospital, which was also located outside the compound and whose patients were predominantly Afghan. As a liminal gate-keeper between an Afghan public and Legation society, the Oriental Secretary was intentionally segregated.

The compound both prominently presented and hid from view its elements. Like the European settlements in colonial India, the Legation compound employed a considerable number of labourers. Chapter 3 shows the presence of house bearers, cooks, washers, cleaners, drivers, Afghan gardeners, water carriers and sweepers. Altogether, the Legation comprised a population of around 100–120 persons.[115] They maintained the mission's critical processes, but were kept out of offices and away from recorded documentation. They lived in areas beyond the Legation's accessible and purposely visible spaces, spatially marginalised in order to prevent the unsettling of the compound's desired effect, by latrines for instance.[116] The Legation's workforce was housed in an isolated corner of the Legation compound in the vicinity of the Legation stables and the garage, economically grouped with horses and other animals, carts, carriages and vehicles away from the expensive and ostentatious structures of the residences. The Legation's spatial structuring sought to highlight the 'magnificent' and simultaneously hide the mundane. At the same time, the Legation compound recreated colonial space, according to which colonial officers organised a South Asian workforce and their dwelling arrangements. In addition to this, a clock was fixed on the water tower: "It is to be provided with chimes so that it can be heard by all on the site. Some such provision is considered necessary in order to have a standard time by which the business of the Legation can be carried on".[117] The Legation turned into a small urban settlement, disciplining its Indian, Afghan and European inhabitants according to imperial time. During Habibullah Kalakani's advance on Kabul, when many of the Legation buildings were damaged, the water tower in particular was used for target practice, suggesting also an act of resistance against the time-keeping regime that it represented.[118]

In addition to these ideas of spatial and temporal structuring, architectural habits that arose from colonial housing in tropical and subtropical climate were copied to Kabul. Most buildings were oriented in a north-easterly direction, with the exception of the houses for the Military Attaché and the Office Superintendent. In India, houses were oriented north to evade the hazardous heat of the sun.[119] Moreover, roofed verandahs intended to offer shade and allow for the flow of cool air.[120] In Kabul, however, natural cooling was needed only for very short periods of time. While Kabul was located at an altitude of close to six thousand feet, similar to the Indian hill stations, it followed a more varied annual climatic cycle. Kabul had four distinct seasons, with short summers, during which temperatures exceeded 100 °F (c. 37 °C) only for about three weeks and with snowy winters and subzero degrees for lengthy spells. Facing north in Kabul meant facing the Hindu Kush and its icy breezes in the winter months. As a result, the Legation was cold and uncomfortable. This design flaw, a "mistake" in Howell's words, was noticed too late.[121] It is best understood by the Indian expertise of Sullivan, the leading architect. Amps did point out Kabul's climate in a paragraph in his report, noting snowfall in December, January and February and that "at no time is the heat great enough to interfere with the work of construction in any way".[122] However, Amps' report on Kabul's meteorological conditions seems to have been disregarded by Sullivan, as several events caused delay to the construction of the Legation. In 1924, the Khost rebellion cut off timber supplies, and in 1925 Afghan passport regulations impeded the movement of Indian labourers. According to Humphrys, the "delay has been due almost entirely to circumstances outside our control".[123] Amps firmly placed blame on "the action of the Afghan Authorities in deliberately holding up transport".[124] Regardless of these circumstances, however, Sullivan did not deliver his first drawings until August 1924, two years after Amps' report, owing "partly to the absence of Mr. Sullivan on leave in England in 1923 and partly to a misunderstanding".[125] It is conceivable that in view of the delays caused, Amps' information was simply lost in the planning process, leading Sullivan to apply the unquestioned principles of colonial architecture in India to the British Legation in Kabul. The need for a central heating system, however, formed part of the Legation structure from the very beginning. The conservatory, too, provided a warm space during winter.

In addition to the import of colonial knowledge and the projection of imperial identity, commentators of the Legation compound have described its many buildings as following a "Home Counties style".[126] According to Bertram, the buildings in the compound, apart from the Minister's residence, reflected a "Surrey idiom".[127] According to Drace-Francis, the Minister's residence "owed much to 1920s Knightsbridge".[128] Mayne commented that the "Georgian-type porch" of the later First Secretary's house "would better suit a western city suburb than Central Asia".[129] The compound was an eclectic mix of metropolitan influences.[130] As a compound, which was informed by discourses of hygiene, security and 'prestige', the Legation drew its inspiration from a variety of colonial, metropolitan and imperial sources. As an act of public diplomacy, it projected this palimpsest of 'British' identities into suburban Kabul. The outward projection also had an inward function. The residential areas recreated a 'home' away from home for diplomats and their families, wives and children. The compound embraced the human life cycle. Some of its houses had nurseries.[131] There were also graves. Here, again, the material construction of the Legation copied processes that inspired architectural designs in Indian hill stations, which reproduced Malls and Strands.[132] Sports facilities, in particular, offered ways to exercise diplomatic bodies in familiar leisurely ways. A tennis court was fitted into the *serais* of the 'second' Legation. The Legation compound included squash and basketball courts as well as spaces for cricket and hockey.[133] There were also two tennis courts and a round swimming pool.[134] Large parts of grass and trees allowed for long walks in the "park-like grounds".[135] The adjacent Wazirabad plain offered riding in the countryside. According to Katherine Himsworth, staying at the Legation was like an "English country-house week end".[136]

Of the total of Rs. 16 lakh in expenditure the most expensive items were the Legation's "water-borne sanitary installation" (Rs. 307,400), followed by the Legation's labour force (Rs. 226,000), the Minister's residence (Rs. 200,000) and the power house (Rs. 125,300).[137] The power generator represented the Legation's embodiment of technological progress. According to Fraser-Tytler: "The Legation is really a great achievement. It has cost £200,000, has taken 5 years to build & is like an oasis of civilisation in a desert of barbarism – a desert which stretches northwards from the Khyber to the Pole, & east & west from Teheran to Pekin. No man so far as I know had ever pulled a [power] plug in Central Asia till Sir Francis [Humphrys], or someone, pulled the first one here some 12 months ago".[138] The use of electricity was, however, limited to lighting and circumscribed by the Legation's *Office Manual*.[139] The water supply and the sanitary installations increased the Legation's autarchy and shielded it further from its neighbouring environments. A septic tank was located outside of the compound in order to minimise the mixing of excrement and drinking water, which, according to diplomatic reports, was a common occurrence in Kabul.[140] A deep source-water well was later built within the Legation compound, which supplied the water tower with drinking water. The Legation Surgeon supervised the septic tank as well as water purification. Before the establishment of the well, the Legation's water supply rested on regular lorry supplies from nearby wells, which were prone to contamination during the many stages of transport.[141] The tube well also ensured the irrigation of the garden and minimised conflicts with the Legation's neighbours over the existing resources in local water channels.[142]

Next to dwellings and working spaces, the compound's garden combined a series of patches, separated by paths and demarcations.[143] It followed European as well as South Asian inspirations. Its sloping terraces constituted "a feature of Central Asian landscapes".[144] It resembled Bagh-e Babur, the gardens of the Mughal emperor Babur in Kabul. It included a long, shallow "ornamental water," similar to architectural structures in India built during Shah Jahan's reign.[145] Fraser-Tytler suggested privately to his mother, that "[n]o one that I can see in Asia, since the Mogul Emperors, has had any idea of symmetry and order, and I believe most of their gardens and monuments were planned by Europeans".[146] According to Fraser-Tytler, Europeans had ordered South Asian nature already in precolonial time. Fraser-Tytler challenged the legitimising authority of the Mughals that informed the design of the Legation garden as well as the Raj as a whole.

The garden allowed for the production of fruits and vegetables on a limited scale. Accounts regarding its productivity vary, but it did not sustain the Legation community. Contemporary accounts contend that "everything had to be brought from India".[147] A standing order from the *Office Manual* prohibited travellers from India to bring "baskets of fruits" as supplements owing to the scarcity of space on the Legation lorries.[148] Still, the garden produced asparagus, peas, lettuce, "English tomatoes", grapes, strawberries, gooseberries, currants, raspberries and loganberries.[149] In his plans for the garden, Amps envisaged the compound to have six large trees each of thirteen kinds, such as oak, chestnut, maple, beech, ash and birch, fifty-six fruit trees in addition to shrubs and small trees.[150] Drace-Francis refers to "noble trees, mainly chenars or oriental planes. Elsewhere were Judas trees, limes, walnuts, almonds, apricots, quinces and fine mulberry trees, both the big white fruit ones, which in dried form provide the basic Afghan winter ration, and the purple-fruited ones".[151] In addition to fruits, there were plenty of flowers, including yellow and dark red roses, narcissus, iris, peony, tulips and eremurus, which were ordered from gardening businesses in both England and India.[152] Given the garden's productivity, methods of composting were introduced from Central India. The "'Indore system' of litter and refuse disposal" addressed the problem of mosquitoes in summer, the recycling of stable bedding and the production of fertiliser for the garden. Developed in India, this gardening practice was transferred to Kabul. H. A. Ledgard, the Surgeon, noted that the scheme worked "admirably" in India, but faced problems due the "difficulties of getting Afghan gardeners to carry out simply worded and clear instructions".[153] The attempted transfer of knowledge broke down because Afghan gardeners allegedly lacked the intelligence to carry it out.[154]

The garden also contained a summer house, which was originally designed to become a centre of diplomatic activity during garden and tennis parties. Contrary to Humphrys' expectations, however, Fraser-Tytler found the summer house was "very ugly".[155] He thought that its purpose was "that the Minister should go there and commune with nature while writing despatches. No one ever used it except to keep tennis nets in".[156] It was consequently demolished to make way for a pergola to facilitate the growing of roses.[157] Acknowledgements of Afghan expertise in growing roses are plentiful. Redpath suggested that talking about gardening could also bring about "a closer acquaintance" with otherwise "secretive and enigmatic" Afghans in diplomatic matters.[158] The garden sought to project empire's ordering of people and nature. When the first plans for the Legation were drawn up, Pears suggested that the Legation "should undoubtedly have a fairly large garden if only to make the entertainment of Kabul Society on a large scale possible".[159] Humphrys agreed and Amps included "what I consider would produce a very satisfactory garden suitable for the prestige of a British Legation in a foreign country".[160] Each year, the Legation hosted a party in honour of the British monarch's birthday. These parties involved a tea party with games of tennis, croquet and bowls attended by several dozen members of the Indian community in Kabul. This was followed by a dinner for members of the Afghan government.[161]

The presence of Indians in particular indicated an overlap of the colonial and diplomatic identities of the Legation. Fraser-Tytler noted in 1937, that "I was glad to find that the Indians, teachers, doctors and so on, were much more at home and less like school boys at a treat. [...] [T]hey should get to look on this place as one to which they can come when asked with the feeling that they are part of the show and not strangers".[162] Fraser-Tytler hoped that the Legation garden might instil in its Indian visitors "a certain pride in the place" and perhaps even quell the politics of Indian nationalism.[163]

The compound's constituent elements and their ordering rested on various forms of colonial knowledge that emerged from the colonial encounter in South Asia. Visible only from a study of the surviving architectural drawings is another inspiration that appears to be specifically rooted in the deep history of colonial cartography of Afghanistan. As a geopolity, Afghanistan was 'made' as a consequence of its interaction with imperial formations, who charted, labelled, indexed, surveyed and measured Afghan spaces according to their own ambitions, objectives and priorities. In this reading, the compound's very geographical outlines constituted a colonial mapping exercise of Afghanistan in reverse. The territorial confines of the Afghan geopolity were superimposed onto the British Legation in Kabul (Figs. 7.2 and 8.1). Afghanistan's major urban centres become the compound's main buildings. The Minister's residence in the south-western corner represents Kandahar, the historical epicentre of the Durrani tribal confederation. As much as visitors entered the Legation compound to first see the Minister's residence, the invasions of Afghanistan in the First and Second Anglo-Afghan Wars had been routed through Kandahar. The Military Attaché's residence becomes Herat, an outpost of Great Game significance in the vicinity of the Persian and Soviet frontiers. In the north-east, the "Married British Clerks Quarters" could be Mazar-i-Sharif as well as Kunduz. Symbolising northern Afghanistan's connectivity to Soviet Central Asia, the compound was accessible through a subsidiary gate here. The Counsellor's residence becomes Kabul, perhaps Ghazni. The compound's south-eastern corner collapses Afghanistan's eastern province, the well-travelled route from Kabul to Jalalabad and Torkham into the shape of the Wakhan Corridor. The four structures here are labelled the "Secretary & Surgeon's Residence", "Three Single British Clerks Q[ua]rt[er]s", the "Garage Sup[erin]t[en]d & British Clerks Q[ua]rt[er]s", as well as the "Office Sup[erin]t[en]d's House". It is conceicable that the North-West Frontier Province, including Peshawar, is also represented among them. Along the architectural rendering of the Indo-Afghan frontier, the Chancery offices stand as one of several border crossings between the Khyber Pass and Chaman in the south. The latter takes the shape of the Legation's main entrance gate, leaving the hospital compound and the Oriental Secretary's Residence in lieu of Quetta in India. Like all hill stations, Quetta was famed for its medical qualities and spelled physical recuperation from life 'in the plains'. Remaining in 'India', the Oriental Secretaries were excised from the Afghanistan of the Legation compound. The compound's eastern half contains most of its structures, including the residences of its political elite. This architectural occupation of Afghanistan echoes eastern Afghanistan's prominence in Indo-Afghan diplomatic relations, whereas the compound's north contains only the military representative's outpost in the Soviet 'sphere of influence'. Beyond the mapping of cities, Afghanistan's geology was also recreated. The Legation's main water canal, running from the south-east to the south-west merges the Kabul and Helmand Rivers into one. The compound's water tower is its Lake Hamun. The sloping garden terraces are the Legation's Hindu Kush, an 'empty' space without buildings or human settlements. The compound built on colonial map-making as the Legation appropriated Afghanistan's geopolitical shape as the borders of the Legation's colonial society within. The British Legation in Kabul became Afghanistan. As 'Afghanistan', the compound populated Afghan space according to the rules of colonial Indian society, and the British Legation in Kabul metaphorically colonised colonialism's own geopolitical rendering of Afghanistan.

As a whole, the Legation was a study in the implementation of colonial difference. The presence of families, dogs and horses, other pets and animals, access to open water, plentifully productive trees, plants and flowers were designed to give the British Legation in Kabul the impression of a paradisiacal place. The Legation was an abode, which ordered Afghan nature in terms of the environment, humanity and international relations.[164] Its self-contained space was built on the reassuring discourses of race, class and labour and brought distance from Kabul's hazardous environment and its 'dirty' inhabitants. The Legation compound was the peaceful counterpart to a harassing environment. It offered recreation and was designed to impress those who laid eyes on it through its productivity, splendour and beauty. In 1941, on the eve of his departure from Kabul, Fraser-Tytler reflected on the imperial meanings attached to the Legation:

[The Legation] gives to the British Minister a position which is far superior to that of any other diplomat in Afghanistan, and fills the minds of all Afghans with a mixture of admiration, envy and respect which they accord to no other foreigner. His house, his servants, his retinue, his carriages, his gardens, his manner of entertaining all combine to impress in a very marked degree on Afghans and foreigners alike that the British Minister is held by his own Government to occupy a position of very considerable importance and respect.[165]

Diplomatic Insurgency, Colonial Revolt and Imperial Violence

Over time, new meanings were added to the Legation's structures. In 1943, Wylie wrote to Anthony Eden, Secretary of State for Foreign Affairs between 1940 and 1945, about the misfit of the Legation's neo-classical presence in Kabul's urban surroundings:

Not only is the group of buildings [...] a most conspicuous affair but it is unfortunately most violently divorced from its local background. [...] [T]he inevitable impression gained after a journey through [Kabul's] streets is one of dirt, dilapidation, slovenliness and extreme poverty. The prevailing tones are [...] grey of crudely dressed stone and brown of omnipresent mud. The British Legation by contrast is of a startling white, it occupies a site no less than 24 acres in extent while within its precincts it houses, as foreign diplomatists are never tired of pointing out – whether in envy or in malice is not clear – 'plusieurs centaines des domestiques'. Many opprobrious epithets have been hurled at these structures by British visitors to Afghanistan.[166]

A caption in Mallam's book states that "[t]he unpopular magnificence was hardly less palatial than the King's own residence".[167] The Legation deliberately rivalled the material representation of Afghan monarchy. Wylie pointed out that the British presence in Kabul was likely to cause the "appearance of tutelage", suggesting that "although the 19th century is dead and gone we are still the power behind the dictator's chair in Kabul".[168] Wylie's "revolutionary comment" unsettled his colleagues in London.[169] I. T. M. Pink at the Foreign Office was "at a loss to understand Sir F. Wylie's criticism":

It is very curious that an ex-Provincial Governor [...] should suggest that the Legation suffers from too much pomp and circumstance. We have always spent a good deal of money on our Missions in Oriental countries, on what I should have thought was the sound principle that in the East people judge by appearances to a considerable extent and that some degree of magnificence is a good investment.[170]

Pink's colleague at the Foreign Office, H. A. C. Caccia, feared that changing the architectural setup of the Legation might show "that the decline of the British Empire had set in, for seeing is believing".[171] To Pink and Caccia, empire manifested itself in architecture. To Wylie, that manifestation unsettled imperial governance. Wylie's point went largely unheeded. On the one hand, diplomatic action was modelled on Indian princely politics and frontier administration. The latter dictated that personal contact with high-ranking Afghan statesmen enabled the 'close touch' and its tutorials in the 'good conduct' of Anglo-Afghan relations. On the other hand, these relations were destabilised by an imperial monument that undermined Afghanistan's setup as a sovereign state. Afghan opposition to the Legation's manifold embodiments of the Raj and its practices surfaced in questions of staffing and in medical activity. To Fraser-Tytler, these acts of resistance were best explained by "the primary impulses to revolt among oriental people":

> There is nothing in this world so exasperating to the inefficient as the 'supreme consciousness of effortless superiority' displayed by the efficient, and in proportion as the former develop and in due course become less inefficient, so do they seek with increasing vehemence to rid themselves of a yoke which in spite of its security carries with it the humiliating stigma of inferiority.[172]

The sheer size of Kabul's largest diplomatic compound and its location outside the city made the Legation "a thing apart".[173] Its premises were also contextualised in an architectural variety of the civilising mission. Its "civilising" factor was meant to generate "emulation to go & do likewise".[174] The Legation's architecture constituted a psychological technology of imperial rule. For R. T. Peel at the India Office, Kabul, New Delhi and "the East" were interchangeable places, as he explained to Olaf Caroe, India's External Affairs Secretary:

Grandeur is part of the Indian tradition and is to be found elsewhere than at Kabul, particularly at New Delhi. It has also been adopted as a policy in Foreign Office posts in the East, although to a lesser extent than in India. Presumably, it is based on the principle that in the East people judge by appearances to a considerable extent and that some degree of magnificence increases our izzat [prestige]. We certainly aimed intentionally at magnificence when we first installed a Legation at Kabul, and I suppose that this helped Humphrys to get through the troubles of 1928-9 without disaster such as befell some of his predecessors in the last century. [...] [E]ven if the grandeur of the Legation annoys the Afghan Government now, there is much to be said for it as a means of impressing the Afghan populace with our importance.[175]

Because of its documented averse affects, Wylie's despatch had to be received as "an interesting if radical point of view[,] and his arguments are worth attention".[176] Mallam supports Wylie's suggestion that the "magnificence" of the Legation made visible imperial India's leading role in Anglo-Afghan relations.[177] In India, however, the Kabul compound was cast in terms of military might. Particularly in times of crisis, such as in 1928/1929 and again during the Second World War, the Legation's structure equated to the potential for imperial violence:

The way in which the Legation dominates Kabul may be a healthy everyday reminder to the Afghan Government of the way in which *British power in India dominates Afghanistan* and of the fact that, while our policy towards Afghanistan is one of friendship and support, *we have beneath our velvet glove a mailed fist* which they might encounter if they intrigue too much with our enemies. Naturally they resent this reminder, but it is perhaps a useful aid to us in keeping the Afghan Government from undesirable political paths.[178]

The threat of diplomatic insurgency met the reality of violent colonial correction.[179]

Decadence, Dysfunction and Late Empire

The Legation compound reified the asymmetries existing in the practice of imperial governance. It stonewalled the principle of egalitarian diplomatic practice between independent states. Wylie's approach to Anglo-Afghan diplomatic relations also revealed fissures in the architectural messages to the Legation's external audiences. For him, the Legation compound was disadvantageously representative of out-dated imperial practice. The means of diplomacy's architecture defeated diplomacy's ends. For others, the time-honoured application of colonial knowledge was beyond questioning. In the 1940s, an embattled Raj remembered Curzon's wisdom, and the crisis of global war reinforced it. As Frantz Fanon observed in a comparative colonial context, "Arab society has often been presented by Westerners as a formal society in which outside appearances are paramount".[180] As much as empire had been the frame of reference for Curzon, his Orientalist rendering of architecture as a ruling device became the ever-narrowing frame of reference for the maintenance of the Legation compound. Elevated to the status of the Legation's aboriginal conceiver time and again, Curzon became its ultimate authority even after death. The debate about the utility of diplomacy's architecture probed the extent of 'good' and 'bad' imperial practice, but the two positions shared the assumption that the Legation did indeed embody empire and spoke in its registers, of the civilising mission or violence, in the eyes of its beholders. The Legation became empire and only empire; and its subjects understood its language.

On the inside, the Legation ordered Afghan space, fields and gardens along the reassuring discourses of race, hygiene and order. The compound accommodated miniature colonial society and its familiar regimes. But, the transfer of colonial knowledge into the compound's construction was often interrupted or inappropriate. Behind the deliberately 'magnificent' façade of its white walls, the compound's inhabitatants struggled with the cold. Its autarchy was challenged in practical terms by a dependence on regular food and petrol supplies and, during construction, on labour and materials. The Legation's 'menial' labourers were cast as unreliable, whose innate tendencies to challenge the Legation's colonial order required constant policing and regulation. As a place that securitised diplomatic society by drawing the borders of extraterritoriality in the shape of a wall, the *serais* as well as the compound, like the British Agency before 1919, also rendered the Legation in the terms of emprisonment and captivity that echoed in the history of Anglo-Afghan relations. Coming to terms in an inhospitable place, the Legation interpreted several places in Kabul in its own historical frames. It rescued the *serais* of the Durand Agreement from an occupation that appeared unbecoming of the imperial practice of international relations that they represented. It was also inspired by Mughal gardens, whose authority it simultaneously rejected. The display of imperial wealth on the outside was often challenged by the possibility of anarchical dysfunction both within and without. And yet, as much as the dearth of fiscal revenue had circumscribed Afghan independence in 1919, the existence of colonial funds prevented the 'true' end of empire. Soon, the emergence of two more independent states exposed tensions in the Legation's layered colonial and imperial identities, unsettling certainties that had guided the compounds's architectural structuring. They are the subject of the next chapter.

NOTES

1. Humphrys to Curzon, no. 6, 3 June 1922, FO 371/8077, N 6381/59/97, 1922, "Accommodation for British Legation at Kabul", TNA and 68(1)-E, F&P, 1922, "Equipment of the British Legation Kabul", NAI.
2. "Note by Kerr Fraser-Tytler on the Situation in Afghanistan", 20 August 1941, file 10, GB165-0326, MECA.
3. Transcript of interview of Horace Phillips, 22 January 1997, 8, https://www.chu.cam.ac.uk/media/uploads/files/Phillips.pdf [accessed: 26 May 2018].
4. Wylie to Eden, no. 10, 2 March 1943, para. 8, IOR/L/PS/12/1733, "Coll 3/143 Medical arrangements in Afghanistan. Visit of Dr Rifki Bey to UK", BL.
5. Squire to Gardener, D.O.No.BLK/9/47(2), 1 November 1947, IOR/L/PS/12/1917, "Coll 4/54(2) British Legation buildings, Kabul: Question of transfer of ownership from Government of India to HMG", BL.
6. Sherard Cowper-Coles, *Cables from Kabul: The Inside Story of the West's Afghanistan Campaign* (London: HarperPress, 2012), 15.
7. Mark Bertram, *Room for Diplomacy: Britain's Diplomatic Buildings Overseas 1800–2000* (Reading: Spire, 2011), 181.
8. Ibid. Transcript of interview of Hugh Michael Carless, 23 February 2002, 5, https://www.chu.cam.ac.uk/media/uploads/files/Carless.pdf [accessed: 26 May 2018].
9. Diana Day and George L. Mallam, *Frogs in the Well* (Moray: Librario, 2010), 134.
10. Nicholas Barrington, *Envoy: A Diplomatic Journey* (London: I.B. Tauris, 2014), 20.
11. William Dalrymple, *The Return of a King: The Battle for Afghanistan, 1839–1842* (London: Bloomsbury), 496.
12. See also "Recollections of a political officer in India (1929–1947)", A. W. Redpath, 85, Mss Eur F226/24, "Redpath, Maj Alexander William (b 1909)", BL.

13. See also Laura Mcenaney, "Personal, Political, and International: A Reflection on Diplomacy and Methodology", *Diplomatic History* 36, no. 4 (2012): 772.
14. Jon Boone, "A Return to Magnificence for British Diplomats", 17 May 2009, https://www.guardian.co.uk/politics/2009/may/17/british-embassy-afghanistan [accessed: 6 February 2013].
15. Dane Keith Kennedy, *The Magic Mountains: Hill Stations and the British Raj* (Berkeley: University of California Press, 1996), 107.
16. "Note by Kerr Fraser-Tytler on the Situation in Afghanistan", 20 August 1941, file 10, GB165-0326, MECA.
17. Ashley Jackson, *Buildings of Empire* (Oxford: Oxford University Press, 2013).
18. Thomas R. Metcalf, *An Imperial Vision: Indian Architecture and Britain's Raj* (University of California Press, 1989), 2; See also Indra Sengupta, "Culture-Keeping as State Action: Bureaucrats, Administrators, and Monuments in Colonial India", *Past & Present* 226, Supplement 10 (2015): 153–177.
19. Jan Morris et al., eds., *Architecture of the British Empire* (London: Weidenfeld and Nicolson, 1986), 11. See also Jan Morris and Simon Winchester, eds., *Stones of Empire: The Buildings of the Raj* (Oxford: Oxford University Press, 1986).
20. E.g. Mark Bence-Jones, *Palaces of the Raj: Magnificence and Misery of the Lord Sahibs* (London: Allen and Unwin, 1973); Philip Davies, *Splendours of the Raj: British Architecture in India, 1660–1947* (London: John Murray, 1985).
21. Thomas R. Metcalf, "Architecture and the Representation of Empire: India, 1860–1910", *Representations*, no. 6 (1984): 50, 61.
22. Quoted in Jakob Hort, *Architektur der Diplomatie: Repräsentation in europäischen Botschaftsbauten, 1800–1920: Konstantinopel, Rom, Wien, St. Petersburg* (Göttingen: Vandenhoeck & Ruprecht, 2014), 591.
23. On the Legation in Tehran, see, for instance, John Gurney, "Legations and Gardens, Sahibs and Their Subalterns", *Iran* 40 (2002): 203–232.
24. Mark Crinson, *Empire Building: Orientalism and Victorian Architecture* (London: Routledge, 1996), 3–4.
25. Hort, *Architektur der Diplomatie*.
26. Stephanie L. Barczewski, *Country Houses and the British Empire, 1700–1930* (Manchester: Manchester University Press, 2014); Robert K. Home, *Of Planting and Planning: The Making of British Colonial Cities*, 2nd ed. (New York: Routledge, 2013); Monica Juneja, "Architectural Memory Between Representation and Practice: Rethinking Pierre Nora's Les Lieux de Mémoire", in *Memory, History, and Colonialism. Engaging with Pierre Nora in Colonial and Postcolonial Contexts*, ed. Indra Sengupta,

GHIL Bulletin Supplement 1 (London: German Historical Institute London, 2009), 11–36; Kennedy, *The Magic Mountains*; Anthony D. King, *The Bungalow: The Production of a Global Culture* (London: Routledge & Kegan Paul, 1984); Metcalf, *An Imperial Vision*.

27. Bertram, *Room for Diplomacy*, 180–183.
28. Note by Denys Bray, 19 December 1921, "Rough note on the proposal for a British Minister at Kabul", S. E. Pears, 24 November 1921, 9, 68(20)-Est, F&P, 1923, "Note by Mr S. E. Pears, C.S.I., C.I.E., on the proposed establishment of a British Legation at Kabul", NAI.
29. Viceroy, Foreign & Political Dept., to Secretary of State for India, copy of telegram, 5 January 1921, no. 40, IOR/L/PS/10/957/2, "File 15/1921 Pt 4 Afghanistan: Kabul Mission 1921; question of consular establishments; British minister at Kabul; Afghan objection to Mr S E Pears; appointment of Major Humphrys", BL. See also 68(2)-E, F&P, 1922, "Establishment of British Consulate in Consulate in Afghanistan. India Office Prints", NAI.
30. Humphrys to Wakely, 24 December 1921, no. 46, IOR/L/PS/10/957/2, op. cit., BL.
31. William Kerr Fraser-Tytler, *Afghanistan: A Study of Political Developments in Central and Southern Asia*, 2nd ed. (London: Oxford University Press, 1953), 199. "Kabul Legation Diary", 36, file 8, GB165-0326, MECA.
32. See Thomas R. Metcalf, *Ideologies of the Raj* (Cambridge: Cambridge University Press, 1994), 171–185.
33. See Chapter 6.
34. Humphrys to Curzon, no. 6, 3 June 1922, N 6381/59/97, FO 371/8077, 1922, op. cit., TNA and 68(1)-E, F&P, 1922, op. cit., NAI.
35. Ibid.
36. Bill Woodburn and Ian Templeton, "From the Bala Hissar to the Arg: How Royal Fortress Palaces Shaped Kabul, 1830–1930", *The Court Historian* 17, no. 2 (2012): 184.
37. Humphrys to Curzon, no. 6, 3 June 1922, N 6381/59/97, FO 371/8077, 1922, op. cit., TNA and 68(1)-E, F&P, 1922, op. cit., NAI.
38. Ibid.
39. The Under Secretary to the Government of India in the Foreign and Political Department to His Majesty's Under Secretary of State for India, India Office, London, no. 2806/73-Est, 16 September 1922, no. 34, IOR/L/PS/10/957/2, op. cit., BL.
40. Note by A. F. L. Brayne, 8 February 1922, 68(9)-E, F&P, 1922, "Menial Establishment for the British Legation in Afghanistan and their emoluments", NAI, emphasis added.
41. Basil John Gould, *The Jewel in the Lotus: Recollections of an Indian Political* (London: Chatto & Windus, 1957), 94.

42. "Account of medical matters in Afghanistan", 8 July 1942, no. 167–168, IOR/L/PS/12/1733, op. cit., BL.
43. Arnold Fletcher, *Afghanistan: Highway of Conquest* (Ithaca: Cornell University Press, 1965), 186.
44. Amin Saikal, *Modern Afghanistan: A History of Struggle and Survival* (London: I.B. Tauris, 2012), 47.
45. "Destruction of the Second British Legation in Kabul", 31 December 1926, file 9, GB165-0326, MECA.
46. Ibid.
47. Ibid.
48. Fraser-Tytler to his mother, 12 April 1923, no. 2–4, file 1/1/1, GB165-0326, MECA.
49. Humphrys to Curzon, no. 6, 3 June 1922, N 6381/59/97, FO 371/8077, 1922, op. cit., TNA and 68(1)-E, F&P, 1922, op. cit., NAI.
50. "Kabul Legation Diary", 48, file 8, GB165-0326, MECA.
51. Humphrys to Curzon, no. 6, 3 June 1922, N 6381/59/97, FO 371/8077, 1922, op. cit., TNA and 68(1)-E, F&P, 1922, op. cit., NAI.
52. "The Legation Fire in Kabul: Help from Neighbours", *The Times*, 31 December 1926, 9.
53. "Destruction of the Second British Legation in Kabul", 31 December 1926, file 9, GB165-0326, MECA.
54. Ibid.
55. Humphrys to Chamberlain, no. 10, 31 January 1927, para. 4, X 1719/246/503, FO 366/841, 1927, "Report on destruction by fire of the British Legation at Kabul", TNA.
56. Ibid. See Ranajit Guha, "Dominance Without Hegemony and Its Historiography", in *Subaltern Studies VI: Writings on South Asian History and Society*, ed. Ranajit Guha (Delhi: Oxford University Press, 1992), 237.
57. "Destruction of the Second British Legation in Kabul", 31 December 1926, file 9, GB165-0326, MECA.
58. Humphrys to Chamberlain, no. 10, 31 January 1927, para. 4, X 1719/246/503, FO 366/841, 1927, op. cit., TNA.
59. "Schedule of alterations proposed in the plans of the new British Legation buildings at Kabul by the Consulting Architect", Humphrys, enclosure no. 4, "Letter from His Majesty's Minister, Kabul, No. 1179, dated the 17th December 1924", no. 84, 212-F, F&P, 1922, "Construction of British Legation Buildings at Kabul", NAI.
60. Ibid.
61. 114-F, F&P, 1924, "Proposed measure for the protection of the British Legation, Kabul, in times of crisis. Question of the installation of a wireless set in the said Legation", NAI. See also Gould, *The Jewel in the Lotus*, 104.
62. "Report on the proposed buildings for His Britannic Majesty's Legation in Kabul, Afghanistan", B. M. Sullivan, 27 September 1922, no. 29, 212-F, F&P, 1922, op. cit., NAI.

63. Gould, *The Jewel in the Lotus*, 47.
64. Schedule II, section (e), C. U. Aitchison, ed., *The Treaties, &c., Relating to Persia and Afghanistan*, vol. 13, A Collection of Treaties, Engagements and Sanads Relating to India and Neighbouring Countries (Calcutta: Government of India Central Publication Branch, 1933), 204.
65. Collectively, the plots amounted to 43 *jarib*, 101 *biswa*, 31 *biswasa* and 13 *zirah*. For copies of the deeds see the following files: IOR NEG 1868, 1930, "File 692 Legation Property in Kabul (including Copies of Deeds)" and IOR/L/PS/12/1917, op. cit., BL; Squire to Bevin, no. 72, 18 June 1949, DO 133/11, 1948, "Embassy Buildings at Kabul and Kathmandu" and File XA01/85 (54/49), FO 366/2793, 1949, "Translation of Sale Deeds covering land which Kabul Embassy is built", TNA; Bertram, *Room for Diplomacy* counts 26 acres; Charles Drace-Francis, "Imperial Impressions", *Historic Gardens Review*, Autumn/Winter 2001, 8–12 counts 27; The following three count 25: Gould, *The Jewel in the Lotus*, 96; Katherine Himsworth, *A History of the British Embassy in Kabul, Afghanistan* (Kabul: British Embassy, 1976); "Recollections of a political officer in India (1929–1947)", A. W. Redpath, 85, Mss Eur F226/24, op. cit., BL.
66. Himsworth, *A History of the British Embassy in Kabul, Afghanistan*, 2.
67. "Note on Building a British Legation in Kabul", Humphrys, 1 August 1922, Appendix C, no. 29, 212-F, F&P, 1922, op. cit., NAI.
68. "Minister's review of the progress of the construction of the new British Legation buildings at Kabul up to mid December 1924", enclosure no. 1, "Letter from His Majesty's Minister, Kabul, No. 1179, dated the 17th September 1924", no. 84, 212-F, F&P, 1922, op. cit., NAI.
69. "Kabul Legation Diary", 40, file 8, GB165-0326, MECA.
70. "Minister's review of the progress of the construction of the new British Legation buildings at Kabul up to mid December 1924", enclosure no. 1, "Letter from His Majesty's Minister, Kabul, No. 1179, dated the 17th September 1924", no. 84, 212-F, F&P, 1922, op. cit., NAI.
71. See note 65 above.
72. Gould, *The Jewel in the Lotus*, 102. See also Boone, "A Return to Magnificence for British Diplomats".
73. Bertram, who follows Himsworth, allocates the distance at 2.5 miles, Drace-Francis at 4 miles.
74. See Home, *Of Planting and Planning*, 129–135.
75. Anthony D. King, *Colonial Urban Development: Culture, Social Power, and Environment* (London: Routledge & Paul, 1976), 125; King, *The Bungalow*, 44.
76. Peter Mayne, *The Narrow Smile: A Journey Back to the North-West Frontier* (London: John Murray, 1955), 122.

77. "Memorandum no. 1140-212-F, dated Simla, the 20th October 1922", no. 30, 212-F, F&P, 1922, op. cit., NAI.
78. Note by W. M. Hailey, 13 October 1922, 212-F, F&P, 1922, op. cit., NAI.
79. David A. Johnson and Richard Watson, *New Delhi: The Last Imperial City* (London: Palgrave Macmillan, 2015).
80. Note by E. B. Howell, 24 November 1926, para. 1., serial no. 21–22, p. 8, IOR NEG 1866, "File 535-R Construction of British Legation Buildings at Kabul. Extension of Agreement of Messrs. L.W. Amps and A. Foster Josephs, Executive Engineer and Assistant Engineer, Kabul Division, Respectively [GOI Foreign and Political Department Printed File 46F/26, Serial Nos 1-60]", BL.
81. "Afghanistan: Annual Report, 1932", para. 271, N 1626/1626/97, FO 371/17198, 1933, "Annual Report on Afghanistan", TNA.
82. Barrington, *Envoy*, 20.
83. Wylie to Eden, no. 10, 2 March 1943, para. 8, IOR/L/PS/12/1733, op. cit., BL.
84. IOR/L/F/8/17/1322, "B. M. Sullivan Esq. Agreement for Service in India as Consulting Architect to the Government of the Punjab", BL.
85. Humphrys to the Foreign Secretary to the Government of India in the Foreign and Political Department, 25 March 1922, 212-F, F&P, 1922, op. cit., NAI.
86. "Forthcoming Marriages", *The Times*, 9 October 1941, 7.
87. Jon Wilson, *India Conquered: Britain's Raj and the Chaos of Empire* (London: Simon & Schuster, 2016), 386–388.
88. IOR/L/F/8/19/1495, "Articles of Agreement as a Civil Engineer in the Military Works Services in India", BL; 46-F, F&P, 1926, "Construction of British Legation Buildings at Kabul. Extension of agreement of Messrs. L W. Amps and A Foster-Josephs, Executive Engineer and Assistant Engineer, Kabul Division, respectively", NAI and IOR NEG 1866, op. cit., BL.
89. 165(2)-A, F&P, 1927, "Budget estimates of the British Legation Kabul for the Year 1928–29"; 313-A, F&P, 1929, "Budget Estimates of the Kabul Legation for the Year 1930–31", NAI.
90. "Report on building construction in Kabul in connection with the proposed British Legation, with notes on materials, conditions and rates", L. W. Amps, 2 August 1922, no. 26, 212-F, F&P, 1922, op. cit., NAI. All following quotes are taking from Amps' report unless specified otherwise.
91. "Report on the proposed buildings for His Britannic Majesty's Legation in Kabul, Afghanistan", B. M. Sullivan, 27 September 1922, no. 29, 212-F, F&P, 1922, op. cit., NAI.
92. Humphrys, no. 373/4, 9 January 1926, 256(2)-A, F&P, 1925, "Budget estimates of the British Legation Kabul for the year 1926–1927", NAI.

93. "Report on building construction in Kabul in connection with the proposed British Legation, with notes on materials, conditions and rates", L. W. Amps, 2 August 1922, no. 26, 212-F, F&P, 1922, op. cit., NAI. All following quotes are taking from Amps' report unless specified otherwise.
94. E.g. Metcalf, *Ideologies of the Raj*, 114–148.
95. "Report on building construction in Kabul in connection with the proposed British Legation, with notes on materials, conditions and rates", L. W. Amps, 2 August 1922, no. 26, 212-F, F&P, 1922, op. cit., NAI. All following quotes are taking from Amps' report unless specified otherwise.
96. "Report on construction, 1 September 1924 to 31 December 1925", Humphrys, no. 6/103, 27 May 1926, para. 4, 19, serial no. 6, IOR NEG 1866, op. cit., BL.
97. Drace-Francis, "Imperial Impressions", 9.
98. Fraser-Tytler to his mother, 19 June 1931, no. 26, file 1/1/4, GB165-0325, MECA.
99. Chamberlain to Gould, no. 27, 30 May 1927, no. 3, FO 402/7, 1927, "Further correspondence respecting Afghanistan: Part VII", TNA.
100. E.g. caption, figure 8.10, Bertram, *Room for Diplomacy*, 181.
101. Barrington, *Envoy*, 20.
102. Bertram, *Room for Diplomacy*, 181.
103. Note by E. B. Howell, 21 March 1927, on Humphrys, demi-official no. 6/117, no. 27, 46-F, op. cit., F&P, 1926, NAI and IOR NEG 1866, op. cit., BL.
104. Humphrys to Howell, demi-official no. 6/117, 21 February 1927, no. 27, 46-F, F&P, 1926, op. cit., NAI and IOR NEG 1866, op. cit., BL.
105. Note by W. M. Hailey, 13 October 1922, 212-F, F&P, 1922, op. cit., NAI.
106. Note by H. Dobbs, 3 February 1922, 68(1)-E, F&P, 1922, "Equipment of the British Legation Kabul", NAI.
107. Ibid.
108. Ibid.
109. "Note on Building a British Legation in Kabul", Humphrys, 1 August 1922, Appendix C, no. 29, 212-F, F&P, 1922, op. cit., NAI. See also Fraser-Tytler to his mother, 2 June 1932, no. 42–43, file 1/1/5, GB165-0326, MECA.
110. "Note on Building a British Legation in Kabul", Humphrys, 1 August 1922, Appendix C, no. 29, 212-F, F&P, 1922, op. cit., NAI.
111. Note by Loch, 1093(3)-A, F&P, 1923, "Kabul Legation Budget estimates for 1922–23 and 1923–24", NAI.
112. King, *Colonial Urban Development*, 123–125. See also Elizabeth M. Collingham, *Imperial Bodies: The Physical Experience of the Raj, c. 1800–1947* (Cambridge: Polity Press, 2001), 99–102.

113. "Building plans", https://www.fco.gov.uk/en/about-us/our-history/historic-views-kabul/building-plans [accessed: 31 July 2012]; "Afghanistan: Kabul", https://roomfordiplomacy.com/afghanistan-kabul [accessed: 18 April 2019].
114. "Construction of New British Legation, Kabul: Revised Project Estimate", L. W. Amps, 22 November 1924, enclosure no. 3, "Letter from His Majesty's Minister, Kabul, No. 1179, dated the 17th December 1924", no. 84, 212-F, F&P, 1922, op. cit., NAI.
115. Letter from Humphrys, no. 241, Kabul, 7 July 1923, no. 59, 212-F, F&P, 1922, op. cit., NAI; "Medical Affairs in Afghanistan", no. 76–98, 1944, IOR/L/PS/12/1733, op. cit., BL.
116. "Statement showing cost of buildings etc. in British Legation, Kabul", Squire to Weightman, D.O.No.1030/46, 15 February 1947, XA01/97D, FO 366/2505, 1947, "Accommodation & Buildings: British Legation, Kabul", TNA.
117. Enclosure 3, Humphrys, no. 6/104, 28 May 1926, para. 27, serial no. 7, IOR NEG 1866, op. cit., BL.
118. "Report on, and estimate of, restoring buildings and services of the British Legation, Kabul, damaged during the attack made on Kabul by Bacha Saqao, 14th to 25th December 1928", R. Wilson, 15 January 1929, FO 366/866, N 1189/1189/603, 1929, "Damage Suffered by Legation Buildings during Recent Fighting near Kabul", TNA and 61-A, F&P, 1929, "Report on, and estimate of cost of, restoring buildings and services of the British Legation, Kabul, damage during the attack made on Kabul by Bacha Saqao in December 1929", NAI.
119. Dane Keith Kennedy, "The Perils of the Midday Sun: Climatic Anxieties in the Colonial Tropics", in *Imperialism and the Natural World*, ed. John MacDonald MacKenzie (Manchester: Manchester University Press, 1990), 118–140.
120. King, *The Bungalow*, 84. See also Metcalf, *Ideologies of the Raj*, 177–181.
121. Note by E. B. Howell, 21 March 1927, on Humphrys' demi-official no. 6/117, no. 27, 46-F, op. cit., 1926, F&P, NAI and IOR NEG 1866, op. cit., BL; Bertram, *Room for Diplomacy*, 181–182; Himsworth, *A History of the British Embassy in Kabul, Afghanistan*, 6.
122. "Report on building construction in Kabul in connection with the proposed British Legation, with notes on materials, conditions and rates", L. W. Amps, 2 August 1922, no. 26, 212-F, F&P, 1922, op. cit., NAI.
123. Humphrys, no. 6/103, 27 May 1926, serial no. 6, IOR NEG 1866, op. cit., BL.
124. "Precis of reports nos. 3-A and 4 on the work of the Kabul division, Public Works Department. From September 1st 1924 to November 30th 1925, by L. W. Amps, Executive Engineer, Kabul Division", no. 6, 46-F, F&P, 1926, op. cit., NAI and IOR NEG 1866, op. cit., BL.

125. Humphrys, no. 6/103, 27 May 1926, serial no. 6, IOR NEG 1866, op. cit., BL.
126. James Stourton, *British Embassies: Their Diplomatic and Architectural History* (2017), 335.
127. Caption, figure 8.9, Bertram, *Room for Diplomacy*, 181. See also images of "House 5, 1991", "House 3, 1991" and "House 2, 1991", https://roomfordiplomacy.com/afghanistan-kabul [accessed: 18 April 2019].
128. Drace-Francis, "Imperial Impressions", 8.
129. Mayne, *The Narrow Smile*, 119; Day and Mallam, *Frogs in the Well*, 134.
130. For visual sources of the Legation's houses, other than the Minister's residence, see Day and Mallam, *Frogs in the Well*, 146–147; "Military Attaché's House", file 2/5 and "Counsellor's House", file 2/7, GB165-0326, MECA.
131. "Schedule of alterations proposed in the plans of the new British Legation buildings at Kabul by the Consulting Architect", Humphrys, enclosure no. 4, "Letter from His Majesty's Minister, Kabul, No. 1179, dated the 17th December 1924", no. 84, 212-F, F&P, 1922, op. cit., NAI.
132. Kennedy, *The Magic Mountains*, 3–4; Metcalf, *Ideologies of the Raj*, 181–185.
133. "Medical Affairs in Afghanistan", no. 76–98, 1944, IOR/L/PS/12/1733, op. cit., BL. Barrington, *Envoy*, 12–25.
134. Mayne, *The Narrow Smile*, 123.
135. Fraser-Tytler to his mother, 21 February 1936, no. 31–33, file 1/1/7, GB165-0326, MECA; Mayne, *The Narrow Smile*, 122.
136. Himsworth, *A History of the British Embassy in Kabul, Afghanistan*, 15.
137. "Construction of New British Legation, Kabul: Revised Project Estimate", L. W. Amps, 22 November 1924, enclosure no. 3, "Letter from His Majesty's Minister, Kabul, No. 1179, dated the 17th December 1924", no. 84, 212-F, F&P, 1922, op. cit., NAI.
138. Fraser-Tytler to his mother, 2 February 1928, no. 25–26, file 1/1/2, GB165-0326, MECA.
139. "Standing Order No. 3: Electric Lighting", 47, IOR/R/12/200, "British Legation, Kabul: Office Manual", BL.
140. See Chapter 6.
141. IOR NEG 1867, "File 429 Arrangement with Capur and Co of Lahore for the Construction of a tube well for the British Legation, Kabul (from 1920); Settlement of their account", BL.
142. Humphrys to Howell, demi-official no. 6/117, 21 February 1927, no. 27, 46-F, F&P, 1926, op. cit., NAI and IOR NEG 1866, op. cit., BL. See also IOR NEG 1869, "File 695A Irrigation of Legation Property and Water Rights (1933–47 Omnibus File)", BL.
143. Drace-Francis, "Imperial Impressions".

144. Note by E. B. Howell, 21 March 1927, on Humphrys, demi-official no. 6/117, no. 27, 46-F, op. cit., F&P, 1926, NAI and IOR NEG 1866, op. cit., BL.
145. Mayne, *The Narrow Smile*, 123.
146. Fraser-Tytler to his mother, 19 June 1931, no. 26, file 1/1/4, GB165-0326, MECA.
147. Squire to A. J. Gardener, D.O.No.BLK/9/47(2), 1 November 1947, IOR/L/PS/12/1917, op. cit., BL.
148. "Standing Order No. 4: Restriction on goods to be taken to and from India by Legation lorry", 48, IOR/R/12/200, op. cit., BL.
149. Drace-Francis, "Imperial Impressions", 9–10.
150. "Note by L. W. Amps, Executive Engineer, Kabul Division, no. 135-2/93", 27 October 1926, no. 21, 46-F, F&P, op. cit., 1926, NAI and IOR NEG 1866, op. cit., BL.
151. Drace-Francis, "Imperial Impressions", 10. See also Mayne, *The Narrow Smile*, 122.
152. Fraser-Tytler to his mother, 17 April 1931, no. 20–21, file 1/1/4, GB165-0326, MECA; "Additional Rose Plants for the British Legation, Kabul", 206-F, 1934, F&P, NAI; Gould, *The Jewel in the Lotus*, 96, 99.
153. "Medical Affairs in Afghanistan", 1943, no. 114–140, IOR/L/PS/12/1733, op. cit., BL.
154. Fraser-Tytler to his mother, 19 June 1931, no. 26, file 1/1/4, GB165-0326, MECA.
155. Fraser-Tytler to his mother, 27 July 1939, no. 91–94, file 1/1/10, GB165-0326, MECA.
156. Ibid.
157. Drace-Francis, "Imperial Impressions", 10.
158. Barrington, *Envoy*, 29; "Recollections of a political officer in India (1929–1947)", A. W. Redpath, 87, Mss Eur F226/24, op. cit., BL.
159. "Rough note on the proposal for a British Minister at Kabul", S. E. Pears, 24 November 1921, 4, 68(20)-Est, F&P, 1923, op. cit., NAI.
160. "Note by L. W. Amps, Executive Engineer, Kabul Division, no. 135-2/93", 27 October 1926, no. 21, 46-F, F&P, 1926, op. cit., NAI and IOR NEG 1866, op. cit., BL.
161. Fraser-Tytler to his mother, 2 June 1932, no. 42–43, file 1/1/5, GB165-0326, MECA.
162. Fraser-Tytler to his mother, 11 June 1937, no. 80–82, file 1/1/8, GB165-0326, MECA.
163. Fraser-Tytler to his mother, 3 June 1937, no. 77–79, file 1/1/8, GB165-0326, MECA.
164. See also Kennedy, *The Magic Mountains*, 47–52.
165. "Note by Kerr Fraser-Tytler on the Situation in Afghanistan", 20 August 1941, file 10, GB165-0326, MECA.

166. Wylie to Eden, no. 10, 2 March 1943, para. 6, IOR/L/PS/12/1733, op. cit., BL. See also Terence Creagh Coen, *The Indian Political Service: A Study in Indirect Rule* (London: Chatto & Windus, 1971), 237.
167. Day and Mallam, *Frogs in the Well*, 146–147.
168. Wylie to Peterson, demi-official no. C-22/41, 12 June 1943, 536-F, EA, 1943, "H.M.'s Minister, Kabul's interviews with the Prime Minister of Afghanistan", NAI.
169. Foreign Office notes on telegram no. 176, IOR/L/PS/12/1934, "Affairs of the Legation Dispensary", BL.
170. FO minutes on telegram no. 176 by I. T. M. Pink, para. 4, ibid.
171. Comments by H. A. C. Caccia on telegram no. 176, IOR/L/PS/12/1934, op. cit., BL.
172. Fraser-Tytler, *Afghanistan*, 193.
173. Note by E. B. Howell, Finance Department, 24 November 1926, no. 22, 46-F, F&P, 1926, op. cit., NAI and IOR NEG 1866, op. cit., BL.
174. Handwritten note by Monteath to Wakely and Peel, signed 3 July 1943, no. 103, IOR/L/PS/12/1733, op. cit., BL.
175. Peel to Caroe, draft letter, 14 July 1943, para. 2, ibid.
176. Minute Paper, signed 24, 25 and 28 June 1943, no. 102, ibid.
177. Day and Mallam, *Frogs in the Well*, 142.
178. Peel to Caroe, draft letter, 14 July 1943, para. 3, IOR/L/PS/12/1733, op. cit., BL, emphasis added.
179. For "insurgent internationalism" or "diplomatic insurgents" see Martin J. Bayly's forthcoming work. See also "epistemic insurgency" in Martin J. Bayly, *Taming the Imperial Imagination: Colonial Knowledge, International Relations, and the Anglo-Afghan Encounter, 1808–1878* (Cambridge: Cambridge University Press, 2016).
180. Frantz Fanon, *A Dying Colonialism* (London: Writers and Readers Publishing Cooperative, 1980), 15.

CHAPTER 8

From Colonial Legation to Postimperial Embassy

1947 AND AFTER

The British Legation had late-imperial decadence ingrained into its fabric. The end of colonial rule brought this inheritance into full view as the gap between historical change in South Asia's political landscape and the Legation's ideational foundations in the 'high imperialism' at the turn of the century widened. In 1919, Afghan independence had shaped the Legation into forming a continuity of empire by means of colonial funds. The independence of India and Pakistan in August 1947 marked the end of the colonial services that had provided the fiscal revenue for the British Legation since its inception in 1922. 1947 initiated another readjustment of empire. With the Raj, the Indian Political Service and the India Office in the process of dissolution by August 1947, the Legation was incorporated into and reorganised within the diplomatic empire of the Foreign Office.

Before 1947, the metropolitan ministries had vaguely compartmentalised Afghanistan in bureaucratic terms. In 1939, William Kerr Fraser-Tytler wrote to his mother: "I wish they'd send [Nevile Montagu Butler] here to act for me, but that is an awful heresy. The idea of letting the diplomatic service get a footing in Kabul causes the India Office to stay awake at nights. But it is bound to come before very long, as I have told Aubrey [Metcalfe, India's Foreign Secretary]".[1] As late as 1946, Giles Frederick Squire wrote that "[t]he interests of His Majesty's Government in Afghanistan are almost entirely concerned with the safety of India as a vital

© The Author(s) 2019
M. Drephal, *Afghanistan and the Coloniality of Diplomacy*,
Cambridge Imperial and Post-Colonial Studies Series,
https://doi.org/10.1007/978-3-030-23960-2_8

317

part of the Empire".[2] Squire seriously considered staffing Kabul with Foreign Office personnel only from 20 February 1947, the same day that saw the announcement of India's independence by June 1948.[3] According to the Secretary Alexander Redpath, the Foreign Office had had only "residual interests in Afghanistan" up until that moment.[4] Now, the Legation had to "[c]hange-over to British Foreign Office procedures".[5] Britain's and India's diplomatic services, that seemed so fundamentally different to its respective members, merged. The potential change in the Legation's recruiting pools was the watershed by which 1947 came to be measured. The nearing end of the Legation's colonial salaries turned independence into a question of continuous employment and career geographies. For many at the Legation, and especially its political leadership, August 1947 primarily threatened a potential rupture in their colonial careers. Whilst the Legation's financial sources changed, the retrenchment of its imperial microcosm was unaffected. Independence and the dismantling of colonial rule did not mean an intellectual or psychological engagement with colonialism itself. Once more, this enabled the harnessing of empire's remnants through another moment of statal independence.

There was a short-lived attempt to engage with the colonial past as past. The Secretary of State for Foreign Affairs ordered the writing up of a memorandum on Anglo-Afghan relations because "in the past the India Office have been inclined to treat the Afghans cavalierly".[6] Written during the unfolding end of the Raj, the historical frame of "A Survey of Anglo-Afghan relations" captured 1947 as the bicentenary of parallel story of imperial rise and decline.[7] In 1747, the "Kingdom of Afghanistan first emerged as an independent, sovereign state", the memorandum stated, but Ahmad Shah Durrani's "success" in establishing Afghan imperial control from northern India to eastern Persia was brief: "In the course of the sixty years following his death [in 1773] the country was rent by internal strife and the empire gradually disintegrated".[8] Fraser-Tytler, by then in retirement, assisted in its production, offering comments and corrections on a draft.[9] He materially contributed to interpretations of the history of Anglo-Afghan relations, which he had shaped himself over almost two decades of service. Unsurprisingly given the circumstances of its production, the attempt of the Foreign Office to come to terms with the colonial past of the British Legation in Kabul was short-lived. It inherited the colonial tradition of Anglo-Afghan international relations as well as the epistemological frameworks in which it was captured. The East India Company's relations with the Afghan Empire became a part of the Foreign Office's intellectual inheritance. The Raj continued to bound thinking about Afghanistan, delimiting at the same time the range for diplomatic engagement. A draft acknowledged that "[t]he Afghans [...] resent the fact that, however much we may try to hide it, the India Office appears to control their relations more than the Foreign Office".[10] This statement admitted the practice of asymmetry which had guided the British Legation in Kabul since its inception. Others found "little, if anything, to quarrel with in the manner in which our policy towards Afghanistan has been conducted by the India Office and the Government of India during the last 100 years".[11] The gradual withdrawal of European colonial officers from the administration of the colonial state between August 1947 and June 1948 brought to light the ambiguities in the diplomatic conduct of Anglo-Afghan relations between 1922 and 1947. They were, however, misrepresented as an anomaly, which history had now corrected: "It is, in a way, a 'hangover' from the earlier period when Afghanistan had no foreign relations and, from the point of view of external affairs at any rate, was virtually an additional Indian State", wrote P. Garran.[12] Coming to terms with the colonial inspiration of the British Legation in Kabul was a drawn-out and uneven process. The Foreign Office came face to face with the messy past of colonial international relations, but struggled to think outside of the historical lessons that the Raj provided.

The chapter picks up the threads of the preceding chapters. Mirroring Chapter 2's discussion of the effects of Afghan independence in 1919 on the Legation's history, it probes the effects of 1947 along the themes of biography, performance, medical humanitarianism and architecture.

BIOGRAPHY AND IMPERIAL TRANSMISSION AFTER EMPIRE

Throughout its life history, the Legation's collective biography shows a community of imperial transmitters who exported colonial technologies of rule from India to the Legation in Kabul, back to India or elsewhere. The Legation was a node in the Indian imperial system where technologies of rule were refined, tested and exchanged among similar colonial and diplomatic enclaves. Long before 1947, its practices were further exported across the Indian Empire, for instance to Iraq, the Arabian Peninsula, business as well as humanitarian organisations. After concluding the Treaty of Kabul in 1921, Henry Dobbs became head of mission in Iraq. Like Afghanistan, the bounded outlines of Iraq were shaped by its interaction with imperial powers. It was described as a "'mere geographical expression' and not a state".[13] Dobbs carried over his experience of shaping the Anglo-Afghan Treaty of 1921 to the making of the Anglo-Iraq Treaty in 1922.[14] The techniques that crafted the confines of Afghanistan's independence in Kabul were themselves further exported into the legal foundations of Iraq's new international status as a League of Nations mandate. In both cases, 'independence' was heavily circumscribed. In 1929, Humphrys followed in Dobbs' footsteps and became High Commissioner. He was instrumental in forging a new Anglo-Iraq Treaty of 1930 that provided the basis for Iraq's admission to the League of Nations as an "emancipated", "independent" member in 1932. At the same time, the treaty secured Britain's "privileged position in Iraq for another quarter-century".[15] Internationally administered empire under the League of Nations transformed into a new imperial relationship. As Susan Pedersen has argued, the true meaning of Iraq's independence emerged as a bargain, in which "internal domination was traded for external concessions[16]:

> What one might call decolonization's Faustian bargain is perceptible in Iraq – a bargain whereby (often unrepresentative) national elites are ceded significant internal authority (including the right to enrich their followers and repress their perceived enemies) through collaboration with, and at the price of ceding a measure of economic and military control to, the former colonial power.[17]

Humphrys was Ambassador until 1935. In an age increasingly dictated by fossil fuels, he became chairman of Anglo-Iraq Petroleum, one embodiment of Iraq's concessions, from 1941 to 1950. The career progression from Kabul to Baghdad was by no means limited to India's imperial services. Fritz Grobba, who had already been Humphrys' German counterpart in Kabul, became Ambassador to Iraq in 1932.[18]

Basil John Gould became an "authority on Tibet". Together with Harry Staunton of the Indian Medical Service, Gould attended the enthronement of the 14th Dalai Lama in Lhasa in 1940. Moreover, several colonial Residencies in the Indian Ocean were headed by former Legation Politicals. William Rupert Hay was Political Resident in the Persian Gulf from 1946 to 1953.[19] Before and after Kabul, Reginald George Evelin William Alban held posts in Bahrain and Aden.[20] Arnold Crawshaw Galloway's record was even more extensive, including government service in Ahwaz, Muscat, Bahrain, Bushire, Kuwait as well as administrative posts with the Bahrain Petroleum Company and the Middle East Navigation Aids Service.[21] In

1947, Alban was Consul at Bandar Abbas while Hay, Galloway and Guy Irvine Pettigrew were Consul-General, Acting Consul-General and Consul in Bushire.[22] William Joseph Moody, the Surgeon, joined the Foreign Office in 1948 and, from 1950, also worked for the Bahrain Petroleum Company.[23] The Legation also supplied humanitarianian organisations on a global scale. From 1941 to 1943, Fraser-Tytler worked for the Red Cross close to home in Scotland. From 1943 to 1946, he headed a mission to Washington and was tasked with the repatriation of prisoners of war from Japanese captivity in the Pacific. The Red Cross also attracted Aileen Knox-Johnston, who later became Fraser-Tytler's second wife, Pamela Eugène Humphrys, Arthur Edward Broadbent Parsons and Terence Creagh Coen.

Far from presenting a fundamental rupture, the end of colonial rule in 1947 saw colonial officers transform into international diplomats once again, who now bridged the end of the Raj and its afterlives. The Legation connected India's old colonial diplomatic service with Foreign Office networks as well as with the emerging diplomatic services of India and Pakistan. 1947 meant the reorganisation of diplomatic cadres both in the metropole and in the postcolonial nation-states. The Legation's political staff were given four choices: to continue employment under the Foreign Office, or choose between government service in India, Pakistan and retirement. Mirza Mumtaz Hasan Kizilbash, the Legation's Commercial Secretary, became Chargé d'Affaires at the Pakistani Embassy in Kabul in 1948.[24] Through him, the Legation's life history forms a part of independent South Asia's international relations, capturing the Legation as a shared, multinational inheritance. Like dozens of other European colonial officers, Alexander Redpath opted for Pakistan, but remained with the British Legation in Kabul for another six months on deputation.[25] Several other colonial officers continued in the Foreign Office diplomatic service. Among them were two former Counsellors—Hay and Roderick Wallis Parkes—and four former Secretaries—Galloway, William Richard Connor Green, Donald Utke Jackson, Patrick John Keen. As much as imperial transmitters translocated ideas of colonial diplomacy through space, creating synchronic instances of colonial diplomacy elsewhere, the ideas shaped at the Legation also travelled through time, creating diachronic instances of coloniality after 1947.

Keen returned to Kabul as early as June 1948.[26] As the most visible continuities, Keen and W. S. Sinclair, the Archivist, were still in Kabul in 1956.[27] Diplomacy's colonial knowledge lingered in other ways, too. The post of Oriental Secretary kept its colonial designation, but now attracted European candidates, including Horace Phillips, Hugh Michael Carless,

Nicholas Barrington and Katherine Himsworth. The formal end of colonialism invited a rediscovery of Afghanistan along old patterns. In 1947, colonial careering did not end; it found other channels. In these, colonial blueprints of othering through observation and reporting flowed. When Carless arrived in Kabul in 1951 as Oriental Secretary, there were "only two hundred yards of tarmac road".[28] He found a "rough and simple society": "It was a medieval country in which nearly everyone wore Oriental clothes. They didn't wear trousers and suits".[29] Biographies kept colonial knowledge and its imperial geographies alive. Phillips had been in the Indian Army. As entrants to the British diplomatic service in the late 1950s and early 1960s, Barrington, David Dain and David Hannay underwent language training at the School of Oriental and African Studies, followed by a posting to Iran. The geographical trajectories of their careers followed Squire's. Hannay considered that "history is a valuable study for a diplomat but I don't think that it is essential".[30] His special subject on the Great Game as an extension of modern European history firmly reinstated empire's historical centre in postcolonial time. According to Dain, in Iran "*we* had great influence, a big part to play as we had over the centuries, through the Gulf, through the history of *our Indian possessions*".[31]

The Embassy inherited the Legation's reliance on South Asian labourers as well as the techniques of their marginalisation. It employed as orderlies Naurez Khan, Harif Gul, Rajwali, Zar Gul, Nazir Din, Faqir Shah and Banat Khan. Naurez Khan had been with the Legation since March 1930. In 1933, he had stopped the armed attack on its diplomats. Habib Shah and Tawwakal Shah were chauffeurs. Habib Shah's service record dated back to 1929. Despite their long and critical service, they were still categorised as the Embassy's "inferior staff".[32] Barrington also mentions "a gentle Goanese cook" in 1959.[33] In the late 1940s and early 1950s, the Legation's Albion lorries were still in use.[34]

Performance and the Colonial Inheritance of the Anglo-Afghan Encounter

Diplomatic practice, rooted in the colonial history of Anglo-Afghan relations, persisted. Squire's Ministership continued under the Foreign Office. In May 1948, he became the first British Ambassador in Afghanistan.[35] Both India and Pakistan had opened Embassies in Kabul in April and May 1948, respectively.[36] The promotion of the Legation to Embassy was not based on a new-found appreciation for Afghan independence. Rank mattered to the colonial state, and it mattered in international relations. As the Indian Empire unravelled, the former colonial governors reluctantly drew level with the diplomatic status shared by empire's former colonial subjects in South Asia.[37] The politics of the 'great powers' and its hierarchies of international entities demanded that the Afghan state requested a British Embassy. Ironically, empire now needed the Afghan government to make that request to keep the imperial heritage of international relations alive. Afghanistan complied, bringing to an end its own long struggle for a diplomatic mission of the highest rank in the imperial capital.

Whilst this was a significant formal change to Anglo-Afghan relations, Squire's frame of reference was his own accreditation as Minister in 1943. In the report on his ambassadorial accreditation in 1948, Squire referred to his despatch of 1943. The ceremonial had not changed, as Squire briefly relayed his escort to the Dilkusha Palace. He dispensed with a long tradition of describing Afghan kings in their emotional and corporeal dimensions. In fact, breaking with previous practices of writing the encounter, Squire's report is almost wholly devoid of a commentary of the proceedings.[38] In view of the reordering of political relations in South Asia after 1947, Squire expressed to Zahir Shah "the sincere hope of His Majesty's Government that every effort would be made to establish cordial relations between Afghanistan and the two new Dominions". As the representative of a now disappearing colonial government, Squire attempted to salvage imperial hierarchies by adopting an advisory role to all three postcolonial states. He introduced this political objective during the accreditation in a way that was reminiscent of Richard Roy Maconachie's speech given to Nadir Shah in 1930. Where his father, Nadir Shah, had bowed, allegedly in acceptance of the colonial officer's directive, Zahir Shah switched topics in 1948. According to Squire:

> The King, however, preferred to keep the conversation on a more personal level and asked me about my recent trip to Mazar-i-Sharif and whether I had succeeded in catching any trout. The King and the Court Minister are both keen and expert fishermen while the Foreign Minister and I make only an occasional and usually not very successful cast and are mere novices.

Zahir Shah's resistance to discussing Squire's vision for postimperial South Asia is an anticolonial rejection of imperial suzerainty. As in 1943, when he effectively removed Francis Verner Wylie from memory and objected to the colonial state's employment of colonial officers as diplomats, Zahir Shah again resisted indications of imperial rule and its remnants by taking control of the conversation. Squire failed to elicit a response from Zahir Shah and, consequently, his cooperation in harnessing the colonial past of the Raj for British diplomacy. In 1929, Nadir Shah had accepted conditions in return for the colonial state's permission to capture the throne of Afghanistan. In 1948, Zahir Shah no longer accepted the former colonial officer as a figure of authority. Reversing the Hegelian logic of the master and the slave, Zahir Shah appeared to recognise that the disappearance of the colonial state's influence over South Asian international relations was only complete when the former colonial subject stopped acknowledging the former colonial master as such. Zahir Shah sent Squire fishing, a physically and mentally rewarding activity that was widely practiced by diplomats at the Legation, proverbially retiring him from colonial office. As much as Afghan bodies were 'put in their place' by the authority of diplomatic writing, Afghans returned the favour on occasion. Squire was faced with the demise of empire in the face of Zahir Shah's embodiment of Afghan independence. He was disappointed at the failure of his political undertaking, but found solace in continuing diplomatic interaction for diplomacy's sake. He hoped that "the many friendships that I have made have helped to strengthen the sincere and friendly relations so happily existing between our two countries. These relations it will be my constant endeavour to maintain and further". The end of Squire's Ministership and the beginning of his ambassadorial tenure performatively displayed the end of the Raj as well as Zahir Shah's diplomatic insubordination. The Legation's practices of writing the encounter had changed with Wylie in 1941. One familiar theme, however, recurred. Squire ended his report with a reference to the mausoleum of Nadir Shah, "which is still under construction". Picking up Wylie's theme of 1941, the reference to the unfinished character of the memorial sought to retrench waning imperial authority in the register of development. Squire's commentary on his accreditation played to familiar themes of incompletion and lack. While Zahir Shah was released from the political adolescence that previous Ministers had imposed on him, Afghanistan was locked in a state of developing in other figurative ways.

Squire was replaced by Alfred John Gardener in 1949, who had previously worked at the 'Afghanistan desk' of the Foreign Office. He was told by R. H. Scott at the Foreign Office that "a new period in Anglo-Afghan relations begins".[39] Although Gardener had not practiced diplomacy in the context of the Legation's institutional history, he was familiar with its records and processes of communication, including those on performing and writing the Anglo-Afghan encounter. In his accreditation report from 1949, Gardener commented that the mausoleum "is still in an unfinished state and work proceeds on it very slowly", copying a familiar trope and adopting the references to unreliable Afghan labour established by his colonial predecessors.[40] Rediscovering techniques of othering, Gardener described Shah Mahmud Khan, the Regent in the absence of Zahir Shah, in an unflattering tone: "At the audience[,] although he made an impressive figure and conducted himself in a most kindly and courteous fashion[,] he did not give me an impression either of great intelligence or forcefulness of character".[41] Gardener's writing invoked Francis Henry Humphrys' descriptions of Amanullah Khan. Gardener also noted Afghan bodily comportment in 1950, returning to descriptions of Zahir Shah "as too weak a character to carry any weight".[42] Maconachie had framed Zahir Shah's political irrelevance in terms of his youth. In Gardener's despatches, the Afghan king of close to two decades, who was now in his forties, still had not grown up in any meaningful political sense. The British Legation, now itself in the shape of an Embassy, lived on in the practices of diplomatic communication, which highlighted Afghan deficiencies under a thin layer of diplomatic moderation. Its attitudes were entrenched in the Embassy's diplomatic business. At the same time, the repetitive, self-contained nature of writing the encounter lessened the experience of cultural distancing, which had characterised previous accounts. Afghan otherness was so fundamental that it did not require lengthy textual performances over and over again.

Medical Humanitarianism

The Legation's hospital had made it stand out from other diplomatic missions. As the literary tropes on Afghan bodies persisted, evident ruptures appeared between the Legation and the later Embassy in terms of its medical humanitarianism. In 1947, Squire deemed the Legation's medical services to be crucial "to all facets of our relations with Afghanistan, diplomatic, social, educational and economic".[43] When the "inevitable separation of British and Indian interests" loomed in March 1947, the British Legation tried to salvage the Raj's "prestige" by means of providing medical assistance to Afghanistan on a broader scale.[44] In addition to the Afghan government's ban, the Legation's metropolitan and Indian sources of funding dried up. The Legation's primary and widely used bodily tool, the dispensary, did not achieve again the same attendance figures as before the Second World War. The explicit connection between the provision of public healthcare and its political relevance for Anglo-Afghan relations disappeared almost entirely from diplomatic communication. Specialised reports by the Embassy's medical officers seem to have stopped after 1948. The annual political review no longer dedicated entire sections to the public healthcare system of Afghanistan or to the health of the Legation's diplomatic personnel. The Legation lost the 'personal touch' that had characterised its colonial diplomacy. The Legation's hospital plan was scaled down to provide medical care only to a small community.[45] The waning of rich textual evidence on bodies after 1947 is striking, but not surprising given that the Legation no longer had access to India's medical services. The annual reports written by the Gardener in 1949 and 1950 make only fleeting references to Zahir Shah's health.[46] Still, ambitions of an imperial nature persisted. Ronald Duncan MacRae saw the potential for a British doctor to become the head of the Afghan medical services. Incidentally, this was also an opportunity to postpone retirement. MacRae's approach was rejected by the Afghan government on grounds that his salary demands exceeded those of other Turkish, Indian and Pakistani doctors already in Afghan employment.[47] Medical humanitarianism in Afghanistan moved into a transnational dimension after 1947.[48] The Legation's archaic humanitarianism primed to serve colonial diplomacy's ends was outpaced and outfunded by global health regimes focussing on Afghan development. Afghanistan joined the UN in 1946, and the World Health Organization in 1948. At the same time, medical students returned home to Afghanistan and other transmitters of colonial knowledge arrived as teachers.

Architecture and the Future of Empire

The material reordering of empire in South Asia challenged the continuity of "British representation to Afghanistan".[49] In February 1946, Squire argued that the Legation should become a joint British-Indian diplomatic mission at the moment of India's independence and continue in much the same way as well as along existing hierarchies. In Squire's thinking, empire would also outlive this moment of independence: "It is true that such a continuance may be illogical, [but] [t]he British Empire is founded on illogical compromises".[50] Empire thrived in the spaces of exceptions that it carved out for itself. Empire would continue to command, as Squire pictured independent India's representative as a diplomatically unequal "Number

Two".[51] Squire was prepared to accept the "very exceptional" Agha Saiyid Bad Shah as an Indian Counsellor for the moment.[52] But, as an expression of the Raj's institutional racism, Squire did not even commit to the principle of accepting representatives of independent India as subordinates owing to the "difficulty of finding suitable Indians".[53] India appeared as a diplomatic void.

Independence brought to light the contradictions between the multiple identities of the Legation between 1922 and 1948. As the idea of Pakistan took shape, the question arose whether the premises of the Legation in Kabul would become part of the 'transfer of power' and its assets be distributed to the colonial successor states or whether it would come to house the diplomatic mission of the metropolitan government. The underlying question was whether the Legation had been 'British' or 'Indian' since 1922. Squire opined in September 1946 that:

> It would be disastrous to hand over the buildings [...]. This Legation has stood since its construction as a monument to Britain's position in the country and has been entirely associated with H.M.G. It may be pretentious and unsuitable, as it is certainly somewhat uncomfortable to live in, but it far outshines all other Legations and Embassies and stands in a class by itself. If we were to hand it over to the Indian Government and move ourselves into an ordinary house in the town we should suffer a tremendous loss of prestige and it would be considered a sure sign in Afghanistan that Britain's day was done.[54]

Abdur Rahim Khan supported Squire in his assessment: "They (the Afghans) see that political relations between India and Afghanistan are carried out by 'His Britannic Majesty's Envoy Extraordinary and Minister Plenipotentiary' and the 'British Legation'—the Legation of His Majesty's Government and not India".[55] Squire's and Khan's assertions that the Legation was entirely representative of the metropolitan government was an attempt to reimagine Anglo-Afghan relations after 1919 as British-Afghan relations. The British Legation now appeared as the 'UK Legation' in files to solidify both this historical reinterpretation as well as future claims to ownership.[56] In March 1947, Squire himself indicated that the Afghan government allegedly held on to the "relic of an old anti-Government of India feeling", referring to past complaints of the Afghan government that the Legation had been staffed by Indian colonial officers, which gave the impression that it was "more representative of the Government of

India than of His Majesty's Government".[57] Squire had encountered these Afghan reservations himself in his own accreditation in 1943.[58] The ambiguity in the identities associated with the Legation buildings constituted a colonial dilemma for the future of British, or UK, diplomacy in Afghanistan.

A meeting at the Foreign Office on 5 March 1947 echoed Squire's concerns and agreed that "for reasons of prestige and in view of the lack of other suitable accommodation" the Foreign Office should attempt to retain the buildings.[59] The fact that India had provided the funds for the land, buildings, personnel and a variety of other connected things, translated into "some difficulty in convincing the Government of our claim to the building".[60] Consequently, the meeting concluded that the British government should be prepared to pay India up to £167,000, covering the original costs for the buildings and land. It also acknowledged that a new Legation would be smaller and more expensive. In 1947, Squire accounted for the sum of Rs. 21.84 lakh (c. £200,000).[61] Meanwhile, the emergence of Pakistan complicated the transfer of power. In July 1947, Gardener, Squire's later successor in Kabul, took part in a meeting at the India Office, which noted that it would constitute "a good bargain" if the Legation could be acquired for £160,000 in view of building costs and the fact that it was "the only accommodation available for diplomatic representation".[62] The "good bargain" became even better in view of the fact that this sum did not include any of the Legation's recurring costs or one-off expenses since 1922, all of which had been funded from colonial expenditure. Moving forward, the British government should "offer to maintain the existing establishment, at U.K. expense, in order to tide of the difficult interim period".[63]

The British proposal for the joint representation of Pakistani, Indian and British interests in Kabul after 14 August 1947 was accepted by India, but rejected by Pakistan.[64] India and Pakistan established separate Embassies, while the British government continued to use the Legation premises after 15 August 1947. In its human foundations, the Legation was partitioned. From the moment of independence, India laid claim to the Legation property. The Foreign Office argued that the Treaty of Kabul of 1921 had been signed by the "British" and Afghan governments, claiming that the Legation had been representing the metropolitan government and not the Indian colonial state all along. It also claimed that the British Legation in Kabul had always and only represented the United Kingdom side of Anglo-Afghan relations; that it had never represented Indian interests in Kabul and that it had not taken diplomatic directives from the Government of India.[65]

8 FROM COLONIAL LEGATION TO POSTIMPERIAL EMBASSY 329

The imperial government in London now tried to disentangle itself from the very contradictions which had guided the setup of the British Legation in Kabul and subordinated Afghanistan's international relations since the signing of the treaty in 1921. The Foreign Office, the argument ran, had "only nominally" been in charge of the Kabul post in order "to *keep up the pretence of Afghanistan's direct relations with H.M.G.* as the Afghan attached great importance to the manifestation their independence and emancipation from the tutelage of the Govt. of India".[66] While individual diplomats both before and after independence identified with empire and its 'possessions' on a personal level, that empire's foundations in colonial funds had to be written out of history in order to secure the usability of the 'prestige' that empire bestowed on 'British' international politics. The acknowledgment of colonialism's past extraction of resources prevented a material connection with empire in the future. In the debate around the ownership of the Legation compound, the future of empire was at stake.

As a member of the Interim Government from 1946, Jawaharlal Nehru had participated in the conversation on the Legation's future. He sought to keep for independent India imperial India's properties.[67] A memorandum drawn up in preparation for Nehru's meeting with Ernest Bevin in May 1949 argued that the Treaty of Kabul contained a pertinent clause:

> [T]he site reverts to them [Afghanistan] if we no longer need it, and the property could therefore not be handed over to the Indians without the consent of the Afghans. Moreover, the Pakistan Government, as part successor to the old Indian Government, should also have a say in the disposal of this property or a share in any compensation we pay for it. In view of the tension between Pakistan and Afghanistan, (and between Pakistan and India), it would give great offence to Pakistan if this property were handed over to India without the prior agreement of Pakistan. Pakistan's political interest in Afghanistan is much greater than that of India.[68]

The Foreign Office exploited the volatility of postcolonial South Asia's international relations in its attempt to hang on to the Legation premises. Introducing Pakistan's claim to the Legation premises served to cover the true ambitions of British diplomacy in Afghanistan: "For all these reasons but *principally for the sake of our prestige in Asia* we are anxious to retain possession of the property at Kabul".[69] The Legation premises instigated postcolonial conflict, which drew its energy from the British wish to harness the Raj's former glory, which had been walled up inside the Legation compound, for the future of British diplomacy in Afghanistan. Having reached the highest levels of the Foreign Office, the case was referred to the Royal Courts of Justice. Although it was now a legal case, the diplomatic officers, who referred it, also included a patriotic-imperial argument in their referral. Unless the premises were kept, "[i]t is considered that it would be highly damaging to United Kingdom prestige not only in Afghanistan but in neighbouring countries and that it would almost certainly be interpreted as a sign that the mantle of the British Government in that part of the world must now be regarded as having been assumed by India".[70]

In their reply, the judges dismissed these arguments. They indicated that the Legation had been used for both United Kingdom and Indian interests, but that the latter constituted "the predominant reason for the use and ownership of the premises".[71] Moreover, they pointed out that according to the Government of India Act of 1915, "Indian revenues could be 'applied for the purposes of the Government of India alone'".[72] The money trail that traced colonial funds from India to Afghanistan gave away the Legation's material foundations as well as its ideological origins. In view of this, the government of the United Kingdom "could not successfully maintain title to [...] these premises and that their ownership is a matter to be decided between the Government[s] of India and Pakistan".[73]

The ambiguous identity of British diplomacy in Afghanistan expressed itself in the debate about the ownership of the Legation premises, but it was also visible in Squire's confusion about who to report to during the last months of British rule.[74] In his farewell despatch, written in 1949, Squire set the tone for the commemoration of the British Legation in Kabul. Shortly before he had been informed of the verdict of the legal officers of the Crown:

> The decision that has now been reached by His Majesty's Government that even the Embassy does not belong to us, and that for the last two years we have been living in it under false pretences will, to the Afghans, be the final proof that *our day indeed is done*. It has been my good fortune to have lived in Afghanistan through all these years when our prestige has been at its zenith. As long as the war lasted Great Britain was the only power that counted for anything in Afghanistan, and the British Legation was the symbol of that power. Its continuance has, in the public eye, obscured the melancholy fact that other powers have now taken our place. Its lovely grounds, never more beautiful than in the present year, have continued to be the centre of attraction for many residents in Kabul. With its passing into other hands there will inevitably pass also the last vestige of British influence in Afghanistan.[75]

Squire ended his last official report by quoting the last lines of Kipling's poem *The Young British Soldier* from 1895. Rudyard Kipling was instrumental in shaping British understandings of Afghanistan, India, empire and the Great Game for generations.[76] For Squire, the end of the Raj resembled nothing less than previous imperial disasters in Afghanistan:

> When you're wounded and left on Afghanistan's plains,
> And the women come out to cut up what remains,
> Jest roll to your rifle and blow out your brains
> An' go to your Gawd like a soldier.

Squire's accreditation in 1948 had foreshadowed his emotions about empire's endings. When his ambassadorial tenure ended in 1949, he retired to a farm in Rhodesia which he named "Asmania", figuratively bringing Kabul into Africa.[77] In London, the Foreign Office noted that Squire appeared to be "disheartened". Its officials thought that Anglo-Afghan relations should be "rebuilt" on a new basis. The file cover of Squire's valedictory despatch notes that:

> This, Sir G. Squire's valedictory dispatch, has a rather melancholy 'twilight' tone; the retiring Ambassador clearly thinks that his departure coincides with the extinction of our influence in the country, and he takes rather the tone of a skipper, who due to circumstances beyond his control is not even permitted the distinction of going down with his rapidly sinking ship. But he leaves us in no doubt, that the vessel is doomed; it is perhaps natural an [ex-ICS] officer who has faithfully represented British interests in the difficult circumstances following upon our 'abdication' of power in India, should take a gloomy view of the future at the present time, when the stability of south Asia, which it was our achievement in India to assure, is gravely threatened on all sides.

The end of colonial rule produced emotional retrospectives. On the minute sheet attached to Squire's despatch in London, the Permanent Under-Secretary noted tellingly:

> The prestige and influence now passing away in Afghanistan were not the prestige and influence of Britain, but of the British Raj in India. In the past, the Afghan attitude to Britain has been governed by the fact that power in India was in British hands, power demonstrated and advertised in Kabul by a magnificent Mission premises built with Indian funds and staffed by officers from Indian Services. If we lose the premises we can console ourselves that,

332   M. DREPHAL

Fig. 8.1 The site plan as palimpsest: Embassy as Legation as Afghanistan (*Credit* Private Collection, Mark Bertram)

since the transfer of power in India, continued occupation of what were symbols of that power put our relations with the Afghans on a false basis.[78]

Regardless of the legal verdict, time was working in favour of the British government in London. The Embassy was now architecturally reorganised on the basis of its Legation predecessor, and the site plan captured the palimpsest of diplomatic identities. The Legation's physical outlines resembled Afghanistan's geography, and the British Embassy supplanted both (Fig. 8.1). In the absence of an Indian-Pakistani agreement, "possession is nine-tenths of the law".[79] Tensions in British-Indian relations informed the advance of the claim to property on Pakistan's behalf. Eric Ralph Lingeman, British Ambassador in Afghanistan in 1952, he sought the reassurance of his superiors in writing that "I hope the Office agrees with me on this point: that if anyone is to move in here it will be the Pakistanis if we have anything to do with it".[80] Lingeman, who had succeeded Gardener, had served in the Indian Army on India's north-western frontier.[81] The involvement of Pakistan in the quest to solve the question of the Legation's ownership was reminiscent of the mechanics of divide and rule, which had marked Indian colonial policy for decades before its end.[82] The aim was to achieve the continued occupation of the Legation premises, an objective worthy of its Curzonian inspiration. Elsewhere, a Foreign Office memorandum summarised the debate around the ownership of the Legation premises in a surprisingly critical tone, noting that the British government "have been shifting their ground from time to time", seeking to "justify their retention of these properties on various legal grounds. [...] Thereafter the main ground on which His Majesty's Government declined to surrender the properties was prestige".[83] The material representations of the former British Legation in Kabul seemed so valuable to some that their retention warranted the construction of counterfactual arguments, exposing the self-serving nature of narratives which contextualised the end of colonial rule as a transfer of power and responsibility from Britain to India and Pakistan. The colonial state had come to an end, and yet the metropolitan government sought to simultaneously own and disown its material and ideological spawn in Kabul. Having lost its claim to ownership of the Legation premises, the British government simultaneously instructed subsequent British Ambassadors in Kabul to acquire alternative property. The contrast between the fiscal generosity with which the Kabul Legation had been constructed in the 1920s from Indian revenues and the financial stringency of the late 1940s could not have been more striking. After 1947, there were no more funds that could be extracted from the colony for the development and maintenance of imperial projection in Kabul.[84] When the colonial state disappeared, it also took away the seemingly never-ending sources for objects designed to further colonial ruling classes.

The distribution of the Raj's material assets was repeated in the spaces of empire globally after 1947. The process was not completed by the 1960s and it included properties in London, Washington, New York, Canberra, Johannesburg, Singapore, Kuala Lumpur, Colombo, Kandy, Rangoon, Nanking, Shanghai, Nepal, Sikkim and Bhutan, Pondicherry, Goa, Jeddah, Kashgar, Kuwait, Meshed, Muscat, Bahrain, Bushire and Shiraz as well as the Consulates in Jalalabad, Kandahar and Zahidan.[85] According to Phillips, the British government claimed the property of the Legation in Tehran, while Pakistan and India traded colonial India's properties in Kathmandu and Kabul.[86] Phillips had been tasked with relocating the East India Company's Residency in Bushire to Bahrain. On 30 September 1963, India and Pakistan agreed that the Legation in Kabul was to be handed over to the government of Pakistan, with India receiving a payout of 82.5% of the book value of Rs. 2,334,339 according to a ratio previously applied to the division of colonial India's assets following Partition.[87] However, Pakistan had already established alternative Embassy premises by that date. In response to the Indian-Pakistan rapprochement, the British Ambassador in Kabul, Arthur James de la Mare, revisited the colonial assumption that Afghans placed importance on "external appearances".[88] If the Legation compound were to be handed over, it would constitute the loss of "political ground": "Some may think that the Afghans look upon this Embassy as a relic of imperialism and would therefore be delighted to see it disappear. That may have been true in the past, but it is certainly not true now".[89] Instead, de la Mare turned the tables of a colonial bad conscience on India and Pakistan:

> It seems to me that if we have to hand over the property *we* should be compensated not only [...] for the amount spent in looking after it, but also for the fact that we have made it possible for the property to remain an asset at all. We have done far more than merely to keep the property in good condition: *we* have preserved an asset which, without our goodwill, would almost certainly now not exist at all.[90]

In a reversal of the historical facts, de la Mare negated India's readiness to take over the Legation premises since August 1947:

Morally, it is very questionable indeed whether they have any right to the property at all; and it is undeniable that if we had abandoned it in 1947 when they could not make up their minds they would have lost everything. So let us not be afraid to speak up for ourselves: we have an excellent case and I think that, far from the Pakistanis and the Indians putting their terms to us, [...] it is *we* who should put terms to *them*. If the bill is worked out on an equitable basis we shall find that we owe them very little, if anything at all. We should be prepared to offer them some financial consideration to clear the title but we should make it plain that during all these years since 1947 it is not *we* who have been beholden to *them*, but *they* who have been beholden to *us*.[91]

The landscape of international conflict left behind by the devolving colonial state was populated by a political movement for an independent state of Pashtunistan and by questions on the futures of Kashmir, Hyderabad and Punjab.[92] This complex, multilateral situation after independence and Partition was instrumentalised in the debate of the ownership of the Legation buildings in Kabul. The international tensions between the independent South Asian neighbours, who were also parties in the transfer of colonial India's material possessions in Kabul, were consciously exploited in order to perpetuate the Orientalist projections inscribed on the Legation structures. Communal thinking upscaled into international relations. It returned colonial notions that colonial subjects were still unreliable caretakers of imperial buildings. Its origins in colonial governance persisted in British diplomatic action long after the end of the colonial state in India. Partition became a tool of empire. De la Mare suggested further that even the recent Indian-Pakistani agreement would not necessarily end Britain's occupation of the Legation, as "we can if we want spin out the negotiations with the Indians and the Pakistanis more or less indefinitely".[93] When Afghans attempted to diplomatically balance competing imperial interests, they were perceived as unreliable partners. In 1920, Dobbs had commented on the "characteristic exhibition of Afghan duplicity" when Amanullah Khan tried to reach an agreement with Russia before entering into treaty negotiations with delegates of the government of India in Mussoorie.[94] Accusing Afghan statesmen of 'playing off' imperial powers in Central Asia against one another was a staple of British perceptions of Afghanistan and implied unreliability. Multilateralism in the hands of colonial subjects was a means of insubordination. By contrast, and in reference to the British diplomatic self, engaging in multilateral diplomacy implied mastering the skills of statecraft. Ultimately, however, it revealed a significant imbalance between British self-perceptions and perceptions of the Afghan state and its representatives, discussed throughout the book. These perceptions were themselves based on latent insecurities induced during times of imperial reconfigurations.

This postcolonial conflict has been buried in the archives under more accessible and openly nostalgic narratives. In 1976, Katherine Himsworth wrote a largely positive *History of the British Embassy* and its buildings, which more recently informed Mark Bertram's *Room for Diplomacy*, which itself informed James Stourton's *British Embassies*.[95] The contents of Himsworth's booklet overlap to a large extent with Barrington's memoirs, yet end on a melancholy note reminiscent of Squire's farewell despatch. The last section of Himsworth's booklet is entitled "The end of an era": "Those days are over. The imperial twilight has deepened into darkness and for those at present in the Embassy life is much more prosaic and colourless".[96] Himsworth finished her story with a reference to the purported material benefits of being an Oriental Secretary at the Legation in Kabul as well as with imagined fears of losing colonial wealth: "We look back with longing to the days when [...] the Oriental Secretary actually possessed silk shirts, ties and dressing-gowns to be looted by bandits".[97] The passage reinforces stereotypes of colonial wealth in danger of Afghan banditry. Fraser-Tytler entertained similar notions at the very beginning of his diplomatic career, describing Afghanistan as "this land of thieves and assassins".[98] The emotional attachment to colonialism's material richness submerges the exploitation of colonial resources for the purposes of British diplomacy in Afghanistan as well as the means applied to ensure the working of colonial materiality in the later Embassy's favour.

In terms of memorialising processes, this also establishes that the Raj had become the focal lens through which to view the British Embassy's past. The further the end of the Raj receded into the past, the more outspoken became references to the Embassy's colonial past. The hazier that past became, the more glorious empire's history appeared. The British Embassy continued to occupy the former Legation premises until Soviet troops departed from Afghanistan in 1989. When it returned to Kabul in 2001, newspaper headlines harked back to the "raj-era embassy".[99] Despite attempts to negate the colonial heritage of the British Legation in Kabul in the immediate aftermath of Indian and Pakistani independence, the social, economic, architectural, horticultural and leisurely traditions of the Raj were clearly visible to all who witnessed the 'British' Legation's materiality in Kabul. The similarities between the colonial lives in the compound at

Kabul on the one hand, hill stations and Residencies in India on the other are also clearly visible to the historian. The British Legation in Kabul was located between colony and empire. The melancholy overtures to George Nathaniel Curzon and the materiality of the compound ultimately sideline the economic realities of the largely unrestrained financing of imperial prestige to further the life and afterlife of the Indian colonial state.

Notes

1. Fraser-Tytler to his mother, 14 July 1939, no. 84–87, file 1/1/10, GB165-0326, MECA.
2. Squire to H. Weightman, No.44/45/F, 1 February 1946, IOR/L/PS/12/1914, "Coll 4/54(1) Future Diplomatic Representation in Kabul (British and Indian)", BL and E 1392/1392/97, FO 371/52290, 1946, "Afghan-Indian relations as regards Legation", TNA.
3. Squire to C. W. Baxter, No.44/45/F, 20 February 1947, IOR/L/PS/12/1914, op. cit., BL.
4. "Recollections of a political officer in India (1929–1947)", A. W. Redpath, 95, Mss Eur F226/24, "Redpath, Maj Alexander William (b 1909)", BL.
5. Ibid.
6. See minutes by S. E. Asia Dept., 1 August 1947, F 10494/9774/97, FO 371/63246, 1947, "Anglo-Afghanistan Relations", TNA. See also F 14857/9774/97, FO 371/63249, 1947, "Anglo-Afghan Relations" and F 108/108/97, FO 371/69451, 1948, "Anglo-Afghan Treaty of 1921", TNA.
7. F 1161/108/97, FO 371/69451, 1948, "Corrections to the Foreign Office Research Department memorandum on Anglo-Afghan relations from 1747 to the present day", TNA.
8. "A Survey of Anglo-Afghan relations", 1, ibid.
9. Ibid.
10. Draft memorandum, Foreign Office, 1947, F 15825/9774/97, FO 371/63250, 1947, "Relations between the United Kingdom and Afghanistan", TNA.
11. See minutes by P. Murray, ibid.
12. Minute by P. Garran, 2 May 1947, E 3984/61/97, FO 371/61465, 1947, "Conduct of Relations with Afghanistan", TNA.
13. Quoted in Susan Pedersen, *The Guardians: The League of Nations and the Crisis of Empire* (Oxford, UK: Oxford University Press, 2015), 264.
14. Ann Wilks, "The 1921 Anglo-Afghan Treaty: How Britain's 'Man on the Spot' Shaped this Agreement", *Journal of the Royal Asiatic Society* (2018); Ann Wilks, "The 1922 Anglo-Iraq Treaty: A Moment of Crisis and the

Role of Britain's Man on the Ground", *British Journal of Middle Eastern Studies* 43, no. 3 (2016): 342–359.
15. Pedersen, *The Guardians*, 269.
16. Ibid.
17. Susan Pedersen, "Getting Out of Iraq—In 1932: The League of Nations and the Road to Normative Statehood", *The American Historical Review* 115, no. 4 (2010): 975–1000.
18. Pedersen, *The Guardians*, 261–286.
19. "Hay, Lt-Col Sir (William) Rupert", *Who's Who 2011 & Who Was Who* (Oxford University Press, 2011).
20. "Alban, Reginald George Evelin William", *India Office and Burma Office List for 1947.*
21. "Galloway, Lt-Col Arnold Crawshaw", *Who's Who 2011 & Who Was Who* (Oxford University Press, 2011).
22. *Foreign Office List for 1947*, 136, 196, 213, 275.
23. "Obituary: Lieutenant Colonel William Joseph Moody", *British Medical Journal* 299, 5 August 1989, 387.
24. "Military Attaché's Summary of Intelligence No. 15 for the fortnight ending 7th August 1948", para. 6, FO 371/69458, 1948, "Military Attache, Kabul: Intelligence Summaries 27 December 1947–9 December 1948. Code 97", TNA.
25. "Recollections of a political officer in India (1929–1947)", A. W. Redpath, 96, Mss Eur F226/24, op. cit., BL; Fraser-Tytler, *Afghanistan*, 275f. The figure 800 is given by Peter Mayne, *The Narrow Smile: A Journey Back to the North-West Frontier* (London: John Murray, 1955), 145–146.
26. "Military Attaché's Summary of Intelligence No. 12 for the month ending 26th June 1948", para. 14, FO 371/69458, 1948, op. cit., TNA.
27. *Foreign Office List for 1956.*
28. Transcript of interview of Hugh Michael Carless, 23 February 2002, 7, https://www.chu.cam.ac.uk/media/uploads/files/Carless.pdf [accessed: 26 May 2018].
29. Ibid.
30. Transcript of interview of David Hannay, 22 July 1999, 1, https://www.chu.cam.ac.uk/media/uploads/files/Hannay.pdf [accessed: 26 May 2018].
31. Transcript of interview of David Dain, 29 September 2003, 3, https://www.chu.cam.ac.uk/media/uploads/files/Dain.pdf [accessed: 26 May 2018], emphasis added.
32. "List of Inferior Staff serving after 15th August, 1947 and of long service prior to that date", W. H. Williams to E. N. Smith, 14 February 1951, 90421/2/51, DO 133/12, 1950, "Embassy Buildings at Kabul and Katmandu", TNA.

33. Nicholas Barrington, Joseph T. Kendrick and Reinhard Schlagintweit, *A Passage to Nuristan: Exploring the Mysterious Afghan Hinterland* (London: I.B. Tauris, 2006), 94; "Barrington, Nicholas John", *Foreign Office List for 1961.*
34. Transcript of interview of Horace Phillips, 22 January 1997, 7, https://www.chu.cam.ac.uk/media/uploads/files/Phillips.pdf [accessed: 26 May 2018].
35. Squire to Bevin, no. 76, 29 May 1948, F 8186/2385/97, FO 371/69464, 1948, "Presentation of Credentials as British Ambassador to Afghanistan by Sir G. Squire", TNA
36. "Military Attaché's Summary of Intelligence No. 9 for the fortnight ending 1st May 1948", para. 9, FO 371/69457, 1948, "Military Attache, Kabul: Intelligence Summaries 27 December 1947–9 December 1948. Code 97"; "Military Attaché's Summary of Intelligence No. 11 for the fortnight ending 29th May, 1948", para. 10, FO 371/69458, 1948, op. cit., TNA.
37. Squire, telegram no. 48, 27 February 1948, FO 983/29, 1948, "Proposed raising of Legation to Embassy Status",TNA.
38. Squire to Bevin, no. 76, 29 May 1948, F 8186/2385/97, FO 371/69464, 1948, op. cit., TNA. All following quotations are taken from this file unless specified otherwise.
39. R. H. Scott to A. J. Gardener, 21 September 1949, F 12979/10110/97, FO 371/75627, 1949, "Estimate of the position that Kabul Embassy has held in Afghanistan since its inception as a Legation after the Treaty of 1921", TNA.
40. A. J. Gardener to E. Bevin, no. 108 (381/19/49), 13 October 1949, IOR/L/PS/12/1915, "Coll 4/54(1) British Diplomatic Representation in Kabul", BL.
41. Ibid.
42. "Afghanistan: Annual Review for 1950", para. 15, FA1011/1, FO 371/92080, 1951, "Afghanistan Annual Political Review for 1950", TNA. See also Bernard S. Cohn, "Representing Authority in Victorian India", in *The Invention of Tradition*, ed. Eric J. Hobsbawm and T. O. Ranger (Cambridge: Cambridge University Press, 2013), 165–209.
43. Squire to Bevin, no. 23, Kabul, 1 March 1947, 13(13)-IA, EA, 1947, "Report by the Legation Surgeon on Medical Affairs in Afghanistan", NAI; "Medical Affairs in Afghanistan, 1947", 19–20, no. 15–23, IOR/L/PS/12/1733, "Coll 3/143 Medical arrangements in Afghanistan. Visit of Dr Rifki Bey to UK", BL.
44. "Afghanistan: Annual Review for 1948", para. 5, 1949, F 1967/1011/97, FO 371/75621, "Political Review of Afghanistan for 1948", TNA.
45. FO 983/36, 1949, "British Embassy Hospital", 1949, TNA. There are occasional files, which seem to have survived for their anecdotal value: Ledwidge to Landymore, 23 March 1955, FO 371/117019, "Request

by Embassy of Soviet Union for doctor of British Embassy in Kabul to attend to two of their officials suffering from a very severe drinking bout", TNA.
46. "Afghanistan: Annual Review for 1949", para. 6, F 1011/1, FO 371/83035, 1950, "Annual Political Review of Afghanistan for 1949"; "Afghanistan: Annual Review for 1950", para. 15, FA1011/1, FO 371/92080, 1951, op. cit., TNA.
47. "Medical Affairs in Afghanistan, 1947", 19, no. 15–23, IOR/L/PS/12/1733, op. cit., BL.
48. Timothy Nunan, *Humanitarian Invasion: Global Development in Cold War Afghanistan* (Cambridge: Cambridge University Press, 2016).
49. "U.K. Legation at Kabul", E.1867/57/97, Ext. 5944, DO 133/9, 1947, "Purchase of buildings by H.M.G. from Govt. of India - Kabul, Afghanistan", TNA.
50. Squire to H. Weightman, No.44/45/F, 1 February 1946, IOR/L/PS/12/1914, op. cit., BL and E 1392/1392/97, FO 371/52290, 1946, op. cit., TNA.
51. Ibid.
52. Ibid.
53. Ibid.
54. Squire to E. P. Donaldson, D.O.No.M.46/46, 27 September 1946, para. 3, IOR/L/PS/12/1914, op. cit., BL.
55. "Extract from a note of 17 March 1947 by Abdur Rahim Khan, Counsellor BLK regarding Afghan reactions to the present political situation in India", 11(12)-IA, EA, 1947, "Future of the British Legation at Kabul", NAI.
56. See note 59 below.
57. Comments by G. F. Squire on Abdur Rahim Khan's note, 17 March 1947, ibid.
58. See Chapter 5.
59. "U.K. Legation at Kabul", E.1867/57/97, Ext. 5944, DO 133/9, 1947, op. cit., TNA.
60. Ibid.
61. "Statement showing cost of buildings etc. in British Legation, Kabul", Squire to Weightman, D.O.No.1030/46, 15 February 1947, XA01/97D, FO 366/2505, 1947, "Accommodation & Buildings: British Legation, Kabul", TNA.
62. "Buildings in the Persian Gulf and elsewhere owned by the Government of India but required by H.M.G. for housing their Representatives after the transfer of power: Minutes of a meeting at the India Office on 16th July, 1947", 21 July 1947, DO 133/9, 1947, op. cit., TNA.
63. Ibid.
64. Note by G. C. L. Crichton, 29 July 1947, 11(12)-IA, EA, 1947, op. cit., NAI; Note by P. N. Krishnaswamy, 30 July 1947, ibid.

65. "File BLK/1/47 [renumbered 0/11/48] Compound and Buildings: Disposal", para. 4, IOR NEG 1871, "Statement of United Kingdom Government's views regarding rights in Diplomatic and Consular Properties formerly maintained in the name of His Majesty's Government but financed wholly or in part by the late Government of India", BL.
66. Note by US NWA, 24 March 1947, 11(12)-IA, EA, 1947, op. cit., NAI, emphasis added.
67. See note by J. Nehru, 13 March 1947, ibid.
68. "Embassy properties in Afghanistan and Nepal", memorandum, 2 May 1949, para. 7, XA01/85 (33/49), FO 366/2791, 1949, "F.O. Minute", TNA.
69. Memorandum on "Embassy premises at Kabul (Afghanistan) and Katmandu (Nepal)", para. 6, XA01/85 (18/49), FO 366/2790, 1949, "Vacating the Kabul & Katmandu premises", TNA, emphasis in original.
70. W. E. Beckett and K. O. Roberts-Wray, XA0 1/85/(46/49), 28 June 1949, para. 4, DO 133/11, 1948, "Embassy Buildings at Kabul and Kathmandu", TNA.
71. "Opinion of the law officers of the crown", 20 July 1949, para. 2, 3, 8, DO 133/11, 1948, op. cit., TNA.
72. Ibid.
73. Ibid.
74. Squire to Crichton, 5 July 1947, 11(12)-IA, EA, 1947, op. cit., NAI.
75. Squire to Bevin, no. 95, 18 August 1949, F 12979/10110/97, FO 371/75627, 1949, op. cit., TNA.
76. See Corinne Fowler, *Chasing Tales Travel Writing, Journalism and the History of British Ideas About Afghanistan* (Amsterdam: Rodopi, 2007), 27–34.
77. Susan Loughhead, *The End Game: The Final Chapter in Britain's Great Game in Afghanistan* (Stroud: Amberley, 2016), 65.
78. Squire to Bevin, no. 95, 18 August 1949, F 12979/10110/97, FO 371/75627, 1949, op. cit., TNA.
79. UK High Commissioner to G. F. Squire, 26 October 1947, IOR/L/PS/12/1917, "Coll 4/54(2) British Legation buildings, Kabul: Question of transfer of ownership from Government of India to HMG", BL.
80. Lingeman to Dalton Murray, 9055/11/52, 26 February 1952, DO 133/12, 1950, op. cit., TNA. See also A. J. Gardener to Dalton Murray, 9 November 1950, file no. 905/5/24/50, ibid.
81. *Foreign Office List for 1953*, 377.
82. E.g. Robin James Moore, *Crisis of Indian Unity, 1917–1940* (London: Clarendon, 1974); Robin James Moore, *Endgames of Empire: Studies of Britain's Indian Problem* (Delhi: Oxford University Press, 1988).

83. "Aide memoire", Nehru to Morrison, No. 2554-P.M., 13 April 1951, DO 35/3069, 1949, "Disposal of embassy property: Law Officers' opinion on Kabul and Katmandu", TNA.
84. Lingeman, 9055/9/52, 16 February 1952, para. 10, DO 133/12, 1950, op. cit., TNA.
85. "Statement showing the present position about possession of Consular and Diplomatic assets held abroad by the un-divided Government of India", FO 366/3256, 1963, "Disposal of Dip & Con assets", TNA.
86. Transcript of interview of Horace Phillips, 22 January 1997, 8, https://www.chu.cam.ac.uk/media/uploads/files/Phillips.pdf [accessed: 26 May 2018].
87. Aide mémoire, 30 September 1963, A. J. de la Mare to C. D. Steel, no. 9057/63, 24 October 1963, ibid.
88. A. J. de la Mare to C. D. Steel, 22 November 1963, no. 9057/63, para. 8, FO 366/3256, 1963, op. cit., TNA.
89. Ibid.
90. Ibid., emphasis added.
91. Ibid., emphasis added.
92. Elisabeth Leake, *The Defiant Border: The Afghan-Pakistan Borderlands in the Era of Decolonization, 1936–1965* (Cambridge: Cambridge University Press, 2016), 104–148.
93. Ibid.
94. Dobbs, No. 178-M.C., 6 August 1920, para. 11, 5, N 127/127/97, FO 371/5381, 1920, "Proceedings of the British-Afghan Conference at Mussoorie, 1920", TNA.
95. Mark Bertram, *Room for Diplomacy: Britain's Diplomatic Buildings Overseas 1800–2000* (Reading: Spire, 2011); James Stourton, *British Embassies: Their Diplomatic and Architectural History*, 2017.
96. Katherine Himsworth, *A History of the British Embassy in Kabul, Afghanistan* (Kabul: British Embassy, 1976), 16.
97. Ibid., 15–16.
98. Fraser-Tytler to his mother, 21 December 1923, no. 25–26, file 1/1/1, GB165-0326, MECA.
99. Eleanor Mayne, "Raj-Era Embassy in Afghanistan to Be Rebuilt", 11 November 2007, https://www.telegraph.co.uk/news/uknews/1569018/Raj-era-embassy-in-Afghanistan-to-be-rebuilt.html [accessed: 12 June 2014].

CHAPTER 9

Conclusions: The Coloniality of Diplomacy

UNENDING EMPIRE AND HISTORY

The history of the British Legation in Kabul provided many continuities for the broader history of Anglo-Afghan diplomatic relations. There were also ruptures along the way. Destruction affected this diplomatic mission, but history enriched its story with meaning and the notion of permanence. Endings of many kinds were the Legation's defining features, which displayed the unravelling of imagined imperial might time and again. The history of British diplomacy's material shells in Afghanistan is a study of precariousness and dysfunction from several points of view. To begin with, the Legation's first quarters in Bagrami were considered unhealthy. In late 1926, the British Legation's premises in the historical *serais* of the Durand Agreement were made uninhabitable by a fire. The mission and its people moved into the neighbouring compound where construction work was still ongoing. Fire was a recurring hazard, even in the new buildings, which were also cold.[1] The Legation compound was easily policed owing to its bounded nature, making it prone to isolation when Afghan governments intended to limit the Legation's engagement with an Afghan public, for instance through the Legation dispensary. The Legation's institutional history is built around the serial destruction of houses and structures, the killing and injuring of people and animals as well as the rupturing of international relations. In order to protect its diplomatic bodies where George Nathaniel Curzon's imperial projection failed to reach, the Legation sought

© The Author(s) 2019
M. Drephal, *Afghanistan and the Coloniality of Diplomacy*,
Cambridge Imperial and Post-Colonial Studies Series,
https://doi.org/10.1007/978-3-030-23960-2_9

refuge in the metaphysical, engraving the motto of Harrow School, *Stet Fortuna Domus*, on the foundation stone of the new buildings.[2] In the winter of 1928/1929, Amanullah Khan's soldiers shelled the Legation. When the Consulate in Jalalabad and its archives were destroyed, Francis Henry Humphrys demanded swift retribution for this "wanton outrage".[3] He recommended the arrest of leaders of the Shinwari tribe in India and demand a ransom for their release, fully aware of the arbitrary legal implications of such action: "In view of possible international complications I recommend that action should be taken to recover the fine before a settled government is re-established in Afghanistan".[4] Anglo-Afghan diplomatic interaction appeared exceptionally "insecure", but also offered spaces of legal exception for imperial policing.[5] The long-term consequences of 1929 led to the killing of Legation employees in 1933. The expression of violence directed at diplomatic bodies in Kabul was historically rooted in the two Anglo-Afghan Wars of the nineteenth century. It was by no means limited to Anglo-Afghan relations, as the killing of the American Ambassador Adolph Dubs in 1979 and the violence in Kabul's diplomatic quarter since 2001 testify.[6] In the wake of the 'War on Terror', the materialisation of Curzon's imperial imagination that was encapsulated in the 'third British Legation' in Kabul reappeared as a fitting imperial backdrop to the 'neo-imperialism' unfolding during the Fourth Anglo-Afghan War. Curzon came to Kabul once again, as the British government considered buying the Legation compound from Pakistan. By then, the Minister's residence was a burned-out shell. Empire and ruin went hand in hand, but empire's selective memory consciously sought to tide over the ruptures that ruin had created. Empire was unending. The continuing rebranding of Anglo-Afghan relations under 'British' and 'UK' labels in the twentieth and twenty-first centuries, does not overcome the repeated transformation and translation of colonial knowledge, ideologies and frameworks. Underneath the superficial reframing of diplomatic relations, imperial genealogies keep empire's inheritances and its asymetries alive.

Making sense of the destruction of the *serais* in 1926, George Kirkbride, the Secretary, wrote: "I wish that some diligent historian of the future, specialising maybe for his tripos on the greatest of all Empires, may care to know something of the quaint old Legation, of its strange setting, of the varied activities pursued within its walls and lastly of its rapid and calamitous end".[7] By the end of 1926, the Legation had already been reincarnated twice. The end of the 'second British Legation' prompted Kirkbride's urge for historicisation. A chapter in the Legation's history had ended, and Kirkbride sought consolation in the idea that the future would return a glorified, larger-than-life rendering of the past. Two decades later, Giles Frederick Squire similarly enlarged the historical record. At the end of his ambassadorial tenure and a prolific colonial career, Squire's valedictory despatch made "sad reading".[8] Squire feared the prospect of the Embassy's colonial compound passing into the hands of previous colonial subjects. To him, "[t]hese buildings, *far exceeding in magnificence anything previously dreamed of or yet constructed in Afghanistan* may have been the envy of many, Afghan and foreigner alike, but they have certainly enormously enhanced the prestige of the British Minister and the Government he represents.[9] The Legation had been staffed and made by the Indian Political Service, which embodied the hedging of viceregal power after 1919. The continuing possession of its compound after 1947 kept the Raj's 'transfer of power' to India and Pakistan open-ended. British diplomacy harnessed the colonial state's "prestige", creating colonial pockets, enclaves and presences in postcolonial time. As the processes of decolonisation kicked in, imperial retrenchment deliberately prevented their completion. The coloniality of decolonisation emerged.

Synchronicity, Diachronicity and Coloniality

In *Orientalism*, Edward Said reflected on the static and dynamic dimensions of knowledge and of the 'Orient' specifically:

> Against this static system of 'synchronic essentialism' I have called vision because it presumes that the whole Orient can be seen panoptically, there is a constant pressure. The source of pressure is narrative, in that if any Oriental detail can be shown to move, or to develop, diachrony is introduced into the system. What seemed stable – and the Orient is synonymous with stability and unchanging eternality – now appears unstable. Instability suggests that history, with its disruptive detail, its currents of change, its tendency towards growth, decline, or dramatic movement, is possible in the Orient and for the Orient. History and the narrative by which history is presented argue that vision is insufficient, that 'the Orient' as an unconditional ontological category does an injustice to the potential of reality for change.[10]

Said and *Orientalism* have filled entire libraries since, such is the contribution of both author and work to the decolonisation of colonial knowledge.

Today, the passage quoted here, especially its last sentence, may run the risk of stating undisputed, established fact. Said was primarily concerned with the construction of knowledge in relation to imperial power. He also hinted at the shaping of the 'Europe', in the process of the colonial encounter. This was the starting point for this book's discussion.[11] Throughout, it has adjusted the lenses previously focused on colonial subjects by colonial masters on colonial masters themselves. Said's rendering of historical change with regard to the 'Orient' holds true for colonial knowledge, its maintainers, carriers and transformers. The book reveals 'British' diplomacy's multiple and intricate colonial origins, links and lasting impacts. It blurs the artificial boundaries that divide the disciplines of colonial and imperial history on the one side and diplomatic and international history on the other. Diplomacy was empire in a different shape. As it was created in the aftermath of 1919, the Legation drew on a 'synchronic essentialism' that captured the constructions of Afghanistan in multiple forms of colonial knowledge. The Legation's protocols were inspired by the political practices of the colonial state in India. Its diplomacy was founded on the history of the colonial state's 'Anglo-Afghan' relations, which were themselves informed by diplomatic traditions from precolonial and colonial India. India was the predominant point of reference in the history of the British Legation in Kabul. It provided the Legation's personnel, its funds, its material, its labour and its political instructions. India inspired the Legation's way of life, its hierarchies and material representations by means of people drafted from colonial services, who brought to Kabul practices common amongst Indian administrators. The Indian colonial state's interaction with Pashtun tribes and Afghanistan informed its approach to diplomacy post independence. The Legation's colonial officers were conditioned by the objectives of the colonial state, which had trained them in the first place. For them, Kabul presented an intersection of British-Indian and cosmopolitan lifestyles. As a result, the diplomat in Kabul was still a colonial administrator and imperial governor. The diplomat and the colonial officer differed only in terms of the place of their service. Through the Legation, the colonial state in India created a presence in Afghanistan to a degree which had not been possible before the installation of the mission in 1922, for instance by establishing and maintaining privileged access to Afghan statesmen and their wives as well as an Afghan public. The Legation was not just a transmitting conduit; it was a colonial space in its own right. The presence of a Legation in Kabul did not signal the beginning of a process of decolonisation; Afghan independence in 1919 was not synonymous with the beginning of a postcolonial era. British diplomacy acknowledged an independent Afghanistan on paper while employing authoritarianism's diplomatic practices developed in colonial India. The Legation's manifold connections with the colonial state in India warrant its description as being colonial in character. It existed *alongside* the Indian colonial state, and was also synonymous with it. The British Legation in Kabul rested on colonial knowledge. The Legation's history paralleled the emergence of Afghanistan from a position of colonial subalternity prior to 1919 to the international recognition of its sovereignty afterwards through to the disappearance of the colonial state from South Asia in 1947. As much as Afghanistan existed as a "para-colonial" state until 1947, the Legation in Kabul was marked by synchronic coloniality that existed simultaneously to colonialism's governing order, albeit spatially removed from it.[12]

As much as undisturbed colonial knowledge flowed from India to Kabul, events in 1919 and 1947 also put pressure on, disrupted and unsettled the stability that the imperial vision of permanence had created for Anglo-Afghan relations. Far from ending and disappearing, knowledge of Afghanistan was transformed. Diplomatic practice rooted in colonial knowledge turned decolonisation into a transformation of empire that ensured colonialism's afterlives. This repurposing of knowledge captures the diachronicity of the Legation's coloniality *through time* in 1919, 1947 and after. In its afterlife, the Legation continued as an Embassy. Its colonial inheritance informed approaches to Afghanistan's international relations even at a time when colonialism in India had already ended. Its colonial past continued to inform British diplomatic practice, its representations and projections after 1948. As recent as 2009, the Embassy commemorated the eightieth anniversary of the 1929 airlift.[13] As British diplomats returned to Kabul after 2001, the Legation's distillation of nineteenth and twentieth-century forms of colonial overrule was invoked. Imperial history still is an essential part of the British Embassy's institutional identity, even if its material representations now forms part of Pakistan's material colonial inheritance. In general, diplomacy draws heavily on its own history. In the specific case of Anglo-Afghan relations that history is intimately tied to its origins in colonial time. Coloniality in its synchronic and diachronic dimensions speaks to empire's conscious and creative resistances to decolonisation and empire's own endings. Diplomacy's power-laden structures, established in colonial paradigms, survive unwittingly and undisturbed.

The book speaks to the specificity of the Afghan experience of statal independence, its making und circumscription, as much as it underlines this case study's universal implications. Through the latter, Afghanistan stands at the centre of historical processes of global relevance rather than at the 'periphery' of empire. The discussion also contributes insights into diplomacy's colonial origins. In the development of diplomacy in the twentieth century as well as in the process of decolonisation, the British Legation in Kabul provides an important transitory and interstitial institution. In the same way that Indian colonial officers in Kabul could perform diplomacy between 1922 and 1947, British diplomats revealed the Orientalist and colonial foundations of diplomatic epistemologies after that date. The mixing of colonial and diplomatic identities articulated by Ernest Satow in 1917 has proven to be particularly resilient. The multiplicity of diplomatic, colonial and imperial identities of international relations in the twentieth century is a strong argument for the rethinking of widely accepted chronologies of international history. Instead of approaching decolonisation from a teleological perspective premised on the notion that the modern world's colonial chapters concluded, coloniality imagines alternative trajectories that speak to the retrenchment and proliferation of empire beyond moments of statal independence. The Legation smoothed the transition from colonial suzerainty to postcolonial diplomatic relations, but it never achieved the point of being entirely decolonial. In this way, the book opens up a field for further research, which investigates the relations of European colonial powers with previous and co-existing colonial entities. The connectivities of Kabul to imperial conduits in Iraq and the Arabian Peninsula are evident from the movement of individuals who also broke free from the immediacy of colonial office into capitalist and humanitarian enterprise. Beyond the links provided by people that directly connect the Legation in Kabul through space—with institutions in existing imperial networks for instance—or through time—with its own incarnations before and after 1919 and 1947—the example of this Legation also prompts the intellectual reconsideration of geographically and biographically disconnected spaces where similar asymmetrical dependencies between imperial formations and nominally independent polities existed in the modern world. From here studies into embassies of all kinds as sites of diplomatic encounter between state and non-state actors opens up. The adoption of the reciprocal principle of embassies as a means for inter-state communication and engagement by postcolonial nations deserves special attention. Rather than appearing as the inevitable outcome of a diffusionist reproduction of 'Western' statecraft, postcolonial approaches to international relations theory and new diplomatic history can work on the excavation of competing ambitions and visions of diplomatic orders.

Coloniality means the temporal entanglement of colonial and postcolonial orders. The coloniality of the modern world exists alongside processes of decolonisation. As empire shaped Afghanistan colonially, independent Afghanistan shaped empire postcolonially. In the case of independent India, decolonisation expressed itself in the alterity of its diplomatic practice in comparison to 'Western' notions of normative statecraft.[14] This anticolonial drive to invent truly independent diplomatic practice becomes understandable in light of latent suggestions that postcolonial freedoms were bestowed, rather than captured. The fact that subordinate diplomatic missions, such as legations, disappeared in the course of the twentieth century and were replaced by embassies is not a question of "fashion"; it was the outcome of a continuing demand for the implementation of an egalitarian diplomatic order that followed the principle of self-determination in international relations.[15] The diplomatic order of the twentieth century was shaped by empire and it resisted the clawing back of sovereignty that had been surrendered during colonising processes the world over. It is, in itself, an expression of colonial knowledge and a product of its gradations of power.

Studying history through the prism of coloniality acknowledges the ability of the colonial encounter to mutually shape all its participants. Coloniality means the interlocking and continued shaping of the postcolonial world as well as postimperial remants of empire. Decolonising diplomacy then demands freeing it from its colonial inheritances. This includes the need to transgress the artificial communal divisions into diplomatic history's 'nations' and 'states' as well as the construction of their inward and outward hierarchies that emerged from and as a result of colonial rule. Decolonisation must entail the scrutiny of the seemingly self-contained denominators that distinguish and separate the 'Afghan', 'British', 'Indian' and 'Pakistani' inheritors of colonial knowledge. The decolonisation of diplomatic history must avoid colonialism's erroneous discursive containers that reinscribe communal boundaries, which supposedly channel colonial knowledge. The book points to the inter-, multi-, transnational vectors of the Legation's inheritance, which was neither singular nor linear. Colonial knowledge also moved transnationally, beyond elites and the state, outside of national archives, through time. To acknowledge the coloniality of diplomacy is only a first step towards the decolonisation of diplomatic history, the histories of inter-state relations as well as of the state itself.

Notes

1. 35-A, F&P, 1934, "Damage Caused by Fire to the Military Attache's House at Kabul", NAI.
2. Humphrys to Chamberlain, no. 4, 5 January 1929, N 562/1/97, FO 371/13990, 1929, "Afghan situation", TNA.
3. Humphrys, memorandum no. 37, 16 April 1929, N 2408/1/97, FO 371/13995, 1929, "Afghan Rebellion", TNA.
4. Ibid.
5. Ibid.
6. James Stourton, *British Embassies: Their Diplomatic and Architectural History* (2017), 332–337.
7. "Destruction of the Second British Legation in Kabul", 31 December 1926, file 9, GB165-0326, MECA.
8. R. H. Scott to A. J. Gardener, 21 September 1949, F 12979/10110/97, FO 371/75627, 1949, "Estimate of the position that Kabul Embassy has held in Afghanistan since its inception as a Legation after the Treaty of 1921", TNA.
9. Squire to Bevin, no. 95, 18 August 1949, ibid., emphasis added.
10. Edward W. Said, *Orientalism* (London: Penguin, 1995), 240.
11. Ibid., 7.
12. Benjamin D. Hopkins, *The Making of Modern Afghanistan* (Basingstoke: Palgrave Macmillan, 2008), 170.
13. Sherard Cowper-Coles, *Cables from Kabul: The Inside Story of the West's Afghanistan Campaign* (London: HarperPress, 2012), 203. See also the anniversary of the 60th anniversary: David Fairhall, "60 Years After, Raj Survivors Recall Our Own Kabul Airlift", *The Guardian*, 15 February 1989, 7.
14. Deep K. Datta-Ray, *The Making of Indian Diplomacy: A Critique of Eurocentrism* (Oxford University Press, 2015).
15. See "legation", Geoff R. Berridge and Alan James, *A Dictionary of Diplomacy* (Basingstoke: Palgrave Macmillan, 2001), 147.

Glossary

amir	king, ruler, governor, commander
ayah	nurse, governess
bagh	garden
bhisti	water carrier
bhoosa	broken straw, husk
biswa	unit measuring 20 biswasas; equivalent to 1/20 jarib ("Glossary", Squire to Bevin, no. 72, 18 June 1949, DO 133/11, 1948, "HMG Embassies at Kabul and Kathmandu: claims to ownership of Government of India", TNA)
chalan	register, list
charas	hashish, cannabis
chowkidar	watchman
cooli	carrier, transporter
Daffadar	rank in Indian Army cavalry regiments, given only to Indians
daftari	office clerk
dhobi (m.), dhoban (f.)	launderer, washer
durbar	court
durzi	tailor
ferrash/farrash	bed-maker, chamberlain, sweeper
firman	order

garam khana	"hot" house (lit.)
godown	warehouse, store
gul khana	greenhouse, conservatory
gumrukh	toll, involving the movement of both goods and people
haj	pilgrimage to Mecca
haji	pilgrim
hakim	physician; but also official, authority, judge
harem	women's quarters
khan	leader; title of a tribal leader
jarib	unit measuring approx. 3600 square yards or 3/4 acre; equivalent to 20 biswas (see above: biswa)
Jemadar	rank in the Indian Army, given only to Indians
jui	irrigation canal
mali	gardener
memsahib	wife of a colonial official
mir munshi	chief secretary; head clerk (of an office)
mistri	mechanic
moulvi	a doctor of Muslim law, an imam
mufti	doctor of Muslim law
mujahideen	someone engaged in 'holy war'
mulki sowar	guard
nazir	overseer
nezam-nama	code of law
purdah	seclusion, separation
rahdari	toll, road or transit duty
Risaldar	rank in Indian Army cavalry regiments, given only to Indians
serai	courtyard with accommodation, especially for travellers and caravans
shah	king
shikar	hunt
sowar	cavalry trooper
surkhi	lime mortar
syce	horse-keeper
Taliban	students

toshakhana	repository of articles received as presents, or intended to be given as presents attached to a government office
ulema	community of religious authorities
yakdan	mail bag

Index

A

Abdul Hadi Khan, 55
Abdul Qaiyum Khan, 195
Abdur Rahim Khan (Counsellor), 145, 147, 327
Abdur Rahman Khan (r. 1880–1901), 50, 51, 63, 65, 193
Accountant, 88
Aden, 182, 320
Afghan. *See* ethnicity
Afridi, 139. *See also* tribe
Agha Saiyid Bad Shah (Counsellor), 145, 327
Ahmed, Akbar S., 11
Ahwaz, 320
Alban, Reginald George Evelin William (Counsellor), 145, 320
Ali Ahmad Khan, 54
Allah Jawaya, 284
Amanullah Khan (r. 1919–1929), 15
  constitution, 14
  rebellion (1928/1929), 4, 15, 195, 243–245. *See also* Habibullah Kalakani (r. 1929)
  reform programme, 14, 15, 63
Amery, Leopold, 142
Aminullah Khan, 286
Amir Ali Shah (Accountant), 89
Amps, Leon Williamson (Resident Engineer), 288–290
Amritsar (Jallianwala Bagh massacre), 48
anarchy, 139, 149
Anglo-Afghan relations, 5
  as British-Afghan relations, 5, 327, 344
  as UK-Afghan relations, 327, 344
Anglo-Afghan Wars
  First, 3, 4, 9, 67, 100, 120, 134, 188, 243, 300
  Second, 4, 9, 65, 67, 68, 134, 135, 137, 193, 243, 300
  Third, 48, 49, 134, 137, 145, 192, 202

Fourth, 4, 344
War of Independence (1919), 49, 183
animals
  bullocks, 289
  camels, 289
  dogs, 301
  donkeys, 289, 290
  elephants, 183, 289, 290
  fly, 240
  horses, 91, 295, 301
  mosquito, 299
  ponies/pony, 91, 173, 196, 289
  sheep, 93
anonymity, 83
appendicitis, 254
Arabia, 128
Archivist, 94
architecture, 277
  as occupation, 301
  classical style, 288
  Indo-Saracenic style, 279
arms, 52, 53, 188, 199
asymmetry, 16, 18, 153, 175, 218. See also imbalance
authoritarianism, 203, 347
autocracy, 54
Aziz Khan, Muhammad, 245. See also Musahiban
  assassination, 245

B
Babur (Mughal emperor), 298
Bacha-i-Saqao. See Habibullah Kalakani (r. 1929)
Baghdad, 194
Bahrain, 320
Baker, Herbert (Architect), 288
Baker (Military Attaché's clerk), 97
Baluch. See ethnicity
Baluchistan, 126, 137, 150

Banat Khan (orderly), 322
Bandar Abbas, 321
Barakzai Muhammadzai. See Musahiban
Barrington, Nicholas (Oriental Secretary), 11, 278, 322
basketball. See sport
Bellew, Henry Walter, 253
Bertram, Mark, 278
Best, Iris (née Bolton), 136
Best, William Hazlitt Duncan (Secretary), 136
Bhutan, 146
Bihar, 127
biography, 81
  life history, 82
  prosopography, 82
body, 242
  diplomatic body, 236
bodyguard. See escort
Bolton, Horatio Norman, 136, 162
Bombay, 182
border-making, 9, 11, 21, 52, 284
bowls. See games
Bowtell-Harris, Capt. (Superintendent), 96
Boyes-Cooper, Alexander (Military Attaché), 128
Bray, Denys, 281
British Legation in Kabul.See also compound
  first (Bagrami), 283
  second (Durand Agreement serais), 283; destruction, 284
  third, 344
Broughton, S. ("lady stenographer"), 97
Brownsdon, Thomas Edward (Attaché), 151
buffer state, 7, 18, 188
Burgess, B.S. (Second Clerk), 96
Burnes, Alexander, 243

Bushire, 320
Butler, Harcourt, 137

C
Caccia, H.A.C., 303
Cairo, 194
Campbell, Robert Neil, 129
Capper, W.B., 133
career geography, 127, 144
Carless, Hugh Michael (Oriental Secretary), 321
Caroe, Olaf, 10, 147
Carter, Harold (Personal Assistant), 82
Carter, J. (Superintendent), 96
cartography, 300. *See also* mapping
Carvello, C. ("lady stenographer"), 97
Cavagnari, Pierre Louis Napoleon, 65, 183, 243
Cecchi, Gino, 285
Central India, 126
Ceremonial Code (diplomatic protocol), 178, 179
Chelmsford, Lord (Viceroy of India, 1916–1921), 48
Chirol, Ignatius Valentine, 132
Cholera, 241, 242
climate, 242, 296
Coen, Terence Creagh, 10, 117, 321
Cold War, 7. *See also* Great Game
Colonial knowledge, 8, 20
coloniality, 21, 348. *See also* postcoloniality; synchronicity
  fiscal, 283, 330; budgets and accounts, 85
compound, 293
  British Legation as, 285
  Minister's residence, 291
  segregation, 286
  spatial structuring, 295
Conolly, Arthur, 3
conservatory, 291

Counsellor, 135, 144
Cowper-Coles, Sherard (Ambassador), 11, 278
Crichton, Gerard Charles Lawrence (Counsellor), 145, 146
cricket. *See* sport
Crombie, G.E., 143, 213
croquet. *See* games
Cunningham, George (Counsellor), 129, 135, 144–146
Curzon, George Nathaniel (Viceroy of India, 1899–1905), 58, 66, 277

D
Dain, David (Third Secretary; Oriental Secretary), 322
Dalrymple, William, 278
Dane, Louis, 58, 65, 125
  Dane Mission, 58
Dar-ul-Aman, 286
Daubeny, Ronald Giles (Secretary), 148
Davies, C.H., 133
Davies, F.G.H., 133
Davies, Francis John, 133
Deane, Harold, 133, 134, 162
death. *See also* suicide
  Alexander Burnes, 243
  Alfred Noel Irvine Lilly, 254
  attack on Legation (1933), "outrage", 87, 245
  casualties during rebellion of 1929, 245
  Geoffrey Herbert Stranger, 97, 245
  Syed Irshad Husain, 90, 245
  William Hay MacNaghten, 243
  Yakub, 245
decoloniality, 20. *See also* coloniality
decolonisation/decolonization, 18, 19, 349
  and coloniality, 345

and linear teleology, 348
as historical period, 25
as process, 20
as transformation of empire, 347
Ashis Nandy on, 20
delinking, 20
Partha Chatterjee on, 20
resistances to, 347
dehumanisation, 92, 252, 285
democracy, 16, 53, 54, 62, 139
dependence, 63, 64, 348
 fiscal, 64
Dera Ismail Khan, 126, 194
despotism, 15, 186
development, 14
 Afghanistan, 61, 64
 and empire, 324
 and independence, 63
 and international hierarchy, 61
 and international relations, 16
 and liminality, 212
 and modernisation, 14
 and sovereignty, 64
 and temporal linearity, 14
Dewe, Douglas Percy (Surgeon), 128
diachronicity, 21, 345, 347
diplomatic history, 21, 23, 24
dispensary. *See also* hospital, 255, 256, 272, 325
 opposition to, 258
Dobbs, Henry, 52, 55, 56, 59–61, 292, 319
 character sketch of Amanullah Khan, 186
 Dobbs Mission, 59, 240
Dodd, Percy Charles Russell (Military Attaché), 128
Dost Mohammed Khan, 4, 120
Drace-Francis, Charles, 290
Dubs, Adolph (US American Ambassador), 344
Dundas, Lawrence, 125

Durand, Mortimer, 280, 284
Durand Agreement, 188
Durand Line, 21, 51, 187–189; international politics of, 198
Durand Mission, 21
Durrani (Afghan) Empire, 56
Durrani, Ahmad Shah (Abdali), 318. *See also* Sadozai
dysentery, 239

E
East Africa, 134
Eden, Anthony, 217
electricity, 297
Elliot, Henry Hawes (Surgeon), 126
Elliott-Lockhart, Percy Clare, 134
Elphinstone, Mountstuart, 8, 20, 67
emotions, 185, 235
 Amanullah Khan, 185
 anxiety, 180, 200; Faiz Muhammad, 214; Francis Henry Humphrys, 184; Richard Roy Maconachie, 192; William Kerr Fraser-Tytler, 142
 discomfort, 206, 211, 220
 fury, 92
 insecurity, 180, 236, 285
 melancholy, 330, 331, 336
 nervousness, 207, 213, 220
 Raj nostalgia, 10, 336
empire, 12
 imperial debris, 19
 imperial formation, 12
 ruin, 19, 344
English Office, 94
equality, 66. *See also* asymmetry
Erskine, Claude Ernest Torin (Military Attaché), 128
escort, 173, 196. *See also* bodyguard
ethnicity, 56, 191, 214. *See also* nationalism

evacuation, 2
  British Embassy (1989), 2, 3
  British Legation (1929), 2, 100, 191
  Pakistani Embassy (1995), 4
  women and children (1923), 100
Ewans, Martin (Ambassador), 11

F
Fagan, Arthur William (Counsellor; Secretary), 135
Fagan, Christopher Sullivan, 135
Fagan, George Hickson, 135
Fagan, Patrick James, 135
Faiz Muhammad, 206
Faqir of Ipi, 52
Faqir Shah (orderly), 322
Farrell, Henry William (Surgeon), 127
Fazal Ilahi, 94
Fazal Rahman (Nazir), 91
fishing, 324. *See also* sport
Fletcher, Edward Walter (Secretary), 148
Forbes, Rosita, 100
Foreign and Political Department, 130. *See also* Indian Political Service
Foster-Josephs, A. (Resident Engineer), 288
Fraser, William Archibald Kenneth (Military Attaché), 128, 189
Fraser-Tytler, James Macleod Bannatyne, 134
Fraser-Tytler, William, 134
Fraser-Tytler, William Kerr (Minister, 1935-1941; Counsellor; Secretary)
  accreditation, 209
  age, 141
  as author, 10, 14
  career, 141, 142, 321
  family, 134
  health, 141

frontier, 8, 12
Frontier Code, 102
Frontier Crimes Regulation, 11, 149

G
Galloway, Arnold Crawshaw (Secretary), 136, 164, 320
Gallyôt, M.R. (Second Clerk), 96
games. *See also* sport, 239
  games ethic, 237
Gandamak, treaty of (1879), 50, 67, 188
Garage Superintendent, 97, 245
garden, 298, 299
Gardener, Alfred John (Ambassador), 324
  accreditation, 325
Garran, P., 319
George V. (r. 1910–1936), 199
Ghulam Nabi Charkhi, 245
  execution, 245
Gibson-Carmichael, Thomas, 134
Goldsmid Mission, 21
Gould, Basil John (Counsellor), 10, 146, 283, 320
Gould, Lorraine, 103
Gould, Richard, 2, 100
Grant, Hamilton, 53, 54, 251
Gray, John Alfred, 254
Great Game. *See also* Cold War
  and Cold War, 3
  as historical subject, 322
  historiographical critique of, 7, 8
  as historiographical mode, 6, 7, 35
  as political determinant, 281
Green, William Richard Connor (Secretary), 148, 321
Griffin, Lancelot Henry Lepel, 136, 146
Griffin, Lepel Henry, 67, 136
Grobba, Fritz, 17, 320

H

Habib Shah (Chauffeur), 322
Habibullah Kalakani (r. 1929), 15, 190
   execution, 193, 203
Habibullah Khan (r. 1901–1919), 50, 51, 63, 65
Hafiz Saifullah Khan (British Agent, Newswriter), 122, 243
Hailey, Hammet Reginald Clode, 135
Hailey, Philip Cotes (Counsellor), 135
Hailey, William Malcolm, 135, 263, 287, 292
Hamilton, Angus, 254
Hannay, David (Third Secretary), 322
Harif Gul (orderly), 322
Harris, Audrey (later Audrey Mander), 100, 125
Harvey-Kelly, Charles Hamilton Grant Hume (Military Attaché), 128
Hashim Khan, Muhammad, 251. *See also* Musahiban
Hayatullah Khan, 48
Hay, William Rupert (Counsellor), 145, 320
Hazara, 290. *See also* ethnicity
health, 142, 143, 211, 237, 250
   mental, 120, 238, 239
   physical, 238, 239
Hentig, Werner Otto von, 143
Himsworth, Katherine (Oriental Secretary), 297, 322, 336
Hindus. *See* minorities
historiography
   as technology of rule, 11
   colonialist, 9, 177
hockey. *See* sport
Hogg, William Peat, 126
Hopkirk, Peter, 3, 7
Hospital, 325. *See also* dispensary
Howell, Evelyn Berkeley, 194, 291
Humanitarianism, 58, 64, 254, 325
Humphrys, Arthur Francis Walter, 133
Humphrys, Francis Henry (Minister, 1922-1929), 320
   accreditation, 182
   career, 139, 320
   family, 133
Humphrys, Gertrude Mary (née Deane), 101, 133, 162
Humphrys, Pamela Eugène (née Wavell), 133, 321
hunting. *See* sport
Hyderabad, 51, 126
hygiene, 241, 242, 282, 289, 297

I

Imam Din, 284
imbalance, 69, 216. *See also* inequality
Inayatullah Khan, 48, 190
independence, 14, 74
   Abdur Rahman Khan and Habibullah Khan, 51
   Afghanistan (1919), 21, 47
   and development, 62
   and empire, 62
   and international relations, 53
   and sovereignty, 52
   and modernisation, 62
   meanings, 64
   recognition, 50, 60
Indian Medical Service, 125
Indian Ocean, 12, 13, 320
   oceanic turn, 13
Indian Political Service, 130, 131. *See also* Foreign and Political Department
   as dynasty, 132
   Indianisation, 125, 146, 147
Indo-Afghan borderland, 8, 11, 52
   international politics of, 187, 188
   intrigue, 188
inequality. *See* equality
infantilisation, 10, 251
insurgency. *See* opposition

INDEX

international history, 7, 11, 18, 23, 24, 26, 71, 284, 346, 348. *See also* new diplomatic history
Iraq, 320
Ireland, 127
irredentism, 56

J
Jackson, Donald Utke (Secretary), 321
Jalalabad, British Consulate.*See also* Kandahar, British Consulate
destruction, 196
Jefferis, M.H. (Resident Engineer), 288
Jenkins, Evan, 133
jihad, 49

K
Kabul, 60
British Agency, 243
British Agent, 122
treaty of (1921), 60, 64, 77, 328, 329
Kalat, 145
Kaltenborn-Stachau, Baron von, 285
Kandahar, British Consulate. *See* Jalalabad, British Consulate
Karachi, 56
Kashmir, 146
Keen, Frederick, 137
Keen, Patrick John (Secretary), 136, 146, 148, 321
Khilafat movement, 60. *See also* nationalism
Khost rebellion (1924), 15
Khyber, 126
Kipling, Rudyard, 127, 331
Kim (novel), 127
The White Man's Burden (poem), 235

The Young British Soldier (poem), 331
Kirkbride, George (Secretary), 284, 285, 344
Knox-Johnston, Aileen, 321
Kuwait, 320

L
labour, 83, 289
Lancaster, Alexander Stalker (Military Attaché), 129
Landi Kotal, 182
language, 290. *See also* minorities
Pashto, 214, 290
Persian (Dari), 214, 290
Ledgard, H.A. (Surgeon), 128, 254
Legation Diary, 101
Legation Ladies, 99
Lewis, Harold Victor (Military Attaché), 128
Lhasa, 320
Lilly, Alfred Noel Irvine (Military Attaché), 128, 254
Lingeman, Eric Ralph (Ambassador), 333
Linlithgow, Lord (Viceroy of India, 1936–1943), 141, 217
Loch, P.G., 293
Lockhart, Robert MacGregor Macdonald (Military Attaché), 129
Lord, Percival B., 253
Lucas, Edmund Stanley Sayer (Surgeon), 127
Lutyens, Edwin, 280

M
Macann, Arthur Ernest Henry (Counsellor; Secretary), 145
MacGregor, R.F.D. (Surgeon), 126
Macnaghten, William Hay, 243

M

Maconachie, Richard Roy (Minister, 1930-1935), 193
  accreditation (1930), 193
  accreditation (1934), 205
  career, 140
MacRae, R.D. (Surgeon), 128, 326
Mahbub Ali Khan (Oriental Secretary), 123–125, 286
Mahmud Khan (Consul in Kandahar), 120
Mahmud Shah (Consul in Jalalabad), 120
Malakand, 124, 126
malaria, 239
Mallam, George Leslie (Counsellor), 10, 278
Mansfield, Ethel Frances Mary, 162
mapping, 128, 300. See also cartography
Mare, Arthur James de la, 334
Marini, Dr., 285
Marseille, 182
Masjidi (gardener), 86
Mayne, Peter, 287
menial establishment, 85
Meshed, 126, 144
Metcalfe, Herbert Aubrey Francis (Counsellor), 145, 146
Military Attaché, 128
Millar, George MacGregor (Surgeon), 126
Milnes, J.H. (Superintendent), 96
Minister, 138
ministerial establishment, 87
minorities. See ethnicity
Miranshah, 194
Mir Munshi, 89
Mirza Mumtaz Hasan Kizilbash (Commercial Secretary), 151, 321
modernisation, 14, 17
  Afghanistan, 15
  and Amanullah Khan, 15
  and diplomacy, 16
  and independence, 63
  and international relations, 16
  as Westernisation, 16
modernity, 14, 15, 18
  and Amanullah Khan, 15
  and diplomacy, 16
  and insurgency, 15
Mohmand. See tribe
Mohammed Daoud Khan, 251
monarchy, 15
Moody, Lucy Eileen, 100
Moody, William Joseph (Surgeon), 128, 321
Morgan, A.W. (Attaché), 151
Mughal rule, 288
Muhammad Aslam Khan (Oriental Secretary), 124, 125
Muhammad Azim, 87, 245
Muhammad Gul Khan, 195
Muhammad Jehangir Khan (Consul in Jalalabad), 120
Muhammad Munif (Nazir), 91
Muhammad Qasim (Accountant), 89
Mujahideen, 2
Murad Khan (*chowkidar*), 93
Musahiban, 193. See also Durrani, Ahmad Shah (Abdali)
Muscat, 320
Muspratt, Sydney Frederick, 183
Mussoorie, Indo-Afghan conference in (1920), 54, 56–58
Muzaffar Khan (Oriental Secretary), 123, 124

N

Nadir Khan, Muhammad. See Nadir Shah, Muhammad (r. 1929-1933)
Nadir Shah, Muhammad (r. 1929-1933). See also Musahiban
  assassination, 202, 205, 245
Najibullah, Mohammad, 2

Nasrullah Khan, 48
nationalism, 56, 66, 203. *See also* language
 India, 288, 300
 Pashtunistan, 56, 335
Naurez Khan (orderly), 87, 322
Nazir, 91
Nazir Din (orderly), 322
Nehru, Jawaharlal, 147, 329
New Delhi, 182, 194, 288
new diplomatic history, 22, 26, 235. *See also* international history
Newswriter, 68, 122, 243
Nicholson, Peter Francis Cobham (Attaché), 151
Nimla, 195
North-West Frontier Province, 137, 138, 149, 150
nursing, 256

O

O'Dwyer, Michael Francis, 124
Operation Enduring Freedom, 4, 8
opposition.*See also* resistance
 to colonial staffing practices, 218
 to Legation architecture, 303
Oriental Office, 88
Oriental Secretary, 121, 122
 segregation, 295

P

palimpsest, 297
paracoloniality, 347. *See also* decoloniality
paramountcy. *See* sovereignty
Paris peace conference (1919), 48
Parkes, Roderick Wallis (Counsellor; Secretary), 145, 146, 321
Parsons, Arthur Edward Broadbent (Counsellor), 144–146, 148, 321
Partition, 335

Pashtun, 56, 139. *See also* ethnicity
Passport Clerk, 90
Pathan. *See* ethnicity
Pears, Steuart Edmund, 77, 140, 175
Peel, R.T., 143, 303
Pennachio, 285
performance, 176
 as colonial archive in action, 177
 as diplomatic writing, 176
 diplomacy as theatre, 176
Peshawar, 56, 67, 127, 182
 district, 123
Pettigrew, Guy Irvine (Secretary), 137, 321
Phillips, Horace (Oriental Secretary), 321, 334
Pink, I.T.M., 216, 302
Piparno, 17
Pollock, George, 134
postcolonialism, 19, 20, 42
postcoloniality, 19. *See also* paracoloniality
Poullada, Leon B., 11
Pratap, Mahendra, 47
prestige, 297, 304, 329–331
princely states, 51, 137, 150, 175, 177, 181, 215
property, 329, 330, 333
public diplomacy, 297
Pulford, Violet, 100

Q

Quetta, 126
Quetta-Pishin, 145

R

Rahmat Khan
 caretaker, 91
 Ministerial Clerk in Jalalabad Consulate, 121
 Nazir, 91

Rajwali (orderly), 322
Rawalpindi, 127
  peace treaty of (1919), 48, 53
Razmak, 194
reciprocity, 4
Red Cross, 321
Redpath, Alexander (Secretary), 137, 148, 318, 321
resistance. *See also* insurgency
  anticolonial, 323
  to dispensary. *See also* dispensary
riding. *See* sport
Rio de Janeiro, British Embassy, 280
Roos Keppel, George, 162
Rowlatt Act (Anarchical and Revolutionary Crimes Act), 48, 49
Royal Courts of Justice, 330
Russell, Alexander Alfred (Secretary), 136, 148
Ryan, Crawford Cecil Lindsay (Counsellor), 135
Ryan, Percival Cecil Hardinge, 135

S
Sadozai. *See* Barakzai Muhammadzai
Sandeman, Robert, 135
sanitation, 241, 298
science, 63
Scott, Edward Jervoise Ferrand (Attaché), 151
Scott-Kerr, Christian Alice, 99
Scott-Kerr, Robert, 134
Scott, R.H., 324
Secretary, 136, 148
security, 87, 244, 282, 297
  bodily, 236
self-determination, 56, 62. *See also* Rawalpindi, peace treaty of (1919)
  in Afghan contexts, 56
  qualification of principle, 55

Shah, Agha Saiyid Bad (Counsellor), 147
Shah Mahmud Khan, 325. *See also* Musahiban
Shah Shuja, 120
Shah Wali Khan, 49. *See also* Musahiban
Shami Pir, 52
Sher Ali Khan (r. 1863–1879), 188
Sher Muhammed (gardener), 92
Sher Zaman Shah (Consul in Kandahar), 120
Shiva Dayal Jha (Accountant), 89
Sibi, 145
Sikandar Khan (Oriental Secretary), 124
Sikhs. *See* minorities
Sinclair, W.S. (archivist), 97, 321
Soraya (queen, wife of Amanullah Khan), 101
sovereignty, 74. *See also* suzerainty
  Abdur Rahman Khan and Habibullah Khan, 50, 51
  Afghanistan (1919), 47
  and empire, 12
  and independence, 52, 63
  and irredentism, 56
  imperial, 177
  limitations of, 59
  sovereignty gap, 16, 64
Soviet occupation, 2, 7, 64
Spain, James W., 11
Spinks, L.H. (Superintendent; Second Clerk), 96
sport, 237, 238, 297
squash. *See* sport
Squire, Giles Frederick (Minister, 1943-1948; Ambassador, 1948-1949), 144
  accreditation (1943), 216
  accreditation (1948), 322
Squire, Mary Irene, 99
state-making, 14, 52, 63

Staunton, Harry, 320
Stein, Aurel, 164
Stenographer, 95
Stoddart, Charles, 3
Stranger, Geoffrey Herbert (Garage Superintendent), 97, 245
Stratil-Sauer, Gustav, 17
subaltern/subalternity, 82, 83
subordination, 82
subsidy, 50, 51, 58–60, 67, 188, 199
suicide. *See* death
Sullivan, Basil Martin (architect), 288, 289
Sultan Mohammad Khan. *See* Musahiban
Superintendent, 94
Surgeon, 126, 256
suzerainty, 49, 51. *See also* paramountcy
Syed Irshad Husain (Mir Munshi), 90, 245
Syed Mahmud Shah (Consul in Jalalabad), 120
Sykes, Percy, 10, 124
synchronicity, 345, 347. *See also* diachronicity

T
Tajik.*See* ethnicity
Taliban, 4
Tank, 194
Tarzi, Mahmud Beg, 54
Tawwakal Shah (chauffeur), 322
technology, 63
Tehran, 144
  British Legation, 280
tennis. *See* sport
theft, 285
Thorburn, Harold Hay (Surgeon), 126
Thornton, Annie, 250, 269
Thornton, Ernest, 250, 269

Tibet, 146
tribe, 9
tropical neurasthenia, 248
Truter (Assistant), 97

U
Uzbek. *See* ethnicity

V
vassal state, 5, 22

W
Wana, 194
War on Terror, 344
Washington, 321
  British Embassy, 280
water, 298
Wavell, Archibald (Viceroy of India, 1943–1947), 133
Wavell, Lady, 133
Wazir Akbar Khan, 4
Waziristan, 126, 194
Wheeler, M.H., 134
Wickham, Edward Thomas Ruscombe (Counsellor), 135, 145, 148
Wickham, William James Richard, 135
Williams, Esme (Personal Assistant), 151
Willingdon, Lord (Viceroy of India, 1931–1936), 138
Wilson, Robert (Resident Engineer), 288
Wilsonian moment, 55, 66
Wilson, Woodrow, 54, 55
Worth, Meredith (Counsellor), 146
Wylie, Francis Verner (Minister, 1941-1943), 143
  accreditation, 212

Y
Yakub (Afghan employee), 245
Yakub Khan (r. 1879), 67

Z
Zahir Shah (r. 1933–1973), 205, 323
Zar Gul (orderly), 322